# Theories of Counseling and Psychotherapy

**Robert Rocco Cottone, PhD,** is a professor of counseling in the Department of Education Sciences and Professional Programs at the University of Missouri—St. Louis. He earned a bachelor's degree in psychology and a master's degree in counseling from the University of Missouri—Columbia, and he earned a PhD from St. Louis University. He is a licensed professional counselor (LPC) in Missouri and a licensed psychologist in Missouri and Arizona. He is certified as a health service provider psychologist by the Missouri psychology licensure authority, and as a family therapist (CFT) by the National Credentialing Academy. Dr. Cottone has written more than 100 articles and chapters, many on theoretical and philosophical issues in counseling and psychology, and he has published six books. He has practiced as a counselor and psychologist for more than 30 years. He is married and has five children, which he counts as his greatest accomplishments. He can be contacted by e-mail at: cottone@umsl.edu

# Theories of Counseling and Psychotherapy

## Individual and Relational Approaches

*Robert Rocco Cottone, PhD*

SPRINGER PUBLISHING COMPANY

NEW YORK

Springer Publishing Company, LLC
11 West 42nd Street
New York, NY 10036
www.springerpub.com

*Acquisitions Editor*: Sheri W. Sussman
*Compositor*: Newgen KnowledgeWorks

*ISBN*: 978-0-8261-6865-8
*e-book ISBN*: 978-0-8261-6866-5

**Instructor's Materials: Qualified instructors may request supplements by e-mailing textbook@ springerpub.com:**
*Instructor's Manual*: 978-0-8261-7208-2
*Instructor's PowerPoints*: 978-0-8261-7209-9

17 18 19 20 21 / 5 4 3 2 1

The author and the publisher of this Work have made every effort to use sources believed to be reliable to provide information that is accurate and compatible with the standards generally accepted at the time of publication. The author and publisher shall not be liable for any special, consequential, or exemplary damages resulting, in whole or in part, from the readers' use of, or reliance on, the information contained in this book. The publisher has no responsibility for the persistence or accuracy of URLs for external or third-party Internet websites referred to in this publication and does not guarantee that any content on such websites is, or will remain, accurate or appropriate.

**Library of Congress Cataloging-in-Publication Data**
Names: Cottone, R. Rocco, author.
Title: Theories of counseling and psychotherapy : individual and relational
    approaches / Robert Rocco Cottone, PhD.
Description: New York, NY : Springer Publishing Company, [2017] | Includes
    index.
Identifiers: LCCN 2017007412 | ISBN 9780826168658 (paper back)
Subjects: LCSH: Counseling psychology. | Psychotherapy.
Classification: LCC BF636.6 .C6727 2017 | DDC 158/.9—dc23
LC record available at https://lccn.loc.gov/2017007412

Printed in the United States of America by McNaughton & Gunn.

*This book is dedicated to my five children:*
*Christopher, Kristina, Maria, Torre, and Cristiana.*

# Contents

## Part V. Cross-Paradigm Approaches

## Part VI. Conclusion

# Contributors

**Amanda K. Bohnenstiehl, MA, LPC, NCC, ACS, DBT-LBC,** is currently working toward her PhD in Counseling at the University of Missouri—St. Louis. She graduated with a Master's of Art in Community Counseling from Loyola University Chicago, and she earned her Bachelor of Science in Psychology from the University of Illinois at Urbana—Champaign. Ms. Bohnenstiehl has been a licensed professional counselor (LPC) in Missouri since early 2012, and she currently provides licensure supervision to Provisional LPCs in Missouri. She has been practicing Dialectical Behavior Therapy since 2010 and as of 2017, is a board certified individual DBT clinician through the Linehan Board of Certification.

**Andrea R. Cox, MEd, PLPC,** is a mental health professional who provides individual, group, and family therapy interventions both in school and clinical settings. Ms. Cox completed her Bachelor of Arts in Psychology from the University of Nevada, Las Vegas. She received her Master of Education in Community Counseling from the University of Missouri—St. Louis, and is currently working to complete the PhD program in Counseling at the same university. Before being a therapist, Ms. Cox worked as an educator for more than 10 years, where she learned the importance of helping children work through behavioral, emotional, and social concerns.

**Ryan Thomas Neace, MA, LPC, NCC, CCMHC,** has a comprehensive background in mental health, entrepreneurialism, and education that spans across several states and more than 14 years. He is currently pursuing a PhD in Counseling at the University of Missouri—St. Louis. He is the founder and director of Change, Inc., a multiclinician private practice in South City, St. Louis, where he resides with his wife and two children.

**Zachary Polk, MS, PLMFT,** has been in the field of behavioral health for the past 6 years, has a background in addiction and systemic studies, and has been a student at the Vancouver School of Narrative Therapy. He earned his master's degree from

Loma Linda University. He is currently working with individuals and couples in private practice at Change, Inc., located in St. Louis, Missouri, where he resides with his wife.

**Christina E. Thaier, MEd, PLPC, NCC,** uses Narrative Theory to teach culturally responsive teaching practices at the University of Missouri—St. Louis, where she is currently pursuing a PhD in Counseling. She works with individuals and couples in private practice at Change, Inc., and is continuing her study of Narrative Therapy through the Evanston Family Therapy Center. In her free time, she writes for fun.

**Holly H. Wagner, PhD, LPC, NCC,** is an assistant professor in the Department of Educational Leadership and Counseling at Southeast Missouri State University. She is a certified school counselor, a nationally certified counselor, and a licensed professional counselor in Missouri. Dr. Wagner has previous work experience as a professional school counselor in a K–8 school setting, the program leader for the school counseling tract at Montana State University, and an assistant professor at the University of Missouri—St. Louis.

# Preface

I feel so lucky to have lived at such an exciting time during the development of the field of counseling and psychotherapy. I have not only been able to observe, but I also have participated in two major theoretical transformations in the field. Trained as a counselor and rehabilitation psychologist, early in my career I was very involved in the delivery of services, primarily to individuals with disabilities, based on what was then defined as the "psychomedical" paradigm of vocational rehabilitation (Cottone & Emener, 1990). The practices of that time were primarily psychological, as I was taught to evaluate, to test, to assess, and to understand individuals as somewhat isolated entities with personalities, intelligence, aptitudes, abilities, and predispositions. As a rehabilitation provider, my work was often about analyzing the person and then trying to find a good fit for the person vocationally. It was a "fit the peg into the hole" mentality.

During my doctoral studies I was lucky enough to have taken a course in marriage and family therapy under the direction of Ray Becvar, a renowned social systems theorist. I was also concurrently working in a setting that allowed much freedom to try new approaches, as it seemed many of the clients at the rehabilitation facility where I worked were either low capacity or low-functioning workers, or they were screened out of the system primarily for social reasons. I began to apply social systems (systemic) principles to the rehabilitation setting, which led me to reframe my understanding of rehabilitation from a psychomedical perspective to a "systemic theory of vocational rehabilitation" (Cottone, 1987). My intent was to develop a coherent and comprehensive theory of rehabilitation based on social systems theory. I think history will show that "a systemic theory of vocational rehabilitation" constitutes the first comprehensive and fully philosophically derived theory of vocational rehabilitation. Although the work is not highly cited, for me, it was a major accomplishment, as it opened my eyes to a new way to address the needs of rehabilitation clients. It also opened my eyes to what I later (1992) defined as "paradigms" of counseling and psychotherapy—big picture theories or metatheories of counseling. Social systems theory was revolutionary when contrasted to the psychomedical framework I was taught early in my career. It required a gestalt-like change in perspective. Relationships were defined as real and treatable processes, and the focus became what happens *between* people. The way I began to conceptualize client problems and to treat them was transformed. I began to study theories aligned with social systems theory—marriage, couple, and family therapies. In effect, I lived through and was part of what might be called a major theoretical dissociation (Cottone, 1992, 2012) from the theory that had predominated practice for years. It was an exciting time, although many of my colleagues were not alert to the developments early on, were not interested, or perhaps did not understand the theory or the movement. So textbooks did not reflect the emerging philosophy, and even to this day, relational approaches to treatment are given less attention in introductory textbooks than they deserve.

The transformation in theory did not stop there. Although social systems theory had its roots in the works of theorists from the 1950s, by the 1980s some credible challenges to social systems theory and its applications arose (see Cottone, 2012). Those challenges were primarily about systems theory's inability to account for unilateral, unprovoked aggression; its circular or reciprocal causal framework did not explain the problems of assault and abuse of women in disproportionate numbers (95% of abuse was estimated to be male-on-female abuse) or abuse of children. Theorists (and I was one of them) began to reassess social systems theory and to revise or even to challenge its causal premises (Cottone & Greenwell, 1992). What emerged was quite compelling. There appeared to be another massive dissociation (development of a new counseling paradigm), another significant change in philosophy that could have a major influence on the theory and practice of counseling and psychotherapy. In 1992, I called the movement "contextualism," but more recently I have more fully embraced the term "social constructivism," or even "radical social constructivism" (Cottone, 2013, in press) to classify and to describe this movement. Social constructivism is a movement in mental health practice that holds that truths (the beliefs of clients, for example) are socially constructed (not individually manufactured) and that belief is "acting with others as if some socially defined concept represents truth" (Cottone, 2011). What clients believe, then, about their problems or their lives derives from the interaction they have with other people. Treatment, therefore, becomes a process of challenging socially held standards and consensualizing new ways of narrating a client's problems and life's story. I was able to participate, again, in a theoretical transformation. How lucky for me.

One of the major reasons I wrote this textbook was to provide the field and readers with a contemporary accounting of these transformations by addressing counseling and psychotherapy approaches according to their "paradigm" alignment. No other text does this. General or introductory coursework in counseling theories and psychotherapy has tended to pay little attention to the relational approaches (social systems theory or social constructivism), focusing primarily on psychological theories. A student had to take a course in marriage, couple, or family therapy to be introduced to the social frameworks (as I did in my doctoral studies). This text allows for an accounting of major "psychological" paradigm approaches, but it also provides clear examples of theories that align with the systemic-relational paradigm and the social constructivism paradigm. It also provides examples of some theories designed purposefully to cross paradigms. In this way, the text is a vehicle for instructors and students to place the relational therapies on an equal footing to the traditional psychological theories that have been emphasized by other authors. This book is my way of sharing my observations and experiences with others.

I hope you find my work interesting and appealing. I wish you well in your studies.

Instructor resources, including a PowerPoint deck and Instructor's Manual, are available to qualified instructors by e-mailing textbook@springerpub.com

## REFERENCES

Cottone, R. R. (1987). A systemic theory of vocational rehabilitation. *Rehabilitation Counseling Bulletin, 30,* 167–176.

Cottone, R. R. (1992). *Theories and paradigms of counseling and psychotherapy.* Needham Heights, MA: Allyn & Bacon.

Cottone, R. R. (2011). *Toward a positive psychology of religion: Belief science in the postmodern era.* Winchester, England: John Hunt Publishing.

Cottone, R. R. (2012). *Paradigms of counseling and psychotherapy.* Cottleville, MO: Author. Retrieved from https://www.smashwords.com/books/view/165398

Cottone, R. R. (2013). A paradigm shift in counseling philosophy. *Counseling Today, 56*(3), 54–57.

Cottone, R. R. (in press). In defense of radical social constructivism. *Journal of Counseling and Development.*

Cottone, R. R., & Emener, W. G. (1990). The psychomedical paradigm of vocational rehabilitation and its alternatives. *Rehabilitation Counseling Bulletin, 34,* 91–102.

Cottone, R. R., & Greenwell, R. J. (1992). Beyond linearity and circularity: Deconstructing social systems theory. *Journal of Marital and Family Therapy, 18,* 167–177.

# Acknowledgments

I am a social thinker, so I believe that what I write is actually a reflection of the relationships throughout my life and career that have affected me. First and foremost, I acknowledge my parents, Salvatore and Francesca Cottone. I was raised in a tradition of love. My father was a brilliant but uneducated man who taught me to see all ideas through a critical and questioning lens. He was a good man, a perfect role model, and a loving father. My mother, Francesca, taught me to have faith in those ideas I chose to believe. She was a devoted wife and mother and a moral beacon and guide. My wife, Molly, has been patient and loving with me through many years of late dinners and lost social opportunities or family time together, all because I was off exploring or writing about my professional discoveries. She has been steadfast in allowing me the freedom to complete my work. To Laura Perkins, my former wife and the mother of my two oldest children, I owe a debt of gratitude as she was an avid supporter of my ideas and my works early in my career. And, of course, I learned the power of relationships not only through my adult relationships, but through my five children, Christopher, Kristina, Maria, Torre, and Cristiana. This book is dedicated to them. I love them dearly, and I want to leave them a body of work that will allow them to know what their father believed.

On the professional side, there have been many friends and associates who have supported and encouraged me. My friend Mark Pope, who was my department chair for 12 years at the University of Missouri—St. Louis, has been an exceptional model of professionalism and professional commitment. He is the consummate politician and a man who models tolerance and inclusion. To my other colleagues who have supported me (there are many), I certainly appreciate the frequent discussions and debates on matters of shared interest. And certainly I owe much to my students. I am energized by them. They motivate me. I love to present ideas and to be challenged by them as they digest and process thoughts that may be alien or revolutionary to them. What a joy to see these bright, young professionals take the challenge of the future of counseling and psychotherapy. Special thanks go to my two graduate assistants during the time this book was written, Ryan Neace and Lukas Presley. I could not have done this without them. They worked tirelessly as I pressed them with deadlines and burdensome tasks. I also owe a special thanks to the contributors who volunteered to help with specific chapters, sharing their knowledge and passion about a theory of choice. They were Amanda K. Bohnenstiehl, Andrea R. Cox, Ryan Thomas Neace, Zachary Polk, Christina E. Thaier, and Holly W. Wagner. Finally, I thank readers who have taken the time to study my works and to understand my ideas. They are not an audience to me. Rather, they are the social network that constitutes my legacy.

# PART 1

# Introduction

Chapter 1 of this text introduces the reader to the importance of theory in mental health professional practice. A definition of *theory* is provided. *Paradigms of counseling and psychotherapy* are defined and introduced, and these paradigms provide an organizing framework for the text.

# CHAPTER

# Overview of Theories and Paradigms of Counseling and Psychotherapy

## OBJECTIVES

- To introduce readers to definitions of theories and paradigms of counseling and psychotherapy

- To raise the question "How does psychotherapy work?" in order to address the mechanism of change through talk therapy

- To address whether counseling and psychotherapy are means of deviance control and engineering for social or client benefits

- To differentiate the concept of *mental health* from the concept of *mental disorder*

- To define the role theory plays in the treatment of mental health issues, problematic personalities, or dysfunctional behaviors

Theories of counseling and psychotherapy are foundational to the practice of mental health professions. In fact, it was the development of theories of treatment through *talk* that is at the core of what professional counselors and psychotherapists do. Regardless of whether the professional has trained as a counselor, psychologist, social worker, marital/family therapist, or psychiatrist, the idea that client problems can be addressed and solved through interpersonal interaction with a trained professional is at the heart of mental health practice. Sigmund Freud's associate, Josef Breuer, invented the "talking cure" (Freud, 1909/undated, p. 13) and first made use of the technique with the founding patient of psychoanalysis, Anna O., a woman suffering from hysteria. It was actually Anna O. who identified the techniques as the "talking cure." Freud, in his 1909 lectures (First Lecture), stated:

> It soon emerged, as though by chance, that this process of sweeping the mind clean could accomplish more than the merely temporary relief of her ever-recurring mental confusion. It was actually possible to bring about the disappearance of the painful symptoms of her illness. (Freud, 1909/undated, p. 13).

Freud later called the process "catharsis." The idea was new at the time. Literally, a person could be cured (in this case cured of hysteria) by talking to another person. Today, the idea that mental problems, or mental disorders, can be solved or cured by a conversation between a client and a therapist is well understood. It is called *psychotherapy*. Since the birth of Freud's Psychoanalysis (based initially on the works of Breuer), there has been an explosion of ideas related to the treatment of individuals with talk therapy.

Most people acknowledge the healing that occurs when they are helped by conversation with caring individuals. Psychotherapy stands apart from general or even empathic conversation because it typically addresses serious and unresolved problems using specially designed techniques. Professional *counseling* or *psychotherapy** (the terms *counseling* and *psychotherapy* are used interchangeably in this text) is not just friendly accepting conversation. It is supposed to be qualitatively different. **It is the process whereby a trained professional uses his or her knowledge of biology, psychology, personality, relationships, and social systems to change behaviors and to solve client problems.** Professionals are paid a fee or salary to change the behavior of clients. In the end, the counselor is typically viewed as an expert and is paid with the expectation that the counselor's interventions produce positive and healthy results for people in need.

The focus of study and ideas about the target for treatment intervention vary significantly across the field. There are a number of *psychotherapy* or *counseling theories*. **A counseling *theory* is an intellectual model that purports certain ideas about underlying factors that affect behavior, thoughts, emotions, interpersonal interactions, or interpersonal interpretations. A theory also must provide a focus of study (e.g., thoughts, behaviors, emotions, relationships, systems of relationships, social agreements) for clinicians using the model. The model outlines the limits of activities used by the clinician to examine and evaluate the client. Once evaluated, it provides specific techniques of intervention that can be used by the clinician to affect the client.** Therefore, a counseling theory is a model of understanding and intervention; it provides the clinician with ways to view and to change a client's behaviors, feelings, thoughts, or interactions. Over the history of mental health treatment, wide variations in the models of treatment have evolved. There are those that are more medically oriented, assuming biological bases for unusual behavior. Some theories purport a psychological nonphysical

---

*Noteworthy or new terms are presented throughout this text in boldface with bold definitions. Boldfaced terms are also noted in bold in the index.

*individual* (e.g., the self) that is the focus of study and target of intervention. Other theories hold that relationships (healthy and unhealthy) are crucial to understanding behavior and should be viewed as treatable. Some clinicians hold that mental problems are housed in language, and treatment should act as a re-narration of a person's life. There is one common thread in all psychotherapy—the counselor is a change agent.

## PARADIGMS OF COUNSELING AND PSYCHOTHERAPY

This textbook recognizes real differences across theories of counseling being applied in the practice of mental health treatment. In 1992, Cottone proposed that counseling theories and psychotherapies could be classified across what he defined as *counseling paradigms*. In an update of his ideas, Cottone (2012) defined counseling paradigms as follows:

> The word *paradigm*, although viewed as trendy by many and viewed as confusing by others, is simply a way of saying "a large, theory-encompassing model." The word *paradigm* is borrowed from Kuhn's (1970) classic work describing scientific paradigms, *The Structure of Scientific Revolutions,* and it is modified in this text to apply to mental health services. . . . Paradigms of counseling and psychotherapy (also called "counseling paradigms") are models that, to a large degree, are mutually exclusive and *based on different professional, political, and philosophical positions* related to the nature of the psychotherapeutic enterprise. Because paradigms in the mental health services account for professional and political issues, as well as practical-theoretical issues, the discussion of theories according to paradigm-relevant issues makes this text unique. Paradigms are larger than theories in counseling and psychotherapy. (Chapter 1, paragraph 1)

Cottone identified four counseling paradigms:

> Four paradigms will be presented in this text, and each paradigm has several theories under its wing. The four paradigms are: (a) the organic-medical paradigm; (b) the psychological paradigm; (c) the systemic-relational paradigm; and (d) the social constructivism paradigm (Chapter 1, paragraph 2)

Paradigms, in other words, provide a big picture—an encompassing organizational framework for understanding the work of counselors and psychotherapists. For example, counselors working in a hospital's psychiatric ward work with psychiatrists and other medical doctors, and they are likely to be involved in medically oriented interventions as well as medically informed psychotherapy. On the other hand, a counselor working at a college counseling center is likely to be working with clients addressing adjustment problems or problems defined in the context of the student's college work; in this case, the likely interventions are more focused on individual psychological adjustment and decision making of the college student. As another example, consider counselors working in a marriage or family counseling center; such counseling typically focuses on the problems in the relationships of clients, like marital problems or family problems. The counselor in a family service agency is usually trained in and applies relationship interventions. Therefore, paradigms provide the overview—they give counselors and psychotherapists information about the focus of treatment, and they recognize the context of mental health treatment.

This text is organized according to the paradigm framework. Part II of the text addresses approaches from both the organic–medical and psychological paradigms. Part III addresses systemic–relational approaches and Part IV reviews approaches aligning with social constructivism philosophy. Theories were carefully chosen in each part to represent the collective philosophy of the paradigm, but they also show ***within-paradigm theoretical variations***, meaning that even within paradigms, each theory provides a unique approach to treatment that varies from other approaches within the paradigm. For example, within the psychological paradigm, Freudian psychoanalysis is unique and quite different from the behavioral approaches addressed in the same part of the book. Also, some psychological theories focus more on feelings of clients, whereas others focus more on thoughts of clients. Therefore, ***within-paradigm variations* are simply therapies that accept similar overall paradigm premises, but they also are different and unique in providing specialized ways to do therapy within the paradigm framework.** Part V addresses *cross-paradigm approaches*—**therapies designed by proponents that purposefully draw tenets, propositions, or techniques from at least two of the identified four paradigms.** Therefore, overall, counseling paradigms provide an organization framework for counseling theories used by mental health professionals.

## HOW DOES PSYCHOTHERAPY WORK?

In *Words Were Originally Magic*, Steve de Shazer (1994), one of the founders of Solution-Focused Brief Therapy, explored the idea that psychotherapy is mysterious or even magical. He quickly challenged the idea that magic is involved. His book's title is actually a phrase of Freud's, who argued that words are a means of human influence. People are influenced all the time by messages around them. There is no magic to it—it is the way people affect each other in everyday interpersonal interchange. Short of physical intervention (e.g., torture, infliction of pain, physical reward), the main method of affecting others is communication with them. Humans are social, and they are proficient with language as their primary social vehicle. So it is no mystery that people can be influenced by communication, and therefore, their behaviors, thoughts, feelings, and relationships are modifiable through language intervention. Where people have problems, language is a means of problem solving.

Sometimes a person's problems are easily addressed through education and logical guidance. Some clients learn easily through a guiding and ethical interaction with someone who cares. Counselors in this regard are teachers—teaching one-on-one. They use logic to explain a situation and to teach the client a new way of thinking, feeling, acting, or interacting, and the client, ideally, learns and responds. The counselor's theory guides the therapy. The theory is the counselor's educational road map, so-to-speak. It provides a framework of understanding and intervention. This is counseling at its best, and at its easiest.

Sometimes the problems of clients are complicated. They have multiple layers of difficulty, and client histories can be described as atrocious. They may have been emotionally, physically, or sexually abused. They may have been harmed either physically or emotionally by nature or by other people. They may suffer serious illness, debilitating disability, or incurable disease. They may be genetically predisposed to act, feel, or think in ways that prevent good social fit in the culture within which they find themselves. These people are in need of attention. They are in need of an educated, guiding hand that can lead them to a better place. Counselors are highly educated professionals who are directed by ethical codes to help people in need. Psychotherapists, no matter what their professional affiliations, are bound by the ethical principles of *beneficence* (**doing good**) and *non-maleficence* (**avoiding harm**; Cottone & Tarvydas, 2016). Counselors are paid to produce results. It is their ethical obligation to do their best to help clients solve problems, no matter how complicated or challenging the problems may be. In this sense, counselors and psychotherapists are social agents. They are given license (literally) to provide treatment to those who need it to better their lives, and to help them find comfort in a community that embraces and supports them. Counselors are treatment professionals with the charge of alleviating the symptoms, pain, and mental disorders of clients. Counselors play the role of social advocates, as counseling is a profession that aspires to embody social responsibility.

The counselor–client relationship cannot be ignored. In fact, the way the magic of psychotherapy happens is the result of the **caring, ethical, guiding, and collaborative relationship** that is established by clients and counselors. Research shows that this relationship can be called the *therapeutic alliance,* and it has been statistically shown to be powerful at producing healthy outcomes in treatment. The concept of therapeutic alliance has its roots in the work of Bordin (1979), who defined the therapeutic "working alliance" as involving interaction between the counselor and the client on goals, tasks, and bond (the interpersonal connection of the client and the counselor). Working alliance was proposed to cross all mental health treatment approaches and was not specific to one type of psychotherapy. The therapeutic alliance (a more contemporary but related concept) may be the most significant factor in producing outcomes in psychotherapy (see Beutler, 2000). Aside from specific treatment approaches, it is one **common factor (a factor that is present in counseling no matter what theory is applied, which also is associated with successful outcomes)** that is influential in human clinical interactions. Common factors are addressed again in the last chapter of this book, Chapter 17.

## IS COUNSELING MANIPULATION?

The best counselors may be those who are master manipulators. How can a therapist always care about clients? Aren't there clients whom counselors do not like? How do therapists always show empathy and regard for clients when some clients' behaviors may be abhorrent to the professionals? Is it not dishonest to act like one cares when one does not really care? Counselors are ethically obligated to serve their clients whether they like them or not. In this sense, psychotherapy can be viewed as a professional strategy— tactics to produce change in clients whether they are motivated or unmotivated to change. In a way, counseling can be thought of as **deviance control**. The counselor can be viewed as a warrior, and the war is against maladaptive behavior, disturbing behavior, harmful relationships, and destructive social systems. The idea that psychotherapy is strategic is an idea that may have some credibility, but it certainly has negative overtones. In general, the concept of manipulation has a negative connotation. It challenges the therapist who is guided by the ethical principles of **veracity (being truthful)** and client **loyalty (being faithful)** (Cottone & Tarvydas, 2016). Yet, it cannot be denied that counselors are expected to get results, and to some degree there must be forethought, planning, and engineering to establish the optimal conditions for changing the clients. Counseling should not be *manipulation* in the negative sense; **it should be a professionally designed activity with the intent of facilitating healthy and functional client outcomes**. This is true whether the client shares values with the counselor, is not likable, or has done something that the counselor finds discomforting. The primary responsibility of counselors is to their clients (Cottone & Tarvydas, 2016). Counselors must enter into relationships with clients with the intent of "doing good" for them, just as lawyers sometimes must serve clients with whom they have serious moral or value differences. Counselors can always rely on technical clinical factors when faced with a situation of moral or value conflict—they can focus on the application of theory to design and to implement methods that can produce changes for the benefit of the client and society in general. Technique, therefore, may be a fall back when counselors are confronted by challenging value or moral conflicts with clients, because some clients act in ways that are disturbing.

## HOW IS MENTAL HEALTH DEFINED?

Mental health is not just the absence of mental disorder. The American Psychiatric Association in 2013 published its widely used *Diagnostic and Statistical Manual of Mental Disorders*, 5th Edition (*DSM-5*), which provides a listing of mental disorders and the criteria used to diagnose them. It is a typology of mental disorders—mental illnesses viewed as within the person. Counselors and psychotherapists are paid to remedy conditions listed in the *DSM-5*, and medical insurance companies are required (in most cases) to pay for medical psychotherapy services for their enrollees so long as the services are provided by a mental health professional licensed to treat such disorders. Any number of counseling theories that apply to treatment of individuals can be used to treat *DSM-5* disorders, and such treatment is likely to be reimbursed by the medical insurance company. A good number of the theories described in this text serve as medical psychotherapies. Insurance companies might refuse to pay for those approaches that are relationship focused (marital or couple therapies) or family relationship focused. Even some relationship focused therapies are being reimbursed by some insurance carriers or **third-party payers (organizations that pay for a client's treatment)**. Generally, then, psychotherapy is designed to lessen, cure, or reduce the symptoms of mental disorders. It is designed to help clients function better. Its goal is to help clients face their challenges with support and comfort. Just as physicians serve patients with physical disorders, psychotherapists serve clients with mental disorders.

Counseling and psychotherapy are not just about treating *DSM-5* disorders. The absence of mental disorder does not necessarily constitute mental health. In fact, many of the therapies presented in this text are undergirded by theories of personality. For example, Freud's (1909/undated, 1940/1949; 1917/1966) psychoanalysis subscribes to a conflict model of personality, meaning that the personality is in an internal conflict (the id vs. the superego) that needs to be resolved. Rogers's (1951) Client-Centered Therapy (now known as Person-Centered Therapy) purports that healthy personalities have self-concepts that are internally *congruent* and capable of *full functioning* psychologically. Perls's Gestalt Therapy holds that the personality should be holistic in its functioning, embracing thoughts, feelings, and behaviors synergistically (see Perls, Hefferline, & Goodman, 1951). Therefore, many of the theories themselves present a framework of mental health, and they are designed to facilitate movement from problematic functioning to healthy functioning.

Some counseling theories have no foundational theory of personality. Rather, they describe some basic propositions about how people operate, and then the therapy derives from the basic propositions. For example, Ellis's (1962) Rational-Emotive

Therapy (now known as Rational Emotive Behavior Therapy [REBT]) assumes that people have a propensity to think irrationally, and rational thinking is preferable and healthier. REBT's basic proposition does not constitute a theory of personality, but it does act as a foundational tenet that guides REBT practice.

As the reader progresses through any study of theories of counseling and psychotherapy, he or she is encouraged to analyze theories on the grounds of his or her internal consistency, theoretical and paradigm alignment, ease of application, context for optimal application, and underlying assumptions about the human condition. This text is designed to facilitate that journey so that readers have a good understanding of the theory itself and have a basic grounding in techniques and applications of the theory in practice.

## IS COUNSELING DEVIANCE CONTROL?

In 1974, Thomas Szasz, a psychiatrist (Figure 1.1), wrote a book entitled *The Myth of Mental Illness*. In that book, he argued that mental illness is a myth. He argued that psychiatry has medicalized problems. He argued that the purview of most social and personal treatment by psychiatrists was that of social and personal problems—problems in living. He stated:

> It is customary to define psychiatry as a medical specialty concerned with the study, diagnosis, and treatment of mental illnesses. This is a worthless and misleading definition. Mental illness is a myth. Psychiatrists are not concerned with mental illnesses and their treatments. In actual practice, they deal with personal, social, and ethical problems in living. (p. 262)

**FIGURE 1.1** Thomas Szasz argued that mental illness is a myth.

*Source*: Photo by R. Rocco Cottone.

Szasz's attack on his own profession was highly credible. He made an articulate and compelling case against the treatment of deviant behavior with medical methods. He argued against the use of the *medical* metaphor when addressing human problem behaviors. His arguments apply not only to psychiatry, but to any mental health professional working with clients exhibiting abnormal behavior.

Consider school counseling. Often school counselors are consulted on a case when a child is manifesting a behavior that is disruptive in some way to the educational process. A child may be overactive in the classroom, sleeping through lectures, or disturbing other students in the class. The child may be insubordinate, threatening, or even aggressive in the school setting. He or she may have a school or test phobia. In such cases, it is the school counselor's role to assess and to intervene to produce some change in the situation. The counselor might act as a therapist, addressing behaviors with the intent of stopping, lessening, or preventing specific problematic behaviors or interactions. In this way the counselor is acting as a means of behavior change to better help the child fit within the educational context. Any problem (deviant) behavior must be brought under control. On the other hand, if the school counselor cannot intervene therapeutically with the student, then there are two choices: (a) encourage the child and parents to seek treatment outside the school from a health professional (e.g., a psychiatrist or pediatrician who might prescribe medication to control the child's behavior); or (b) act to make a case against the child remaining in the regular educational setting, thereby screening the child from the standard classroom. Regardless, the counselor's role in such cases is the control of behavior outside the norm of acceptable regular classroom demeanor. This is certainly a constricted view of the school counselor's role, as some would argue that the school counselor's role is much broader and may involve educational, preventative, and **strength-focused (focusing on success)** activities. Sometimes the disciplinary role in the school gets blurred with the counselor role, and certainly, in some cases, counselors may be primarily a means of deviance identification and control.

The disease model of mental disorder and its treatment in the form of psychotherapy may have done the field of counseling an injustice from the very beginning. Szasz followed up his book on the myth of mental illness with a book entitled *The Myth of Psychotherapy* (Szasz, 1978). In that book, he argued against viewing psychotherapy as a medical intervention. He stated: "The promiscuous use of the term *psychotherapy* is an important sign of the debauchment of the language of healing in the service of dehumanizing and controlling persons by technicizing and therapeutizing personal relations" (p. 215). He argued for a new terminology to replace the concept of *psychotherapy* based in logic and rhetoric. He believed that psychiatrists (and now all mental health professionals) should act less like physicians and should recognize their role in social and moral action (Szasz, 1974). Counseling and psychotherapy, in other words, cannot be isolated from the social, political, and moral context within which they exist. In fact, the term *counseling* may better represent the de-medicalized version of traditional *psychotherapy*.

In this text, theories listed under the systemic–relational and social constructivism paradigms appear better positioned to acknowledge and to address fully the social context of treatment, whereas organic-medical and purely psychological approaches appear less sensitive to the social nature of problem formation and solutions, consistent with Szasz's critique of psychotherapy.

## CONCLUSION

This chapter serves as an introduction to theories of counseling and psychotherapy. It addresses some issues about the therapeutic enterprise, and it asks some questions that should whet the appetite of the reader. Paradigms of counseling and psychotherapy were defined and constitute the organizational framework of this book. Questions were raised about the nature of psychotherapy, how it works, whether it is simply a conversation or something like interpersonal manipulation, and whether its purpose is to treat mental disorders. Some of the answers to these questions are embedded in the chapters that follow. Also, following the challenge of Szasz (1974, 1978), the social nature of human discomfort and psychotherapy must be recognized and addressed by both philosophy and method. The next chapter begins by presenting the most medical of the psychotherapies, Psychiatric Case Management, which is then followed by Freud's Psychoanalysis—the first psychological psychotherapy.

# REFERENCES

American Psychiatric Association. (2013). *Diagnostic and statistical manual of mental disorders* (5th ed.). Arlington, VA: American Psychiatric Publishing.

Beutler, L. E. (2000). David and Goliath. When empirical and clinical standards of practice meet. *The American Psychologist, 55*(9), 997–1007.

Bordin, E. S. (1979). The generalizability of the psychoanalytic concept of the working alliance. *Psychotherapy: Theory, Research & Practice, 16*(3), 252–260.

Cottone, R. R. (1992). *Theories and paradigms of counseling and psychotherapy.* Needham Height, MA: Allyn & Bacon.

Cottone, R. R. (2012). *Paradigms of counseling and psychotherapy.* Cottleville, MO: Author. Retrieved from https://www.smashwords.com/books/view/165398

Cottone, R. R., & Tarvydas, V. M. (2016). *Ethics and decision making in counseling and psychotherapy* (4th ed.). New York, NY: Springer Publishing.

de Shazer, S. (1994). *Words were originally magic.* New York, NY: W. W. Norton.

Ellis, A. (1962). *Reason and emotion in psychotherapy.* Secaucus, NJ: Lyle Stuart.

Freud, S. (1909/undated). *Five lectures on psycho-analysis.* New York, NY: W. W. Norton.

Freud, S. (1949). *An outline of psycho-analysis.* New York, NY: W. W. Norton. (Original work published in 1940)

Freud, S. (1966). *Introductory lectures on psycho-analysis.* New York, NY: W. W. Norton. (Original work published in 1917)

Kuhn, T. S. (1970). *The structure of scientific revolutions* (2nd ed.). Chicago, IL: University of Chicago Press.

Perls, F., Hefferline, R. E., & Goodman, P. (1951). *Gestalt therapy: Excitement and growth in the human personality.* New York, NY: Dell.

Rogers, C. R. (1951). *Client-centered therapy.* Boston, MA: Houghton Mifflin.

Szasz, T. S. (1974). *The myth of mental illness: Foundations of a theory of personal conduct.* New York, NY: Harper & Row.

Szasz, T. S. (1978). *The myth of psychotherapy.* New York, NY: Anchor.

# PART II

## Organic–Medical and Psychological Paradigm Approaches

This part of the book is devoted to approaches that align with the most traditional philosophies at the base of counseling theories. The organic medical paradigm of counseling and psychotherapy is historically based in pre-Freudian medicine. It is an approach that has evolved into what is considered the classic American psychiatric approach to treatment, especially as aligned with the biological psychiatry movement (which seeks to define organic, biological, and biochemical bases for behavior). The biological psychiatry movement assumes physical causation for deviant behavior or misbehavior, and it treats deviant behavior or misbehavior accordingly as organically based mental disorders. This philosophy is actively applied in some geographic locales where local medical schools purport an overarching biological psychiatry philosophy. Nonmedical mental health providers, in most cases working with a psychiatrist of this bent, will do what is called "Psychiatric Case Management," which is a counseling approach that defines and describes the activities of nonmedical personnel involved in cases treated by psychiatry. Chapter 2 thoroughly describes Psychiatric Case Management.

The other chapters in this section of the book are classically *psychological*. Psychological theories, almost across the board, identify some nonphysical aspect of self (such as an ego, self-concept, deviance, or personality), and then treatment methods are developed to address the problem that is at the root of unacceptable, unusual, or problematic behavior. The approaches in this chapter cover a broad array of philosophies within the psychological paradigm. Psychoanalytic, humanistic, behavioral, and cognitive behavioral approaches are presented.

# CHAPTER

## 2

# Psychiatric
# Case Management

## OBJECTIVES

- To introduce Psychiatric Case Management as a full-fledged and highly applied theory of counseling

- To describe the biological psychiatry movement at the base of this approach to counseling

- To give counselors and psychotherapists a good introductory understanding of the basic terminology in psychiatric practice

- To outline the practice of Psychiatric Case Management for nonmedical mental health practitioners

- To outline criticisms of this approach

Psychiatrists are primarily suited to working within the boundaries of organic–medical propositions and tenets, meaning they are trained as medical professionals addressing physical health issues. But other mental health professionals can be involved in therapeutic work, with clients being treated by psychiatrists who hold strictly to a biological understanding of mental disorders. Psychiatric Case Management, as a counseling approach and as described in this chapter, can be used by psychiatrists. However, it can also be used by psychologists, mental health counselors, marital and family therapists, social workers, and other mental health professionals when there is involvement of a physician overseeing medical treatments. However, nonmedical practitioners are limited when serving patients receiving medical treatments. Nonmedical practitioners are limited to noninvasive, nonradioactive, or other nonphysically involved diagnostic techniques. Also, they cannot perform treatments involving medications, **electroconvulsive therapy** (ECT or electroshock therapy), or other physically or legally restricted treatments. **ECT involves application of electricity to neural networks in the brain through electrodes positioned carefully on the skull, with the intent of shocking the brain's electrical activity so that a new pattern of activity can emerge that replaces old patterns associated with symptomatic behavior.** Regardless, nonmedical mental health professionals can be actively involved in the diagnostic and treatment processes. The science of psychiatry is not finely developed; by medical standards, psychiatric diagnostic processes are inexact (Woodruff, Goodwin, & Guze, 1974). Consequently, once global physical causes can be **discounted (*ruled out*)**, the diagnostic process for any mental health professional is very much the same. Behaviors will be observed in a diagnostic interview situation. The patient's history, family background, medical and psychological record, and other pertinent information will be used. And the diagnosing professional will derive an impression as to the nature of the disorder. The diagnostic classificatory scheme most used in the United States is that of the American Psychiatric Association's (APA) *Diagnostic and Statistical Manual of Mental Disorders* (5th ed.; *DSM–5*; APA, 2013). The *DSM-5* defines a mental disorder as follows:

> A mental disorder is a syndrome characterized by clinically significant disturbance in an individual's cognition, emotion regulation, or behavior that reflects a dysfunction in the psychological, biological, or developmental processes underlying mental functioning. Mental disorders are usually associated with significant distress or disability in social, occupational, or other important activities. (p. 20)

Furthermore, the *DSM-5* states:

> An expectable or culturally approved response to a common stressor or loss, such as the death of a loved one, is not a mental disorder. Socially deviant behavior (e.g., political, religious, or sexual) and conflicts that are primarily between the individual and society are not mental disorders unless the deviance or conflict results from a dysfunction in the individual. (p. 20)

Obviously, an internal perspective of causation is purported. A disorder is viewed as "dysfunction *in the individual*" [emphasis added].

Actually, the *DSM-5* is more liberal about defining the causes of disorder than what might be acceptable according to a strict biological psychiatry view of mental disorder (see Hedaya, 1996; Panksepp, 2004). Biological psychiatry is a movement in psychiatry that holds that biological and organic factors must be primary in any definition of disorder, in diagnosis, and in treatment. The *DSM-5* may be less extreme in holding to a strict biological framework, primarily due to the political lobby of psychology that has influenced *DSM-5* definitions. The *DSM-5* does allow for *psychological* factors in the definition of disorder. Comparatively, a strict biological psychiatry (see Shagass et al., 1986, for an example of empirical studies in this area) is less accepting of nonbiological explanations. Even assuming a strict biological psychiatry, a thoroughly trained nonmedical mental health professional should be able to make the important distinctions related to **differential diagnosis (choosing one diagnosis vs. another diagnosis when a number of competing diagnoses are under consideration)**. Differential diagnoses can be made by nonmedical practitioners in a majority of the cases seen in everyday practice, with physicians being consulted when there are signs of **organicity (some physical finding such as brain damage, endocrine dysfunction, or substance effects)** or problematic diagnoses, or when medical treatments are needed. Some conditions, such as organic mental disorder (brain dysfunction), will have a clear-cut organic **etiology (origin or cause)**. Other mental disorders may not have such a clear-cut etiology; however, there is the expectation that science will define the biological/organic causes of a disorder if given enough time and adequate resources.

Probably the most comprehensive and accessible resource on current practices in psychiatry is *Kaplan and Sadock's Synopsis of Psychiatry* (Sadock, Sadock, & Ruiz, 2015), now in its 11th edition (originally authored by Kaplan and Sadock; the current authors honor the textbook founders with the founders' names in the book title). This text provides a broad view of psychiatric practice, and it describes many organic–medical diagnostic and treatment approaches. It also addresses types of psychotherapy, approaches to treatment of specific mental disorders, and psychopharmacology. Readers are referred to the Kaplan and Sadock work for in-depth discussions on topics such as medical assessment, psychiatric interviewing, mental status assessment, psychiatric diagnosis, psychiatric report writing, and medication management, many of which are discussed briefly in this chapter. The Kaplan and Sadock text also describes many commonly used psychosocial treatments, which are more clearly aligned with the other paradigms in this text; they will not be discussed in any systematic way in this chapter.

Because no outstanding contemporary proponent of the organic–medical paradigm has emerged, there is no one proponent of Psychiatric Case Management listed in this chapter. Consequently, no biographical sketch is included in this chapter, unlike other therapy-specific chapters in this text. Many individuals through the history of psychiatry have contributed to what can be classified as organic–medical Psychiatric Case Management. Most notably, the American physician Benjamin Rush has been defined as a significant figure in the history of psychiatry. This chapter, rather than reflecting one person's theory of counseling, however, is an integration of ideas from theorists and practitioners, as well as from observations of current psychiatric practices. It is a best attempt to present a contemporary counseling theory consistent with current, individually focused, organic–medical propositions and tenets.

## THE FOUNDATIONAL THEORY

### The Target of Counseling

The target of Psychiatric Case Management is the individual patient and his or her mental condition. A mental condition is assumed to have a physiological correlate, although the etiologies (clear-cut causative factors) of mental conditions are unknown. Mental health professionals must identify **symptoms (complaints expressed by patients)** and **signs (behaviors observed by the diagnostician)** consistent with diagnoses of mental disorders. A diagnosis, from a strict organic–medical stance, is identification of a disease. As Woodruff, Goodwin, and Guze (1974) stated:

> When the term "'disease'" is used, this is what is meant: a disease is a cluster of symptoms and/or signs with a more or less predictable course. Symptoms are what patients tell you; signs are what you see. The cluster may be associated with physical abnormality or may not. The essential point is that it results in consultation with a physician who specializes in recognizing, preventing, and, sometimes, curing diseases. (pp. x–xi)

They further stated:

> It is hard for many people to think of psychiatric problems as diseases. For one thing, psychiatric problems usually consist of symptoms—complaints about thoughts and feelings or behavior disturbing to others. Rarely are there signs—a fever, a rash. Almost never are there laboratory tests to confirm the diagnosis. What people say changes from time to time, as does behavior. It is usually harder to agree about symptoms than about signs. But whatever the psychiatric problems are, they have this in common with "real" diseases—they result in consultation with a physician and are associated with pain, suffering, disability, and death. (pp. x–xi)

Woodruff et al. went on to describe diagnoses as "conventions," useful categorizations, which have explicit definitions and predictable courses. Woodruff and his associates were very empirical in providing a classification schema, including such categories as schizophrenia and affective (mood) disorders within the psychiatric diagnostic realm, but avoiding such classifications as certain personality disorders, which they claimed were studied too little to provide conclusive guidance as to their diagnostic usefulness.

From an organic–medical standpoint, then, an individual's disease is diagnosed according to an accepted psychiatric nosology (classification), and then it is targeted for treatment. Box 2.1 provides a list of some common psychiatric terms and their definitions.

The biological psychiatry movement is currently active in the profession. Trimble and George (2010) in their text *Biological Psychiatry* describe affiliations within the movement. They stated:

> The Society for Biological Psychiatry and its journal were founded in 1954 and the first World Congress of Societies of Biological Psychiatry was held in 1974. The World Federation of Societies of Biological Psychiatry today has 50 affiliated nationalities and nearly 5000 members. (Introduction and Preface to the Third Edition, 2010)

Trimble and George have been outspoken advocates for the biological psychiatry movement, as have several other authors (e.g., Hedaya, 1996; Panksepp, 2004).

## The Process of Counseling

Psychiatric Case Management often begins once there has been at least a provisional diagnosis and when severe unmanageable symptoms, if present, have been stabilized. Psychiatric Case Management counseling has four purposes: (a) to ameliorate or reduce any factors (internal or external to the individual) that may stress the individual, thereby preventing the triggering of maladaptive physiological responses and **exacerbation (worsening)** of symptoms; (b) to educate the patient and his or her family (if a family is

# BOX 2.1 Some Brief Definitions of Psychiatric Terms

**Abstract thinking:** Ability to think in a high-level associative way. To say that an apple and an orange are both fruits is an example of a high-level abstraction. To say that they both can be eaten is an operational similarity and is more concrete than abstract.

**Affect:** Emotional expression associated with environmental stimuli, usually as observed by another person. For instance, smiling when smiled at in an interview is appropriate affect. Showing no emotion when told a funny joke or a sad story is *flat* affect. Limited emotional expression is *blunted* affect. Demonstrating an unanticipated emotional response is called *inappropriate* affect. *Labile* affect is quickly changing.

**Blocking:** Referring to halted thought processes, for instance, when one stops a thought in mid-sentence.

**Circumstantial thought:** Speaking in circles, irrelevantly, and coming to a point on questioning only after much irrelevant speech.

**Clang associations:** Rhyming thoughts or speech.

**Compulsion:** A distressful predisposition to act a certain way, for example, a handwashing compulsion, where the patient washes his or her hands excessively.

**Content of thought:** The patient initiated topics of conversation, usually during a diagnostic interview. Delusional, hallucinatory, and obsessional material is considered significant to content of thought.

**Deja vu:** A feeling one has been someplace where one has not been.

**Delusion:** A false conclusion. Common delusions are persecutory ("They are trying to hurt me"), paranoid ("They are out to get me"), somatic ("There's something inside of me eating my organs"), of influence ("They are trying to affect my thinking"), of reference ("They are talking about me on TV"), and systematized delusions (which are well developed and held together by a logical thread).

**Depersonalization:** Losing one's sense of self.

**Depression:** A low mood.

**Dysthymia:** A pattern of depressions, generally not extreme.

**Echolalia:** Mimicking sounds.

**Echopraxia:** Mimicking motions or postures.

**Elation:** A high emotional feeling, the opposite of depression.

**Euphoria:** Extreme elation.

**Euthymia:** Normal mood.

**Feelings of unreality:** A sense of loss of touch with one's world.

**Flight of ideas:** Pressured speech combined with loose associations.

*(continued)*

## BOX 2.1    Some Brief Definitions of Psychiatric Terms (*continued*)

**Flow of thought:** Whether the person speaks in a way that is spontaneous, smooth, logical, and coherent, without internally produced interruptions, blocking, looseness of associations, circumstantiality, or tangentiality.

**Functional disorder:** Disorder having to do with one's operation in an environment, as opposed to organic disorder, which relates to one's bodily structure.

**Grandiosity:** A false sense of importance.

**Hallucinations:** False perceptions involving any one or more of the five senses—auditory (hearing), visual (seeing), tactile/kinesthetic (feeling), gustatory (tasting), or olfactory (smelling).

**Histrionic:** Extremely dramatic.

**Hypomanic:** A pattern of elevated mood, bordering on mania.

**Illusion:** A distorted perception.

**Insight:** One's understanding of one's situation.

**Jamais vu:** Feeling one has not been someplace where one has been.

**Judgment:** One's ability to make basic social decisions.

**Loose associations:** A thought sequence where there is little logical thread, which is manifested to the extreme in a word salad (expression of unrelated words in a sequence).

**Mania:** An extreme psychotic euphoria.

**Memory:** Retention of information. Immediate memory involves retention of materials for seconds, short-term memory involves retention for minutes or hours, and long-term memory involves retention for a day or longer.

**Mood:** Emotional state as described by a patient. Usually down (dysthymic), up (euphoric), or normal (euthymic).

**Mute:** Lack of speech.

**Neologisms:** A new word, usually totally newly constructed or a combination of other words. For example, "nulicious" combines nutritious and delicious.

**Neuroleptic drugs:** Powerful antipsychotic medications.

**Neurosis:** A disorder usually causing significant distress to oneself but not to others. It is typically characterized by excess anxiety and other symptoms, such as depression.

**Obsession:** A distressful predisposition to think about something.

**Organic/organicity:** Having to do with the physical makeup of the body, as opposed to functional concerns, which relate to one's operation in an environment. Organicity is often used to refer to brain damage.

(*continued*)

## BOX 2.1  Some Brief Definitions of Psychiatric Terms (*continued*)

**Orientation:** Being knowledgeable about one's surroundings, specifically related to one's person, place, time, and situation. Oriented times three means oriented to person, place, and time. Oriented times four means oriented to person, place, time, and situation.

**Paranoia:** Extreme suspiciousness or a feeling that someone is out to cause one harm.

**Perseveration:** A recurring thought or action that appears out of the conscious control of the patient and is usually associated with brain damage or organicity.

**Pressured speech:** When one speaks forcefully, as if a thought must be pushed out.

**Prodromal symptoms:** Symptoms that precede a full-blown active phase of a disorder.

**Prognosis:** An educated medical prediction.

**Psychosis:** An invented reality, often manifested by hallucinations, delusions, or operational incoherence.

**Residual symptoms:** Symptoms that follow a full-blown active phase of a disorder.

**Scanning:** Visually hyperactive. Looking around quickly.

**Sign:** An observed behavior or finding that supports a diagnosis.

**Somatization:** Undue focus on body functioning or disorders, often without evidence of organicity.

**Suicidal potential:** The presence of suicidal ideas, plans (how it will occur), and intentions (when it will occur).

**Symptom:** A complaint by a patient of diagnostic significance.

**Tangential thought:** Going off the topic and never answering questions.

**Tardive dyskinesia:** A relatively permanent neurological disorder (brain damage) that results from the use of powerful antipsychotic medications.

**Vigilance:** Overalertness regarding environmental stimuli.

involved) about the disorder and how best to adjust to the disorder; (c) to monitor the effects of medications (both main effects and unwanted side effects); and (d) to assess the mental status of the individual to detect and to record the presence of symptoms and signs, which is necessary to analyze the overall effect of treatment and to adjust treatments accordingly. Box 2.2 gives a sample of psychiatric diagnostic criteria from *DSM-5*, and Box 2.3 gives a sample mental status examination tool.

The process of Psychiatric Case Management is an ongoing process of individual counseling and assessment, where the patient meets with a counselor to discuss his or

## BOX 2.2 *Diagnostic and Statistical Manual of Mental Disorders* (5th ed.; *DSM-5*) Criteria for Diagnosis of Schizophrenia

The following criteria are listed in the *Diagnostic and Statistical Manual of Mental Disorders* (5th ed.; *DSM-5*), published by the APA (2013, p. 99).

### Criteria

A. Two (or more) of the following, each present for a significant portion of time during a 1-month period (or less if successfully treated). At least one of these must be (1), (2), or (3).
   1. Delusions
   2. Hallucinations
   3. Disorganized speech (e.g., frequent derailment or incoherence)
   4. Grossly disorganized or catatonic behavior
   5. Negative symptoms (i.e., diminished emotional expression or avolition)
B. For a significant portion of the time since the onset of the disturbance, level of functioning in one or more major areas, such as work, interpersonal relations, or self-care, is markedly below the level achieved prior to the onset (or when the onset is in childhood or adolescence, there is failure to achieve expected level of interpersonal, academic, or occupational functioning).
C. Continuous signs of the disturbance persist for at least 6 months. This 6-month period must include at least 1 month of symptoms (or less if successfully treated) that meet Criterion A (i.e., active-phase symptoms) and may include periods of prodromal or residual symptoms. During these prodromal or residual periods, the signs of the disturbance may be manifested by only negative symptoms or by two or more symptoms listed in Criterion A present in an attenuated form (e.g., odd beliefs, unusual perceptual experiences).
D. Schizoaffective disorder and depressive or bipolar disorder with psychotic features have been ruled out because either (1) no major depressive or manic episodes have occurred concurrently with the active-phase symptoms, or (2) if mood episodes have occurred during active-phase symptoms, they have been present for a minority of the total duration of the active and residual periods of the illness.
E. The disturbance is not attributable to the physiological effects of a substance (e.g., a drug of abuse, a medication) or another medical condition.
F. If there is a history of autism spectrum disorder or a communication disorder of childhood onset, the additional diagnosis of schizophrenia is made only if prominent delusions or hallucinations, in addition to the other required symptoms of schizophrenia, are also present for at least 1 month (or less if successfully treated).

her concerns and present status. Assessment occurs continually through the process of counseling, but it is useful and recommended that formal mental status assessments should be accomplished and recorded at least on a monthly basis during **outpatient (nonhospital)** treatments. Educational interventions with the patient and with other involved individuals should occur soon after diagnosis. For hospitalized patients (inpatient treatment), educational interventions should occur before discharge.

## Counselor Role

The counselor role in Psychiatric Case Management is threefold: a counselor must be a monitor, educator, and problem solver. As a *monitor*, the counselor must be an expert at identifying symptoms and signs consistent with a mental disorder. He or she must also be able to recognize signs that are *prodromal* (typically preceding) or *residual* (typically following) acute exacerbations of a mental disorder. **An acute exacerbation is a short-term worsening of symptoms,** and it is during exacerbations that symptoms and signs more clearly meet diagnostic criteria. The counselor must also be knowledgeable about medications and medication interactions in order to identify main (wanted) effects and unwanted side effects of the medications and to understand the signs of appropriate or inappropriate medication.

---

## BOX 2.3 Mental Status Examination

Ask the client: "What symptoms have you experienced in the last 48 hours?"

Record response: _____

Ask the client: "What symptoms have you experienced in the past?"

Record response: _____

*Orientation to:* Person ( ); place ( ); time ( ); situation ( ).

*General behavior:*

Eye contact: present ( ); absent ( ).

Normal motor activity ( ); increased motor ( ); decreased motor ( ); agitation ( ); tremor ( ); tics ( ); peculiar posturing ( ); unusual gait ( ); repetitive acts ( ); seductive posturing ( ); angry outburst ( ); impulsive ( ); hostile ( ); withdrawn ( ); evasive ( ); passive ( ); aggressive ( ); naive ( ); dramatic ( ); manipulative ( ); dependent ( ); uncooperative ( ); demanding ( ); negativistic ( ); vigilance ( ); scanning ( ); other ( )—describe: _____

*Content of thought:*

Check if present and describe frequency, intensity, duration:

____ Delusions (paranoid, influence, somatic, grandeur, of reference, systematized, or other):

____ Hallucinations (auditory, visual, olfactory, gustatory, kinesthetic):

____ Obsessions:

____ Compulsions:

*(continued)*

## BOX 2.3 Mental Status Examination (*continued*)

___ Phobias:

___ Suicidal thoughts or plans:

Assaultive or homicidal thoughts:

___ Antisocial attitudes:

___ Suspicious:

___ Feelings of unreality:

___ Thoughts of running away:

___ Somatic (bodily) complaints:

___ Guilt ideas:

___ Ideas of hopelessness/worthlessness:

___ Excessive religiosity:

Sexual preoccupation:

___ Blames others:

___ Other:

*Speech and flow of thought*:

Goal directed ( ) OR loose ( ); circumstantial ( ); tangential ( ).

Spontaneous ( ) OR blocked ( ).

Deliberate ( ) OR pressured ( ).

Check if present: neologisms ( ); clang associations ( ); flight of ideas (loose + pressured) ( ); perseveration ( ); echolalia ( ); echopraxia ( ); excessive ( ); reduced ( ); slow ( ); loud ( ); soft ( ); mute ( ); slurred ( ); stuttering ( ).

*Affect* (emotional tone observed and defined through observation by the interviewer):

Appropriate ( ); inappropriate ( ). If inappropriate, check flat ( ); blunted ( ); elated ( ); labile ( ); angry ( ); histrionic ( ); anxious ( ); silly ( ); depressed ( ).

*Mood* (emotional state as subjectively described by client):

Euthymic (normal) ( ); dysthymic (depressed) ( ); euphoric (elated) ( ).

## Cognitive Mental Status Assessment

*Immediate memory and concentration*:

Ask client to subtract 7s backward from 100 in a serial fashion. Record responses:

____ ____ ____ ____ ____ ____

Ask client to subtract 3s backward from 20 in a serial fashion. Record responses:

____ ____ ____ ____ ____ ____

Ask the client to repeat the following sequences of numbers and check if correct:

2-5 ( ); 3-8-4 ( ); 7-4-8-3 ( ); 8-2-0-1-4 ( ); 8-2-1-9-0-4 ( ); 3-9-7-2-8-4-1 ( ).

*(continued)*

## BOX 2.3 Mental Status Examination (*continued*)

Ask the client to reverse the following sequences—check if correct: 5-8 ( ); 4-9-1 ( ); 2-7-3-6 ( ); 6-1-0-5-8 ( ); 5-2-8-9-1-4 ( ).

*Short-term memory:* Ask the client to tell you what he or she had for breakfast; record response: _____

*Long-term memory:*

Ask client to name five recent U.S. presidents; record response: _____

*Current knowledge:* Ask client to name one major recent news event; record response: _____

Ask client to name the state's governor: record response: _____

Ask client to name a local city's mayor: record response: _____

*Abstract thinking:*

Ask client to explain the saying:

1.  A rolling stone gathers no moss: _____
2.  The grass is always greener on the other side:_____

*Insight and judgment:* Poor insight ( ); poor judgment ( ).

*Other symptoms of neurological significance:*

Headaches: no ( ); yes ( ), frequency, intensity, duration: _____

Dizzy spells? describe:

Any recent changes in the following: walking ( ); talking ( ); vision ( ); hearing ( ); memory ( ); balance ( ); thirst ( ); sense of direction ( ); sleep ( ); handwriting ( ); sexual responsiveness ( ).

Explain:_____

Have any of the following phenomena occurred: dropping things out of hands ( ); reaching for something and missing while looking ( ); deja vu ( ); jamais vu ( ); forgetting what was said in mid-sentence ( ); forgetting names of common things (such as a pencil, cup, lamp, etc.) ( ); uncontrollable hand trembling ( ).

Describe:_____

Do any of the following illnesses run in the family: epilepsy ( ); Parkinson's disease ( ); Alzheimer's disease ( ); schizophrenia ( ); depression or manic depression ( ); alcoholism ( ); Down's syndrome ( ); neurological disease ( ).

Describe:_____

Has the client ever experienced: ringing in the ears ( ); pain when moving the head ( ); contact with poisonous chemicals ( ); recent loss of control of bowels or bladder ( ); pain or numbness in any part of the body ( ); head injury ( ).

Describe:_____

Diagnostic impression: _____
_____
_____

As an *educator*, the counselor must be able to teach clients and other significant individuals in the patient's life about the disorder and its clinical course. Manifestations of the disease must be communicated in a way that is helpful, and not frightening, to patients and their families. The latest research findings on the disorder should be communicated, and the **prognosis (a prediction of the probable course and outcome of the disease)** must be presented in an understandable way. The counselor must educate the patient and others about the importance of medical treatment compliance, and about the likelihood of future exacerbations.

As a *problem solver*, the counselor must be prepared to direct the patient when problems arise and to assist the patient in the everyday management of stressors. Internal and external stressors must be managed. For example, the tendency of depressive patients to catastrophize must be monitored, and the counselor must be directive about solving problems associated with a tendency to interpret concerns out of proportion. External factors, such as employment concerns, the drug culture, family stressors, and so on, must be understood and addressed appropriately in counseling. The counselor must be willing and able to assist patients to develop reasonable solutions to the everyday problems associated with life with a mental disorder.

## Goals of Counseling and Ideal Outcomes

The primary goal of counseling is the lessening or control of symptoms and/or signs of disorder. A secondary goal is to assist patients to make realistic decisions related to lifestyles and goals, in order for them to accommodate their conditions. It is understood that many mental disorders will have lifetime consequences, and it is imperative that patients understand and adjust to their disorders. Just as a patient with diabetes must make adjustments in his or her life according to the dictates of diabetic treatment, so too must the individual with a mental disorder make adjustments to his or her disability. Ideally, symptoms and signs will remit through treatment and, through prudent follow-up care and lifestyle adjustments, there will be no recurrence of acute symptoms.

# GENERAL PROCEDURES

## Assessment

Although seemingly simplistic, the diagnostic process in psychiatry is a much more complicated matter than matching a patient's symptoms to a diagnostic category. Each listing of a disorder in the *DSM-5* (APA, 2013) has a section entitled "Differential Diagnosis" that provides a list of competitive diagnoses with similar symptoms or signs. This list of other possible diagnoses is useful in factors associated with one diagnosis compared to another diagnosis. The differential diagnosis process is quite complex and involves an analysis of the person's family background (which may have genetic as well as social/economic implications), levels of education and intelligence, environment factors (present and past, so that environmental triggers may be identified), and other factors.

The psychiatric examination is characterized by a thorough interview with a specialized examination of the person's mental status and symptomatology. The diagnostic interview will provide in-depth questioning about such matters as the claimant's medical and psychiatric history, family history (medically and otherwise), educational background, vocational history, symptom history (including the frequency, intensity, and duration of symptoms or complaints), social history, military experience, drug or alcohol abuse history, and other relevant historical matters. Once a thorough background has been accomplished, a physician may physically examine the patient, most usually performing a thorough neurological examination, to rule out (discount) neurological disorder. Then a complete mental status examination will be accomplished in the physician's office. The mental status examination will explore, in an objectified way, the patient's general behavior (e.g., dress, grooming, psychomotor activity), content of thought, flow of thought, affect (the evaluator's assessment of mood within the interview context), mood (the patient's assessment of his or her recent mood), neuroadaptive functioning and daily activities (such as sleep, sex, self-care), memory, concentration, ability to abstract, the patient's insight into his or her problems, basic social judgment, and orientation to person, place, time, and situation. It is the manifestation of symptoms or signs during the mental status examination that is the most trustworthy interview-related diagnostic indicator. For example, if a patient of average intelligence is unable to subtract 3s sequentially starting from 20, then this may be viewed as a sign of poor concentration. Additionally, if the claimant describes a dysphoric mood, appears to have a depressed or flattened affect to the evaluator, shows signs of sleep and appetite disturbance, shows retarded psychomotor activity, and continually complains about not being able to get motivated, then these factors should lead to consideration of a mood disturbance (e.g., depression). On the other hand, if the patient complains of dysphoric mood, but does not demonstrate consistent behaviors during the mental status examination, then the evaluator must question either the nature and severity of the concern or the credibility of the complainant. There may be no severe mental impairment or distress, or there may be other signs or symptoms that will take the diagnostic process another direction. Regardless, the mental status examination is an important tool in the medical diagnostic process.

Once an assessment has been made, the evaluator must weigh all data and formulate some impression about the nature of the disorder. The *DSM-5* (APA, 2013) provides guidance for how this takes place. Conditions are listed hierarchically based on their prominence in the clinical picture. An example of the format for recording such impressions is as follows:

F32.2 Major Depression, Single Episode, Severe
F10.20 Alcohol Use Disorder moderate
F60.7 Dependent Personality Disorder (Provisional, rule out Borderline Personality
   Disorder) (American Psychiatric Association, 2013)

The numbers assigned to each diagnosis constitute the *DSM-5* "codes" for classification; they are a shorthand summation of disorders. In many cases when, for instance, a client should not know a diagnosis for fear of misunderstanding it, and when that patient may have access to insurance forms or other sources of such information, a code alone may be used.

From an organic–medical perspective, the major purpose of differential diagnosis is differential treatment.

## Treatment/Remediation

Once diagnosed, it is the responsibility of the treating professional to provide or to obtain appropriate medical treatment for the patient, which should include psychotherapy or supportive counseling, as well as follow-up. Differential treatment follows differential diagnoses, so in many instances, different types of treatment will be used across standard diagnostic categories. However, in most cases, organic–medical treatment involves some form of medication. In addition, psychotherapy or supportive counseling is common. The ultimate responsibility for medication management rests on the shoulders of the physician, although in practice, other mental health professionals may provide information to the physician so that the process may be interactive among involved professionals on the case.

## Case Management

The case management of an individual receiving organic–medical psychiatric treatment involves skillful interprofessional communication. Aside from the assignment of medical responsibilities to an attending physician, all involved professionals are responsible to ensure effective, ethical, and appropriate treatment.

Nonmedical counselors or psychotherapists coordinating nonmedical treatments on cases receiving medical attention must be able to regularly observe the patient and to report the patient's status in oral or in written forms to other involved professionals. (See Box 2.4 for a sample psychiatric case report.) The treating counselor must be prepared to do crisis intervention and to coordinate emergency services when necessary. He or she should be well-versed in medical treatments, especially related to medication *side effects* (unusual or unwanted effects) as opposed to main or wanted treatment effects. There must be a continual monitoring of symptomatology. Physical and social environmental stressors must be identified and controlled or lessened, when possible. The treating counselor must be alert to community resources and should be knowledgeable about the availability of services and the means for obtaining services for patients.

Case notes should be detailed, precise, and thorough. One of the clearest signs of the incompetency of a Psychiatric Case Management professional is the failure to record in ongoing case notes the frequency, intensity, and duration of symptoms and signs of a disorder. Progress from a Psychiatric Case Management perspective cannot be assessed unless attention is focused on the presence, absence, or degree of symptom behaviors. Regular and thorough mental status examinations should be performed. Monitoring of medication and other treatment compliance is critical.

Counseling sessions should be regularly scheduled in order to prevent or to lessen any internal or external factors that may negatively affect progress toward goals. The Psychiatric Case Management professional must be educated, competently trained, and medically sophisticated. He or she must be an able communicator and an astute observer as well as a skilled counselor.

## BOX 2.4   Example of a Psychiatric Report

The following psychiatric report is based on a real report of a seriously ill patient. However, the material has been extensively modified to protect the rights of the patient.

### Psychiatric Evaluation of an Active Schizophrenic

Identification: The patient is a 29-year-old single White male, referred for a psychiatric examination by a mental health agency.

*Expressed complaint:* "My father wants me to see you."

*Patient description of current status:* The patient states he was never in "analysis." His doctor falsely said that he had a neurological disorder. His whole problem

*(continued)*

## BOX 2.4   Example of a Psychiatric Report (*continued*)

was "temporal mandibular joint syndrome." This condition made his brain concentrate on his jaws. He feels like he has two mouths. The jaw condition caused "an input into my brain." The patient said others may think of a spouse but he thinks of his brain itself. He says he was never given a diagnosis but he made his own diagnosis of his jaw condition. Nervous conditions come from the jaw and send signals of pain up his spinal cord to his brainstem. Abraham Lincoln had the same disease, according to what television told him. He also needs glasses. He requested glasses from the welfare agency. He diagnosed his own eye condition as "congenital familial cataracts." This condition causes him to put more effort into his vision than others. When asked about medications, he states he took Haldol (an antipsychotic drug) a year ago. He has been off of Haldol 1 year. It had no effect whatsoever. It was a major tranquilizer. It took his thoughts about society away from him. He had the correct idea about society, which is that education in society is for training animals, not people. He calls himself a "philosophical scientist." He went on to say that his hearing is bad as well as his vision.

Obtained medical records indicate he has been hospitalized at the state institution on four occasions. He was seen there in a psychotic state each time with features of paranoia, grandiosity, bizarre behavior, threats to murder the U.S. president, attempts to become a refugee to Russia or Cuba, delusions that the government had placed "control boxes in my brain," that the government owes him large sums of money, and that news people are after him. Diagnoses varied from atypical psychosis to paranoid schizophrenia. There was repeated documentation for pernicious cannabis abuse. He had been smoking marijuana since he was age 13. It brought about his quitting high school. He had been treated with oral neuroleptics as well as intramuscular injections of Haldol. He was, at one point, thought to have tardive dyskinesia, but this was never proven. Although there was no acting-out behavior reported, he was known to sleep with a gun. He had responded to neuroleptics but proved to be noncompliant and had recurrences. Delusions of influence by microwave radar, radio, and television were also reported in other admissions to the state hospital. Paranoid preoccupations with television brainwashing to control him were reported. Medical and neurological studies were found to be unremarkable. Other neuroleptic treatments than Haldol included treatment with Navane. Psychological testing revealed a full-scale IQ of 100.

*Medical history:* He reports he broke his leg 4 or 5 years ago. He was hit on the head with a bottle at a bar. No history of skull fractures, subdural hematoma, or concussion.

*Contributing social, developmental, and family factors:* The claimant was born and raised in a Midwestern urban area. He has one brother and one sister. He stated: "My family, between you and me, has signs of mental instability. My sister and mother are irrational. My brother is retarded and epileptic. My father believes whatever the government tells him." He stated that his father has "no intelligence." Of his childhood, he states, "I was mentally deprived as a child of correct sensory input. My mind was conditioned and brainwashed. I woke up to

(*continued*)

## BOX 2.4   Example of a Psychiatric Report (*continued*)

intelligence when I was 24. I am improving since then in mental nonpsychotic thinking." He mysteriously reports that he had "put on makeup as a psychotic. I have a human life in the micro-cosmos." His language tends to be grandiose as well as extremely tangential. He repeats that, "I am single in psychosis. Two people mingle their souls together in marriage contracts." He stated that he has never married in order to avoid becoming single and then psychotic. He completed 2 years of high school and dropped out. He quit because he "abhorred the word *education*." He stated that he is "a doctor and a scholar. I deal with people who are psychotic." He could not give a clear account of his occupational history. "I worked on lawns as a child. I mean flowers." He stated he went to a technical school, worked in some filling stations, worked for a department store, and worked in a car manufacturing plant for 2 years. He was a vendor at the city stadium for 3 months 1 year ago. He's done no regular job for more than a year. He doesn't remember how long ago. He now lives in an apartment by himself. His father paid for 2 months' rent. He had been living with his parents. His parents will be cutting him off if he doesn't get a job or some sort of benefits. He denies any police record. He could give no description of social attachments or interactions. His habits include a pack of cigarettes a day. He denies ever using illicit drugs or alcohol, entirely contradictory to the medical records.

*Mental status assessment*:

*Observed general behavior:* A 29-year-old White male, appearing about his stated age. He is 5 feet, 8 inches tall, and weighs 140 pounds. Blood pressure was 120/ 80; pulse 80; respirations 16. There was no eye contact. He was clean with adequate personal hygiene. No unusual mannerisms. Psychomotor activity was within normal limits. He was markedly digressive in speech. He was suspicious and became angry from time to time as he discussed paranoid preoccupations with the government, society, and education. He tends to be histrionic.

*Flow of thought:* Extremely tangential to a point of being almost unintelligible. Neologisms and complex, disorganized phraseology is noted. He is illogical and irrelevant. He definitely shows loosening of associations.

*Content of thought:* Multiple delusional systems. Extremely poor reality testing. His body is controlled by brain boxes installed by the government. The government wants to slow down his thinking so that he will not reveal their plots against him and others. A door has been placed in his brain. "The circuitry of my intelligence has been cross-fired." He is forced to get false brain signals. He has to protect himself in order to evade persecutors from the government. Television warns him and threatens him. His intelligence is too powerful to be eliminated by the government, however. Grandiosity pervades the entire interview. No suicidal ideas were elicited. No homicidal ideas were elicited.

*Mood and affect:* Mood is dysthymic, with blunted affect. He is indignant and angry about his father's requests of him. At times he appears histrionic.

*Orientation and cognition:* He is oriented times three, but not to the purpose of the examination. Judgment and comprehension are extremely poor. If he found a

*(continued)*

## BOX 2.4    Example of a Psychiatric Report (*continued*)

stamped addressed letter on the sidewalk, he would open it. He could interpret simple proverbs, such as "the grass is always greener." Memory: digit span was 6 of 7 forward, and 4 of 6 backward; he recalled three of three items within 1 and 5-minute delays; he had cereal for breakfast. He could name five presidents—Washington, Lincoln, Kennedy, Nixon, and Reagan. Concentration: serial seven subtractions from 100 were accurate to 79. He could name three major cities and one current news event. Insight is extremely limited—when asked about his condition, he stated, "I believe I am in excited isocratic suffrage."

*Functional limitations:*

*Social:* He is severely socially constricted and isolated. Related to his relations to others, he stated: "I am very opinionated, according to others. I sense hostility to me due to people wanting to degrade American life. My brain is overwhelmed to see and hear the sights. I have pain from my back due to electrical discharges from my jaws going to my left occipital lobe."

*Daily activities:* He spends his day in his apartment and walking the streets. He says he spends most of his 16 waking hours every day killing the bugs in his apartment and studying "diseases and pathogens." He said he is too busy "teaching myself what I am deprived of." He doesn't eat much, and he depends upon his family for meals and shopping. He doesn't manage money. He says he has "no expenses."

*Ability to concentrate on simple tasks:* Extremely limited, distracted, extremely delusional, hallucinating at times.

*Diagnosis:*

Schizophrenia, paranoid type, active.

*Prognosis:*

This man is actively psychotic. He is delusional, hallucinatory with marked tangentiality, loss of reality testing, grandiosity, delusions of influence and persecution. He is totally without insight. He has shown no sustained remission despite four hospitalizations at the state hospital. He is noncompliant with medications. He is unpredictable, unable to make useful contact, unable to communicate socially. He is bizarre in attitude. Flow of thought is illogical. He is socially withdrawn. Prognosis is extremely poor. He would ideally be treated with long-term institutionalization. Repeat hospitalizations are predictable. He is not capable of self-sufficiency, self-support, or adequate nutrition. Hygiene contrarily appears relatively appropriate. He is unable to relate with peers, family, or figures of authority. He is not competent to manage any benefits provided him.

Thank you for this interesting referral.

Sincerely yours,
T. Smith, MD
ABPN Diplomate in Psychiatry

## SPECIALIZED TECHNIQUES

Probably the most comprehensive list of techniques associated with the organic–medical paradigm is provided by the APA (1984) in its book entitled *The Psychiatric Therapies*. In that book, five classifications of organically based therapies are defined: (a) pharmacotherapies; (b) nutritional therapies; (c) electroconvulsive therapies; (d) psychosurgery; and (e) other somatic therapies, which include disulfiram (Antabuse) treatment for alcoholics, the use of stimulants for children with attention deficit disorder, hormone therapy, sleep-deprivation therapy for treatment of depression, and the like. Other treatment types are also addressed in the text; they are classified as psychosocial therapies, which include psychotherapy, group therapy, family therapy, biofeedback, and other approaches that are more closely aligned with the other paradigms in this text. A more contemporary text for the selection of treatments according to *DSM-5* diagnoses is the book by Reichenberg and Seligman (2016), which provides a compendium of approaches across diagnostic categories.

The most commonly used of these organic–medical techniques is ***pharmacotherapy***, also commonly referred to as ***medication therapy, psychiatric chemotherapy***, or ***drug therapy***. Pharmacotherapy is the most comprehensive and widely used medical treatment method in psychiatry. Medications are used to control anxiety symptoms, mood disorders (such as bipolar disorder and major depression), psychoses (such as schizophrenia), or other disorders where certain chemicals have been found to control or lessen symptoms. Treatments by medications are probably the most effective way to quickly lessen symptoms and to modify behavior. However, it is not without controversy (see Haley, 1989; Szasz, 1974; see Figure 2.1).

**FIGURE 2.1**  Thomas Szasz, Salvador Minuchin, Jay Haley, and Mary Goulding (from left to right) were among those who questioned the traditional approach to psychiatric conditions.
*Source:* Photo by R. Rocco Cottone.

*ECT*, also called *electroshock therapy (EST)*, is another commonly used treatment that is almost exclusively used today with severe mood disorders such as depression or bipolar disorder (manic-depressive illness). ECT involves systematized and exact electrical stimulation of portions of the brain. With disorders such as severe unmanageable depression, ECT has been found to be highly effective (APA, 1984). Controlled studies have demonstrated that it is quick and effective in reducing severe depressive symptoms, thereby preventing suicide and other self-inflicted harm in severely depressed patients. With regular follow-up maintenance treatments, it can also prevent relapse. Regardless, it is a controversial technique that arouses much public criticism, debate, and scrutiny.

*Nutritional therapy* is less controversial than its counterparts at face value. When used prudently, it is a more natural biological approach to mental disorder (albeit a less effective or inappropriate approach with many disorders). Nutritional therapy is used when there are nutritional deficiencies (e.g., soluble vitamin deficiencies in alcoholics) by increasing the amount of needed nutrients in the body. There are also several nutrients or food contents that have been implicated in certain disorders by their presence, for example, allergens. In these cases, nutritional therapy requires deletion of certain foods from the diet. Some nutritional substances may also be toxic if overingested, and nutritional therapy helps to ensure that dietary intake is controlled.

*Psychosurgery* is the severing, removal, or invasive stimulation of brain tissue or connective fibers. One of the most well-known psychosurgical procedures is *prefrontal lobotomy*, which involves severing connections between the prefrontal lobes of the cerebrum and the remainder of the brain. It was used primarily with aggressive and assaultive patients. Today, lobotomies are infrequently performed, although, with medical advances, more specialized, surgical procedures have been developed to sever, remove, or stimulate certain portions of the brain implicated in certain disorders. At present, especially with mood disorders, it is viewed "as a treatment of last resort," and then only under special considerations (APA, 1984). Time will be the truest test of developments in psychosurgery.

Overall, these common medical approaches are implemented by trained medical practitioners with the intent of modifying behavior at the biological level. There are serious side and main effects to these treatments, and counselors involved in psychiatric case management must be thoroughly knowledgeable about such effects.

## Recent Developments or Criticisms

To a large degree, the fate of psychiatric case management depends on the fate of the organic–medical philosophy in psychiatry. The organic–medical approach to psychiatry has been attacked in many ways from many sources. For example, psychologists more aligned with the psychological paradigm criticize organic–medical adherents on the grounds that the organic–medical perspective denies what they believe is the predominance of psychological and social factors at the root of human behaviors. For example, behaviorists have challenged the organic–medical approach by demonstrating that by affecting the environment of the individual with a severe disorder (such as childhood autism) they can have a significant positive effect on the behavior (Lovaas, 1987). Additionally, some psychologists argue that psychological factors, such as poor self-concepts or environmental psychological deprivations, are at the root of what the psychiatric profession has labeled as mental disorder. In fact, psychologists define such problems not as diseases, but as "maladjustments," and they usually use normative behavioral frameworks as standards for assessment.

Probably the most credible challenge to organic–medical ideas has come from the psychiatrist Thomas Szasz (1970, 1974, 1978). As mentioned in Chapter 1, Szasz (1974) described the idea of "mental illness" as a *myth*. He claimed that misbehavior should be seen just as that—a behavioral deviation—and it should be treated as such. He has argued convincingly that the medicalization of human social and psychological problems is an injustice to the treated person and to society. He argued that the actual role of the psychiatrist is akin to that of a *judge*, and he felt, unless there was clear-cut organic etiology, that the treatment of social and behavioral problems was outside of the realm of medicine. He argued instead for a social, psychological, and linguistic understanding of behavioral disturbances.

Another source of criticism from within the profession of psychiatry has come from the community psychiatry movement (see McQuistion, Sowers, Ranz, & Feldman, 2013). The community psychiatry movement has taken psychiatry out of the hospital and into the community in order to redefine the boundaries of psychiatry to include the social and psychological spheres. The community psychiatry movement downplays the medical aspects of its work and emphasizes the social and psychological aspects of mental disorder. It has expanded the province of psychiatry to include nonmedical social and cultural factors.

Regardless, strict organic–medical practitioners argue that just because etiology is unknown does not mean something is not a disease (Woodruff et al., 1974). They argue that practitioners must be empirical in their approach to human problems, and if the evidence solidly supports the contention of biological or chemical causation, even if such a contention has not been proven, then they assert that it is imprudent to treat such concerns as anything but medical. In fact, there have been many studies that support the idea of genetic linkage to some of the most severe *mental disorders*, such as schizophrenia, bipolar disorder (manic-depressive illness), alcoholism, and others (see the summaries according to disorders in Woodruff et al., 1974). Further, some research demonstrates a predominance of genetic factors in defining personality predisposition, separate from the actual mental disorder (Tellegen et al., 1988). The results of empirical studies of *twin concordance rates* **(the rates at which both individuals in twin pairs manifest a personality trait or a disorder)**, for example, convincingly support the idea that genetics is a primary factor in the development of some mental disorders. With the most severe disorders, there is a higher concordance rate among identical twins than fraternal twins, and an even greater difference between identical twins and nontwin siblings, even if the individuals in a twin pair or siblings are reared in separate environments.

There has been a remedicalization effort going on in psychiatry, primarily apparently for political reasons. Psychiatrists, by aligning with the organic–medical position, appear to be attempting to differentiate themselves clearly from other nonmedical mental health professions, such as psychology. For example, in 1989, the Association for the Advancement of Psychology circulated a document entitled "Psychiatry Declares War on Psychology" written by Rogers Wright and Charles Spielberger, both past presidents of a division of the American Psychological Association. In that document, Wright and Spielberger (1989) stated:

> Another aspect of psychiatry's war on psychology is reflected in its efforts over the past decade to "medicalize" itself, i.e., to identify with organized medicine. This has, at times, gone to ridiculous extremes in asserting an organic basis for every type of problem or misbehavior that troubles humankind. Though many "explanations" are given to justify these efforts,

the predominant driving force seems to be economic, reflecting "skyrocketing" medical costs which have contributed to the declining role of psychiatry as the intervention of choice in the treatment of troubled human beings. The "medicalization" strategy not only blatantly attempts to carve an exclusive turf for psychiatry, but it is also designed to enhance the probability of reimbursement for "medical/psychiatric" services, while limiting the consumer's freedom of choice and disenfranchising psychologists from many health care delivery plans. (p. 2)

It appears that battle lines have been drawn over the provincial rights of the mental health professions, and psychiatry is defending itself by means of its medical roots. Any remedicalization by psychiatry will likely drive it further from its competitors and toward a purely organic–medical approach to treatment, which will have consequences for mental health professionals practicing Psychiatric Case Management.

## STUDENT–MENTOR DIALOGUE

**Student:**  I was surprised to see this approach to treatment as the first approach in a book on counseling and psychotherapy. It was out-of-sync with my expectations. I thought a book on psychotherapy would be exclusive to approaches counselors, psychologists, social workers, and marriage/family therapists could use. Are you sure this approach belongs in a book on counseling and psychotherapy?

**Mentor:**  Yes. This is an approach to treatment that is largely ignored in textbooks on counseling and psychotherapy, even though in practice it is widely encountered by clinicians who primarily work in settings offering clients psychiatric consultation. Most community mental health centers or hospitals involve psychiatric treatment. Psychiatric Case Management certainly meets the criteria for a "counseling theory" or "therapy," as it is grounded philosophically and has a set protocol or structured method for assessing and treating clients. It has prescribed interventions for prescribed problems. It directs clinicians to be alert and to observe the client's behavior in an objectified way that allows for a strict medical or biological interpretation of maladjustment. So it definitely fits as a counseling approach that is highly applied but not well recognized by academics and textbook authors.

**Student:**  But can a nonmedical professional actually participate as a full partner in this kind of treatment?

**Mentor:**  To a large degree, the answer to this question depends on the attitude of the psychiatrist who is involved in the case. If the psychiatrist comes from a strict "biological psychiatry" framework, then the psychiatrist may communicate a message that nonphysician clinicians must take a backseat. That means that the counselor or psychotherapist will be viewed as an adjunct or secondary partner in treatment. On the other hand, a psychiatrist trained with a more "community psychiatry" philosophy will be willing to work side-by-side with a nonmedical clinician on a case. The community movement in psychiatry fully acknowledges the contributions of clinicians who address psychological and social factors affecting clients. A counselor in this situation will have a voice at the table when conferences or meetings are held to address a client's progress. Counseling and psychotherapy will not be viewed as add-on treatments—rather, Psychiatric Case Management will be considered a front-line treatment strategy. It is easy to assess whether a psychiatrist is more accepting of Psychiatric Case Management, because the psychiatrist will depend on, and work with, the nonmedical professionals to define the status and progress of the client they treat. Medical treatments will be refined to address the client's functioning and to facilitate healthy functioning of the client in some setting (rather than just trying to remove or lessen symptoms).

**Student:** Can a counselor or psychotherapist do Psychiatric Case Management in the absence of a treating psychiatrist?

**Mentor:** Yes, definitely. In many cases, an independently practicing counselor or psychotherapist can work with a client and communicate with the client's primary care doctor to provide information on the diagnosed mental condition and recommended treatments. Most primary care doctors appreciate the involvement of mental health professionals on their cases, as it provides a trained observer of the client's behavior in another context and can help the physician prescribe or adjust medications according to the perspective of the mental health professional. This happens quite frequently in practice. For example, a client may be seriously depressed; the counselor then writes a summary assessment and sends it to the primary care doctor with release forms for sharing treatment information. The counselor or psychotherapist may not be able to prescribe or recommend a medication based on the professional's *scope of practice* **(the limits by law of a treatment provider's acceptable interventions or activities)**, but the counselor can generally recommend consideration of prescription of a medication to treat the diagnosed mental disorder. Also, some mental disorders do not necessarily require medical interventions (such as a *personality disorder*, **which is a condition that is socially problematic and not typically responsive to medical interventions**). A counselor treating some diagnosed mental disorders can fully treat the conditions using nonmedical methods.

**Student:** How does a student of counseling and psychotherapy prepare to do this kind of work?

**Mentor:** It is important to take coursework that thoroughly addresses psychopathology and diagnosis. Counselor trainees also should take courses that treat the diagnostic process, including doing a full historical interview with the client or knowledgeable client advocate, and the counselor should be able to do a complete mental status examination that allows for one-on-one observation of the client in a controlled interpersonal context. The counselor must have an understanding of diagnostic terminology, applying information from the *DSM-5* diagnostic categories. The counselor should be well practiced at differential diagnosis, so seeking practicum and internship sites that provide supervision of diagnostic work is imperative. And, ideally, the diagnostician should also be a treatment professional that follows the diagnosed client through treatment, so the validity of both the diagnoses and treatment processes can be assessed. Student clinicians interested in this kind of work should seek training sites that provide in-depth training in Psychiatric Case Management.

## CONCLUSION

This chapter has introduced a type of counseling theory that is closely associated with the organic–medical paradigm. The presentation in this chapter is purposefully purist and extreme in its interpretation of Psychiatric Case Management; it is hoped that readers will get a precise picture of how paradigm-specific developments translate to the practice of counseling and psychotherapy. It is a contention of this presentation that Psychiatric Case Management is widely practiced in the mental health field, although, historically, it has not been strictly defined or recognized as a counseling theory. With the medicalization of the psychiatric profession, and with the clinical emphases predominating in other mental health professions (e.g., clinical psychology, clinical mental health counseling, clinical marital and family therapy, and psychiatric social work), it is assumed that Psychiatric Case Management will proliferate and develop into a widely acknowledged and applied counseling approach.

## REFERENCES

American Psychiatric Association. (1984). *The psychiatric therapies*. Washington, DC: Author.

American Psychiatric Association. (2013). *Diagnostic and statistical manual of mental disorders* (5th ed.). Arlington, VA: American Psychiatric Publishing. Excerpts reprinted with permission from the American Psychiatric Association. All Rights Reserved.

Haley, J. (1989). The effect of long-term outcome studies on the therapy of schizophrenia. *Journal of Marital and Family Therapy*, 15, 127–132.

Hedaya, R. J. (1996). *Understanding biological psychiatry*. New York, NY: W. W. Norton.

Lovaas, O. I. (1987). Behavioral treatment and normal educational and intellectual functioning in young autistic children. *Journal of Consulting and Clinical Psychology, 55*, 3–9.

McQuistion, H. L., Sowers, W. E., Ranz, J. N., & Feldman, J. M. (Eds.). (2013). *Handbook of community psychiatry*. New York, NY: Springer-Verlag.

Panksepp, J. (2004). *Textbook of biological psychiatry*. Hoboken, NJ: Wiley-Liss.

Reichenberg, L., & Seligman, L. (2016). *Selecting effective treatments: A comprehensive, systematic guide to treating mental disorders* (5th ed.). Hoboken, NJ: Wiley.

Sadock, B. J., Sadock, V. A., & Ruiz, P. (2015). *Kaplan and Sadock's synopsis of psychiatry: Behavioral sciences/clinical psychiatry* (11th ed.). Philadelphia, PA: Wolters Kluwer.

Shagass, C., Josiassen, R. C., Bridger, W. H., Weiss, K. J., Stoff, D., & Simpson, G. M. (1986). *Biological psychiatry, 1985*. New York, NY: Elsevier.

Szasz, T. S. (1970). *The manufacture of madness*. New York, NY: Harper & Row.

Szasz, T. S. (1974). *The myth of mental illness* (rev. ed.). New York, NY: Harper & Row.

Szasz, T. S. (1978). *The myth of psychotherapy*. Garden City, NY: Anchor Press/ Doubleday.

Tellegen, A., Lykken, D. T., Bouchard, T. J., Wilcox, K. J., Segal, N. L., & Rich, S. (1988). Personality similarity in twins reared apart and together. *Journal of Personality and Social Psychology, 54*, 1031–1039.

Trimble, M., & George, M. S. (2010). *Biological psychiatry* (3rd ed.). West Sussex, England: Wiley.

Woodruff, R. A., Goodwin, D. W., & Guze, S. B. (1974). *Psychiatric diagnosis*. New York, NY: Oxford University Press. Excerpt reproduced by permission of Oxford University Press, USA.

Wright, R., & Spielberger, C. D. (1989). *Psychiatry declares war on psychology*. Washington, DC: Association for the Advancement of Psychology.

# CHAPTER

## 3

# Psychoanalysis: Breaking New Ground

## OBJECTIVES

- To present the groundbreaking work of Sigmund Freud as a way to introduce a theory that has influenced the mental health field significantly and pervasively

- To provide an historical perspective to give the reader a context for understanding and adopting the ideas that Freud presented

- To give some biographical information on Freud to give readers a sense of his personal history and how his history may have influenced his ideas

- To list basic tenets of the theory and the basic concepts used in conceptualizing and addressing a client's concerns

- To offer a dialogue on the theory, as between a student and a mentor, on the significance of the theory for the mental health enterprise

- To discern criticism and current/recent developments in application of psychoanalysis

*Psychoanalysis* was developed by Sigmund Freud, MD. **Psychoanalysis is the term used by Freud to represent his therapeutic model—a model that focuses on the internal workings of the individual self.** The first time the term appeared in print was in 1886. With publication of two of Freud's major works, *The Interpretation of Dreams* in

1900 and *The Psychopathology of Everyday Life* (published in journal form in 1931 and in book form in 1901), psychoanalytic ideas were publicized. Freud's works represent a break with the traditions that preceded them in a way that facilitated a reframing of the cause and cure of emotional maladjustments. Before Freud's time, emotional concerns were thought to have spiritual (e.g., demons and/or possession) or physical causes (such as lesions on the brain). Although Freud was a physician, he defined and refined the concept of *psyche* **as a nonphysical personal aspect of an individual's self**. His work represents a milestone in the development of the discipline of psychology. Freud was clearly a *transitional theorist* **(a theorist who crossed from one paradigm to a new paradigm),** as he broke new ground theoretically and maintained close linkage to biological thinking, yet developed ideas that are aligned with present-day *psychological* theory. Therefore, his theory is less purely psychological than many of the theories that followed, as there is an obvious linkage to biological theory. Clearly, however, his works act as a bridge between biological and psychological perspectives of mental disturbance and treatment methods (Cottone, 2012).

## SIGMUND FREUD: A BIOGRAPHICAL SKETCH

Sigmund Freud
*Source*: Wikimedia Commons.

A complete chronology of Sigmund Freud's life and a brief narrative biography were published by Gay (1966, 1989). These two publications were used in the writing of this section as primary sources for describing Freud's life.

Sigismund (Sigmund) Schlomo Freud was born in 1856 in what is now Pribor, Czechoslovakia. His family later settled in Vienna, Austria, where Freud spent his youth. In 1873, Freud enrolled at the University of Vienna, where he studied medicine. He earned his medical degree in 1881. Between entering the University and finishing his degree, Freud developed a passion for research. Actually, his degree was slow to come because of his involvement in research at the university.

In 1882, Freud met his future wife, Martha Bernays. Although Freud and Martha Bernays were secretly engaged in 1882, they delayed wedding plans because Freud lacked a stable income. Subsequently, he accepted a position at the Vienna General Hospital and later set up a private medical practice in 1886. During this time, he continued to do research and, in fact, wrote a paper about the then unexplored properties of cocaine. Later in 1886, Freud and Martha Bernays were married.

Over Freud's early professional years, he met several individuals who would have lasting effects on his theory. One was a French neurologist, Jean-Martin Charcot, who studied hysteria and was a proponent of hypnosis. Freud also came into contact with Josef Breuer, a prominent internist, who would later coauthor a book with Freud, *Studies on Hysteria* (Breuer & Freud, 1895, republished in Gay, 1989). In fact, Anna O., a woman with bizarre and hysterical symptoms, who was a patient of Breuer's, would be the "founding patient of psychoanalysis" (Gay, 1989, p. xxxii). Gay (1966) stated that Anna O. "demonstrated to Freud's satisfaction that hysteria originates in sexual malfunctioning and that symptoms can be talked away" (p. xii).

It was in the 1890s that Freud's ideas about the *psychical* causes of certain symptomatic behaviors began to mature. Through those years, he wrote several brief works that helped form his ideas. It was in 1900 that his classic work, *The Interpretation of Dreams*, was published; it received a *cool* reception and sold only 351 copies in its first edition (Gay, 1966). *The Psychopathology of Everyday Life*, a second major publication, was published in book form in 1901 and received a *wider audience* (Gay, 1966, p. xiv).

In 1902, Freud accepted an appointment as an associate professor at the University of Vienna. In the years that followed, Freud was very productive. He worked with difficult patients and often wrote case studies or articles on the problems he encountered. His ideas began to have more influence, especially in Vienna. Later, contacts were made with two individuals who would hold important places in the psychoanalytic and psychotherapy movements. First was Carl Jung, from Zurich, Switzerland, who was supported by Freud to become a leader in the psychoanalytic movement. Jung later disagreed with Freud in an acrimonious split over issues of the role of the sexual drive, libido, in the formation of a class of emotional disturbances called *neurosis*. Second, there was Alfred Adler of Vienna, an early adherent of Freud's, who also later differed with Freud over the issue of primary drives at the root of emotional disturbance. These two individuals went on to develop theories that competed with psychoanalysis but also paralleled Freud's ideas by maintaining a strong allegiance to ideas of the unconscious.

World War I stalled the spread of psychoanalytic ideas, as academic matters gave way to the priorities of war. However, Freud was prolific even under the tension of seeing his sons go to war. (All of his sons survived the war.) In 1915, for instance, Freud began to deliver a series of lectures on his theories, published in 1917 as *Introductory Lectures on Psycho-Analysis* (S. Freud, 1917/1966). That work clearly described his ideas and helped him to secure a wide audience (Gay, 1966). However, the growth of Nazi Germany and the successful German invasion and occupation of Austria in 1938 had a serious personal effect on Freud. He was forced under the influence of anti-Semitism to leave Vienna near the end of his life. He left Vienna after his daughter, Anna, "was summoned to Gestapo headquarters." She suffered distress over the incident, but was physically unharmed (Gay, 1966, p. xxii). Freud and his family moved to London in 1938.

Freud was extremely prolific, leaving many well-articulated written positions related to psychoanalysis. His influence on what is now the psychotherapeutic field cannot be overemphasized. Freud recognized the gap in theory relevant to human functioning (because neither the biology of the day nor the religion of the time could adequately explain abnormal human behavior), and he filled the gap in a way that created a new perspective. Although his theory has been critiqued by many, its place in history is well secured. Freud died in 1939.

# THE FOUNDATIONAL THEORY

## The Target of Counseling

Freud's conception of the self is very structural. He views the internal workings of the mind, the *psyche*, as **organized but dynamic**. Essentially, **the psyche is composed of three major sections: the conscious, the preconscious, and the unconscious** (Figure 3.1). The *conscious* **(a level of awareness)** was compared to the unconscious by S. Freud (1940/1949) as follows:

> [The conscious] is the same as the consciousness of philosophers and of everyday opinion. Everything else psychical is in our view "the unconscious." We are soon led to make an important division in this unconscious. Some processes become conscious easily; they may then cease to be conscious, but can become conscious once more without any trouble: as people say, they can be reproduced or remembered. This reminds us that consciousness is in general a highly fugitive state. What is conscious is conscious only for a moment. (p. 16)

The *unconscious,* on the other hand, is **a deep-seated symbolic reservoir**. It is manifest only at times when individuals are in a sleeplike state, for example, through the process of dreaming or hypnosis. Otherwise, what is unconscious is unknown. However, there is a psychical process termed the *preconscious*, which is a **part of the psyche between the two extremes of the conscious and the unconscious**. The material in the preconscious is retrievable; it is "capable of becoming conscious" (S. Freud, 1940/1949, p. 17). Describing the relative nature of conscious, preconscious. and unconscious material, S. Freud (1940/1949) stated:

> The division between the three classes of material which possess these qualities is neither absolute nor permanent. What is preconscious becomes conscious, as we have seen, without any assistance from us; what is unconscious can through our efforts be made conscious, and in the process we may have a feeling that we are often overcoming very strong resistances. (p. 17)

It was precisely his understanding and definition of the unconscious that led Freud to develop his psychoanalysis. However, the human being could be psychologically held captive by his or her own unconscious; therefore, a means to free up the material stored there was necessary. That is precisely what psychoanalysis is all about.

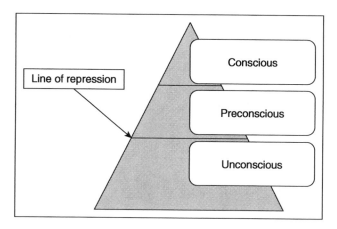

**FIGURE 3.1**    The three parts of the psyche.

However, Freud's conception of a structured psyche divided into three parts was not adequate for understanding the interplay of conscious and unconscious material that he observed in everyday life. He needed a *dynamic*—**a means of movement among the unconscious, the preconscious, and the conscious.** At the same time, he needed a way to conceptualize the idea of *self* that incorporated biological and cultural factors. The means to this end was the development of **three dynamic aspects of self: the id, the ego, and the superego** (see Figure 3.2).

**The *id* is the aspect of self most linked to biology and heredity.** It is, consistent with Darwin's (1859/1984, 1874) theory of natural selection, **sexually and aggressively motivated.** Rather than logic, it is driven primarily by libido, the life force. In a sense, the id represents the prurient, selfish, hedonistic aspects of humans. It is motivated primarily by two instincts: the sexual instinct and the aggressive instinct (what Freud first called the "destructive" instinct). The id lives deep in the unconscious.

**The *superego*, on the other hand, is an aspect of self that is developed primarily through cultural rather than biological means.** Although the superego is present from birth (as a far-evolved extension of the id), it is malleable, especially in the first 6 years of life. It lives primarily in the conscious part of the psyche. It is influenced mainly by the individual's relationships with his or her parents, and consequently, it represents parental instructions or commands. In this way, **it is the cultural conscience (moral code) of the personality—the civilized aspect of the personality.** However, where civilization prevents the expression of unreigned sexual and aggressive activity, the superego becomes the antithesis of the id. In this way, the superego and the id are antagonistic in the personality. If the superego and the id are in un-remediated conflict, then disintegration of the personality can occur (where integration of the personality reflects the constructive, adaptive sense of human functioning). The superego is actually a close extension of the ego, and it is thereby vulnerable to weakness in the ego.

**The *ego* is the rational mediator of biological and cultural influences on the personality.** S. Freud (1940/1949) said that the ego "acts as an intermediary between the id and the external world" (p. 2). It has the "task of self-preservation" (p. 2), and, if it is strong, it maintains control over oppositional forces in the personality. S. Freud (1940/1949) stated,

> The ego strives after pleasure and seeks to avoid unpleasure. An increase in unpleasure that is expected and foreseen is met by a signal of anxiety; the occasion of such an increase, whether it threatens from without or within, is known as a danger. (p. 3)

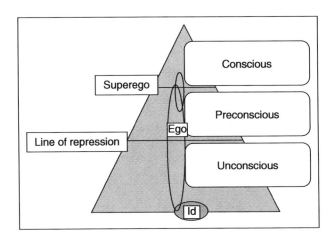

**FIGURE 3.2**  Locations of the dynamic aspects of the personality—id, ego, and superego.

Therefore, when the ego is conscious and alert to potential difficulties arising from cultural versus biological conflicts, it experiences anxiety, a chief characteristic of *neurosis*. **Neurosis is mental distress in which the ego is still organized and moderating opposing forces, but it is still vulnerable**. If, on the other hand, the ego were to give over to the id–superego conflict, a *psychosis* might emerge. **In psychosis, unrelenting sexual and aggressive instincts from the unconscious predominate, and contact with the external world is lost.**

The ego is a close relative of the id. It evolves from the id and reflects the social requirement for human survival. Without the ego, the human would be purely animalistic. Luckily, there is a line of repression between the unconscious and the preconscious parts of the psyche that helps to keep the id and the ego separate. In fact, the ego lives primarily in the conscious and the preconscious, retreating to the unconscious mainly during periods of somnolence in order to reorganize without the influence of external factors. When internally or externally threatened, however, the ego's main defense mechanism is *repression*. **Repression represents the ego's retreat from the unconscious while abandoning in the unconscious any threatening psychological material. Repression is a way of pushing down threatening or dangerous psychological material.** What Freud proposed was a picture of the self—represented by a psyche divided into three parts (the conscious, the preconscious, and the unconscious) and affected by three dynamic mechanisms—the id, the ego, and the superego. The interplay of conscious and unconscious material is reconciled by the biological and cultural demands on the organism that are moderated by the ego. In order for there to be psychological health, there must be a strong, healthy ego (see Figure 3.2).

## The Process of Counseling

The process of psychoanalysis is the process of uncovering the psychological history of the individual and removal of symptomatology through a "talking cure." Psychoanalysis began when Freud's colleague, Josef Breuer, described to Freud his treatment of Anna O., a woman who showed severe physical symptomatology without physical correlates. In his account of his treatment of Anna, Breuer (Breuer & Freud, 1885, as published in Gay, 1889) described how her symptoms (which included paralysis of certain body parts) were affected by discussion of their origins. Her symptoms were especially affected when Anna was in a hypnotic state. In fact, as part of her disorder, Anna entered into a hypnotic state regularly in the evenings. Breuer stated:

> These findings—that in the case of this patient the hysterical phenomena disappeared as soon as the event which had given rise to them was reproduced in her hypnosis made it possible to arrive at a therapeutic technical procedure which left nothing to be desired in its logical consistency and systematic application. Each individual symptom in this complicated case was taken separately in hand; all the occasions on which it had appeared were described in reverse order, starting before the time when the patient became bed-ridden and going back to the event which had led to its first appearance. When this had been described the symptom was permanently removed.
>
> In this way her paralytic contractures and anaesthesias, disorders of vision and hearing of every sort, neuralgias, coughing, tremors, etc., and, finally her disturbances of speech were "talked away." (p. 72)

Psychoanalysis was born. Although Breuer is credited with the first "talking cure," it was Freud who recognized the implications of his work and developed the procedures described by Breuer into a comprehensive theory of treatment of mental disorder. **Catharsis was used by Freud as the technical term for** *talking cure.* (The term *talking cure* was actually coined by Anna O. in her description of her own treatment.) **Catharsis is a "purging of the mind, a sort of unburdening of the mind,"** according to Brill (1921/1949, p. 8).

The process of psychoanalysis, then, is a process of providing an atmosphere in which the patient can explore his or her history without constraint, revealing his or her most intimate memories, especially those memories surrounding the emergence of symptomatic behavior.

To understand Freud's process of therapy, it is important to understand his theory of personality. For Freud, the sexual instinct predominated in the emergence of neurosis. He even felt that Breuer, in his presentation of Anna O.'s case study, underplayed the role sexuality held in the emergence of her symptoms. Of course, others disagreed with Freud on the role of the sexual instinct in the development of mental disorder (such as Adler and Jung), and one has to wonder why Freud so steadfastly held to his position. The answer may be threefold: (a) in the privacy of the therapeutic relationship, patients probably spoke openly about sexual issues, as they were probably sexually frustrated by a restrictive cultural and societal attitude, which probably prevented people from acknowledging, much less discussing openly, their sexual urges; (b) the findings of Freud's self-explorations, including his interpretations of his own dreams, were highly sexual, and these subjective experiences were viewed as representative of biological processes common to all humans; and (c) Freud's views on the sexual instinct were consistent with Darwin's theories. Moreover, Freud's ideas, being seminal, were largely initially ineffectively challenged by alternative viewpoints. Freud viewed the **sexual drive** (manifested quantitatively by **libido**) as resulting from processes in the darkest but most basic reaches of the human nature.

What this all means is that humans, according to S. Freud (1940/1949), must be viewed as highly sexual beings. Since birth humans primarily seek pleasurable sensations and sexual stimulation. Freud postulated several stages in **childhood psychosexual development: oral, anal, phallic, and genital phases.** These stages are critical to psychical functioning, because libido can become *fixated* (**disproportionally distributed**) to objects associated with the stages of development. S. Freud (1940/1949) stated:

> During the study of sexual functions we have been able to gain a first, preliminary conviction, or rather a suspicion, of two discoveries which will later be found to be important over the whole of our field. Firstly, the normal and abnormal manifestations observed by us (that is, the phenomenology of the subject) need to be described from the point of view of their dynamics and economics (in our case, from the point of view of the quantitative distribution of the libido). And secondly, the aetiology of the disorders which we study is to be looked for in the individual's developmental history—that is to say, in his early life. (p. 13)

A fixation may occur at a particular stage of development and the individual may be **cathected (charged with libidinal energy)** to particular objects associated with the fixation at that stage of development. Such fixations have a dramatic effect on "adult erotic life" (p. 10), as, under external stress, the individual may psychologically **regress (return)** to that level of functioning.

Libidinal frustration, when the libido is deprived of satisfaction, leads to regression of psychological functioning associated with a childhood stage of psychosexual development, and symptomatically, the individual demonstrates behaviors consistent with fixations at that stage. In this way, childhood development, frustrations during psychosexual development and subsequent fixations, and later libidinal frustration and regression are closely associated with neurosis and symptomatic behavior.

The process of self-exploration through psychoanalysis, then, must take a person back to those points where symptomatic behaviors first emerged, which likely are linked to early childhood developments.

## Counselor Role

The primary role of the therapist, beyond providing an atmosphere for full exploration of the client's history, is to help to strengthen the client's ego. S. Freud (1940/1949) stated: "The ego is weakened by the internal conflict and we must go to its help" (p. 30). The importance of the ego in mental health is clearly communicated by Freud in the following passage:

> According to our hypothesis it is the ego's task to meet the demands raised by its three dependent relations—to reality, to the id and to the super-ego—and nevertheless at the same time to preserve its own organization and maintain its own autonomy. The necessary precondition of the pathological states under discussion can only be a relative or absolute weakening of the ego which makes the fulfilment [sic] of its tasks impossible. The severest demand on the ego is probably the keeping down of the instinctual claims of the id, to accomplish which it is obliged to maintain large expenditures of energy on anticathexes. But the demands made by the super-ego too may become so powerful and so relentless that the ego may be paralysed, as it were, in the face of its other tasks. We may suspect that, in the economic conflicts which arise at this point, the id and the super-ego often make common cause against the hard-pressed ego which tries to cling to reality in order to retain its normal state. If the other two become too strong, they succeed in loosening and altering the ego's organization, so that its proper relation to reality is disturbed or even brought to an end. We have seen it happen in dreaming: when the ego is detached from the reality of the external world, it slips down, under the influence of the internal world, into psychosis. (pp. 29–30)

Essentially, the psychoanalyst must assist the ego by making it aware of the conflicts and the challenges from both biological and cultural sources, so that the ego can mediate these forces and make decisions for adaptive living. The psychoanalyst expects "complete candour" on the part of the ego (S. Freud, 1940/1949), and in return there is discretion on the part of the therapist. The fundamental rule for the client is:

> He is to tell us not only what he can say intentionally and willingly, what will give him relief like a confession, but everything else as well that his self-observation yields him, everything that comes into his head, even if

it is disagreeable for him to say it, even if it seems to him unimportant or actually nonsensical. . . . thus [he will] put us in a position to conjecture his repressed unconscious material and to extend, by the information we give him, his ego's knowledge of his unconscious. (p. 31)

This knowledge is critical to reconciliation of the internal forces that heretofore have led to disintegration of the personality. The therapist's *interpretation* (the meaning placed on the client's described experiences by the therapist) is critical to going beyond the stage of recognition on the part of the client. The therapist's tasks can be summarized as follows: (a) the therapist should produce ego self-knowledge in the client and (b) the therapist must accurately interpret material from the client's unconscious. If done effectively, it is assumed that symptoms diminish or disappear.

There are many traps in the process of psychoanalysis that make the therapist's task difficult, but there is one ally that proves to be of special importance. That ally is *transference*. According to S. Freud (1940/1949), **transference is the phenomenon by which the client actually sees in the therapist a "reincarnation of some important figure out of his childhood or past, and consequently transfers on to him feelings and reactions which undoubtedly applied to this prototype"** (p. 31). Often, the image of a client's parents are transferred onto the therapist. Transference can be positive or negative, just as feelings toward parents can be positive or negative. Regardless, *transference allows for the restructuring of the superego*, as it takes the individual back to an earlier time when relations had a significant impact on the formation of the personality. In this sense, transference gives the client a second chance. The newly educated superego (educated under the watchful eye of a trained therapist) can undo the mistakes of earlier learning—literally undermining fixations and cathected libido. By respecting the patient's individuality, the therapist can help to reconstruct the personality so that libidinal drives are more fully reconciled with the injunctions of a newer, more accepting superego. Consequently, the patient, through transference, relives a part of his or her past in the relationship with the therapist. Subsequently, the client is given a new opportunity. However, the role of the therapist through the transference process is a tricky one, as **the therapist might be trapped by his or her own transferences in relation to the client (this is called *"countertransference"*).** In this case, a therapist might be unable to extricate himself or herself from his or her own personality, thereby becoming a victim of his or her own unreconciled libidinal impulses. For example, a male therapist confronted by a female client who views the therapist through transference as a strong father figure might succumb to his own sexual feelings, just as a disturbed father might when confronted seductively by a loving daughter. (Remember Freud's theory was very sexual, and he even defined the child–parent relationship as highly incestuous at the unconscious level.) Therefore, the therapist must constantly battle with countertransference, which could lead to actions that would be counterproductive to the psychoanalytic task.

## Goals of Counseling and Ideal Outcomes

The main goals of psychoanalysis are ego self-knowledge and ego strength. S. Freud (1940/1949) stated: "What we desire . . . is that the ego, emboldened by the certainty of our help, shall dare to take the offensive in order to reconquer what has been lost" (p. 35). Furthermore, Freud stated:

> We serve the patient in various functions, as an authority and a substitute for his parents, as a teacher and educator; and we have done the best for him if, as analysts, we raise the mental processes in his ego to a normal level, transform what has become unconscious and repressed into preconscious material and thus return it once more to the possession of his ego. (p. 38)

Obviously, the ego takes precedence in the healthy personality, and it is the therapist's goal to put the ego in its rightful place as a rational voice and a moderator of divergent forces in the personality.

# GENERAL PROCEDURES

## Assessment

Assessment in psychoanalysis is first a medical process, as originally conceived. The individual patient is examined (if not physically then through a complete history) regarding the symptoms from which he or she wants relief. Symptoms are viewed in a classic medical sense as indicators that something is wrong internally. Although there is no analogy to *germs* in the physical sense, psychoanalysts proceed from the assumption that something is wrong with the inner workings of the patient. Some basic hypotheses can be made based on psychoanalytic assumptions (such as an overcontrolling super-ego or an unremitting libidinal drive), but these hypotheses are held in suspension until a clear exploration of the patient's unconscious processes is undertaken.

## Treatment/Remediation

Treatment is taken to remediate the ego, to strengthen it, and to reveal conflicting forces in the personality. Treatment may involve analyzing dreams; *hypnosis* **(a technique used to facilitate a client's trance as a means to access unconscious material)**, although Freud used hypnosis less and less in his later years; *free association* **(the process of allowing the client to respond spontaneously and in an unrestricted way to either the analyst's cues or to self-concentration on symptoms)**; and other means of releasing repressed material. The intent is to clarify the events associated with symptomatic behavior, with the aim of reconstructing those events psychologically.

## Case Management

Case management is an ongoing process of analysis, interpretation, and reanalysis. The patient and the analyst may meet several times a week, sometimes for several years. As the client's history (especially the symptomatic history) must be fully understood and brought to conscious light, it takes a concerted effort and a long-term commitment to successfully undergo psychoanalysis. This commitment must be understood from the beginning of therapy, and it is incumbent on the therapist to communicate clearly the potential benefits and dangers of undergoing psychoanalysis. Owing to the potential cost and commitment in time, it is also wise for the therapist to describe alternative treatment methods. In that way, the client is fully informed before consenting to psychoanalytic psychotherapy.

Psychoanalysis usually takes place in a comfortable office. The client is allowed to be comfortable and may recline on a couch or sit in a nearby chair. The analyst usually sits in a way that he or she can observe the patient, although it is ideal if the patient cannot observe the analyst. Note taking during sessions is important, as these notes help the analyst to uncover unconscious processes. Sessions ordinarily last from 30 to 50 minutes.

## Specialized Techniques

There are several techniques associated with psychoanalysis that are briefly described. It should be remembered that learning psychoanalysis is not an easy task. It takes many years of training, supervised experience, and personal analysis under the direction of a trained analyst. In this light, the following techniques are offered as a didactic means to help represent Freud's theory of counseling and psychotherapy. The list is not meant to be a comprehensive accounting of psychoanalytic techniques, nor is it meant to be an adequate means to direct beginning therapists. Students interested in becoming psychoanalysts should seek direction from trained analysts at approved psychoanalytic training centers.

Some of the techniques consistent with psychoanalysis are:

1. *The cathartic method.* As mentioned earlier, catharsis is the technical term for the talking cure. A major task of the therapist is to allow for a free flow of information from the client's ego to the therapist. The intent is to free the client through open discussion. As Brill (1921/1949) stated:

> Every hysterical symptom represents some mental or emotional disturbance that has taken place in the person's life in the past; there were occurrences of a disagreeable and painful nature which every individual likes to forget. Their [psychoanalysts'] idea was that if a patient can recall the unpleasant situation which gave origin to the symptom and live it over, so to say, he loses the symptom; that words are almost equivalent to the action, and that in going over some painful experience in the past there is what they called an abreaction . . . in which the painful emotions associated with the experience were liberated and thus ceased to create physical disturbances. (p. 8)

By means of the cathartic method, symptoms are overcome.

2. *Free association.* Arlow (1989) stated that Freud developed free association as a technique as follows:

> Because many of his patients could not be hypnotized, he dropped hypnosis in favor of forced suggestion, a technique of recollection fostered by the insistent demanding pressure of the therapist. Among other things, this technique produced artifacts in the form of sexual fantasies about childhood, which the patient offered the therapist as if they were recollections of actual events. Taking advantage of his new operational concepts of the dynamic unconscious and the principle of strict psychic determinism, Freud reduced the element of suggestion to a minimum by a new technical procedure in which he asked his patients to report freely and without criticism whatever came into their minds. (p. 34)

By simply allowing a client to tell everything that comes to his or her mind, the therapist can "trace all the forces that were responsible for the symptoms" (Brill, 1921/1949, p. 15). Patients are simply asked to maintain attention on the task at hand, as they let their minds roam freely among the images and thoughts associated with problematic behaviors. Once revealed, the therapist constructs interpretations of these recollections that can help the client to understand his or her own internal work-ings. Thus, the client's internal processes can be brought under conscious ego control.

3. *Facilitating and interpreting transference.* The analysis of transference is a classic psychoanalytic technique. It assumes, according to Arlow (1989),

> At a certain stage in the treatment, when it appears the patient is just about ready to relate his current difficulties to unconscious conflicts from childhood concerning wishes over some important person or persons in his life, a new and interesting phenomenon emerges. Emotionally, the ana-lyst assumes major significance in the life of the patient. The patient's per-ceptions of and demands upon the analyst become inappropriate, out of keeping with reality. The professional relationship becomes distorted as he tries to introduce personal instead of professional considerations into their interaction. Understanding transference was one of Freud's major discoveries. He perceived that in the transference, the patient was uncon-sciously reenacting a latter-day version of forgotten childhood memories and repressed unconscious fantasies. (p. 39)

Through the development of transferences, resistance and defenses come forward as a means to protect the ego from unconscious material. Yet it is the "working through" (Arlow, 1989, p. 39) of such resistances and defenses that is important to a resolution of conflicts within the personality. Through the process of analysis, the therapist attempts to make the transferences understood so the client can experience in the present what occurred in the past. The intent is awareness, and, at the same time, a rebuilding of the superego with fuller acceptance of the client's biological needs. S. Freud (1940/1949) stated:

> If we succeed, as we usually can, in enlightening the patient on the true nature of the phenomena of transference, we shall have struck a powerful weapon out of the hand of his resistance and shall have converted dangers into gains. For a patient never forgets again what he has experienced in the form of transference; it carries a greater force of conviction than anything he can acquire in other ways. (p. 34)

The analysis of transference, therefore, plays a major role in the psychoanalytic process.

4. *Dream interpretation.* While discussing dream interpretation, S. Freud (1940/1949) stated:

> But what makes dreams so invaluable in giving us insight is the circum-stances that, when the unconscious material makes its way into the ego, it [the unconscious] brings its own modes of working along with it....It is only in this way that we learn the laws which govern the passage of events in the unconscious and the respects in which they differ from the rules that are familiar to us in waking thought. (p. 24).

**Dream interpretation is the process whereby the analyst provides meaning to the dream experience described by the client.**

Freud felt that symptoms and dreams were similar as they involved unconscious material amenable only under circumstances in which the ego was reclining.

Essentially, dreams reflect conflicts among the forces in the personality. The therapist requests that the patient recall his or her dreams in depth. In that way, the analyst can take notes and attempt to piece together aspects of the dream that may clarify repressed wishes and impulses. The interpretation of dreams is founded on the idea that what is unconscious can be known and understood if one understands the basic biological drive of the human being. Dreams are interpreted in light of the biological instincts of sex and aggression.

These four techniques can be considered foundational to Freud's psychoanalysis.

## Recent Developments or Criticisms

To a degree, what has been presented here represents Freud's theory up till the day he died, but it is not in any sense a complete accounting of his ideas and their later implementation. There are a number of issues that cannot be covered in such a short summary that should not be overlooked. Readers, for instance, are directed to the work of Anna Freud (Sigmund's daughter); her book *The Ego and the Mechanisms of Defense* (A. Freud, 1936) is a classic psychoanalytic text that describes *ego defense mechanisms* **(a personality's means of self-preservation)**, such as repression, introjection, and projection. Freud's later emphasis on *insight* **(a spontaneous clear-cut moment of understanding)** as a means to awareness should not be overlooked, either. As Fine (1973) stated: "Freud's early emphasis on catharsis has been almost entirely superseded by his later emphasis on insight and the subsequent stress on the reorganization of the character structure" (p. 21). In this sense, one of the valued outcomes of therapy is a patient's **insight** into his or her functioning (which translates to **a deep-felt awareness that is unlikely to be forgotten**). Readers are directed to Freud's own works for further exploration of these issues, and to those works of his contemporary and subsequent adherents for a more complete and recent explication of his theory.

Freud's ideas have been lauded and criticized. Critics argue that his ideas, although at the time viewed as scientific, are actually reflections of Freud's own subjective experiences. Thus, his theory is viewed as nonobjective. Behaviorists, for example, argue that Freud's concepts are not objectively measurable, and therefore, they are not viewed as useful according to behavioral or objectively measurable criteria.

Freud's emphasis on sexuality is also a point of contention. Although it can be argued convincingly that sexuality plays an important part in the survival of the species and in human (especially young adult) motivation, the fact that Freud subjugated all aspects of human psychological growth, development, and functioning to the sexual drive seems to deny the other nonsexual aspects of humanness.

Feminist theorists have also launched a credible attack on Freud's ideas, especially the role Freud gave to the concept of **penis envy—the idea that women envy and desire the male sexual organ**. This concept openly espouses male superiority and implies the subordination of female personality development to that of the male. Freud's position, by today's standards, is extraordinarily sexist.

Freud's view of human nature is quite pessimistic. His theory fully recognizes that human cruelty and abuse are realities. Freud viewed human beings as sexually and aggressively driven and, especially when confronted by patients who have committed unconscionable crimes, his perspective offers a logical framework for assessment and understanding.

It is clear from his works that Freud viewed people as entities that exist to a large degree separately and independently. In fact, his emphasis on the need for individuals to be autonomous is revealing of his view of the human as a separable unit. Society, too has a thing-like quality, as the human is continually confronted by conflicts between biological and cultural pressures (as if culture exists as a discrete phenomenon). Freud's view of nature and reality, then, is very structural and concrete. It separates biology, psychology, and culture, yet it is dynamic in its descriptions of how these factors interrelate. The term *psychodynamic* to describe Freud's psychoanalysis, therefore, is quite appropriately reflective of biological, psychological, and cultural "things" in motion.

Contemporary discourse on psychoanalysis is acknowledging that there are different branches of psychoanalysis "including ego psychology, interpersonal theory, self-psychology, and various relational theories" (Luborsky, O'Reilly-Landry, & Arlow, 2011). In a sense, psychoanalysis has evolved and developed off-shoot approaches that, at least to some degree, hold to some of Freud's original ideas. There is also a divergence when addressing the psychology of the individual, versus the psychology of the therapeutic relationship. Luborsky et al. (2011) stated: "A 'one-person' psychology focuses exclusively on the mental reactions of the patient, whereas a 'two-person' psychology considers the treatment as emerging from the interaction between two individuals" (p. 27). There are definitely branches of psychoanalysis that focus on the therapeutic relationship as the vehicle for change. Luborsky et al. (2011) concluded: "This emphasis on the patient's real interaction with the analyst was a radical departure from the less involved stance of the classical analyst" (p. 27). It seems ironic that psychoanalysis, a classic psychological theory, has evolved into forms that emphasize the study of relationship over internal analysis of the individual client.

Regardless of developments and criticisms, Freud's ideas broke new ground. Psychoanalysis thus represents a milestone, especially as viewed from the perspective of the psychological paradigm of mental health services.

## STUDENT–MENTOR DIALOGUE

**Student:**  What are your thoughts on Sigmund Freud?

**Mentor:**  I think Freud's place in the history of psychotherapy is well-secured. He was a genius of the *intrapersonal* (inside the self), and he was masterful at presenting his very complex theory in a way that he received much attention. So as an historical figure, he will be viewed always as a major contributor to psychology and psychiatry.

**Student:**  But what about his theory—what do you think about his ideas?

**Mentor:**  Well, I find his ideas very interesting and also a bit perturbing. His ideas are multilayered and complex, which makes for a very complicated form of therapy. It takes years to be trained in psychoanalysis. It is also typically a long-term therapy, which means it might take many sessions or even years for a client to gain "insight" into his or her inner psychological workings. It doesn't fit well with a medical treatment enterprise that seeks a "quick fix" or quick cure. It also seems very pessimistic of the human condition, which may be disappointing to those who prefer to view humans in a positive light. But his theory certainly explains some heinous acts; it helps provide an interpretive framework for behavior that appears highly aggressive, destructive, abusive, or sexually exploitive. Other theories have a difficult time explaining intentional and sadistic abuse of others, for example. Freud's theory does provide an understanding of such behavior.

**Student:** How does it explain such aggressive and sexual exploitive behaviors?

**Mentor:** Freud's fundamental theory holds that there is an unconscious process that is driven by biological needs to aggress and to reproduce—two drives housed in the "id" and necessary for survival of the individual and his or her genes. This is an offshoot of Darwin's theory, which was prominent and gaining attention when Freud was developing his theory. So at a base level, humans are driven to reproduce potentially at the expense of social relations. Freud defined, though, an opposing force in the personality—one that is affected by social interaction—the superego. If there is a strong ego, the conflict between biological and social influence is moderated in a healthy way, so the individual does not become overly constrained emotionally (as in an overactive superego and neurosis) or under-controlled (as in an overactive id and psychosis). There is a balance between internal forces that represents mental health. That's why Freud's model is viewed as a conflict model— the personality is in internal conflict.

**Student:** Why is there such an emphasis on the unconscious in his model? Is everything significant to human behavior happening inside of us at a place that is unknown to us?

**Mentor:** Freud made a choice to focus on the unconscious process and fantasy (so-to-speak) as opposed to actual conflict outside of the personality. For example, he rejected the idea that children were abused (sexually or otherwise) to the degree it was influential in affecting their mental health. He wrote to a friend about abuse of children and essentially discounted actual abuse as unlikely. He wrote to a friend that "widespread perversions against children are not very probable" (readers should see the discussion of this matter in Cottone, 2011). Freud proposed that children were not really seduced by adults, they just unconsciously fantasized such seduction. Unconscious process is foundational to his theory. He also wrote at a time when hypnosis was getting attention— Mesmer's work influenced him and he learned to use hypnotic trance in exploring what was below client consciousness. The development of hypnosis as a practice and technique appeared to have a significant influence on his theory.

**Student:** So what do you see as good about this theory?

**Mentor:** It's the first—the very first—comprehensive and coherent theory of personality that acknowledges non-physical aspects of self (the psyche, id, ego, superego) that can be interpreted as affecting behavior. No one, to that date, did what Freud did in a way that gained widespread attention. He also gave us the first non-medical, nonreligious, and psychological treatment intervention for affecting deviant behavior. His theory offers much to clients who want to self-explore and who have the capacity to use insight to address their actions. In this model, insight is cure, and some people clearly show the capacity to use insight in assessing and directing their own behaviors. Psychoanalysis would be an ideal therapy for a client who has the resources, time, and interest in exploring thoughts, feelings, and emotions at a level that is deeper psychologically than what can be accessed through approaches that do not analyze the farthest reaches of human consciousness. It certainly is an interesting theory to study. It is elegant in its complexity and in its focus on the therapeutic relationship as a microcosm of unconscious processes.

**Student:** Thank you.

## CONCLUSION

This chapter has served as an introduction to counseling theories associated with the psychological paradigm. The development of psychoanalysis was a milestone in the development of the mental health service field. It was revolutionary for its time and has been unequaled in its influence on the way human nature is viewed. As a transitional psychotherapy, it provides a good example of how groundbreaking ideas can lead to development of comprehensive, competitive viewpoints of human nature, mental health, and treatment.

## REFERENCES

Arlow, J. A. (1989). Psychoanalysis. In R. Corsini & D. Wedding (Eds.), *Current psychotherapies* (4th ed., pp. 19–62). Itasca, IL: F. E. Peacock. Excerpts republished with permission of Cengage Learning.

Breuer, J., & Freud, S. (1989). Studies on hysteria: Case I: Fraulein Anna O. In P. Gay (Ed.), *The Freud reader* (pp. 61–86). New York, NY: W. W. Norton. (Original work published in 1895)

Brill, A. A. (1949). *Basic principles of psycho-analysis.* New York, NY: Washington Square Press. (Original work published 1921). Excerpt republished with permission of University Press of America.

Cottone, R. R. (2011). *Toward a positive psychology of religion: Belief science in the postmodern era.* Winchester, UK: John Hunt Publishing.

Cottone, R. R. (2012). *Paradigms of counseling and psychotherapy.* Cottleville, MO: Author. Retrieved from https://www.smashwords.com/books/view/165398

Darwin, C. (1874). *The descent of man and selection in relation to sex* (2nd ed.). Chicago, IL: Rand McNally.

Darwin, C. (1984). On the origin of species by means of natural selection. In R. Jastrow & K. Korey (Ed. & Commentator, respectively). *The essential Darwin* (pp. 57–228). Boston, MA: Little, Brown & Co. (Original work published in 1859)

Fine, R. (1973). Psychoanalysis. In R. Corsini (Ed.), *Current psychotherapies* (pp. 1–33). Itasca, IL: F. E. Peacock.

Freud, A. (1936). *The ego and the mechanisms of defense.* New York, NY: International University Press.

Freud, S. (1900). *The interpretation of dreams* (Standard ed., Vol. 4). New York, NY: W. W. Norton.

Freud, S. (1901). *The psychopathology of everyday life* (Standard ed., Vol. 6). New York, NY: W. W. Norton.

Freud, S. (1949). *An outline of psycho-analysis.* New York, NY: W. W. Norton. (Original work published in 1940)

Freud, S. (1966). *Introductory lectures on psycho-analysis.* New York, NY: W. W. Norton. (Original work published in 1917)

Gay, P. (1966). Freud: A brief life. In J. Strachey (Ed. and translator), *Introductory lectures on psycho-analysis.* New York, NY: W. W. Norton.

Gay, P. (1989). Sigmund Freud: A chronology. In P. Gay (Ed.), *The Freud reader.* New York, NY: W. W. Norton.

Luborsky, E. B., O'Reilly-Landry, M., & Arlow, J. A. (2011). Psychoanalysis. In R. J. Corsini & D. Wedding (Eds.), *Current psychotherapies* (9th ed.). Belmont, CA: Brooks/Cole, Cengage.

# CHAPTER

## 4

# Adlerian Therapy:
# The Individual Psychology
# of Alfred Adler

*Robert Rocco Cottone and Holly H. Wagner*

## OBJECTIVES

- To provide a brief biological sketch of the founder of Adlerian psychotherapy

- To define the basic tenets of Alfred Adler's theory of personality and therapy

- To outline the crucial elements of a theory that conceptualizes mental disorder from a psychological framework, but that is very alert to, and acknowledging of, social influence

- To provide a historical context for the development of Adler's ideas

- To give a summary of techniques and applications of Adlerian psychotherapy

- To describe current and recent developments as well as criticisms of Adlerian psychotherapy

The "Individual Psychology" of Alfred Adler represents a unique approach to addressing psychological problems and a break from the tradition from which it emerged. Although Adler was a member of Freud's circle (Ansbacher, 1962) and a contemporary of Freud (he was 14 years younger), he did not view himself as a disciple of Freud, and he strongly made the case that he had significant theoretical disagreements with Freud dating back to the beginning of their interaction (Ansbacher, 1962). Although he adopted Freud's ideas about the **"*psyche*" (an internal psychological structural aspect of the self),** he significantly differed from Freud regarding the nature of conflict in the personality and the basis for *neurosis,* **a term that reflected psychological disturbance deriving from conflict within the personality.**

Adlerian theory is used today in several settings. School counselors have embraced this approach, as they have found it to be a useful framework for working with children and adolescents. Adlerian theory is congruent and effective with contemporary approaches within school counseling and the American School Counselor Association (ASCA) National Model (Lemberger & Nask, 2008; Wagner & Elliott, 2014; Ziomek-Daigle, McMahon, & Paisley, 2008). Adler's theory is grounded on the idea that childhood experiences are crucial to psychological development, and that children, who are by nature in an inferior position to parents and other adults, strive to achieve some sense of superiority. In addition, counselors and psychotherapists acknowledge the flexibility in the approach that has evolved from the framework that Adler offered. Therefore, the model is adopted by practitioners who value flexibility in choosing techniques to apply to counseling and psychotherapy. There is also a very active Adlerian society with a well-respected journal. Adlerian theory has been modified to accommodate changes in the mental health enterprise, and it can be used by professionals who work within managed care as well as general mental health settings. Alfred Adler's thinking was progressive and, indeed, ahead of his time. Although he may have been "out of step with his contemporaries," today, however, his theory is widely applicable to the field of psychotherapy within many populations and contexts. The current emphasis on multiculturalism, social justice, common factors in therapy outcomes, and strengths-based approaches lends itself to congruence with Adlerian theory and the revolutionary thinker who was Adler (Carlson, Watts, & Maniacci, 2006a, p. 40).

## ALFRED ADLER: A BIOGRAPHICAL SKETCH

Alfred Adler
*Source:* Wikimedia Commons.

Adler was born in 1870 in Vienna. He was the third of seven children born to Hungarian Jewish immigrants. His father was a grain trader. Adler developed rickets at a young age, a disease that impaired his physical development. Serious health issues helped him form his career interests, and at a young age he decided to study medicine. The facts that he was ill at a young age and also witnessed his brother's death influenced significantly his theory of personality development. For example, he felt psychological compensation deriving from feelings of inferiority was a powerful motivator.

He studied medicine at the University of Vienna and started his medical practice as an eye doctor. He later changed his specialty to neurology and then he switched to the closely related developing specialty of psychiatry.

In 1902, on the invitation of Sigmund Freud, Adler joined a weekly discussion group on psychoanalytic ideas, meeting at Freud's house. The group later was the foundation for the Vienna Psychoanalytic Society of which Adler became president. However, because of serious philosophical differences with Freud, Adler left the society in 1911 with several colleagues. Adler's disagreement with Freud was profound and centered on the influence of external factors affecting the psyche—especially social factors, which became a theme of Adler's later works. Adler believed that feelings of inferiority were motivational and he also viewed the individual holistically, using the concept of Individual Psychology to imply that the human is indivisible. His ideas diverged significantly from Freud's ideas of internal conflict because of *libidinal* **(sexual and aggressive)** *impulses* driving personality development. Adler was much more external in his understanding of factors affecting behavior, and he began to place the individual in a social context with *social interests* (Bickhard & Ford, 1976). Under the strain of prejudice toward Jews, Adler left Vienna and took a teaching job at Long Island College of Medicine in the United States (in the early 1930s).

Overall, Adler's work represents a psychological theory that clearly acknowledges the influence of social factors on the personality. He held to Freud's idea of the human "psyche," but otherwise he cannot be viewed as a disciple of Freud. Adler's work is significantly different from Freud's work on substantive grounds, and the fact that they shared a common interest in analytic work as framework for psychiatric treatment is where their similarities appear to end.

Adler was married and had four children, two of whom became psychiatrists. He died in 1937.

# THE FOUNDATIONAL THEORY

## The Target of Counseling

Referring to the psyche and to an individual's conception of a goal in life, Adler (1929/1969) wrote:

> In each mind there is the conception of a goal or ideal to get beyond the present state, and to overcome the present deficiencies and difficulties by postulating a concrete aim for the future. By means of this concrete aim or goal the individual can think and feel himself superior to the difficulties of the present because he has in mind his success of the future. Without the sense of a goal individual activity would cease to have any meaning. (p. 2)

Adler (1924/1999) assumed that there was *striving* at the foundation of all human motivation. In a chapter dated 1914 in a book first published in 1929, he stated:

> The conclusion thus to be drawn from the unbiased study of any personality viewed from the standpoint of individual-psychology leads us to the following important proposition: every psychic phenomenon, if it is to give us any understanding of a person, can only be grasped and understood if regarded as a preparation for some goal. (Chapter I, para. 11)

Accordingly, humans are driven to achieve some goal, so his theory is a "drive" theory, and a major driving force within the personality was the need for compensation—one is compensating for some weakness or deficiency.

Ansbacher (1968) described three basic concepts that he believed provided a summary of Adler's theory: (a) style of life, (b) goal striving, and (c) social interest. Related to the concept of style of life, Ansbacher stated that the human is a biological and psychological unit. Everything that a human experiences is experienced by the whole biological and psychological unit and constitutes the *style of life* of the person. In other words, according to Ansbacher, **one's motivations, dreams, memory, and perception are all embodied in the organism as a whole and constitutes the *style of life* (sometimes called the *lifestyle* or *life-plan*).** The lifestyle is a cognitive map of sorts. It is the underpinning of the personality. Goal striving is crucial to the theory, as Adler believed that the healthy human was always striving and motivated to some goal. Adler believed that upward striving was crucial to mental health and driven by compensation for weakness or feelings of inferiority and the intent to be superior. *Goal striving,* **therefore, is the personality's means of self-motivation**; it is the motor that drives the human psychological machine, so to speak. Adler used the German word *Gemeinschaftsgefühl,* **meaning social interest or community feeling,** to describe one of the major tenets of his theory. *Social interest* **is the *innate aptitude* (Ansbacher, 1968) to engage other humans in a meaningful way.** To Adler, problems were social, and problem solving required full involvement with other people to define ways to address difficulties. In the end, social interest is communal—it requires a commitment beyond the self to other people. Furthermore, social interest entails having a sense of equality toward other people. Adlerians encourage this attitude within their clients and, in essence, promote social equality and justice through their work, while inspiring their clients to carry forth this virtue (Corsini, 2007).

The style of life develops in a way that fully incorporates the social context in the developmental process. Mosak and Maniacci (2011) described the importance of the family constellation in the development of the cognitive map that becomes a lifestyle. They said, "The family constellation constitutes the primary social environment" (p. 78). Within the family, children have subjective experiences that are foundational to their worldview. Mosak (1954) described components of the lifestyle as: (a) the self-concept; (b) the ideal self; (c) the *Weltbild,* **or *"picture of the world"*;** and (d) the person's ethical code, which defines what is right or wrong.

Mental disorder, from the perspective of Adlerian theory, represents a lack of social interests and, therefore, a lack of connection. This includes neurosis, psychosis, criminality, addiction, suicides, and perversions according to Ansbacher (1968). The psychotherapist's task is to address these issues by addressing the underlying style of life and by encouraging and strengthening social interests.

Adler (1924/1999) believed that mental disorder derived from the earliest of age as a striving for superiority that has gone awry. He believed that children, who are in an inferior (subordinate) position to parents and others, are driven by inferiority to establish a sense of superiority. The child possesses a feeling of inferiority toward parents and others. Where the *will to power* drives the person to selfish interests rather than social interests, the individual is set on a life course that is unhealthy and potentially destructive. The style of life in these cases must be reconfigured to one that embodies social interests. If one is not able to establish a healthy personality configuration, one can go through adult life with what might be called an "inferiority complex."

## The Process of Counseling

Although Adler's theory is quite different from Freud's in its focus on childhood experience of inferiority and the drive to superiority (vs. Freud's focus on the psychosexual development of children), Adler still embraced the psychoanalytic method and credits Freud and his colleague Breuer with its development. Adler (1924/1999) wrote:

> Eventually Josef Breuer hit upon the idea of questioning the patient, first in the case of hysterical paralysis, concerning the meaning and development of his own disease. He, and Freud, used this method without any preconceptions and confirmed the outstanding presence of memory-lacunae preventing both the patient and the physician from obtaining a real insight into the causes and the history of the disease. The attempts to formulate inferences with regard to the forgotten material from the knowledge of the psyche, the pathological traits of character, the phantasies and the dream-life of the patient, were successful and led to the creation of the psychoanalytical method and view-point. Thanks to this method Freud was able to trace back to earliest childhood the roots of nervous diseases and to disclose a number of psychical phenomena, such as repression and transference. (Chapter II, para. 2)

Obviously, Adler appreciated Freud's Psychoanalysis as a major contribution to the practice of medicine. He adopted several of Freud's core concepts about the psyche and the method of analysis in his own works.

Adler (1924/1999) wrote:

> At this place let me go out of my way to endorse an old fundamental conception of all who know human nature. Every marked attitude of a man can be traced back to an origin in childhood. In the nursery are formed and prepared all of man's future attitudes. Fundamental changes are produced only by means of an exceedingly high degree of introspection or among neurotics by means of the physician's individual psychological analysis. (Chapter I, para. 25)

The process of counseling is that of deep exploration of the individual psyche under the guiding influence of the counselor or psychotherapist (identified as the physician in the quote).

The process of Adlerian counseling involves four stages: establishment of the therapeutic relationship (stage 1), assessment and investigation (stage 2), interpretation and insight (stage 3), and reorientation and reeducation (stage 4) (Tinsley, Lease, & Giffin Wiersma, 2016). In stage 1, the counselor works to build trust and rapport with the client. This is of the utmost importance, as all subsequent stages are built on the successful laying of this therapeutic foundation. Stage 2 includes the lifestyle assessment, whereby lifestyle convictions, basic mistakes, and private logic are uncovered and explored through a focus on how past relationships (family, early relationships) are influencing current and future ways of being. In stage 3, the counselor and client make meaning of the client's lifestyle and together they develop awareness (insight) of what is serving and not serving the client to adopt healthy and adaptive functioning in life. Finally, in stage 4, the counselor assists the client in reorienting and reorganizing initially held beliefs to allow creative new ways to come forth that ultimately serve in strengthening positive self-concept, connection, and social interest.

## Counselor's Role

The role of the counselor is that of analyst, collaborator, and encourager. Counseling is one-on-one (dyadic), meaning it is the counselor in relation to the client. The role of the therapeutic relationship is emphasized. The counselor establishes a comfortable and collaborative environment in which the client's deepest memories of childhood can be explored. Any memories of childhood events are of importance, especially those that were relationship enhancing or destructive. The analyst is mindful of any overt or implied discussion of goals, of striving, or of feelings of inferiority, because they are keys to addressing the individual's style of life. Any client attitude that is *asocial* (showing no social interest) or *antisocial* (showing a sense of entitlement over others) are explored. Any healthy social interest is also important to analyze, as such an interest may be key to reorganization of the psyche.

The counselor, through empathy and compassion, seeks to understand and gain insight into the client's private logic. *Private logic* is a client's personal way of making sense of reality and is based on the client's subjective experience of the world, his or her self, and his or her lifestyle convictions. The counselor seeks to understand and bring awareness to the client's *basic mistakes* (assumptions or beliefs held because of one's private logic). The counselor relies heavily on *encouragement*, demonstrating faith and confidence in the client's ability to "reorient" himself or herself to a healthier way of living (lifestyle) through increased social interest and connection (Mosak & Maniacci, 1999).

## Goals of Counseling and Ideal Outcomes

Therapy is designed to create a sort of cognitive reorganization or reorientation. This reorganization reflects recognition that the lifestyle needs to be changed, or unhealthy behavior within a functional lifestyle needs to be modified. Adlerian psychotherapy is an *insight-oriented therapy* (a therapy that seeks to provide the client the opportunity to gain awareness as a primary precursor to behavior change) although Adlerians (e.g., Mosak & Miniacci, 2011) argue for a nontraditional definition of insight. Classically, insight is viewed as a prerequisite to change—a precursor to effective action on the part of the client. Most insight-oriented therapies purport that insight is the mechanism of change. Adlerians have taken the position that the insight encouraged by the Adlerian counselor is about "understanding translated to constructive action" (Mosak & Maniacci, 2011, p. 89). They have merged the idea of intellectual insight with the need for the client to demonstrate different, more constructive behavior. In the absence of behavior change, an Adlerian might argue that there has been no insight.

The primary goal of psychotherapy is to facilitate insight so that a client can change the lifestyle, which, for whatever reasons, has led to unhealthy behavior.

Adler (1924/1999) stated:

> Our science demands a markedly individualizing procedure and is consequently not much given to generalizations. For general guidance I would like to propound the following rule: as soon as the goal of a psychic movement or its life-plan has been recognized, then we are to assume that all the movements of its constituent parts will coincide with both the goal and the life-plan. This formulation, with some minor provisos, is to be maintained in the widest sense. It retains its value even if inverted: the properly understood part-movements must when combined, give the picture of an

integrated life-plan and final goal. Consequently we insist that, without worrying about the tendencies, milieu and experiences, all psychical powers are under the control of a directive idea and all expressions of emotion, feeling, thinking, willing, acting, dreaming as well as psycho-pathological phenomena, are permeated by one unified life-plan. Let me, by a slight suggestion, prove and yet soften down these heretical propositions: more important than tendencies, objective experience and milieu is the subjective evaluation, an evaluation which stands furthermore in a certain, often strange, relation to realities. Out of this evaluation however, which generally results in the development of a permanent mood of the nature of a feeling of inferiority there arises, depending upon the unconscious technique of our thought-apparatus, an imagined goal, an attempt at a planned final compensation and a life-plan. (Chapter I, paras. 15–16)

Individual Psychology's focus on the style of life, or "life-plan," as described by Adler, cannot be understated. It becomes the focus of treatment. It is the framework from which the counselor or therapist defines the target for intervention. It is a defining concept both theoretically and therapeutically.

Mosak and Maniacci (2011) stated: "Although the life-style is the instrument for coping with experience, it is very largely nonconscious" (p. 80). The Adlerian therapist, like the psychoanalyst, uses *interpretation* to facilitate the client's insight and to help to address nonconscious issues. **Interpretation is the therapist's description to the client of his or her understanding of the client's feelings, thoughts, actions, or relationships.** It is meant to be a stimulus for client self-analysis. It is the counselor's intention to facilitate a client **"aha" experience (a *eureka* experience)**, which ideally is followed by a change to healthier client behavior.

Rudolph Dreikurs (1961), who viewed psychotherapy and counseling differently, believed that Adlerian "counseling" targeted behavior that occurred within a functional or acceptable lifestyle. Changing the lifestyle is not the intent of counseling (where counseling's goal is to work with a healthy person addressing difficult problems), whereas lifestyle change is the intent of psychotherapy (where personality dysfunction requires a realignment of the personality) from Dreikurs's point of view. Dreikurs was largely responsible for infusing Adlerian principles and ideas within the United States and the context of the school system. Adlerian–Dreikursian classroom management strategies are used in education to promote a democratic classroom and academic achievement (Dreikurs, Grunwald, & Pepper, 1998; Soheili et al., 2015).

## GENERAL PROCEDURES

In a chapter titled "The Individual Psychological Treatment of Neurosis" (Adler, 1924/1999), Adler described in detail the process and challenge of doing psychotherapy with a dysfunctional person. He described the problems associated with inferiority and a dysfunctional life-plan. He addressed the need for the therapist to be active and even aggressive at challenging the destructive lifestyle of the client. He described "a compensatory psychic superstructure, the neurotic modus vivendi" (Chapter 4, para. 1) of the neurotic, and the struggle of the therapist to address the psychotherapeutic challenge presented by such a psychological structure (a boundary of sorts). An apparent means of the neurotic to free himself from the danger that counseling represents, he or she may become aggressive, oppositional, or defiant. The therapist is then faced with addressing these means of self-preservation. These client defenses are ironic because they come at the cost of moving forward to a healthier lifestyle.

In a sense, Adlerian psychotherapy holds to classic psychoanalytic procedures. There is a dyadic counselor–client relationship, an intense focus on childhood development, an in-depth analysis of psychological injury that causes a person to be bound psychologically to an unhealthy anchor, and a technique aimed at doing the hard work to raise the anchor into the open, in which it can be examined while it does not impede movement. The Adlerian psychotherapist's interpretations, however, focus on the client's inferiority feelings, selfish superiority strivings, maladaptive or distorted life-plans, and the need to re-organize the style of life to a healthy alternative.

The Adlerian psychotherapists must be firm, clearly directed by Adlerian theory, and able to recognize and to counter any defensive maneuvers of the client. Adler, following Freud, adopted the concept of unconscious process, which can impede the psychotherapeutic process. Adler (1924/1999) said:

> While the patient is imagining himself to be fighting for his superiority the physician can demonstrate to him the one-sidedness and sterility of his attitude. One of the greatest difficulties in treatment is the fact that the patient, although he may possess the proper insight into the nature of the neurotic mechanism, still partially maintains his symptoms. This he does until another of the neurotic artifices is disclosed, perhaps the most important namely, that the patient makes use of the unconscious in order to be able to follow the old goal of superiority and his old preparations and symptoms in spite of his recognition of them. (Chapter XIX, paras. 3–4)

In such cases, it is the Adlerian psychotherapist's role to affirm the destructive influence of distorted thinking and to delve deeply into the defensive methods of the client. At the same time, it is crucial for the therapist to educate, to encourage, and to inspire the client to adopt a more healthy sense of striving, one that is less selfishly focused on accomplishing superiority at the expense of others, and one that is socially sensitive and responsible.

## Specialized Techniques

Although Adler (1924/1999) wrote about how to address such psychological problems as organ inferiority, war neurosis, paranoia, psychosis, compulsions, sleep disturbance, insomnia, and other issues, contemporary Adlerian psychotherapists have defined and described specialized techniques that can be applied in general counseling contexts.

Mosak and Maniacci (2011) provided a list of techniques or methods of treatment. They include: (a) acting "as if"; (b) task setting; (c) creating images; (d) catching oneself; (e) the push-button technique; and (f) the "aha" experience. Using Mosak and Maniacci's outline, the techniques are expounded upon in the following paragraphs.

**Acting "as if"** is a technique that requests that the client do something different from what has been done in the past. Mosak and Maniacci (2011) described a situation in which someone is asked to wear different clothing to experience a difference—personally and even socially. The idea is that action is crucial to change, and the acting "as if" technique actually gets the client doing something different. It is like acting a part in a play that represents something healthy and not unhealthy.

Depending on the problems presented by a client, or the intention of treatment, **"task setting"** is a technique that allows collaborative definition of goals of treatment. However, the goals of task setting are very specific—small steps, so to speak—that allow the client to achieve some success in a way that does not engage the defensive process. For example, someone with social anxiety might be asked to say "hello" to one new stranger every day. Tasks should be simple and it is the counselor's job to encourage (perhaps gently) the client to achieve the tasks.

**"Creating images"** is a technique used to give the client a visual picture of something that is meaningfully related to the client's problem or goals. So someone who is overburdened by a *pile of work* might be asked to imagine himself or herself as a bulldozer, pushing through what has to be done. Or, a person afraid to swim might be asked to imagine himself or herself as a dolphin enjoying the gentle waves off of a beautiful coast line.

**"Catching oneself"** is a self-monitoring technique. It requires that the client recognize situations in which he or she reverts back to unhealthy behavior and stops an action that would lead to previously maladaptive behavior. Someone with an eating disorder might catch himself or herself approaching the refrigerator, and once recognized, the client would be asked to stop and resist the old behavior. In the end, the idea is to help clients avoid such situations (Mosak & Maniacci, 2011).

The **"push-button technique"** is akin to using a switch to turn off an emotion or feeling and to replace it with something that is healthier. The client rehearses the opposite of unwanted behavior, and then, like turning on a light, the client pushes the button to turn a room from dark to light.

The **"aha" experience** is encouraged by the counselor. When a client has an insight, even a slight awareness of something that has meaning in defining a healthier lifestyle, the counselor encourages such recognition. Since the Individual Psychology of Adler is an insight-oriented psychotherapy, it is important for the counselor to acknowledge any meaningful client self-awareness.

## Adlerian Application to Children and Adolescents

It is noteworthy that Adler took a special interest in the treatment and education of children. In 1930, he wrote *The Education of Children*, a book that outlines how children should be guided. He stated: "On account of the immaturity of children, the question of guidance—never wholly absent in the case of adults—takes on supreme importance" (Chapter I, para. 1). In his book, he detailed his views on the educational significance of the striving for superiority. He believed the superiority drive should be directed and that children should know the importance of *social feeling*. He defined the *inferiority complex* and described how children should be educated to prevent such a complex. He defined the child's position within his or her own family as crucial to psychological development. He addressed the school context and how it can positively or negatively influence a child, as can other *outside influences*. He also addressed educating parents on the psychological development of their children. A basic theme of his book is the need to raise children with *social mindedness*, a concept that is aligned with the development of the healthy lifestyle. It is obvious that Adler recognized the importance of parent education, early learning, prevention, and psychoeducation in the psychological development of the child, and he held the family and schools in high regard as contexts for positive education of the child. This is outlined further as the tasks of life, as applied to children, as follows.

## THE TASKS OF LIFE

In efforts toward understanding the lifestyle, Adler viewed humans' unique approaches to life through the lenses of the **life tasks**. These tasks included: **the work task, the social task, and the sexual** (intimacy or love) **task**. Some writers have gone on to recognize two additional tasks, the **self-task** and the **spiritual task** (Mosak & Maniacci, 1999). Developmentally, these tasks can be applied practically with children in order to assess and interpret healthy functioning and areas of needed growth. In childhood and adolescence, the five tasks can be simplified to three, and correspond with the three main socializing contexts for children (Vernon, 1999): the work task (school), the social task (friends), and finally the love task (family). School, friends, and family comprise the lifestyle of a child. The child's task of work is fulfilled within the context of school, as school becomes the major avenue to contribute and succeed during the earlier stages of life. The social task of connecting, finding a sense of belonging, and *fitting in* comes by the process of making and keeping friends. Finally, the child first comes to understand love through his or her family. The family provides the initial blueprint for relationships through family dynamics and constellation, birth order, and sibling relationships. However, the family of origin eventually gives way as the child develops intimate relationships forged outside of the family and the adult child creates a family of his or her own.

## GOALS OF MISBEHAVIOR

Dreikurs et al. (1998) outlined the *goals of misbehavior* as a framework to aid counselors and educators in understanding children's attempts at achieving certain common goals from a discouraged (rather than an encouraged) frame of reference. The four goals are: attention (being seen, noticed), power (being in control), revenge (hurting others because of being hurt), and display of inadequacy (withdrawing to helplessness) (Carlson, Watts, & Maniacci, 2006b). Once adults identify and recognize the child's underlying goal of his or her behavior, the child may be redirected to achieve the goal in a different way. The aim within counseling and education, ultimately, is to assist children in meeting these goals from an encouraged place, thereby meeting the same goal using adaptive behavior. For example, a child who has the faulty goal that he belongs only when being noticed, served, or attended to (attention) may constantly interrupt in class and speak out of turn (misbehavior). When the teacher connects the misbehavior to the goal, she can then allow the child to meet this goal by asking the child to help her, to involve him in class activities, and to give him attention for positive behavior. This response allows the child to meet his goal from an encouraged frame of reference.

> Adlerian therapy attempts to reeducate counselees within their social context in order for them to experience their role in society as one of equally giving to and receiving from others. When counselees are aware and cognizant of destructive patterns that do not enhance their ability to contribute to society, they can then attempt to change their behavior and meet their goals from a place of encouragement. (Wagner & Elliott, 2014, p. 9)

## ENCOURAGEMENT

Adler believed that **encouragement, in essence, the act of promoting courage within someone else**, was the cornerstone of therapy and could inspire clients toward growth, healthy adaptation, and functioning in life. Adlerian counselors working with youth use encouragement to promote the inner courage within these youth, thereby bolstering their self-concepts and self-esteem, as well as reorienting their lifestyles to reflect more positive beliefs regarding themselves, others, and the world (Mosak & Maniacci, 1999; Wagner & Elliott, 2014). Although Adler believed that humans are always striving for superiority and a sense of belonging, he recognized perfection as a *final fictional goal, one that could limit and harm the individual if not reoriented*. Therefore, Adlerian counseling serves to help youth find "the courage to be imperfect." Through the process of encouragement, young clients find the courage within themselves to accept their imperfections and build on what is already working (Tinsley et al., 2016).

## Recent Developments or Criticisms

Mosak and Maniacci (2011) stated, "Although Adlerian psychology was once dismissed as moribund, superficial (i.e., an 'ego psychology'), and suitable mainly for children, it is today considered a viable psychology" (p. 77). As a psychotherapy, it garners support from theoreticians and practitioners alike, who value the work of Adler and his insights into human psychological functioning.

In 1989, Lundin published *Alfred Adler's Basic Concepts and Implications*, a book that detailed the foundational theory and also defined the state of the theory to that date. In fact, at mid-century there was a renewed interest in Adler's work, which until that time in America had achieved secondary status to Freud's psychoanalysis. In 1952, with the foundation of the American Society for Adlerian Psychology and the publication of two Adlerian journals, there was an increase in interest in and popularity of Adler's work. To this day, the *Journal of Individual Psychology* is a viable outlet for the ideas of Adlerians and those interested in Adler's ideas. In fact, Adlerian therapy has been transformed to some degree by those who hold that it has applications beyond the Individual Psychology initially drafted by its founder. For example, issues like aging, trauma, play therapy, distance counseling and technology, and treatment of sexual minorities have been addressed in the journal (Bloom & Taylor, 2015; Close, 2015; Hjertaas, 2013; Taylor & Bratton, 2014).

Moreover, recently there have been some theoreticians that have attempted to align Adlerian theory to the emergent social constructivism paradigm of mental health services (see Cottone's [2012] definition of social constructivism). Constructivist philosophy is based on an idea that relationships are crucial to all understanding. In its extreme, constructivists do not believe that individuals exist in any psychological form. However, theorists like Watts (2003) have argued that Adlerian theory is a form of relational constructivist theory. Although Watts makes a compelling case, he grounds his arguments in the works of contemporary Adlerian theorists rather than in the seminal works of Adler himself, whose position is very clear in grounding Individual Psychology to the individual psyche.

Adlerians tend to want Adler's theory to have something for everyone. In practice, the theory allows for great flexibility of approaches, including full acknowledgment of the influence of the family and the social environment. Therefore, it is not constrained to a fully internal model of psychological influence, akin to theories such as Freud's. Nevertheless, it need not be so malleable as to lose its core tenets, and some contemporary writers appear to be pushing the limits in that regard. Stein (2008) spoke to the importance of maintaining the purity of Adler's original ideas by regarding Adler's seminal writings on the theory. Furthermore, Stein asserted the importance of being trained in the study of Adlerian theory through being the client as well as practitioner. "We need to encourage more Adlerians to learn the unique art of depth psychology, a process that can change the direction of people's lives, that reaches their mind, heart, and soul, that frees them to live creatively and become their best selves. Adler offers us inspiration and the tools necessary to achieve the valuable cause he promotes" (2008, p. 7). Stein purported that Adlerians must complete a "personal study-analysis" (p. 5) of themselves with the help of a "congruent mentor" (p. 7) in order to effectively guide clients in achieving insight into their lifestyles. It is only then that an Adlerian clinician can truly be helpful to others (Stein, 2008).

Another criticism or limitation of Adlerian psychotherapy is the fact that it has not been as widely researched as other approaches, such as cognitive behavioral therapy. Additional research could advance the theory further and allow it to gain a broader field of acceptance. Some practitioners also find the lifestyle assessment to be cumbersome and time-consuming, giving way to the use of more time-limited, brief approaches (Tinsley et al., 2016).

## STUDENT–MENTOR DIALOGUE

**Student:** So often one hears that Adler was a student of Freud. It appears, from the chapter material, that this is only partially true.

**Mentor:** Although Adler was a contemporary of Freud and followed Freud's lead on the idea of psychoanalysis as a treatment method, Adler was not in agreement about some fundamental ideas about human functioning. Adler, throughout his career, recognized the influence of the family on a child's functioning. He focused on the power dynamics in childhood relationships, such as the superior position of parents to children, sibling relationships, and the child's rebellion to inferiority feelings. Adler believed in the developmental influence of social dynamics of families, and he rejected Freud's ideas of psychosexual stages and concepts such as the Oedipus and Electra complexes. He believed there was a natural tension between the individual's need to strive to superiority and the developmental process all children experience in relationship to authority figures. Yet, Adler adopted Freud's ideas of the psyche and of the unconscious process. There was definitely tension between Adler and Freud, and their relationship was strained to the degree that Adler left Freud's inner circle of theoreticians. In some of his writings he appeared perturbed that people viewed him as a student of Freud.

**Student:**  How would you place Adler in the history of psychotherapy?

**Mentor:**  Adler's work is groundbreaking in its recognition of social factors influencing the psychological process. He recognized the influence of families. He recognized the power in interpersonal relationships and social connection. He described the tension that arises in child and adolescent development, which explains adolescent defiance. He was astute to the idea that healthy individuals are able to negotiate through the developmental relational quagmire to arrive at a psychological place that allows for social interests and social responsibility, rather than self-centeredness. He focused on the ideal of a healthy style of life—which he defined clearly as socially responsive action. So he provided a clear picture of the healthy personality. He has to be classified as a highly social psychological theorist. This means that his theory clearly reflects the influence of relationships, but it also is founded on classic psychological theory with psychic structure and even an unconscious process.

**Student:**  So would you classify this as a relationship theory?

**Mentor:**  No. Adler's theory is clearly a psychological theory. It is not akin to the more purely relational theories that do not focus on the individual at all; rather, the purer relational theories focus on relationships as the focus of treatment. Individual Psychology, although the name was meant to imply holism, must be viewed as just what it says it is—a psychology of the individual. It is, however, the most social of the classic psychological theories emerging from the works of Freud and other early psychoanalysts.

**Student:**  Is this approach still used today?

**Mentor:**  Yes, it is still a very recognized and used approach. One of the benefits of this theory is its application to working with children and adolescents. Adler was very sensitive to the need for prevention and early intervention and work in the schools. His work has been embraced by some school counselors, school psychologists, and school social workers who believe it has direct application to work with children and adolescents in the school setting. It helps to explain the influence of family relations on childhood behavior. It is positive in its ideal of social interest. So it has much to offer any child or adolescent counselor who works with children who often have a difficult time negotiating the social environments of home and school. It also helps to address inferiority feelings, which are not uncommon in a school-aged population. Of course, it still applies to work with adults, as just about any psychological disorder can be interpreted as a conflict of personal and social interests.

**Student:** It sounds like you are sold on Adler's theory. Do you have any general criticisms?

**Mentor:** Well, it can be criticized on a number of fronts. One general criticism is that it has morphed into a theory that can be described as unhinged from the original works of Adler. What I mean by this is that it is all things to all therapists who use it. In some applications, it does not appear to hold true to its origins and it seems to have become something that it is not. For example, some say it is a relational theory principally, when in fact, its linkage to classic psychological theory is unmistakable. So as a general criticism, it can be said that new generation Adlerians have denied or ignored the roots of the theory and are making it something that philosophically it cannot and should not be. Historically and practically, it is an elegant psychological theory that helped to point psychotherapy in the direction of full recognition of social factors affecting psychological functioning. That is a great accomplishment. It does not need to be something else. Also, Adler, like just about all theorists who address social issues from a psychological standpoint, never clearly defines how social relationships actually distort the psyche. It is just assumed that sick relationships do some sort of psychological damage. But the mechanism of damage is unclear. A more pure relational theorist would simply say that harmful interaction affects the individual's ability to enter subsequently into other relationships in healthy ways. Adler is saying that a harmful social environment damages the psyche, which then somehow translates to damaged future social relationships. There is a layer of theory in this explanation that is structural (the structure of the psyche), and yet the nature of the structural damage and its implications are unclear.

## CONCLUSION

The Individual Psychology of Alfred Adler provides a rich theoretical foundation for what has developed into Adlerian psychotherapy. Adler's work is the most sensitive to relationship influence of the classic psychological theories emerging from the works of Freud. Adler recognized the importance of relationships in the development of children, and he viewed the education of children at an early age on matters of social feelings and social responsibility as crucial to psychological well-being. He delimited the concept of inferiority complex, and he defined striving for superiority as a basic human drive that is, for healthy individuals, linked to a strong connection to others through social interests. His theory is positive, as he defines a healthy personality as achievable through healthy connection with others.

Adler's theory was unique for its time, and it has stood the test of time, as it is still respected and used in clinical and educational practice today.

# REFERENCES

Adler, A. (1930). *The education of children*. [Vitalsource ed.]. Retrieved from http://www.vitalsource.com

Adler, A. (1969). *The science of living*. Garden City, NY: Anchor. (Original work published in 1929)

Adler, A. (1999). *The practice and theory of individual psychology*. Abingdon, Oxon, UK: Routledge. (Electronic version. Original work published in 1924)

Ansbacher, H. L. (1946). Adler's place today in the psychology of memory. *Journal of Personality, 15*, 197–207.

Ansbacher, H. L. (1962). Was Adler a disciple of Freud? A reply. *Journal of Individual Psychology, 18*, 126–135.

Ansbacher, H. L. (1968). Introduction. In A. Adler's, *The science of living* (pp. vii–xxii). Garden City, NY: Anchor. (Original Adler work published in 1929)

Bickhard, M. H., & Ford, B. L. (1976). Adler's concept of social interest. *Journal of Individual Psychology, 32*, 27–49.

Bloom, Z. D., & Taylor, D. D. (2015). New problems in today's technological era: An Adlerian case example. *The Journal of Individual Psychology, 71*(2), 163–173.

Carlson, J., Watts, R. E., & Maniacci, M. (2006a). The contemporary relevance of Adlerian therapy. In J. Carlson, R. E. Watts, & M. Maniacci (Eds.), *Adlerian therapy: Theory and practice* (pp. 21–41). Washington, DC: American Psychological Association. doi:10.1037/11363-002

Carlson, J., Watts, R. E., & Maniacci, M. (2006b). Why should psychotherapists be excited about Adler? In J. Carlson, R. E. Watts, & M. Maniacci (Eds.), *Adlerian therapy: Theory and practice* (pp. 7–19). Washington, DC: American Psychological Association. doi:10.1037/11363-001

Close, R. E. (2015). Adlerian counseling in a virtual world: Some implications of Internet practice for the development of gemeinschaftsgefühl. *The Journal of Individual Psychology, 71*(2), 155–162.

Corsini, R. (2007). What does Alfred Adler have to teach to contemporary psychologists? *PsycCRITIQUES*. doi:10.1037/a0007604

Cottone, R. R. (2012). *Paradigms of counseling and psychotherapy*. Retrieved from https://www.smashwords.com/books/view/165398

Dreikurs, R. (1961). The Adlerian approach to therapy. In M. I. Stein (Ed.), *Contemporary psychotherapies* (pp. 80–94). Glencoe, IL: The Free Press.

Dreikurs, R., Grunwald, B. B., & Pepper, F. C. (1998). *Maintaining sanity in the classroom: Classroom management techniques* (2nd ed.). Philadelphia, PA: Taylor & Francis.

Hjertaas, T. (2013). Toward an Adlerian perspective on trauma. *Journal of Individual Psychology, 69*(3), 186–200.

Lemberger, M. F., & Nash, E. R. (2008). School counselors and the influence of Adler: Individual psychology since the advent of the ASCA national model. *Journal of Individual Psychology, 64*(4), 386–402.

Lundin, R. W. (1989). *Alfred Adler's basic concepts and implications*. New York, NY: Routledge.

Mosak, H. (1954). The psychological attitude in rehabilitation. *Archives of Rehabilitation Therapy, 2*, 9–10.

Mosak, H., & Maniacci, M. (1999). *A primer of Adlerian psychology: The analytic-behavioral-cognitive psychology of Alfred Adler*. London, UK: Brunner-Routledge.

Mosak, H., & Maniacci, M. (2011). Adlerian psychotherapy. In R. J. Corsini & D. Wedding (Eds.), *Current psychotherapies* (9th ed., pp. 67–112). Belmont, CA: Brooks/Cole, Cengage.

Soheili, F., Alizadeh, H., Murphy, J. M., Bajestani, H. S., & Ferguson, E. D. (2015). Teachers as leaders: The impact of Adler-Dreikurs classroom management techniques on students' perceptions of the classroom environment and on academic achievement. *The Journal of Individual Psychology, 71*(4), 440–461.

Stein, H. T. (2008). Adler's legacy: Past, present, and future. *Journal of Individual Psychology, 64*(1), 4–20.

Taylor, D. D., & Bratton, S. C. (2014). Developmentally appropriate practice: Adlerian play therapy with preschool children. *The Journal of Individual Psychology, 70*(3), 205–219.

Tinsley, H. E., Lease, S. H., & Giffin Wiersma, N. S. (2016). *Contemporary theory and practice in counseling and psychotherapy*. London, UK: Sage.

Vernon, A. (1999). *Counseling children and adolescents*. Denver, CO: Love.

Wagner, H. H., & Elliott, A. (2014). Adlerian adventure based counseling to enhance self esteem in school children. *Journal of School Counseling, 12*(14), 1–12.

Watts, R. E. (2003). Adlerian Therapy as a relational constructivist approach. *The Family Journal, 11*, 139–147. doi:10.1177/1066480702250169

Ziomek-Daigle, J., McMahon, G., & Paisley, P. O. (2008). Adlerian-based interventions for professional school counselors: Serving as both counselors and educational leaders. *Journal of the Individual Psychology, 64*(4), 450–467.

# CHAPTER

## 5

# Person-Centered Therapy

## OBJECTIVES

- To introduce the reader to the theoretical approach of Carl Rogers—a counseling theory that focuses on feelings

- To provide a biographical sketch of Carl Rogers, the creator of Person-Centered Therapy (PCT)

- To outline the theory of personality that undergirds PCT

- To provide the basic counseling philosophy and the approach used to engage clients in counseling

- To define the basic methods of PCT

- To summarize criticisms of the approach and to provide a student–mentor dialogue on the philosophy and practice of PCT

Person-Centered Therapy (PCT) was developed originally as a "nondirective" or "client-centered approach" by Carl Rogers, PhD, in the early 1940s. As a therapeutic approach, it has had a pervasive impact on the fields of counseling and psychology. It is one of the purest examples of a therapy focused on feeling and emotion as a means of change and personal development. As a therapy, it is very process oriented, emerging from "the necessary and sufficient conditions for therapeutic personality change" (Rogers, 1957), which are elaborated later in this chapter. As a philosophy, it is founded on a positive perspective of mental health, deriving from the view that humans have a tendency toward full functioning. As it has evolved, the original *Client-Centered Therapy* has become a *person-centered* approach, reflecting Rogers's unyielding faith in human growth through human interaction and downplaying the clinical context in which *therapy* usually occurs. In this text, for historical purposes and to reflect the changes in the approach itself, whenever a reference is made to foundational ideas originally closely aligned with Rogers's early theoretical conceptions, the title *Client-Centered Therapy* is used. On the other hand, when relating to later theoretical developments or the evolution of Rogers's approach, the title *PCT* will be used. Readers should not be confused by this dual method of referring to Rogers's therapy; rather, the dual approach reflects significant developments in Rogers's thinking over the years. It should help to clarify the ambiguities of evolved meanings for individuals wishing to better understand his theory.

## CARL RANSOM ROGERS: A BIOGRAPHICAL SKETCH

Carl Ransom Rogers
*Source*: Wikimedia Commons.

Carl Ransom Rogers was born in 1902 in Oak Park, Illinois. His father was trained as an engineer at the University of Wisconsin. His mother was a homemaker. His earliest years were spent in an upper-middle-class neighborhood in Oak Park (Kirschenbaum, 1979). His family later moved to a farm in nearby Glen Ellyn, Illinois, where Rogers spent his later childhood and adolescent years. His family was very religious.

Rogers was a very bright young boy and skipped one year in school. He was an excellent student in grade school and in high school (Kirschenbaum, 1979). He later attended the University of Wisconsin at Madison and majored in agricultural studies. Before leaving Wisconsin, he married a childhood playmate, Helen Elliott. He subsequently enrolled at Union Theological Seminary in New York, where he attended on scholarships. While in the seminary, Rogers enrolled in education and psychology courses at nearby Columbia University, which significantly influenced him. He later left the seminary, preferring to study at Columbia University's Teachers' College (in 1926), where he would take coursework in educational psychology. He received his MA degree in 1928 and his PhD degree in 1931, both from Columbia University. His doctoral dissertation was entitled *Measuring Personality Adjustment in Children Nine to Thirteen Years of Age*.

After attaining his PhD, Rogers remained in New York working as a psychologist until 1940; he then accepted a position at The Ohio State University to be a Professor of Clinical Psychology. At Ohio State he became thoroughly engrossed in academic life, while maintaining a schedule that allowed him to counsel students and supervise counselor trainees. Under the pressure of teaching, he felt obligated to develop his own position on counseling, and in late 1940, he presented a paper at the invitation of the

University of Minnesota that he described as significant to the development of Client-Centered Therapy. The reaction to his paper inspired his first major work, *Counseling and Psychotherapy: Newer Concepts in Practice* (Rogers, 1942), which today is viewed as a classic. In 1945 he moved to the University of Chicago, lured by an opportunity to develop a counseling center. It was while he was teaching and counseling at the University of Chicago that Rogers published his book *Client-Centered Therapy* (Rogers, 1951), which is foundational to his position on human growth, understanding, and change. His years at Chicago were very productive, and it was there that he became widely recognized. However, as if driven by a "pioneering spirit," Rogers accepted a position developed for him at the University of Wisconsin (see the discussion of his move in Kirschenbaum, 1979). At Wisconsin, Rogers applied his theory to severely disturbed psychotics. His time and work at Wisconsin, which produced outcome studies with mixed findings, proved to be very personally stressful, primarily due to serious disagreements among his colleagues (see Gendlin, 1988; Kirschenbaum, 1979). He later left the University for La Jolla, California, where he remained until his death in 1987. In La Jolla, he was a fellow with the Western Behavioral Sciences Institute.

Rogers received many distinguished awards in his lifetime. He was awarded the American Psychological Association's "Distinguished Scientific Contribution" award in 1956. Because of the application of his theories to the study of peace, he was nominated for a Nobel Peace Prize. He was truly an outstanding theoretician and counselor, and his impact upon the field of counseling and psychotherapy will be long-lasting.

# THE FOUNDATIONAL THEORY
## The Target of Counseling

In describing the foundational theory, the focus will be on Rogers's earliest expositions of his theory. Rogers's Client-Centered Therapy, as originally conceived, was a therapy focusing on the individual and upon the self. The "self" and the "self-concept" are foundational constructs that reflect Rogers's early ontology—**the self as an identifiable aspect of individuality**. (Although in his later years, Rogers moved away from viewing the individual in structural terms, his thinking never completely reconciled a structural concept of self with a process orientation in therapy.) Rogers (1951) defined the self-structure as follows:

> The self-structure is an organized configuration of perceptions of the self which are admissible to awareness. It is composed of such elements as the perceptions of one's characteristics and abilities; the percepts and concepts of the self in relation to others and to the environment; the value qualities which are perceived as associated with experiences and objects; and the goals and ideals which are perceived as having positive or negative valence. It is, then, the organized picture, existing in awareness either as figure or ground, of the self and the self-in-relationship, together with the positive or negative values which are associated with those qualities and relationships, as they are perceived as existing in the past, present, and future. (p. 501)

Furthermore, in describing the development of the self from childhood, Rogers stated: "The child . . . begins to perceive himself as a psychological object, and one of the most basic elements in the perceptions of himself as a person who is loved" (p. 502). It is noteworthy in these quotations that the self is predominant as a personality construct. It is an organizing principle in Rogers's theory of personality. It is a means of understanding his philosophy. The *self* **is viewed as an organized pattern of perceptions,** yet Rogers stated that the self is also "fluid" to a degree. In this way, the self is not immune to experience. **It is not so structured that it is unalterable. Yet the self is more constant than perception.** It provides continuity to the personality. As such, the personality becomes amenable to counseling.

## The Process of Counseling

Rogers's exposition of the "necessary and sufficient conditions for therapeutic personality change" in 1957 is perhaps the best summary of his foundational theory of change. Those six conditions, paraphrased in the following, are useful for understanding both his theory of personality and his ideas about therapy. In effect, the six conditions define how the self is positively affected in an interpersonal context. The six conditions are:

1. Two persons are in psychological contact.
2. The first, who shall be termed the client, is in a state of incongruence, being vulnerable or anxious.
3. The second person, who shall be termed the therapist, is congruent or integrated in the relationship.
4. The therapist experiences unconditional positive regard for the client.
5. The therapist experiences an empathic understanding of the client's internal frame of reference and endeavors to communicate this experience to the client.
6. The communication to the client of the therapist's empathic understanding and unconditional positive regard is to a minimal degree achieved.

According to Rogers (1957), if all of these six conditions are met over a period of time, they are *sufficient* to be associated with healthy personality change.

The terms *empathy* and *unconditional positive regard*, introduced in the six conditions, will be more fully defined in a following section entitled Counselor Role. The terms *psychological contact*, *congruence*, and *incongruence* require further immediate elaboration.

*Psychological contact*, as defined by Rogers (1957), means that when two people interact, "each makes some perceived differences in the experiential field of the other" (p. 96). According to Rogers, **the difference that one person makes in interaction with another person** does not necessarily have to be consciously recognized—it can be *subceived* (sensed at a nonconscious or even an organic–physical level). But at some level, there must be some effect due to the interpersonal relationship.

*Incongruence* is a term that Rogers used to describe psychological maladjustment. Rogers (1951) felt that psychological maladjustment exists "when the organism denies to awareness significant sensory and visceral experiences, which consequently are not symbolized and organized into the gestalt of the self structure. When this situation exists, there is a basic or potential psychological tension" (p. 510). **When a person essentially denies to conscious awareness his or her own sensory or visceral experiences,** he or she is denying important information to the self. Such experiences must be fully recognized for psychological health. Rogers believed that all such "sensory and visceral experiences" should be symbolically and consistently incorporated into "the concept of self" (p. 513). **When experiences are in a *consistent relationship with the self*, there is psychological *congruence*.** As an example, assume for a moment that a young man accidentally brushes up against another young man in skin-to-skin contact. Skin-to-skin contact is arousing to humans, and unless perceived through other sense organs, humans cannot identify the sex of the individual with whom they have made contact. In the case of the young man, if he felt aroused by the skin contact with the other man, he could: (a) accept the arousal, and depending on his sexual orientation, incorporate the experience into the self-structure (if heterosexual, the arousal could be viewed as simply a natural response to physical stimulation.); (b) deny the experience to awareness, thereby pushing aside sensory data, which potentially could cause distress when confronted with similar data in the future; or (c) accept the arousal, and misinterpret it as an absolute sign of unitary sexual orientation, which could produce discomfort in a person who has viewed himself as heterosexual. (Response "c" effectively requires denial of past arousal when in contact with females.) Response A is a congruent response. Responses B and C are incongruent responses.

In effect, Rogers developed a picture of the human being that includes a ***real self* (involving sensory and visceral experience and, ultimately, what one *feels*) and a *perceived self* (which may be consistent or inconsistent with experience).** When there is awareness of the real self, and there is consistency between the real and perceived self, there is congruence.

It is also true that the individual has a *self ideal* (Rogers, 1951, pp. 140–142). **The self ideal is a concept of self related to what one hopes or dreams of being.** Ideally, an individual's real, perceived, and ideal selves should all be consistent; when they are not consistent, a person may manifest psychological distress in some form.

Clearly, the focus of treatment in Client-Centered Therapy is the individual. The *self* is a psychological construct that endures and represents a predisposition to act. Rogers's early theory relied heavily on the definitions of structures—the real, perceived, and ideal selves. Rogers's focus on the individual "self," his unyielding faith in

**FIGURE 5.1**    An incongruent self-concept. The real, perceived, and ideal selves are disjointed.

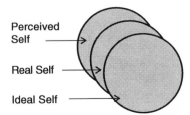

**FIGURE 5.2**    A congruent self-concept. The real, perceived, and ideal selves are congruent, as concentric circles.

human nature, and his continuous study of the process of individual change through psychotherapy reveal his emphasis on the individual as a primary locus of study.

In summary, in his early work, it is clear that the individual self constitutes a sort of object of intervention. The actions of the therapist are designed to produce a directional change, from incongruence to congruence. The cause of psychological maladjustment is directly defined—that is, distress results from incongruence that occurs when experiences are denied or not organized into the self-structure. Change occurs by someone (a counselor or psychotherapist) affecting internal psychological processes and facilitating self-growth.

## Counselor Role

Professional expertise as a Client-Centered Therapist is best gained through training in qualitative and quantitative scientific methods; Rogers (1951, 1987) is quite explicit about his faith in and reliance on the scientific method. However, he recognized that paraprofessionals could apply Client-Centered Therapy concepts successfully without extensive training. Related to assessment, all clients are viewed as inherently rational, possibly incongruent, and changeable. Positive outcomes occur when necessary and sufficient therapeutic conditions for personality change are met within an interpersonal context. And failure is often viewed as: (a) a failure of the counselor to build a therapeutic relationship; (b) reflecting the fact that a certain type of client cannot be helped (i.e., failure associated with, as Rogers [1951] stated, a "certain classification of personality diagnosis"); and (c) reflecting the inability (failure?) of the counselor to accept fully certain types of clients (Rogers, 1951, p. 189). Related to the role of the counselor, Raskin and Rogers (1989) stated:

> The basic theory of person-centered therapy is that if the therapist is success-ful in conveying genuineness, unconditional positive regard, and empathy, then the client will respond with constructive changes in personality orga-nization. Research has demonstrated that these qualities can be made real in a relationship and can be conveyed and appreciated in a short time. (p. 170)

One of the primary tasks of the counselor is to demonstrate the necessary and sufficient conditions for therapeutic personality change.

*Empathy* basically is defined as **the therapist's ability to accept and to experience as much as possible the feelings and attitudes of the client.** Essentially, the therapist should attempt to *feel* from the client's perspective, and although it can never be known whether this has been accomplished, the fact that the therapist expresses interest in such understanding is viewed as adequate for facilitating change.

*Unconditional positive regard* **relates to a positive, nonjudgmental, and accept-ing attitude conveyed by the therapist.** In effect, no matter how the client acts at the moment of therapy, the therapist must convey that the client is respected as a human being, and, even if the therapist cannot agree with something a client says or does, the therapist can accept him or her fully, as a person, without judgment.

*Genuineness* **and** *congruence* **are practically equivalent** concepts related to the ther-apist's role in the therapeutic relationship. **Congruence**, as stated earlier, **relates to con-sistency between the real and perceived selves.** The therapist must have the ability to understand and to express his or her own feelings in an open and unfettered way. The therapist must be aware of, and must not deny, his or her real self during the therapeu-tic encounter. For example, Raskin and Rogers (1989) addressed the issue of therapist fatigue as follows:

> An effective way of dealing with the common occurrence of therapist fatigue is to express it. This strengthens the relationship because the therapist is not trying to cover up a real feeling. It may act to reduce or eliminate the fatigue and restore the therapist to a fully attending and empathic state. (p. 172)

Accordingly, the therapist must be fully human in therapy, just as he or she expects the client to be fully human. Ultimately, the therapist must be a model of *congruence* and open communication.

## Goals of Counseling and Ideal Outcomes

Probably the clearest explanation by Rogers of the ideal outcome of therapy is contained in his book *On Becoming a Person: A Therapist's View of Psychotherapy* (Rogers, 1961). In that book, Rogers describes how **a fully functioning person** can emerge from therapy:

> For the client, this optimal therapy would mean an exploration of increasingly strange and unknown and dangerous feelings in himself, the exploration proving possible only because he is gradually realizing that he is accepted unconditionally. Thus he becomes acquainted with elements of his experience which have in the past been denied to awareness as too threatening, too damaging to the structure of the self. He finds himself experiencing these feelings fully, completely, in the relationship, so that for the moment he is his fear, or his anger, or his tenderness, or his strength. And as he lives these widely varied feelings, in all their degrees of intensity, he discovers that he has experienced himself, that he is all these feelings. He finds his behavior changing in constructive fashion in accordance with his newly experienced self. He approaches the realization that he no longer needs to fear what experience may hold, but can welcome it freely as part of his changing and developing self. (p. 185)

**A fully functioning person is a fully feeling and experiencing person**. At first glance, Rogers's conception of full functioning appears very similar to Abraham Maslow's concept of "self-actualization" (Maslow, 1954, 1968, 1971). About the same time Rogers was developing his ideas related to personality change and therapy, Maslow was developing his ideas related to personality development and motivation, and Maslow was refining the concept of self-actualization. Both ideas appear to have been founded on an earlier work by Goldstein (1934/1959), who first adequately defined the term *self-actualization*. But there are differences between Rogers's and Maslow's concepts, which were made clear by Rogers (1961, 1963). These differences help to bring to light what Rogers viewed as the ideal outcome of therapy. Figure 5.3 shows Maslow's hierarchy of needs pyramid.

*Self-actualization* **is a concept that describes what Maslow (1954) believed was a state of being: the ultimate in human mental and emotional maturation.** Self-actualization results from the natural tendency for humans to grow and develop psychologically as their basic or foundational needs are met. **Self-actualization represents a description of the epitome of mental health—a level of "being," not "becoming."** Self-actualized individuals can be viewed as having "arrived." Rogers's (1961) conception of "the fully functioning person," on the other hand, is less fixed. He stated: "It seems to me that the good life is not any fixed state.... It is not a condition in which the individual is adjusted, or fulfilled, or actualized" (pp. 185–186). Although Rogers's and Maslow's

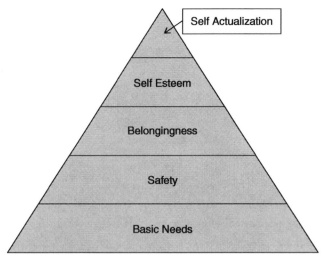

**FIGURE 5.3** Maslow's "Hierarchy of Needs."

conceptions of mental health are similarly founded on the idea that if basic conditions are met, individuals will naturally tend toward optimal psychological adjustment, there is a glaring difference in their final views of optimum functioning. In contrast to ideas such as Maslow's, **Rogers defined full functioning as "a process, not a state of being. . . . It is a direction, not a destination" (p. 186).** In summarizing his position, Rogers stated:

> The good life, from the point of view of my experience, is the process of movement in a direction which the human organism selects when it is inwardly free to move in any direction, and the general qualities of this selected direction appear to have a certain universality. (p. 187)

In this sense, the fully functioning person is free to become whatever he or she can. From Maslow's view, the outcome of growth is viewed as more clearly predestined.

Accordingly, the Client-Centered Therapist is basically viewed as a facilitator of growth and movement toward *the process* of full functioning. This is a position that was unchanged by Rogers even as he moved toward a more person-centered approach (Rogers, 1987).

## GENERAL PROCEDURES

### Assessment

Diagnosis, in the classic organic–medical sense, is completely avoided in Client-Centered Therapy. In fact, Rogers (1951) made an explicit case against diagnosis, indicating in some ways that it can be deleterious to the therapeutic relationship. Rogers felt that diagnosis placed the locus of evaluation on the therapist, instead of the client; he felt the client should be self-evaluative. Also, Rogers believed that the traditional process of diagnosis has social implications; for instance, one implication is that the client should be controlled by a professional who should accept the role of manager of the client's life. Rogers felt both of these implications of classic diagnosis warranted its avoidance. On the other hand, he viewed the *process* of therapy and diagnosis as one—as an evolving process. Rogers (1951) stated:

> In a very meaningful and accurate sense, therapy is diagnosis, and this
> diagnosis is a process which goes on in the experience of the client, rather
> than in the intellect of the clinician. (p. 223)

Rogers stated that only the client can diagnose, since "the client is the only one who
had the potentiality of knowing fully the dynamics of his perceptions and his behavior"
(p. 221). Accordingly, the process of diagnosis is an ongoing process accomplished primarily by the client.

## Treatment/Remediation

The focus of treatment is the individual. Treatment occurs in a therapeutic relationship.
Although the therapeutic relationship can be extended to include other individuals in
groups or families, the primary focus of attention in therapy is upon an individual's
experiences in the here and now, reflecting the match between the experienced, perceived, and ideal selves. When the six necessary and sufficient conditions for therapeutic personality change are met, a positive outcome is expected (Rogers, 1957). These
conditions may be met in settings other than one-to-one counseling, such as group
counseling (Raskin & Rogers, 1989).

## Case Management

The Client-Centered Therapist makes every effort to make the client comfortable.
Sessions are held at mutually agreed-upon times, and the therapist makes every effort
to accommodate the client's needs and desires. This is not to say that the client dictates
the mechanics of therapy, but rather, the client's position is respected.

The audio- or videotaping of sessions is encouraged with the permission of clients.
Counselors, especially beginning counselors, will find recordings of sessions of special usefulness in understanding the client's values and experiences. Case notes should
reflect what occurs in counseling, using language consistent with the basic theories of
personality and change. Care is taken to be nonjudgmental, and case notes and tape
recordings are used to facilitate the process of subsequent therapy sessions. Therapy
is scheduled in a way that is compatible with expressed client needs and the organizational constraints of the therapist.

## Specialized Techniques

Client-Centered Therapy is a therapy founded on both belief and trust. As Rogers
(1951) stated, there is belief "that the individual has a sufficient capacity to deal con-
structively with all those aspects of his life which can potentially come into conscious
awareness" (p. 24). There is trust that the therapeutic relationship will bring forth
the tendency toward full functioning in each individual. It is a therapy founded on a
positive view of human nature. This translates at the level of practice to communication that allows the client and therapist to be fully human, expressive of feelings, and
nonjudgmental. The therapist does not give advice or interpretations. Instead, he or
she reflects personally what the client has said, or, through techniques such as paraphrasing, the therapist facilitates, reflects, and/or mirrors the client's own interpretations. In this way, the client is more self-directive within the therapeutic relationship,
and since the client is fully accepted by the therapist, the client can be fully revealing,

without fear of being judged or devalued. Through the client-centered approach, a therapist helps a client to come face-to-face with the client's real self.

Beyond the more global methods used in therapy, such as empathy and unconditional positive regard, specific techniques consistent with Client-Centered Therapy and exhibited by Rogers in his therapy sessions are:

1. **Paraphrasing verbalizations—restating what a client has said in different words.** This is done often as both a means of checking what has been communicated for accuracy and as a means of cueing further responses. Example: "I understood what you said to mean. . . ."

2. **Paraphrasing nonverbal messages as feelings—stating in words, which are reflective of feelings, what the therapist observes** in a client's behavior. Example: "I see the pain that comes through in your tears. . . ."

3. **Acknowledging through nonverbal behaviors—responding to the client through actions.** Rogers appeared to use head nods and movements to signify that he was listening and attending to the client. The use of nonverbal behavior is also a means of recognizing the statements and actions of the client. Example: After a client states, "I feel more accepting of my aggressive feelings," the therapist might nod and respond "umm-hmm."

4. **Self-disclosure—revealing something about oneself as a therapist** as a means of making psychological contact and as a means of being congruent. Example: "I sometimes have trouble expressing my feelings, too."

5. **Expressing emotions—stating in the here and now what the therapist is feeling.** Example, "I am feeling a little concerned about what you just said, and I'm not sure what it means."

## Recent Developments or Criticisms

The therapeutic process of Client-Centered Therapy, as it was originally conceived, was best summarized by the term *nondirective*. In fact, the term *nondirective* preceded the use of the term *client-centered*, and for a period immediately following 1951 both terms were used synonymously (e.g., Rogers, 1951). Rogers (1951) stated, while talking about the philosophical orientation of the counselor: "He can be only as 'nondirective' as he has achieved respect for others in his own personality organization" (p. 21). However, the term *person-centered* was used by Rogers in his latest works, reflecting his faith in the individual and the need to view individuals from a positive, nonclinical standpoint. His ideas in his later years became much more egalitarian, much less concerned with maladjustment, and much more reflective of his deep faith in humanity. Sanford (1987), speaking of the evolution of the "client-centered" approach to the "person-centered" perspective, described the therapeutic process as follows:

> The organismic growth in the concept of the therapeutic experience brought with it not only a wider field of functioning for the client, but a broadening of the concept of the therapist, functioning in the climate of the person-centered approach, and compatible with the metaphor of companion on a journey—a more experienced and mature companion, but quite different from an expert or a doctor who prescribes a remedy, or a wise person who knows the "'solution" and will bring the patient around to it in due time, or at least will reveal in the process the causes of the illness or dilemma. (p. 191)

Rogers was an optimist, and his ideas were a manifestation of a deep-seated belief in the process of human growth through human interaction (Sanford, 1987). In fact, his work is well respected by some in the field of speech communication, as it positively contributed to a philosophy about dialogue as a mode of communication (see the excellent discussion by Cissna & Anderson, 1990, on this topic). As Cissna and Anderson (1990) stated:

> Carl Rogers was raised an American psychologist. As an American, he was taught that the individual is inherently important and that the pursuit of that which enhances the individual is the greatest value. As a psychologist, he was trained not only in a scientific method founded on prediction and control and on operationalism, but also in the belief that the real stuff of human life and of therapy is psychological. Against that training, Rogers struggled all his life to find a vocabulary in which he could express the reality of relationship as he experienced it. Though a psychologist, his focus was beyond the psyche, and on dialogue. (p. 139)

In one sense, Rogers can be viewed as an interactionist, although he lived at a time when the language of psychology and psychotherapy was focused almost exclusively upon the individual. In this way, Rogers appears to be a theoretician locked into an emphasis on the individual, although, paradoxically, his work recognized fully the use of relationship as a process unto itself. This is meant both as a compliment to Rogers and as a criticism of his work. He broke new ground by emphasizing the therapeutic relationship, yet he was bound to a theory that focused on the "self" as a final arbiter of truth.

Probably a more compelling reason that Rogers moved away from the term *nondirective therapy* as applied to his theory was his encounters with behaviorists. Rogers was best known at a time when behaviorism was on the rise in American psychology. In fact, it seemed that the behaviorists (e.g., Skinner) and the humanists (e.g., Rogers) were often viewed as opposing camps, or schools of psychology. In the heat of debate, Rogers was confronted by the fact that humans could be behaviorally conditioned to respond in ways reflective of self-expression—that is, reinforced by the behaviors of the therapist. Greenspoon (1955) produced data from study that showed that subject responses could be modified by nonverbal vocalizations ("mmm-hmm" and "huh-uh"), behaviorally increasing subject responses in expected directions. Effectively, he demonstrated that nonverbal behaviors typical of "nondirective" therapists could clearly be directing client response, for example, in the direction of more affective expressions. Greenspoon and Brownstein (1967), speaking of nonbehaviorally oriented psychotherapists as cognitive theorists, stated:

> Though the behaviorist has not accepted the construct of awareness, he has attended to the variables that affect the verbal responses from which the cognitive theorist has inferred awareness, as well as to the function of the verbal response itself. The behaviorist has tended to accept the verbal response per se and to investigate the antecedent conditions that produced it. At the same time he has also been willing to consider any unique functions of the verbal response that may apply to the behavior under consideration. The cognitive theorist, on the other hand, has not accepted the verbal response per se but rather has used it to infer awareness, which he then attempts to relate to the behavior under observation. (p. 305)

The behaviorists argued that therapists should simply focus on behavior, its antecedents, and consequences, while refraining from inferring other causes (see Greenspoon & Simkins, 1968). In fact, Rogers was involved in a debate with B. F. Skinner, the preeminent behaviorist (recorded during the 1956 American Psychological Association convention), which subsequently appears to have affected his position about the *directive* nature of his therapy. Rogers, confronted with arguments (and data from Greenspoon, 1955) that client-centered therapists condition responses in clients, responded as follows, according to Kirschenbaum (1979):

> Rogers, in the symposium with Skinner and on other occasions, acknowledged that the client-centered therapist is engaged in the reinforcement and control of the client's behavior. To a group of graduate students at the University of Rochester, he said, "... if you think of therapy as operant conditioning and certainly there is enough evidence in that field to make us think very seriously about the meaning of that—then I've come to feel that perhaps my hypothesis would be that effective therapy consists in the reinforcing of all experienced feelings. So then when you have reinforced all the feelings of the individual, then he can be all of those and he can be himself." To Skinner at the APA he said, "As therapists, we institute certain attitudinal conditions, and the client has relatively little voice in the establishment of these conditions. We predict that if these conditions are instituted, certain behavior consequences will ensue in the client. Up to this point this is largely external control, no different from what Skinner has described.... But here any similarity ceases." (p. 273)

In effect, the behaviorists mounted a credible challenge to Rogers's conception of nondirective therapy. And it appears that Rogers modified his theory to acknowledge the directive aspects of his work.

Another criticism of Rogers's Client-Centered Therapy related to diagnosis. Rogers's position is that diagnosis and treatment are one, and that everyone has the capacity to grow toward full functioning. To a large degree, Rogers's (1951) position on diagnosis and assessment ignores the obvious. First, for therapy to occur, there must be some degree of incongruence. Otherwise, what would mask as therapy would actually be two congruent persons in dialogue (which would be quite acceptable from a friendly conversational standpoint, but fails in the real sense of treatment). Two congruent persons in dialogue can hardly be conceptualized as therapy, which almost always occurs in an authoritative context. Assessment, in the sense that there must be a measure of client incongruence, is a prerequisite to therapy, and, although formal diagnosis and assessment are not operationalized in the process and techniques of Client-Centered Therapy, they are implicit in the therapeutic context. Additionally, although a client-centered therapist might view himself or herself as nonjudgmental, the fact that he or she has faith in the client's own resources, and communicates such, is a judgment that cannot be escaped. The client-centered therapist's assessment of individuals seeking treatment is always the same—that is, each person is viewed as having the capacity for growth and self-enhancement. *All* clients are assessed as having growth potential, which should not be misunderstood to mean that assessment has not occurred. This position appears naive if one accepts that there are genetic predispositions that may impede a client experiencing emotion in an unfettered or unimpaired way. Ultimately, a truly nonassessing therapy would have to be grounded upon a theory of personality that did not make distinctions about mental health versus mental maladjustment; Client-Centered Therapy is not such a therapy.

Rogers was also criticized by Albert Ellis, who vehemently disputed Rogers's six necessary and sufficient conditions for therapeutic personality change as neither individually necessary nor cumulatively sufficient to produce change in clients (Ellis, 1958). Ellis argued that each one of the conditions, or all of the conditions, can be absent, and individuals still can improve from a psychological standpoint.

Regardless of criticisms, Rogers's PCT is one of the most significant contributions to the psychotherapy literature. In fact, as researchers have begun to identify factors across different therapies that influence outcomes positively, the importance of the therapeutic relationship emerges as a crucial factor. Bordin (1979) first defined the importance of the therapeutic relationship by identifying what he called the "working alliance." More recently, researchers have identified the *therapeutic alliance*—**factors present in counselor–client interaction that are positively correlated to desirable outcomes** (cf., Ackerman & Hilsenroth, 2003; Baldwin, Wampold, & Imel, 2007; Castonguay, Constantino, & Holtforth, 2006; Lambert & Barley, 2001). These factors mimic some of Rogers's core conditions, such as empathy and unconditional positive regard. At some level, Rogers intuitively identified factors so basic to success in therapy that those factors are significant regardless of the theory of personality or psychotherapy that is applied. Some of those therapeutic alliance factors are: "trust, acceptance, acknowledgement, collaboration, and respect for the patient" (Beutler, 2000, p. 1005).

Rogers made a major impact at both the theoretical and philosophical levels. In one sense, he has been a moral conscience of the field of counseling and psychotherapy, always reminding theoreticians that people need to feel valuable and wanted, which comes through clearly in the evolution of his theory to a more person-centered approach. He also identified some very basic interpersonal skills that may apply to effective therapy no matter what theory is applied.

## STUDENT–MENTOR DIALOGUE

**Student:** What are your thoughts on Carl Rogers's Person-Centered Therapy?

**Mentor:** Well, against the backdrop of dominant psychoanalytic thinking and the rising tide of behaviorism, Rogers's theory holds a very significant historical place. His ideas represent a linkage to humanistic philosophy, which contrasts with the negativity of psychoanalytic philosophy (which paints a negative picture of human nature), or behavioral philosophy (which defines humans as devoid of free will). Rogers, along with several other counseling theorists (e.g., Perls, 1969), proposed that humans at their very basic level are "good," and capable of lofty achievement. He developed a positive theory of personality (people will be motivated to a higher level of functioning if certain conditions are met), and he developed a process of counseling that represents a means to help clients access their foundational selves. It is a theory that informs counselors to build on the emotional experiences of clients so that clients may be aware of their deepest and most basic feelings.

**Student:** So this is a theory that really focuses on the client's innermost feelings?

**Mentor:** Yes. It is focused on the internal psychological functioning of the client—how the client operates inside himself or herself. It directs counselors to focus on client feelings primarily, rather than client thoughts or behaviors.

**Student:** There has been significant criticism of Rogers's ideas that might influence a counselor applying his approach.

**Mentor:** Regardless of the criticism, Rogers's approach is widely practiced, as it is a very simple formula for successful treatment—six easy-to-learn conditions that must be present in counseling. Beginning counselors find this approach very simple and attractive, because, in-a-sense, the therapist is guided to be a caring person, and most counselors and psychotherapists tend to be caring people. Good listening skills are also required by the skillful person-centered therapist, and those skills are typically taught in early classes in training programs for mental health professionals. Also, Rogers's ideas hold some weight against criticism, as recent research on *common factors*—**factors associated with effective treatment across different psychotherapies**—continues to show the influence of trust and acceptance as crucial factors, and these are inherent in PCT. Some studies identify the "therapeutic alliance" as important in this regard, and Rogers may have inadvertently (not directed by research but by a theory of personality) identified some alliance factors.

**Student:** Is this not a useful theory for some clients?

**Mentor:** Rogers had some difficulty getting psychotic clients to respond to his treatment, although, to his credit, he tried. In some cases, highly disturbed clients did respond, it just took an inordinate amount of time, making such intervention impractical. So clients who have clear communication skills and the capacity to identify their feelings would be best served by this approach. Those that are cognitively or emotionally impaired may not respond well.

**Student:** So you see this as a viable counseling approach?

**Mentor:** Most definitely. It certainly can produce remarkable results with clients who are out of touch with their own feelings.

# CONCLUSION

Rogers's PCT is a classic example of a therapeutic approach consistent with the psychological paradigm that emphasizes what the client feels (as opposed to thinking or behavior). It is also consistent with the internal model of the psychological paradigm, since it focuses on the internal workings of the individual, as is evident in such concepts as "self" and "self-concept." However, in Rogers's later years he began to move away from the idea of treating disturbance of the self-concept and toward the idea of growth through interpersonal dialogue. He began to view dialogue itself as growth-enhancing when certain conditions were present, and he began to see that his ideas had applications beyond clinical settings to a truly person-centered way of social interaction. As Sanford (1987) stated, his ideas evolved from a means for facilitating a "fully functioning self" to enhancement of a "fully functioning self within the society," which involves "social awareness/ involvement" (p. 191).

# REFERENCES

Ackerman, S. J., & Hilsenroth, M. J. (2003). A review of therapist characteristics and techniques positively impacting the therapeutic alliance. *Clinical Psychology Review*, 23(1), 1–33.

Baldwin, S. A., Wampold, B. E., & Imel, Z. E. (2007). Untangling the alliance-outcome correlation: Exploring the relative importance of therapist and patient variability in the alliance. *Journal of Consulting and Clinical Psychology*, 75(6), 842–852. doi:10.1037/0022 -006X.75.6.842

Beutler, L. E. (2000). David and Goliath: When empirical and clinical standards of practice meet. *American Psychologist*, 55, 997–1007.

Bordin, E. S. (1979). The generalizability of the psychoanalytic concept of the working alliance. *Psychotherapy: Theory, Research & Practice*, 16, 252–260.

Castonguay, L. G., Constantino, M. J., & Holtforth, M. G. (2006). The working alliance: Where are we and where should we go? *Psychotherapy: Theory, Research, Practice, Training*, 43(3), 271–279. doi:10.1037/0033-3204.43.3.271

Cissna, K. N., & Anderson, R. (1990). The contributions of Carl R. Rogers to a philosophical praxis of dialogue. *Western Journal of Speech Communication*, 54, 125–147.

Ellis, A. (1958). *Critique of requisite conditions for basic personality change*. Paper presented at the meeting of the American Academy of Psychotherapists, August 9, 1958, in Madison, WI.

Gendlin, E. T. (1988). Carl Rogers (1902–1987). *American Psychologist*, 43, 127–128.

Goldstein, K. (1959). *The organism: A holistic approach to biology derived from psychological data in man*. New York, NY: American Book. (Original work published in 1934)

Greenspoon, J. (1955). The reinforcing effect of two spoken sounds on the frequency of two responses. *The American Journal of Psychology*, 68, 409–416.

Greenspoon, J., & Brownstein, A. (1967). Awareness in verbal conditioning. *Journal of Experimental Research in Personality*, 2, 295–308.

Greenspoon, J., & Simkins, L. (1968). A measurement approach to psychotherapy. *The Psychological Record*, 18, 409–423.

Kirschenbaum, H. (1979). *On becoming Carl Rogers.* New York, NY: Delta. Excerpt used with permission from Howard Kirschenbaum.

Lambert, M. J., & Barley, D. E. (2001). Research summary on the therapeutic relationship and psychotherapy outcome. *Psychotherapy: Theory, Research, Practice, Training, 38*(4), 357–361.

Maslow, A. H. (1954). *Motivation and personality.* New York, NY: Harper & Bros.

Maslow, A. H. (1968). *Toward a psychology of being.* New York, NY: D. Van Nostrand.

Maslow, A. H. (1971). *The furthest reaches of human nature.* New York, NY: The Viking Press.

Perls, F. (1969). *Gestalt therapy verbatim.* Menlo Park, CA: Real People Press.

Raskin, N. J., & Rogers. C. R. (1989). Person-centered therapy. In R. J. Corsini & D. Wedding (Eds.), *Current psychotherapies* (pp. 155–194). Itasca. IL: F. E. Peacock. Excerpts republished with permission of Cengage Learning.

Rogers, C. R. (1942). *Counseling and psychotherapy: Newer concepts in practice.* Boston, MA: Houghton Mifflin.

Rogers, C. R. (1951). *Client-centered therapy.* Boston, MA: Houghton Mifflin. Excerpts used with permission from Frances Fuchs, trustee of the Natalie Rogers Separate Property Trust.

Rogers, C. R. (1957). The necessary and sufficient conditions for therapeutic personality change. *Journal of Consulting Psychology, 21,* 95–103.

Rogers, C. R. (1961). *On becoming a person: A therapist's view of psychotherapy.* Boston, MA: Houghton Mifflin. Copyright © renewed 1989 by David E. Rogers and Natalie Rogers. Excerpts used by permission of Houghton Mifflin Harcourt Publishing Company. All rights reserved.

Rogers, C. R. (1963). The concept of the fully functioning person. *Psychotherapy: Theory, Research and Practice, 1,* 17–26.

Rogers, C. R. (1987). Rogers, Kohut, and Erickson: A personal perspective on some similarities and differences. In J. Zeig (Ed.), *The evolution of psychotherapy* (pp. 179–187). New York, NY: Brunner/Mazel.

Sanford, R. C. (1987). An inquiry into the evolution of the client-centered approach to psychotherapy. In J. Zeig (Ed.), *The evolution of psychotherapy* (pp. 188–197). New York, NY: Brunner/Mazel.

# CHAPTER

6

# Rational Emotive Behavior Therapy

## OBJECTIVES

- To introduce a counseling theory that is highly focused on how people think both in problem formation and in problem solution

- To provide a historical backdrop to the theory of Albert Ellis by providing a concise biography

- To present the Rational Emotive Behavior Therapy (REBT) model in workable form

- To outline the basic techniques and case management methods

- To update the theory with contemporary ideas from those adopting to this model

Rational-Emotive Therapy (RET) was developed by Albert Ellis, PhD, in 1955 (Ellis, 1989a). One of his major publications presenting his approach was a book entitled *Reason and Emotion in Psychotherapy* (Ellis, 1962). In that book, Ellis defined his basic therapeutic approach. Since that time, Ellis and his associates have been prolific in defining and communicating the basic tenets of RET. Many publications have appeared in print, and RET is a highly researched therapeutic approach. RET, as the name implies, is a highly *cognitive* **(perception plus language)** approach for understanding behavior and for doing therapy. Interestingly, in the 1990s, Ellis changed the name of his therapy to "Rational Emotive Behavior Therapy" (REBT) using the new title in the revised edition of *Reason and Emotion in Psychotherapy* (Ellis, 1994). Ellis (1995) stated: "So, to correct my previous errors and to set the record straight, I shall now call it what it has really always been, rational emotive behavior therapy (REBT)" (p. 5). He changed the name because he believed that the old title was "misleading" and that RET "omits the highly behavioral aspect that rational-emotive therapy has favored right from the start" (p. 86). Ellis believed that the therapist should implement not only techniques to change maladaptive thoughts, but should also implement techniques to produce a new set of actions and what he called "an effective new philosophy" (Ellis, 1994, p. 79).

## ALBERT ELLIS: A BIOGRAPHICAL SKETCH

Albert Ellis.
*Source*: Photo by R. Rocco Cottone.

Albert Ellis was born in Pittsburgh, Pennsylvania, in 1913. At an early age, Ellis suffered from an illness called nephritis, and he almost died from complications following an infected tonsil (Dryden, 1989). Between the ages of 4 and 9 years, he was hospitalized nine times, which affected his schooling and curtailed his involvement in physical activities. In fact, throughout his life, Ellis has been affected by illnesses. In middle age, he was diagnosed as diabetic, a lifelong condition that required a significant lifestyle adjustment. Beyond facing his illnesses, Ellis learned early in life to be helpful to others. He viewed his mother as "a neglectful woman in her own nice way," and he took an active role in his family, especially helping with his younger siblings. Consequently, he adopted a helping attitude early in life. In fact, Ellis said in an interview in 1989,

> I always seemed to have been the kind of person who, when unhappy, made an effort to think about and figure out ways to make myself less unhappy. In a way I was a born therapist, for myself. It certainly came naturally to me. Later on, I used this problem-solving tendency to help my friends with their problems, but first I used it with myself. (Dryden, 1989, p. 540)

Although he had much to be sad about, he apparently learned that he could make himself less unhappy through effort, and he applied this basic philosophy to his own life and later in his relationships with others.

Ellis grew up and completed his college education in New York City. He earned a business degree at the City College of New York. In 1943, he earned an MA from Columbia University in clinical psychology and started a private practice in counseling about the same time. He later (1947) earned a PhD degree in clinical psychology from Columbia University. He was trained in classic psychoanalysis, but he felt uncomfortable using psychoanalytic techniques. His disenchantment with psychoanalysis later led to the development of REBT.

Ellis frequently told stories at his workshops about how he overcame his fear of women—a story that not only reflects a personal philosophy but also reflects on the development of REBT. At the age of 19 years, to overcome his fear, he forced himself "to talk to a hundred girls in a row in the Bronx Botanical Gardens during the period of one month" (see Dryden, 1989). Subsequently, he married and divorced twice, followed by a long period of living single, and then in 2004 he married for the third time, staying in the relationship till his death in 2007. He was a model of his own theory, in that he believed that thinking and acting—or, in other words, cognition and action—rule over the emotions. Ellis's views were derived from his readings of the philosopher Epictetus, who carried forth ideas from earlier philosophers about disturbances deriving from *one's view* of things.

Ellis held several clinical and teaching positions, but for most of his career he was in private practice while directing his institutes in New York (e.g., the Institute for Rational-Emotive Therapy). He taught at Rutgers University and New York University. He worked for a while as the chief psychologist of the New Jersey State Diagnostic Center, and also as a chief psychologist at the New Jersey Department of Institutions and Agencies. He was a consultant to the Veterans Administration.

Dr. Ellis received the award for Distinguished Professional Contributions from the American Psychological Association in 1985. He was a fellow of several prestigious professional organizations. Ellis was a prolific writer, and his bibliography filled 16 pages of the *American Psychologist* in a 1986 issue of the journal (Ellis, 1986). He has been one of the most influential theorists in the field of counseling and psychotherapy. Dr. Ellis died on July 24, 2007, in New York at the age of 93 years.

# THE FOUNDATIONAL THEORY

## The Target of Counseling

Ellis (1989a) has simplified his theory into an A-B-C-(D) model of thinking and feeling (Figure 6.1), which to a large degree presents his therapeutic approach and the target of therapy.

According to this model, people are born with the potential to think rationally or irrationally, that is, to hold rational beliefs (rB) or irrational beliefs (iB). People, being cognitive beings, tend to perceive and think more or less concurrently with their feelings and behaviors. In fact, Ellis believed that when a human is confronted by an antecedent event (A), it is the cognitive event or belief (B) associated with the event that results in emotional consequences (C). Essentially, the way one thinks affects the way one feels and behaves. However, when the emotional consequences are self-defeating, then they

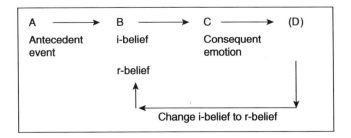

**FIGURE 6.1**  Ellis's A-B-C-(D) model of thinking and feeling.

are most likely the result of iB, which can be actively disputed (D) in therapy either by a trained professional or by the client himself or herself, once the client is taught how to identify and to dispute irrational thoughts (Ellis & Harper, 1975).

Ellis (1962, 1989c) emphasized how people interpret what happens to them; this is true as the basis of his theory of personality and as the foundation of his theory of psychotherapy. Accordingly, when a person exhibits severe emotional maladjustment, it is assumed that it has stemmed from some "magical, empirically unvalidated thinking" (p. 199). According to Ellis, it is the disputation of iB by way of ideas firmly grounded in the *logico-empirical tradition* (the scientific tradition that assumes that there are facts that are true and knowable) that can help to minimize or even to lessen emotional maladjustment. The therapist, and subsequently the client himself or herself, must actively attack those thoughts and images that result in emotional distress. According to Ellis (1989c), as people have a tendency to think irrationally, it takes "hard work and practice" to straighten out such "crooked" thinking (p. 200).

REBT is very focused on the individual client. Theoretically, attention is primarily on the way the individual thinks (*cognitive primacy*—meaning that cognition is primary over feelings or behaviors), with secondary but localized attention on how the individual feels and acts (Schwartz, 1982, 1984). Although individuals can be significantly affected within the A-B-C-(D) model of therapy, Ellis viewed irrationality as constitutionally rooted in human nature (Ziegler, 1989). The cause of maladjustment appears to be linear, although his later works pointed to an interactive framework (e.g., Ellis, 1990, 1994). Although Ellis (1989b, 1994) argued for the simultaneity of thoughts, behaviors, and emotions, according to his foundational theory cognition supersedes behavior and emotion as a linear, causative factor of emotional maladjustment.

There is a clear conception of mental health versus mental maladjustment. Ellis (1962) stated:

> Sustained negative emotions (other than those caused by continuing physical pain or discomfort) are invariably the result of stupidity, ignorance, or disturbance; and for the most part they may be, and should be, eliminated by the application of knowledge and straight thinking. For if perpetuated states of emotion generally follow from the individual's conscious or unconscious thinking; and if his thinking is, in turn, mainly a concomitant of his self verbalizations, then it would follow that he is rarely affected (made sad or glad) by outside things and events; rather: he is affected by his perceptions, attitudes, or internalized sentences about outside things and events. (pp. 53–54)

Maladjustment is associated with "crooked thinking." Adjustment is associated with "straight thinking."

## The Process of Counseling

Ellis (1989c) stated that people have a "tendency to irrational thinking, self-damaging habituations, wishful thinking, and intolerance" (p. 197), which can be exacerbated by the social environment. Ellis held that about 80% of the personality is determined by heredity. Nevertheless, he felt that people can learn to change their thinking so that the outcomes of their thinking can be positive and nondistressing. A therapist, then, must essentially target a person's beliefs, point "B" as presented in the A-B-C-(D) diagram, in order to change the client's "most basic values," if, in fact, those values keep the client "disturbance prone" (Ellis, 1989c, p. 198).

Ellis (1989a) claimed that almost all irrational ideas seen in therapy can be summarized by three "basic" iB: (a) "I must be liked by all people," (b) "You other people must treat me nobly and think the way I do," and (c) "You must give me exactly what I want when I want it." Notice the word *must* is present in each basic iB. Ellis believed that *shoulds* and *musts* are at the foundation of dogmatic and irrational thinking. Accordingly, they *must* be disputed in therapy. Ellis (1989a) also stated that if a client can actively dispute his or her own iB so that he or she begins to think rationally in a spontaneous way, then an "E" can be added to the A-B-C-(D) model. The "E" stands for an "effective new philosophy" (Ellis, 1994, p. 79) based on rB and actions.

## Counselor Role

Ellis essentially saw therapy as educational. His approach is active. He believed, in fact, that in the early stages of counseling the therapist may do more talking than the client. Although not ignoring what the clients have to say, Ellis (1989c) made it clear that the therapist should be stern, focused, and convincing in efforts to demonstrate irrational ideas that are at the foundation of a client's distress. Ellis (1989c) argued that therapists should not be "thrown" by distress; rather, they should use distress and emotion to prove to clients that they (the clients) are bound to irrational thinking, thereby distressing themselves. All the while, the therapist must continually check to see whether the client is understanding what is being taught. Clients must learn the three basic insights (Ellis, 1989a) of REBT: (a) we basically upset ourselves through our beliefs; (b) no matter when or where our crooked thinking began, previous distress does not cause subsequent distress; and (c) if we change our iB continually through work and practice (behaviorally) we think rationally.

## Goals of Counseling and Ideal Outcomes

Although symptom removal is a goal of REBT, it is not the final goal. Ellis (1989c) stated: "The usual goal of RET, therefore, is not merely to eliminate clients' presenting symptoms but to help rid them of other symptoms as well and, more importantly, to modify their underlying symptom-creating propensities" (p. 199). As the way one thinks is at the root of the symptom-creating propensities, one's thinking must be modified.

# GENERAL PROCEDURES

## Assessment

From the very early sessions of REBT, the therapist makes a concerted effort to understand the *ideas* behind the emotions manifested and described by the client. Although traditional means of assessment may be used, they are less important from an REBT perspective than a face-to-face dialogue. The therapist does a great deal of questioning, talking, and educating in the early sessions. Ellis (1989c) stated, about the early actions of therapists:

> In most instances, they quickly pin the client down to a few basic irrational ideas. They challenge the client to validate these ideas, show that they

contain extralogical premises that cannot be validated; logically analyze these ideas and make mincemeat of them; vigorously show why they cannot work and why they will almost inevitably lead to renewed disturbed symptomatology; reduce these ideas to absurdity, sometimes in a highly humorous manner; explain how they can be replaced with more rational theses; and teach clients how to think scientifically, so they can observe, logically parse, and minimize any subsequent irrational ideas and illogical deductions that lead to self-defeating feelings and behaviors. (pp. 215–216)

The therapist, then, as early as the assessment process, takes an active directive role. Assessment is thereby directly tied to therapy, targeted to the definition of iB, and quickly followed by an educational attitude and approach to the client.

## Treatment/Remediation

Treatment is action oriented. As discussed in the section Recent Developments or Criticisms, Ellis (1989a) has become much more behavioral in his approach, although he makes it clear that thinking, and not behavior, must be changed so that there are lasting results.

Treatment is highly educational. Yet the therapist can challenge the client to act and think in different, more productive ways. The idea is to remediate—to provide learning experiences to assist in the undoing of self-defeating thinking. Whatever is effective in bringing about a change in attitude and thinking is considered reasonable as a technique from the REBT perspective. Therefore, *implosive techniques* **(where a client is asked to submerge himself or herself in situations that create uncomfortable feelings, in order to implode—explode inwardly—the overwhelming thoughts and emotions associated with the situation),** classically behavior-oriented techniques, skill training, role-playing, and so on, are viewed as useful, optional techniques when directed by the therapist. However, these techniques are always viewed as secondary to disputation of iB, which is the mainstay remediator according to REBT.

## Case Management

The setting for REBT is the therapist's office, usually informally arranged, so that the therapist and the client can sit without barriers between them. The therapist is encouraged to be down-to-earth, using language that the client can understand. Tape recording of sessions is highly encouraged and, in fact, clients are encouraged to bring their own voice-recording devices so they may record sessions, and thereby have an audio file to listen to subsequent to the session. In this way, clients may study the teachings and directives of the therapist, benefiting additionally from what occurred in the therapist's office (Ellis, 1989c). Although a warm relationship is valued in therapy, it is not viewed as necessary (Ellis, 1962). Therefore, therapists are encouraged to be rational and in control throughout the treatment. They can be "feeling" in therapy, but not at the expense of rationality. If a client cries, for instance in the therapy session, the therapist would not necessarily attempt to be empathic; instead, he would remain rational and in control, maintaining the focus on the ideas that led to the crying. Case notes should be used to record hypotheses about how the client thinks, to record the client's iB the therapist believes he or she has uncovered, and to record the actions taken by the therapist in the form of directives, homework assignments, arguments, and so forth.

## Specialized Techniques

Related to specific techniques, Ellis (1989a) listed a number of techniques, some of which are direct offshoots of REBT, and others that were developed by other theorists/therapists. Some of those techniques are:

1. *Positive visualization, imaging, and thinking.* Clients are asked to think, imagine, or to get a mental picture of a positive outcome as a result of rational thinking.

2. *Reframing.* The therapist redefines a bad situation into a good one.

3. *Referenting.* The therapist helps the client to see the whole picture rather than just a part of the picture.

4. *Thought stopping.* The therapist acts to stop or block a thought as a means of temporary relief.

5. *Semantics.* The therapist helps the client to change his or her basic language, that is, to make it more positive.

6. *Proselytizing.* To proselytize is to attempt to convert someone. In RET, the therapist attempts to convert the client to a more rational way of thinking.

7. *Problem solving.* The therapist defines options for solving problems based on rational rather than irrational thinking.

8. *Cognitive distraction techniques.* The therapist attempts to distract the client into such activities as sports, art, or politics. The distraction is a means of temporary relief.

9. *Emotive techniques.* The therapist assists the client in being self-provocative, dramatic, or even evocative. For example, a client may be asked to give a forceful disputational speech during therapy.

10. *Rational-emotive imagery.* The client is asked to imagine, in an irrational way, the worst thing that can possibly happen and then to change the feeling in an implosive way through a change from irrational to rational thinking.

11. *Shame-attacking exercises.* The therapist actively disputes thoughts preceding shame feelings, and may even ask the client to go into public and to do something shameful while disputing shameful irrationalities in order to prevent shameful feelings.

12. *Relationship establishment.* The therapist attempts to demonstrate positive regard for the client, while teaching the client to like himself or herself. This is a valuable technique, but it is not necessary for producing lasting personality change.

13. *Humor.* The therapist attempts to reduce irrationality to absurdity.

14. *Role-playing.* The client is asked to role-play certain behaviors and ways of thinking or interacting.

15. *Stories, fables, and analogies.* Rational ideas are dramatized through therapist storytelling or use of analogies.

16. *Group therapy.* In group situations, clients can see the advantages of rational thinking and the disadvantages of irrational thinking while learning how to dispute their own and other individuals' irrationalities.

17. *Behavioral techniques.* Techniques such as in vivo desensitization or the use of reinforcers or punishments can be used to affect immediate behavioral change, which should be followed by the development of an effective new philosophy.

18. *Skill training.* Active training of skills in the following areas can be used as adjuncts to RET: assertiveness, sexual functioning, communication, and social relations.

Essentially, Ellis wanted people to make a profound philosophical change as well as to change behavior. The preceding techniques are examples of concrete ways therapists can achieve behavioral, emotional, or philosophical change in clients.

## Recent Developments or Criticisms

Ellis (1989c) described RET as "a comprehensive cognitive-affective behavioral theory and practice of psychotherapy" (p. 197). It is interesting that Ellis used both the terms *affective* and *behavioral* in his descriptions of his approach. Actually, he has become more behavioral in his most recent years, although his earlier works focused more on the impact of cognition on the way people feel and act. His approach is becoming similar to the methods of theoreticians who are developing integrative approaches (Meichenbaum, 1990). In fact, looking over the list of techniques used by the rational-emotive therapist, one must ask, "How does this differ from purely behavioral therapy?" Ellis answered such questions by stating that the major difference is the focus on thinking as the factor underlying behavior. Change in behavior alone does not solve problems. The problems will reemerge unless a deeper change in philosophy and thinking occurs. This is consistent with his early stated holistic philosophy about human nature, but paradoxically, it is also a reflection of reduction of human nature primarily to thinking rather than feeling or acting. Nevertheless, Ellis (1989c, 1990) has recently argued that his therapy should not be viewed as simply rationalistic— he has come to view thinking, feeling, and behaving as interactive—and therefore, REBT trainees are taught to focus on all aspects of humanness as they attempt to produce changes. Regardless, Ellis's critics (e.g., Schwartz, 1982, 1984) have convincingly argued that Ellis, in his writings, clearly gives primacy to cognition.

It is the issue of holism versus reductionism that brings to light an observation that can be commonly viewed when studying well-known counseling theories. It seems that major theorists, to a large degree, isolate some aspect of human functioning, focus on it, and target it as an intervention while, at the same time, ironically, downplaying its structure as a thing or target of change. This is clearly the case with Ellis's REBT related to the primacy of cognition, and even more specifically related to the issue of rationality. It is implicit in his approach that rationality and irrationality are treated as logically distinct—at least as extremes on a continuum—if not as things unto themselves. In fact, Ellis (1989c) has defined irrational thinking as "absolutistic," whereas he has defined rational thinking as "non-absolutistic" (p. 213). Yet Ellis in his theoretical writing also links rationality and irrationality to their consequences in a way that one's thinking and the consequences of one's thinking are almost indistinguishable. If a way of thinking becomes self-defeating, it is considered irrational. In this sense, rationality and irrationality are relativistic, behavioral concepts. As a criticism, then, it appears that Ellis has hedged his own definition, and the concepts of rationality versus irrationality can be viewed as either distinct, absolute, and personality-relevant, or as relative behavioral concepts. In either case, the theory is vulnerable; if irrationality is relative to behavior, then it is always secondary or at least conditional to behavior, and, therefore, behavior should be the focus of study and not thinking. On the other hand, if rationality and irrationality are viewed as personality-relevant, absolute concepts, then his theory is seriously flawed in not providing a complete theory of personality (see Ziegler, 1989). In effect, one must construct a theory of personality around Ellis's writing, because he does not clearly and concisely lay out such a theory, as other theorists have done (such as Freud, Rogers, and others). Ellis (1989c) agreed with similar criticisms, as he has stated: "RET is not a 'fully developed, comprehensive personalogical system.' It is mainly a theory of personality change, and even in that respect it could be, and I hope that eventually will be, more fully developed and comprehensive" (pp. 203–204).

Another criticism of Ellis's REBT is the assumption that all disorders derive from similar irrational thinking. Therapists subscribing to Beck's (1976) "Cognitive Therapy" criticize Ellis's position by offering an alternative position. While discussing differences and similarities between RET and Cognitive Therapy, Beck and Weishaar (1989) stated,

> A profound difference between these two approaches is that cognitive therapy maintains that each disorder has its own typical cognitive content. The cognitive profiles of depression, anxiety, and panic disorder are significantly different and require substantially different approaches. RET, on the other hand, assumes that all psychopathology has a similar set of underlying irrational beliefs. (p. 288)

Cognitive therapists view cognition as a much more complex process than the REBT adherents.

Essentially, critics of Ellis have forced him to revise, or at least restate, his thinking. To a degree, Ellis's restatements or revisions have shed light not only on REBT's strengths, but also on its weaknesses. Nevertheless, REBT is a useful and effective means for changing the way clients think and behave, and as such, it is a valuable counseling theory.

## STUDENT–MENTOR DIALOGUE

**Student:**   What is Albert Ellis's major contribution to the field of counseling and psychotherapy?

**Mentor:**   Well, Dr. Ellis certainly provided the field with a formula for addressing concerns from a more rational or thinking framework. He believed that the way people think is crucial to their mental health and to interpretation of the situations they encounter. He did not provide a complete theory of personality, as did Freud or Rogers, as examples. Rather, he made some basic assumptions about how people operate and then moved from those assumptions to a means of changing behavior. His approach is more about changing the way people think and behave rather than addressing why it is people think the way they do. He just assumes that people have an inherent tendency to think "crooked," meaning to think irrationally. He doesn't assume much about the personality beyond the tendency to think irrationally.

**Student:** So his approach is more about treatment than interpretation of behavior, correct?

**Mentor:** Yes. He gave counselors an easy formula to use when addressing the problems clients present. It's literally A, B, C, and (D). So it makes it easy, especially for beginning therapists, to implement his technique. Rationality, however, may be viewed by some as a controversial standard, as what is the ultimate criterion for rationality? It's unclear. Originally, Ellis reverted to the logical-empirical tradition (Western science) to help define what is rational, but that shows a bias toward that cultural framework, and may best apply only to clients who emerge from Western cultural contexts. Ellis's theory is rooted in *logical positivism* (see Popper, 1959), which **purports that science directs that there are objective knowable truths that apply in all situations**. He later backed off this position a bit (see Ellis, 1994, 1995), but his foundational theory is clearly based on Western science.

**Student:** So you are saying this is a culturally biased approach that is not useful to clients from culturally diverse backgrounds.

**Mentor:** To some degree. If the cultural background of the client is not wholly rooted in Western tradition, this approach may not be well received. In Eastern traditions, for example, thinking is more *collectivist* (meaning **there is agreement among members of a group of significant other involved people**). In such a case, applying an individually oriented psychological theory may not serve the client well. So the definition of "rational" would have to derive from the group agreement about what is "right" or "good" for the client. This is in contrast to the Western mind-set where the client is viewed as alone in his or her deliberations and thoughtfulness, and that the individual client is not burdened by the significant influence of others. The counselor is the primary connection to the logical and rational world, and therefore the counselor has the most influence in educating the client about what "should" be.

**Student:** Isn't it ironic that the theory disputes "musts" and "shoulds" while prescribing what "must" be—the logical and the rational?

**Mentor:** Yes, this is a paradoxical weakness of the model. But, in the end, a theory "must" be judged on how helpful it is to clients, and research and practice has shown that this approach is very useful and is viewed as very helpful by many clients. It's a well-researched approach that produces results in the direction that the therapist defines as healthy.

**Student:** But wasn't Ellis a bit brash in his approach with clients—he seemed to indoctrinate his clients?

**Mentor:** Ellis made no excuse about indoctrinating or proselytizing (converting) his clients. He made it very clear that he wanted to convert his clients to a rational and healthy way of thinking and behaving, and he was honest and forthcoming in defining the goals of treatment. There was no hidden agenda for Ellis. In this sense, he was very honest, even if he was a bit abrupt.

**Student:** So you believe Ellis made a significant contribution to counseling and psychotherapy.

**Mentor:** Yes, no doubt. He has made a major contribution and his legacy is rich and well-recognized.

**Student:** Thank you.

## CONCLUSION

Ellis's REBT is a classic example of a therapeutic approach consistent with the psychological paradigm. REBT emphasizes what a client is thinking as related to his or her problems (as opposed to feeling or behaving). REBT is also consistent with the internal model of the psychological paradigm, since it focuses on the internal workings of the individual, as is evident in such concepts as "rational and irrational beliefs."

## REFERENCES

Beck, A. T. (1976). *Cognitive therapy and the emotional disorders.* New York, NY: International Universities Press.

Beck, A. T., & Weishaar, M. E. (1989). Cognitive therapy. In R. J. Corsini & D. Wedding (Eds.), *Current psychotherapies* (pp. 285–320). Itasca, IL: F. E. Peacock.

Dryden, W. (1989). Albert Ellis: An efficient and passionate life. (An interview with Albert Ellis.) *Journal of Counseling and Development, 67,* 539–546.

Ellis, A. (1962). *Reason and emotion in psychotherapy.* Secaucus, NJ: Lyle Stuart.

Ellis, A. (1986). Bibliography. *American Psychologist, 41,* 380–397.

Ellis, A. (1989a, May). *A one-day workshop on rational-emotive therapy.* Paper presented at the Saint Anthony's Medical Center-Hyland Center, St. Louis, MO.

Ellis, A. (1989b). Comments on my critics. In M. E. Bernard & R. DiGiuseppe (Eds.), *Inside rational-emotive therapy: A critical appraisal of the theory and therapy of Albert Ellis* (pp. 199–233). San Diego, CA: Academic Press.

Ellis, A. (1989c). Rational-emotive therapy. In R. J. Corsini & D. Wedding (Eds.), *Current psychotherapies* (pp. 197–238). Itasca, IL: F. E. Peacock. Excerpts republished with permission of Cengage Learning.

Ellis, A. (1990, December). *The revised ABCs of rational-emotive therapy (RET)*. Paper presented at the second "Evolution of Psychotherapy" conference, Anaheim, CA.

Ellis, A. (1994). *Reason and emotion in psychotherapy*. Secaucus, NJ: Birch Lane Press.

Ellis, A. (1995). Changing rational-emotive therapy (RET) to rational emotive behavior therapy (REBT). *Journal of Rational-Emotive and Cognitive-Behavioral Therapy, 13*, 85–89.

Ellis, A., & Harper. R. A. (1975). A *new guide to rational living*. North Hollywood, CA: Wilshire Book Company.

Meichenbaum, D. (1990, December). *Cognitive-behavior modification: An integrative approach in the field of psychotherapy*. Paper presented at the second "Evolution of Psychotherapy" conference, Anaheim, CA.

Popper, K. R. (1959). *The logic of scientific discovery*. New York, NY: Basic Books.

Schwartz, R. M. (1982). Cognitive-behavior modification: A conceptual review. *Clinical Psychology Review, 2*, 267–293.

Schwartz, R. M. (1984). Is rational-emotive therapy a truly unified interactive approach? A reply to Ellis. *Clinical Psychology Review, 4*, 219–226.

Ziegler, D. J. (1989). A critique of rational-emotive theory of personality. In M. E. Bernard & R. DiGiuseppe (Eds.), *Inside rational-emotive therapy: A critical appraisal of the theory and therapy of Albert Ellis* (pp. 27–45). San Diego, CA: Academic Press.

# CHAPTER

## 7

# Gestalt Therapy

## OBJECTIVES

- To introduce readers to a therapy that clearly focuses on the internal workings of the individual, but emphasizes the thinking, feeling, and behavior of the individual holistically

- To provide a brief biographical sketch of Fritz Perls, the founder of Gestalt Therapy

- To outline the underlying philosophy and basic principles that guide the Gestalt therapist

- To list criticisms and recent developments in the Gestalt Therapy movement

## THERAPY FOCUSING ON THINKING, FEELING, AND BEHAVIOR

Gestalt Therapy was developed by Frederich S. Perls, MD. The beginning of Gestalt Therapy is identified best by the writing of Perls's classic work, *Ego, Hunger, and Aggression*, which was originally viewed as a revision of Freud's Psychoanalysis. It was written in 1941 and 1942 and was published in South Africa in 1946. The book was later published in England in 1947 (F. Perls, 1947/1969a). Perls also wrote several other books, including *Gestalt Therapy Verbatim* (F. Perls, 1969b), and *Gestalt Therapy*, with two associates (F. Perls, Hefferline, & Goodman, 1951). As **the word *Gestalt* implies viewing organisms holistically**, Gestalt Therapy focuses not only on what one thinks or feels, but also on behavior—all viewed in the here-and-now. In this way, this therapy is unique as a counseling theory, while also offering a distinct perspective of mental health.

# FREDERICH (FRITZ) PERLS: A BIOGRAPHICAL SKETCH

Fritz Perls, Berlin, 1923
*Source:* Gestalt Therapy Press.

Frederich (Fritz) Salomon Perls was born in Berlin in 1893. His autobiography, a free-floating integration of his life and this theory, entitled *In and Out of the Garbage Pail* (F. Perls, 1969c), describes little of his younger years, especially the years in Germany before he earned an MD. After earning his MD at the Frederich Wilhelm University in Berlin in 1921, he received training in Psychoanalysis in Berlin, Frankfurt, and Vienna. He later (in 1926) worked under Kurt Goldstein at the Institute for Brain Damaged Soldiers. Goldstein is widely known for his holistic view of organisms and his definition of the term *self-actualization* (Goldstein, 1934/1959). At that time, Gestalt psychology, a movement in psychology that addressed perception holistically, was receiving much attention in intellectual circles, and Perls was introduced to the work of Gestalt psychologists while he worked with Goldstein. As a part of his psychoanalytic training, he was analyzed by Wilhelm Reich, a leading theoretician and psychoanalyst of his day. In his autobiography, Perls described himself as a "mediocre psychoanalyst" (F. Perls, 1969c, p. 1), and yet he recognized his role as a "possible creator of a 'new' method of treatment" (p. 2).

After leaving Germany because of the rising influence of Hitler, Perls moved to Amsterdam in 1933 and then to South Africa (in 1934), where he established a psychoanalytic institute in Johannesburg. Under the influence of Gestalt psychology, and disenchanted with how unyielding psychoanalysts were, Perls began to develop a different position. In the early 1940s he wrote his classic book, *Ego, Hunger, and Aggression* (F. Perls, 1947/1969a), which was partially coauthored by his wife, Laura Perls. With the publication of this book, Gestalt Therapy was born. It is interesting that the title of the book reflects Perls's early holistic thinking—ego reflecting thinking, hunger reflecting feeling, and aggression reflecting behavior.

Perls later left South Africa (in 1946) with the rise of Apartheid (see the discussion of this in F. Perls, 1969c). He then settled in New York, where he established the New York Institute for Gestalt Therapy (in 1952). The remainder of Perls's life was essentially spent training therapists, writing, giving workshops, and establishing training centers. He set up the Cleveland Institute of Gestalt Therapy in 1954. He moved to California and was associated with the Esalen Institute between 1964 and 1969. Shortly before his death, he established an institute in Vancouver, British Columbia.

Perls is best remembered as a lively figure who provided a unique philosophy and perspective about mental health and psychotherapy. His work incorporates an emergent European philosophy and a deep understanding of human suffering, which probably reflects his years of clinical experience as a physician and as a psychotherapist. His theory is one of the most creative accomplishments in the history of psychotherapy.

Perls died in California in 1970.

# THE FOUNDATIONAL THEORY

## The Target of Counseling

The target of Gestalt Therapy is the individual perceiver as he or she lives (flows through) life. The individual is continually forming **figures (*gestalts*)** out of the background that is composed of the social and physical environment. In this process, it is important for the individual to maintain a *sense of self*—**an awareness of one's boundary with the outside world**. F. Perls et al. (1951) defined the self as follows:

> Self may be regarded as at the boundary of the organism, but the boundary is not itself isolated from the environment; it contacts the environment; it belongs to both, environment and organism. Contact is touch touching something. The self is not to be thought of as a fixed institution, it exists wherever and whenever there is in fact a boundary interaction. (p. 373)

It is through awareness at any moment that the individual can fully experience his or her world. Yet this boundary between self and others is not impermeable. There is a constant interplay of the inside and the outside world through awareness of boundary contact. As Kempler (1973) stated:

> Healthy coordinated awareness flows ceaselessly between two points and is itself continually being modified. The healthy awaring apparatus moves back and forth between internal knowledge and an object outside the person and then back again to the deepest knowledge within relative to the object. (p. 258)

**Awareness of one's boundary in the present is analogous to mental health.** It is a type of mental flexibility that allows one to live continually in the present, fully cognizant of self and others. F. Perls (1970a) stated: "To me, nothing exists except the now. Now = experience = awareness = reality. The past is no more and the future not yet. Only the now exists" (p. 14). There is emotional disturbance when (a) the individual is unable to differentiate self from others, (b) the individual's self splits or (c) the individual unduly focuses on the past or the future. Therapy then is a process of dialogue with the individual to help him or her understand the boundaries of the self, to reintegrate parts of the self, and/or to experience life in the present.

## The Process of Counseling

The process of Gestalt Therapy is best exemplified in several general principles, which follow. Gestalt Therapy is essentially a process of maintaining these principles actively in counseling. The principles are:

1.  *Holism*. According to Gestalt principles, **"the whole is greater than the sum of its parts."** This is an underlying principle of Gestalt Therapy as well as Gestalt psychology (F. Perls et al., 1951). Consequently, during therapy, one of the major tasks is to help the client get a whole sense of the self. Although the personality is viewed holistically, polarities are present. *Polarities* **are parts of the personality that are opposites,** yet they complement each other (Yontef & Simkin, 1989). One major aspect of the process of Gestalt Therapy, then, is a **process of integration—or centering—in order to allow natural polarities to exist**, while healing the splits arising from

dichotomous forces. F. Perls (1947/1969a) gave the example of Robert Louis Stevenson's Dr. Jekyll and Mr. Hyde as extremes in the personality of one person. These extremes, in this case one good and one evil, represent polarities of the personality.

Gestalt therapists essentially attempt to bring polarities into a larger context, that is, within a phenomenological whole.

According to F. Perls et al. (1951), splits in the personality may be manifested as: (a) *retroflections* **(where a person acts on herself or himself as a target when, instead, the environment should be acted on; retroflections essentially split the self into "doer" and "done to");** (b) *introjections* **(something from the outside has been incorporated into the organism, but has not been fully accepted or accommodated by the organism—psychologically the equivalent of undigested food);** and (c) *projections* **(there is a part of one's own personality that is externalized but is not seen as part of the organism—for instance, seeing one's own sexual urges in another person's behavior).** Dichotomous thinking and splits in the personality go hand in hand, and Gestalt Therapy attempts to allow dichotomies to be viewed as complementary polarities, thereby preventing further disintegration of the personality. For example, a man who is unable to integrate the feminine aspects of his personality is doomed to dichotomous thinking—that is, feeling he is either a man or a woman. Gestalt Therapy would fully encourage integration of this man's femininity into his picture of himself, his gestalt, just as it would encourage integration of the masculine aspect of a woman's personality into a larger picture of a whole personality.

2. *Figure and ground.* In the social realm, the idea of figure and ground is easily understood as that of **self and environment.** To have a sense of gestalt, one must differentiate oneself from one's context, while being able to connect or separate (contact or withdraw) appropriately from the environment. (The environment is often composed of other individuals). **In** *confluence* **(fusion) the distinction between figure and ground (self and others) becomes unclear.** An example would be an adult woman living a life to please her mother because, separate from the mother, she has no sense of self. The opposite of confluence is **isolation, where all connectedness with others is lost.** The socially constricted individual is considered "isolated," as there is no real contact made with others.

*Contact* **is the process of getting through the boundary of another person** (F. Perls, 1969b). It involves sensory stimulation, **contiguity (closeness in time),** and may involve talking and moving; it involves a "full engagement with whatever is interesting at that moment" (E. Polster & Polster, 1973). It occurs in therapy by means of "dialogue" (Yontef & Simkin, 1989). *Dialogue* **is the process of making contact through interpersonal interaction**—of sensing "me" and "not-me" while interacting with another. In order to make contact through dialogue, the therapist must be fully present, reflective of self and the others, committed to the interaction, and focused on actions and feelings as well as words. Making contact with another person is a useful means to a better understanding of one's self. It is in the interpersonal realm that one can truly come to know the self.

3. *Here and now.* The Gestalt therapist continually focuses on **the present.** There is nothing but the here and now (F. Perls, 1969b). The Gestalt Therapy process is designed to help the client focus on the present, with the aim to bring about awareness. According to Yontef and Simkin (1989), *awareness* **is a sense of self and**

**environment (figure and ground) in the here and now** involving "full sensorimotor, emotional, cognitive, and energetic support" (p. 333). For example, if a mother is feeling a split between her protective mother instinct and her anger at her abusive adult child (a retroflection), a therapist might point out the conflict by making the mother aware that when she speaks of her child, she speaks lovingly, but she also clenches her fist in anger. The therapist might then ask her to focus on the fist, to feel the anger in the here and now, and to let it flow through the rest of her body so that feelings, verbalization, and expressions are consonant with a more holistic picture of the self. The goal of such an exercise is to bring therapy into the present, and to help the client gain insight. *Insight* **is a special type of awareness that is an immediate sense of unity of the otherwise split personality**. Awareness is the only goal of Gestalt Therapy.

4. *Therapy is horizontal, not vertical*. In other words, the therapeutic relationship is an *"I–Thou" relationship*, **where two people are equals in dialogue** rather than one person being one-up and the other being one-down in the client–therapist relationship (in the classic psychoanalytic sense of the therapist being in control). Therapy, then, is ideally a process of co-experience, in which the therapist has awareness in the here and now, as he or she facilitates the client's experience in the here and now.

5. *Awareness in the here and now leads to change*. The therapist is continually designing experiences for the client that bring both the therapist and the client fully into awareness of the here and now. It is through awareness that clients have the opportunity to take full responsibility for themselves. Once the person has a sense of figure and ground (self and others) and when dichotomies are recognized as polarities within a larger gestalt whole, then the person can move forward and make decisions necessary to solve problems.

These five basic principles guide the process of Gestalt Therapy.

As is evident in the five basic principles of Gestalt Therapy, the focus is on the individual perceiver. Describing the Gestalt psychology movement, E. Polster and Polster (1973) stated:

> The gestalt psychologists investigated the dynamics of the act of perceiving. They theorized that the perceiver was not merely a passive target for the sensory bombardment coming from his environment; rather, he structured and imposed order on his own perceptions. Basically, he organized perceptions of the incoming sensory stream into the primary experience of a figure as seen or perceived against a background, or ground. (p. 29)

Although there is a constant interplay between figure and ground in the definition of self (Kempler, 1973; F. Perls et al., 1951), the individual organism is the organizer of experience. The human being is viewed as an active organism experiencing life at a contact boundary with an ever-changing environment. Although the organism is in contact with an ever-changing world, without a structured sensing organism, there can be no perception. Therefore, the focus is clearly on the individual human organism and his or her perceptions in interaction with the environment.

Gestalt theory derives from a *phenomenological* **(meaning things that are perceived and consciously experienced)** position or philosophy. It does not deny an external reality. It is fully consonant with an assumption that the "background" exists, just as the perceiving organism exists, and that there is contact between the organism as a thing and the external world as a continually flowing process. In this sense, it is a position that assumes the presence of an objective ever-changing external world and a bounded psychological entity (e.g., the individual or the ego).

Clearly, the focus of Gestalt Therapy is on the individual. Individuals, although not assessed in a classic organic–medical diagnostic sense, are evaluated through a process of therapy, where there is a constant interplay between the client and the therapist. The cause of disturbance is viewed as a lack of awareness, primarily deriving from disturbance between the individual perceiving human organism and the environmental contact boundary. Change occurs within the individual through an interpersonal process, where essentially the therapist *catalyzes* **(stimulates and facilitates)** the inherent potential for growth in the client. Therapists must adhere to the basic principles consistent with Gestalt Therapy philosophy in order to catalyze change in a client.

## Counselor Role

The role of the Gestalt therapist is distinct in many ways from other therapies. Proponents of the Gestalt approach view it largely as an art form, and Perls himself avoided viewing or presenting his therapy as a set of techniques. Rather, Gestalt Therapy purists view the work of the therapist as implicit in the basic principles of Gestalt Therapy, listed in the previous section. They allow for much variability in the way the therapist approaches a client, but always with adherence to the basic principles. In this way, there is an *implicit* philosophy of intervention. As Naranjo (1970) stated:

> The Gestalt therapist places more value in action than in words, in experience than in thoughts, in the living process of therapeutic interaction and the inner change resulting thereby than in influencing beliefs. (p. 48)

The therapist's style of presentation, what he or she does, is as much Gestalt Therapy as is what the therapist says. The therapist essentially attempts to engage the client in dialogue—to make contact with the client to bring him into the present, while maintaining a philosophical allegiance to the basic principles of holism and centeredness. F. Perls et al. (1951) stated:

> Our view of the therapist is that he is similar to what the chemist calls a catalyst, an ingredient which precipitates a reaction which might not otherwise occur. (p. 15)

In this sense, the therapist enters into a process called *therapy*, with the intent of making contact with the client. As long as the basic Gestalt Therapy principles are adhered to, therapy is viewed as productive.

## Goals of Counseling and Ideal Outcomes

Gestalt Therapy is not a problem-solving therapy (Yontef & Simkin, 1989). It is a therapy that is best used with individuals who seek self-growth and understanding. Clients faced with the need to solve a problem immediately would be ill served by Gestalt Therapy. On the other hand, a basic premise of this therapy is that individuals who are in touch with themselves, who are aware in the present, and who have a good clear sense of self and environment, when confronted by decision making are able to make decisions that are congruent with their needs and self-concepts. In this sense, awareness and self-understanding are prerequisites to effective living.

According to Yontef and Simkin (1989), "in Gestalt therapy, the only goal is awareness" (p. 337).

Related to outcomes, F. Perls et al. (1951) stated:

> The criteria of therapeutic progress cease to be a matter of debate. It is not a question of increased "social acceptability" or improved "interpersonal relationships," as viewed through the eyes of some extraneous, self-constituted authority, but the patient's own awareness of heightened vitality and more effective functioning. (p. 15)

*Awareness* **is viewed as both content and process. It is a deep understanding, while it is also a means of understanding.** It is a process by which attention and awareness become one, although as an outcome it is a definition of selfhood. In a sense, one's self is what one experiences in awareness.

Where awareness may appear to be overstated as an outcome of therapy, it is reflective of Perls's faith in the self and in full experience in the present. He was an optimist, and his position can be viewed as humanistic, especially when contrasted with Freud's negative view of the human nature (from which Perls's ideas were an outgrowth). Where Freud viewed life as a struggle, Perls viewed life as an opportunity.

# GENERAL PROCEDURES

## Assessment

As Gestalt Therapy is present focused, the therapist is not directed to do history taking. From the very beginning of therapy, the therapist, rather than diagnosing the patient in the classic sense, seeks to guide the client in exploration of himself or herself in the present. Yontef and Simkin (1989) stated:

> Rather than maintaining distance and interpreting, the Gestalt therapist meets patients and guides active awareness work. The therapist's active presence is alive and excited (hence warm), honest, and direct. Patients can see, hear, and be told how they are experienced, what is seen, how the therapist feels, what the therapist is like as a person. Growth occurs from real contact between real people. Patients learn how they are seen and how their awareness process is limited, not primarily from talking about their problems, but from how they and the therapist engage each other. (pp. 338–339)

Diagnostically, then, it is assumed that the client is not fully integrated at some level. Several therapeutic hypotheses may be formed. It may be that the client's self is split in some sense—through a retroflection, introjection, or projection. This is similar to the idea that some aspect of self is being denied (consciously, or, more likely, unconsciously), and the split in the personality needs to be healed. Or it may be hypothesized that the patient is living in the past or the future, while denying primary experience in the here and now. Or it is possible that the client's experience is dichotomized in some way, where the self and others are viewed as not one at the contact boundary, but separate and distinct—not complementary, but contradictory. In this way, wholeness is lost, and the individual needs to be centered at the point and moment of interpersonal contact in therapy. These are hypotheses the Gestalt therapist uses in working with clients. However, using these hypotheses is not synonymous with classic diagnosis. In Gestalt Therapy, there is no final determination or interpretation. **Diagnosis is the process of Gestalt Therapy. It is not separable. The therapist never is bound to one view of the client.** The therapist enters into dialogue to facilitate growth in his or her own personality and the client's personality—to take the client and himself or herself to full experiencing and awareness in interpersonal interaction. Where Carl Rogers is loving, Perls is making love. Where Albert Ellis is defining the irrational, Perls is living irrationality with the client. All concerns are "brought to" and "lived in" the present.

## Treatment/Remediation

According to Enright (1970), the basic task of the therapist in remediation is "to help the patient overcome the barriers . . . that block awareness, and to let nature take its course...so he can function with all his abilities" (p. 108). Furthermore, Enright described how the therapist must have a watchful eye, focusing on "splits" in the patient's attention—for example, where *organismically* **(related to the actions of the physical body)** the individual is acting (even unconsciously) in a way that is incongruent with his or her words and actions. Voice tone, motoric actions, gestures, and all nonverbal cues are hints as to the organismic functioning, to which the client may not be consciously attending. Enright stated:

> My task begins when these other "unconscious" activities begin to stand out in the total gestalt and vie with the verbal content. I then encourage the patient(s) to devote some attention to these other activities, asking him to describe what he is doing, seeing, feeling. I make no interpretations but simply draw awareness to these phenomena, and let him make of them what he will. (pp. 108–109)

It is noteworthy that ideally, but not necessarily, interventions, such as the one just described, are noninterpretive. Whenever possible, the patient should make interpretations of his or her own behavior.

## Case Management

*Case management* **is the process of maintaining contact with the client while facilitating the interpersonal relationship consistent with Gestalt Therapy principles.** The therapist is not viewed as the one in control per se. The principle of the "I-Thou" relationship holds at the level of case management. The therapist mutually works through the business aspects of counseling with a client. The therapist recognizes the client's responsibility for himself or herself. This is not to say that the therapist is inactive and nondirective. In fact, the Gestalt therapist can be very active in therapy by teasing, cajoling, frustrating a client, and reflecting back to the client his or her response. In this sense, the therapist acts not only as a catalyst (as stated earlier), but also acts as a mirror, reflecting the client back on himself or herself. It is valued when the client is aware, but it is also valued for the therapist to make observations whether the client is aware or not. These observations of a trained therapist are considered valid and reflective of what the client feels, thinks, and does. In this sense, one-upness (one person being in charge) of the therapeutic relationship is not escaped, although it is downplayed in ongoing case management activity by means of the "I-Thou" principle.

Gestalt Therapy also can be accomplished in group settings, as long as the group facilitator fosters the basic Gestalt Therapy principles described previously.

Audio or video recording of sessions is encouraged. Audio and video recordings may be helpful to the therapist in assessing inconsistencies in the patient's thoughts, feelings, and actions. Such recordings, however, do not substitute for therapy in the here and now, which is a primary focus of therapeutic activity. Notes are not taken during sessions, as such activity may interfere with the contact between client and counselor. However, notes should be recorded after the session reflecting what happened in therapy, to cue the therapist's memory before future meetings.

## Specialized Techniques

Perls did not like to view his work as technique. He felt that the use of the term *technique* sounded manipulative and controlling. However, if one observes Perls, there is no question that he uses several methods to engage and to influence the client. Some of the methods that follow were described by Levitsky and Perls (1970), and others have been observed in Perls's videotaped works:

1. *Paraphrasing client's nonverbal behaviors.* A Gestalt therapist does this in two ways. First, a Gestalt therapist might simply **describe a behavior operationally**, which then cues a client's own interpretation; for example, "Your foot is moving." Second, a therapist might **interpret a person's nonverbal activity**: "You are pouting like a little girl." In both of these cases, the paraphrase is meant to reflect back to the client those behaviors of which the client might not be aware.

2. *Misparaphrasing client's nonverbal behaviors.* This appears to be manipulative at face value, and it is used usually in an effort to engage resistant clients. By **interpreting a client behavior in a way that the client is likely to disagree**, the client is engaged in interaction, and dialogue usually ensues. For example, to a resistant and disengaging ex-convict, the therapist might say, "I interpret your silence as deep-seated feelings of concern for me." As the resistant client may be perturbed as to dispute the interpretation, it is hoped that interpersonal contact with the client can be initiated.

3. *Focusing questions.* **Focusing questions are questions designed to get the client to attend to certain experiences.** The classic Gestalt Therapy focusing question, described in Yontef and Simkin (1989, p. 341), is: "What are you aware of (experiencing) now?" Any question that brings the client into contact with his or her own experience in the present is considered a focusing question, such as "How are you feeling now?" or "What are you thinking now?"

4. *The empty chair technique.* **This is a method in which the therapist asks the client to view an empty chair and to pretend that another person is in the chair, or that some aspect of the client's own personality is in the chair, and then the client is asked to have a dialogue with the empty chair.** This is essentially an integrating technique, used to help the client deal with retroflections, introjec-

tions, or projections at the root of splits in the personality. A classic example of how this technique could be used in therapy is that of "top-dog" and "underdog" (Levitsky & Perls, 1970), which is considered a classic dichotomized split in the personality. The concept of top-dog roughly translates to the psychoanalytic concepts of superego, the "shoulds" and "oughts" in the personality. According to Levitsky and Perls (1970), the underdog is "passively resistant, makes excuses, and finds reasons to delay" (p. 145). Levitsky and Perls stated that: "When a division is encountered, the patient is asked to have an actual dialogue between these two components of himself" (p. 145). The patient simply imagines the response, and replies in a continuing dialogue until some insight or awareness is gained.

5.   *Enactment.* Yontef and Simkin (1989) described **enactment as having the patient "put feelings or thoughts into action"** (p. 342). **"Playing the projection" is a classic enactment** described by Levitsky and Perls (1970). Playing the projection is an enactment of an attitude that the client perceives as reflective of another person's personality (when in fact it may be a projection of the client's own personality), and, once enacted, the client is asked "whether this is possibly a trait he himself possesses" (p. 146). **Exaggeration and reversal are other types of enactment. Exaggeration is where the person is asked to exaggerate some feeling, thought, or movement. Reversal is where the person is asked to act the part of some aspect of his or her personality that is not usually manifested**—for example, playing the exhibitionist if one is timid (Levitsky & Perls, 1970).

6.   *"Stay with it" commands.* **These are commands made by the therapist for the client to continue to feel, experience, and act in a way that is integrative of the personality.** Yontef and Simkin (1989) describe this as allowing the patient to build and to deepen his or her awareness. "Stay with it" commands follow expressions by the client that appear to be insights or which can lead to awareness.

These are just several techniques that are consistent with Gestalt Therapy.

## Recent Developments or Criticisms

One of the obvious criticisms of Gestalt Therapy is that it borders on game playing with the client (see Patterson, 1973). In fact, in the hands of an unethical or improperly trained practitioner, it could easily be viewed as cruel or teasing, instead of constructive and fruitful. Also, the idea of full interpersonal contact with another person can easily be used as a rationale for having sexual relations with clients, which is absolutely unethical according to the codes of conduct for the mental health professionals (Cottone & Tarvydas, 2016). In addition, because there is no objectified measure of outcome ("awareness" is a subjective phenomenon), it is difficult to dispute its effectiveness or even to document its potential harm. Regardless, Gestalt Therapy is a process-oriented therapy, and as such it offers the ethical practitioner a means to make meaningful interpersonal contact with a client.

The interpersonal contact issue is an important one. Gestalt Therapy makes full use of the therapeutic relationship, as it is recognized that one lives in a very social world, where figure and ground reasonably translates to self and others. The interpersonal nature of Gestalt Therapy is a strength, from a practical, therapeutic standpoint, but it is also a theoretical weakness. Although Gestalt Therapy fully recognizes the interpersonal relationship therapeutically, it is constrained by its emphasis on the individual as a perceiving entity. Theoretically, the perceiver is reified, and relationships only act to help define the perceiver. F. Perls (1969b) described the nature of a living perceiving organism in the following quotation: "What is an organism? We call **an organism any living being, any living being that has organs, has an organization, that is self-regulating within itself. . . . The organism always works as a whole**" (p. 5). Without the perceiver, there can be no construction of figure against ground. Therefore the individual always works from an internal frame of reference. Perls described the relationship of the organism to the environment as follows:

> Now let's talk a bit more about the relationship of the organism to its environment, and here we introduce the notion of the ego boundary. A boundary defines a thing. Now a thing has its boundaries, is defined by its boundaries in relation to the environment. In itself a thing occupies a certain amount of space. Maybe not much. Maybe it wants to be bigger, or wants to be smaller—maybe it's not satisfied with its size. We introduce now a new concept again, the wish to change based upon the phenomenon of dissatisfaction. Every time you want to change yourself, or you want to change the environment, the basis always is dissatisfaction. (p. 7)

Although the ego boundary is not described by Perls as a fixed thing, the thingness of his definition cannot be denied. In fact, there is much similarity between Perls's definition and Freud's definition of ego, which Perls himself addressed (F. Perls, 1947/1969a). F. Perls (1947/1969a), speaking of the human being, stated:

> He achieves this subjective integration by the process of identification— the feeling that something is part of him or that he is part of something else. . . . Thus I agree with Freud that the Ego is closely related to identification. (p. 140)

Consequently, the perceiver, as an internally *identified* organism, cannot be completely affected by external relationships, which is a position that requires one to believe that both relationships and individuals are distinct and dichotomous to a degree, which is inconsistent with the holistic philosophy of Gestalt Therapy. In this way, Gestalt Therapy has not fully integrated the concept of the individual "organism" into a more pure interpersonal dynamic. Or in other words, if individuals are so easily influenced within the Gestalt Therapy interpersonal context, why are they not viewed as malleable processes instead of internally directed organisms? This kind of inconsistency is unacceptable and is more readily reconciled by a more complete process-oriented, interpersonal construction of self, where self is viewed fully within relationships. Until recently, Gestalt therapists appeared to be unaware, or at least unclear, about this philosophical inconsistency, which made the theoretical foundation vulnerable. Readers fully understand this criticism when introduced to the counseling theories within the systemic-relational or social constructivism paradigms. However, Gestalt therapists have recently begun to recognize and address the powerful influence of relationships in treatment. Yontef and Jacobs (2008) stated: "The past decade has witnessed a major shift in Gestalt therapy's understanding of personality and therapy. There has been a growing, albeit sometimes controversial, change in understanding the relational conditions for growth, both in general and (especially) in the therapeutic relationship" (p. 351). Therefore, to some degree,

Gestalt therapists are modifying the theory to adjust to recognition of the importance of relationship in health and treatment.

Another criticism of Gestalt Therapy is its emphasis on "awareness." It can be argued that distressed individuals are already over-aware, and that facilitating more awareness is counterproductive in such cases. E. Polster and Polster (1973) addressed this concern, and essentially rebutted the concern by differentiating self-consciousness with aware-ness, where self-consciousness is defensive and awareness is integrative.

Perls was vulnerable to criticism that he was teasing and even inhumane in applica-tion of his technique, although he can be classified as a humanist according to his opti-mistic view of human nature. Attempts have been made to *humanize* the technique of Gestalt Therapy. For example, E. Polster (1990) developed a style of therapy that incor-porates a humanistic interpersonal spirit with the sometimes confrontive techniques of Gestalt Therapy. E. Polster, in effect, attempted to facilitate the goals of Gestalt Therapy by emphasizing the "power of simple human exchange." He demonstrated how one can be loving and confrontive at the same time. Similarly, Yontef and Jacobs (2008) stated:

> There is . . . a greater realization of how shame is created in childhood and triggered interpersonal relationships. . . . As Gestalt therapists have come to understand shame and its triggers more thoroughly, they have become less confrontive and more accepting and supportive. (p. 351)

Gestalt therapists have come to recognize that aggressive confrontation may be ill-advised with clients who may be defined as vulnerable in such an interpersonal exchange.

To the credit of the latest generation of leaders of the Gestalt Therapy movement, the approach is becoming more clearly delineated and refined. Gestalt Therapy proponents have been active and effective in clarifying the Gestalt position related to techniques and processes. Perls appeared to have had a difficult time communicating his ideas in

## STUDENT–MENTOR DIALOGUE

**Student:**   It seems like Perls's ideas about therapy changed dramatically over his career.

**Mentor:**   Yes, that's true. He started as a psychoanalyst and then began to change his ideas about therapy, most likely under the influence of Kurt Goldstein, who proposed the idea of self-actualization; Goldstein also viewed organisms (living things) holistically. Like Rogers, Perls can be classified as a humanist—meaning he viewed human nature positively at its most base level, with the intent of therapy to free people to be who they really are. This certainly is more consistent with the teachings of Goldstein about holism and actualization than with the ideas of Freud. So, yes, his theory and way of counseling was transformed dramatically over the course of his career.

**Student:**   Was Perls confrontational in his approach?

**Mentor:**    As a personality, Perls had a definite presence. He seemed at times to be playful in therapy, teasing clients or even perturbing them to get reactions. At times he was even charming. I sense he was intent on bringing out people's most base responses, so he could then acknowledge them or address any inconsistent behaviors in a way that could help the client gain some insight. Gestalt Therapy can be confrontational, but it doesn't have to be. However, the counselor has to be assertive about any inconsistencies that are relevant to the client's personality functioning. In this sense, the therapist must be assertive, but not necessarily challenging in any aggressive way. With vulnerable clients—those that have a deep sense of shame or guilt—the Gestalt counselor should be very cautious about confrontation, as confrontation could act to trigger unhealthy or even damaging emotional reactions. So with some clients, confrontation would be ill-advised.

**Student:**    Did he maintain any ideas from psychoanalytic thought?

**Mentor:**    Most definitely. He maintained the idea of ego, and he certainly targeted the individual "self" as the focus of treatment. His theory of personality is all about holism and internal consistency, and his therapy is about healing splits and polarities. That's not unlike Freud's ideal of the strong ego mediating competing internal forces in the personality (the id and the superego). But Perls's style of therapy was quite distinct from psychoanalysis. It purports an egalitarian counselor–client relationship—the "I–Thou" relationship. The psychoanalytic relationship is much less egalitarian and is reflective more of the therapist's authority.

**Student:**    How would you summarize Perls's contribution to the field of psychotherapy?

**Mentor:**    Well, Perls taught a lesson about the need to view people holistically. There is a message inherent in his work that counselors should not divide clients up into pieces—behavior, feelings, thoughts, or relationships. Counselors should address behavior, thoughts, and feelings all at the same time. This appeals to modern day proponents of holism as a philosophy and practice. Holism is a philosophy that acknowledges the complexity of human functioning and human relations. And his theory of personality is fairly elegant in that regard, as he lays out how people should be "together" so-to-speak. When we speak about people "having it together," we are talking the language of Gestalt Therapy.

a simple, straightforward manner, and the burden for clear conceptualizations of his position has fallen on others. His adherents have, to a large degree, ferreted out the basic principles and techniques consistent with Perls's underlying philosophy (see M. Polster, 1987, for a clear and concise summary). And now they are addressing criticisms as well.

## CONCLUSION

Gestalt Therapy is an approach that helps to produce an integration of a client's feelings, thoughts, and actions into his or her perception of self. It is extremely useful in helping clients to grow and change while being aware of their behaviors and feelings. It helps clients to live fully in the present. It is a counseling theory that clearly fits within the psychological paradigm, and, specifically, the internal model of the psychological paradigm. Its focus on feeling, thinking, and behaving is unique among therapies aligned with the psychological paradigm. As an approach, it has evolved and continues to enjoy recognition as a mainstay theory of personality and psychotherapy.

## REFERENCES

Cottone, R. R., & Tarvydas, V. M. (2016). *Ethics and decision making in counseling and psychotherapy*. New York, NY: Springer Publishing.

Enright, J. B. (1970). An introduction to gestalt techniques. In J. Fagan & I. L. Shepherd (Eds.), *Gestalt therapy now* (pp. 107–124). New York, NY: Harper & Row.

Goldstein, K. (1959). *The organism: A holistic approach to biology derived from psychological data in man*. New York, NY: American Book. (Original work published in 1934)

Kempler, W. (1973). Gestalt therapy. In R. Corsini (Ed.), *Current psychotherapies* (pp. 251–286). Itasca, IL: F. E. Peacock.

Levitsky, A., & Perls, F. (1970). The rules and games of gestalt therapy. In J. Fagan & I. L. Shepherd (Eds.), *Gestalt therapy now* (pp. 140–149). New York, NY: Harper & Row.

Naranjo, C. (1970). Present-centeredness: Technique, prescription, and ideal. In J. Fagan & I. L. Shepherd (Eds.), *Gestalt therapy now* (pp. 47–69). New York, NY: Harper & Row.

Patterson, C. H. (1973). *Theories of counseling and psychotherapy* (2nd ed.). New York, NY: Harper & Row.

Perls, F. (1969a). *Ego, hunger, and aggression*. New York, NY: Vintage/Random House. (Original work published in 1947)

Perls, F. (1969b). *Gestalt therapy verbatim*. Lafayette, CA: Real People Press. Excerpts used with permission from Real People Press.

Perls, F. (1969c). *In and out of the garbage pail*. Lafayette, CA: Real People Press.

Perls, F. (1970a). Four lectures. In J. Fagan & I. L. Shepherd (Eds.), *Gestalt therapy now* (pp. 14–38). New York, NY: Harper & Row.

Perls, F., Hefferline, R. E., & Goodman, P. (1951). *Gestalt therapy: Excitement and growth in the human personality*. New York, NY: Dell. Excerpts used with permission from Gestalt Journal Press.

Perls, L. (1970b). One Gestalt therapist's approach. In J. Fagan & I. L. Shepherd (Eds.), *Gestalt therapy now* (pp. 125–129). New York, NY: Harper & Row.

Polster, E. (1990, December). *Gestalt therapy: Humanization of technique*. Paper and demonstration presented at the second "Evolution of Psychotherapy" conference in Anaheim, CA.

Polster, E., & Polster, M. (1973). *Gestalt therapy integrated*. New York, NY: Random House.

Polster, M. (1987). Gestalt therapy: Evolution and application. In J. Zeig (Ed.), *The evolution of psychotherapy* (pp. 312–322). New York, NY: Brunner/Mazel.

Yontef, G. M., & Jacobs, L. (2008). Gestalt therapy. In R. J. Corsini & D. Wedding (Eds.), *Current psychotherapies* (8th ed., pp. 342–382). Belmont, CA: Brooks/Cole.

Yontef, G. M., & Simkin, J. S. (1989). Gestalt therapy. In R. Corsini & D. Wedding (Eds.), *Current psychotherapies* (4th ed., pp. 323–361). Itasca, IL: F. E. Peacock. Excerpt republished with permission of Cengage Learning.

# CHAPTER

## 8

# Behavior Therapy and Cognitive Behavioral Therapy

## OBJECTIVES

- To introduce Behavior Therapy as a psychological approach to treatment that assumes that mental health problems derive from external forces that impinge the individual

- To provide a framework for treatment based on principles of learning and the philosophy that behavior is externally motivated and influenced

- To give readers a basic understanding of behavioral principles, specifically based on classical and operant conditioning models of learning

- To provide the theoretical underpinnings for behaviorally focused psychotherapy

- To introduce techniques using either classical or operant conditioning as their learning model base

- To extend Behavior Therapy by addressing the effect of cognition on the therapeutic formula

- To summarize the Cognitive Behavioral Therapy (CBT) movement and to identify basic approaches and techniques that fall within the banner of CBT

117

# THERAPY FOCUSING ON BEHAVIOR

This chapter is organized slightly differently from the other chapters in this part of the text, primarily because Behavior Therapy is not easily associated with one outstanding proponent. There are several theoreticians and researchers who are most often associated with behavioral approaches in counseling and psychotherapy. Therefore, the focus of the beginning of the chapter is on the empirical works of two major researchers, Ivan P. Pavlov and Burrhus F. Skinner, who developed learning theories that have serious implications for the treatment of emotional concerns. These learning theories will be summarized at some length, because it is imperative that counselors have a good understanding of them before attempting to do Behavior Therapy.

It is also noteworthy that the term *Behavior Therapy* does not represent one consensually agreed-on position in the mental health services. There is no predominant unifying "Behavior Therapy" as the beginning of this chapter title implies. In fact, there are a number of different schools of Behavior Therapy, each distinct in its own way, yet each subscribing to an **external view of human influence, meaning that behavior is viewed as resulting primarily from factors outside the individual, in contrast to other psychological theories that focus on internal factors (the id, the self-concept, the mind).** The other chapters are held together logically by works of one predominant theorist; this is not the case with Behavior Therapy.

After the basic learning theories—classical conditioning and operant conditioning—are described, two specialized counseling methods are presented in the Specialized Techniques section of the chapter. They are Wolpe's (1973) "Systematic Desensitization" and Kazdin's (1977) "Token Economy." There are a number of reasons why these two approaches have been chosen. First, each represents a counseling technique associated with one of the two different learning theories—that is, Systematic Desensitization is closely aligned with classical conditioning, and Token Economy is an approach closely aligned with operant conditioning. Second, both have been found to be reasonably effective and well-researched methods, which is consistent with the operational philosophy of behaviorism (Watson, 1924/1930). And third, they are applied in diverse settings. Systematic Desensitization is used in office settings predominantly. Token Economies are often applied in institutional settings.

Related to the use of Token Economies in institutional settings, it can be argued that such an approach does not constitute counseling or psychotherapy in the usual sense. However, counselors should have some preparation in this area, so that they have a clear vocabulary and understanding of how operant techniques are applied to human beings, even if they are not directly involved in day-to-day management of a Token Economy program. This is especially important for beginning practitioners working at psychiatric rehabilitation facilities or in programs for the severely intellectually deficient.

This chapter, then, provides a discussion of two learning theories and two specialized techniques (deriving directly and respectively from the learning theories) that can be applied in mental health settings.

Additionally, this chapter addresses the Cognitive Behavioral Therapy movement, both historically and practically. Cognitive Behavioral Therapy, or CBT, has taken the Behavior Therapy movement (which is focused on external factors affecting behavior) across the internal versus external locus of influence boundary. It addresses how **cognition, which is an internal psychological process involving language and perception,** can be associated with behavioral techniques to improve case conceptualization and to affect treatment outcomes positively. Toward the end of the chapter, a section on CBT will provide readers with a foundation for application of the cognitive process to otherwise understood behavioral interventions.

# IVAN P. PAVLOV AND BURRHUS F. SKINNER: BIOGRAPHICAL SKETCHES

## Ivan P. Pavlov

Ivan Pavlov
*Source*: Wikimedia Commons.

Ivan P. Pavlov was born in 1849 in the town of Ryazan in Russia. His father was a priest, and Pavlov attended a local seminary, where he felt he had excellent teachers. In 1870, he entered Petersburg University and studied natural history, with a major in physiology and a minor in chemistry. He later studied medicine with the intent of becoming a professor, rather than practicing medicine. By the age of 41 years, he was appointed to a position as a professor in a medical academy and also worked as a researcher and department head at an institute for experimental medicine. There he carried out physiological research. However, he became interested in psychological processes and how nervous system activity was affected by sensory stimuli. Through his experiments, he learned that otherwise noninfluential objects could be made to influence physiological processes by means of association with activating stimuli. Although he considered himself a physiologist, he spent a good number of his years studying mental processes.

According to Marx and Hillix (1973), in 1904, Pavlov was awarded the Nobel Prize for his "investigations of glandular and neural factors in digestion" (p. 97).

Pavlov died in 1936.

## Burrhus F. Skinner

B. F. Skinner
*Source*: Wikimedia Commons.

Burrhus F. Skinner was born on March 20, 1904, in Pennsylvania. His father was a lawyer, and his mother was a homemaker. At an early age, he was known to be inquisitive, having a fascination with mechanical things (Kirschenbaum & Henderson, 1989). He also loved to read and write.

Skinner majored in literature at Hamilton College in Clinton, New York, with the intent of being a fiction writer. But after receiving awards and graduating Phi Beta Kappa, he spent a year writing fiction and "discovered the unhappy fact that I had nothing to say" (as cited in Kirschenbaum & Henderson, 1989, p. 79). He became intrigued with the writings of Bertrand Russell and John Watson, which changed his career course. He pursued and received his PhD degree in psychology from Harvard University in 1931. He received several post-doctoral fellowships there, and later taught psychology (from 1936 to 1945) at the University of Minnesota, as well as from 1945 to 1947 at Indiana University where he was chairman of the Department of Psychology. In 1947, he took a professorship at Harvard University, where he actively taught until 1974 and where he remained as Professor Emeritus of Psychology until his death in August 1990, at the age of 86 years.

Skinner was a man who believed and acted his own theory. He strongly felt that humans could condition themselves to achieve certain behaviors, and he was known for keeping charts of his own behavior and presenting himself with rewards for achievements. He strongly believed that humans are externally controlled, and that freedom, as an internal psychological phenomenon, is a result of external conditioning. He was prolific throughout his life; one of his last publications, *Recent Issues in the Analysis of Behavior* (Skinner, 1989), is a contemporaneous and readable summary of his ideas. Skinner received the American Psychological Association's Distinguished Scientific Contribution Award in 1958. In 1968, he received the National Medal of Science, and in 1971 the Gold Medal of the American Psychological Association. He was a member and fellow of several scholarly and learned societies.

Skinner is widely known to have taken up the banner of "behaviorism," and his work will have a lasting effect on experimental psychology and the field of counseling and psychotherapy.

## THE FOUNDATIONAL THEORY
### Classical (Respondent) Conditioning

Ivan Pavlov has been credited with developing classical conditioning theory. Classical conditioning is best understood as *learning through association*—**one object becomes psychologically linked with a second object through a process of repeated and simultaneous pairings of the two objects.**

As a physiologist, Pavlov was interested in the physiological reactions of animals under experimental conditions (e.g., the salivation responses of canines). However, he also was intrigued by the psychological phenomena, which he uncovered in his work. Pavlov (1916/1957) described how certain objects can be psychologically associated with food to excite a salivation response in an animal:

> It has been proved that any agent of the external world can be made a stimulus of the salivary gland. Any sound, odour, etc., may become a stimulus that will excite the salivary gland exactly in the same way as it is excited by food at a distance. As to the precision of the fact, there is no difference whatever; it is only necessary to take into account the conditions in which the fact exists. What, then, are the conditions which can become stimuli of the salivary gland? The chief condition is coincidence in time. The experiment is performed as follows. We take, for example, a certain sound which has no relation to the salivary gland. This sound acts on the dog. Then we feed the dog or introduce acid into its mouth. After several repetitions of this the sound itself, without the addition of food or acid, begins to excite

the salivary gland. There are altogether four or five, at most six conditions under which any stimulant, any agent of the external world, becomes a stimulus of the salivary gland in the dog. Once this is so, once it has become a stimulus under a definite series of conditions, it will always act with the same precision as food or as any rejected substance introduced into the mouth. . . . Actually this is a law-governed reaction of the organism to an external agent effected through the medium of a definite part of the nervous system. (pp. 397–398)

In the preceding passage, Pavlov was essentially describing classical conditioning—the association of a stimulus (sound) with an object (food in this case), so that the stimulus produces the same reaction as the original object.

There are certain animal responses that are physiologically based (respondents). For instance, a hungry dog salivates when presented food. Human infants, for instance, respond with fear when they hear a loud noise. When a response is physiologically based, it is considered as an unconditioned response (UCR). No conditioning of any sort is necessary for the response to occur. It occurs quite naturally when certain stimuli are present. **(A** *stimulus* **is a condition that affects the organism through any of five senses—visual, auditory, olfactory [smell], gustatory [taste], and tactile/kinesthetic [touch].)** In effect, when an organism's senses are confronted by certain stimuli, certain unconditional responses can be predicted. Specific stimuli that produce UCR are called unconditioned stimuli (UCS).

> Time ⟶
> Unconditioned stimulus ⟶ Unconditioned response

In all cases, there is a direct correspondence between the presentation of an unconditioned stimulus and a UCR.

What Pavlov found was that when a stimulus that otherwise produced no noticeable effect (a neutral stimulus [NS]) was associated with an unconditioned stimulus (which always produced an UCR), the NS could be made to produce a very similar response. For instance, when a bell is repeatedly and simultaneously rung at separate presentations of food powder to a hungry dog, the bell becomes associated with the food powder. Over time, the bell alone will produce a salivation response much like the salivation response of the dog when food is present. In effect, the NS (the bell), which otherwise would not produce a salivation response in a dog, can be made to produce salivation. Diagramatically, this type of learning through association looks as follows:

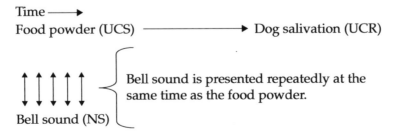

Time ⟶
Food powder (UCS) ⟶ Dog salivation (UCR)

↑↑↑↑↑  Bell sound is presented repeatedly at the
↓↓↓↓↓  same time as the food powder.

Bell sound (NS)

The bidirectional arrows (◄──►) above the words "Bell Sound (NS)" represent the *repeated* sounding of the bell (the NS) when food powder is placed in sensory perception of the dog. *Also, the bell sound is made at the same time that the food powder is presented.* In other words, there must be *temporal contiguity* **(closeness in time)**—both the UCS and the NS must be presented at about the same time. This is a basic principle of classical conditioning—as Pavlov described it—"coincidence in time." Therefore, *repetition* of the NS and *temporal contiguity* (coincidence in time) between the NS and the unconditioned stimulus are two basic classical conditioning principles.

It is noteworthy that if the bell is rung *after* the food powder is presented, the conditioning effect is not as strong. **Presenting the NS after the UCS (*backward conditioning*)**, therefore, is not as effective as presenting the NS at the same time as the UCS. Also, **the NS can be presented immediately before the presentation of the UCS (*forward conditioning*)** and the NS will have near or as good an effect as with simultaneous NS and UCS presentation.

Once the NS has been associated with the unconditioned stimulus through temporal contiguity and repetition, the NS takes on properties of its own for producing a response in the organism. The NS, therefore, becomes a conditioned stimulus (CS), which produces a conditioned response (CR) that is very similar to the UCR. In the previous example, the sounding of the bell alone (without food powder presentation) would produce salivation almost to the degree that the food powder produced salivation in dogs. Diagrammatically, classical conditioning looks as follows:

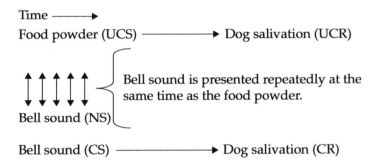

This diagram shows how the bell sound has been conditioned through temporal contiguity and repetition to produce a response of salivation. In this way, the bell sound (a NS that has become a CS), on its own, produces a salivation response (CR). Pavlov showed that dogs could be made to salivate on presentation of CS. In effect, an animal's nervous system can be taught to react to otherwise neutral stimuli through a process of associational learning.

A more meaningful and personal example is that of thunder and lightning and the fear response evidenced in young children. As mentioned earlier, loud noises produce fear responses in humans. Thunder, of course, can be quite frightening, even when a human is physically protected from the elements. But lightning is really not dangerous to a human when the human is in safe quarters. In fact, flashes of light as a general rule do not produce fear responses in humans. People are frequently confronted with light flashes in everyday life, and although a flash of light may orient a person, it will not usually produce fear. But it is well understood that lightning can cause a fear response in children. Actually, it is not the flash of lightning that causes the fear—it is the association of the lightning with thunder that produces fear in children, even in the safety of their homes. Diagrammatically, the association of lightning and the fear response to thunder look as follows:

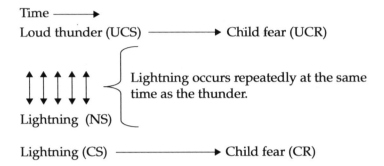

As is presented in this example, lightning flashes can produce a fear response in children that is very similar to the fear response resulting when there is a loud thunderclap. Classical conditioning has occurred. Almost every time there is thunder, lightning precedes it (forward conditioning). There is repetition and temporal contiguity between thunder and lightning. After such conditioning occurs, lightning will produce fear even in the absence of the sound of thunder.

As was mentioned earlier, there must be *temporal contiguity* **(the lightning and thunder must happen about the same time)** or at least forward conditioning—**the lightning comes slightly before the thunder.** If the lightning, however, were to occur after the thunder (backward conditioning) it would not have the same effect. The ease of conditioning, in the lightning and thunder example, reflects the power of forward conditioning.

The importance of this kind of learning through association was not fully explored as applied to humans by Pavlov. It was John B. Watson, credited with being the "Father of Behaviorism" (Watson, 1924/1930; Watson & Rayner, 1920), who recognized the consequences of Pavlov's ideas for human behavior. Watson, in a classic experiment, attempted to condition a fear response in a young child, Little Albert. Using classical conditioning principles, Watson and Rayner (1920) associated the presentation of a white rat (as an NS) to the presentation of a loud, frightening noise (remember human children react to loud noises in an unconditioned manner). See the following diagram:

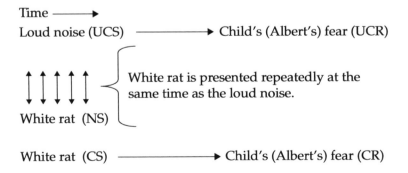

Over time, the child came to associate the presentation of the white rat with the loud noise to the degree that the white rat, alone, produced a fear response. Not only did the child fear the white rat, but his fear *generalized* **(spread) to become associated with other similar objects**. Jones (1924b) reported:

> Albert, eleven months of age, was an infant with phlegmatic disposition, afraid of nothing "under the sun" except a loud sound made by striking a steel bar. This made him cry. By striking the bar at the same time that Albert touched a white rat, the fear was transferred to the white rat. After seven combined stimulations, rat and sound, Albert not only became greatly disturbed at the sight of a rat, but this fear had spread to include a white rabbit, cotton wool, a fur coat, and the experimenter's hair. It did not transfer to his wooden blocks and other objects very dissimilar to the rat. (pp. 308–309)

Watson's intent, however, was to go beyond the actual conditioning of fear in a child. He wished to show that fear could be unlearned, just as it could be learned. Unfortunately, Little Albert was "adopted by an out-of-town family" shortly after he was conditioned to fear white rats (Watson, 1924/1930); deconditioning of the fear never was accomplished! It was left to one of Watson's students, Mary Cover Jones (1924a, 1924b), to demonstrate how fear could be unlearned through classical conditioning principles. Jones (1924a) described how deconditioning of a child's fear could be accomplished by using food as a stimulus to produce a response incompatible to fear:

> During a period of craving for food, the child is placed in a high chair and given something to eat. The feared object is brought in, starting a negative response. It is then moved away gradually until it is at a sufficient distance not to interfere with the child's eating. The relative strength of the fear impulse and the hunger impulse may be gauged by the distance to which it is necessary to remove the feared object. While the child is eating, the object is slowly brought nearer to the table, then placed upon the table and, finally, as the tolerance increases, it is brought close enough to be touched. Since we could not interfere with the regular schedule of meals, we chose the time of the mid-morning lunch for the experiment. This usually assured some degree of interest in the food and corresponding success in our treatment (pp. 388–389).

Essentially Jones extended classical conditioning principles to the deconditioning of fear. She associated an unconditioned stimulus (food) that produced a pleasant UCR (satiation) with the former CS (a white furry animal) that produced an unwanted CR (fear). The diagram shows the extension of classical conditioning for reasons of deconditioning:

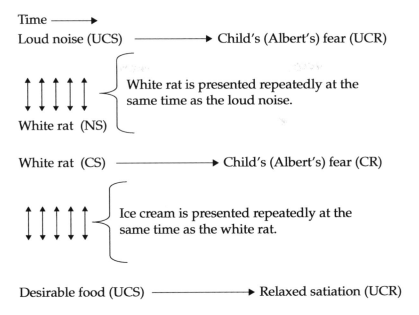

Time ——→

Loud noise (UCS) ————————→ Child's (Albert's) fear (UCR)

White rat is presented repeatedly at the same time as the loud noise.

White rat (NS)

White rat (CS) ————————→ Child's (Albert's) fear (CR)

Ice cream is presented repeatedly at the same time as the white rat.

Desirable food (UCS) ————————→ Relaxed satiation (UCR)

The child's satiation and pleasant responses to food proved to be, to some degree, *incompatible* with the fear response. Through contiguity and repetition the child was *deconditioned* to the previously conditioned fear response. After eating ice cream with the white rat present several times, he came to be relaxed in the presence of the white rat.

Through Watson's work (Watson & Rayner, 1920) and the works of Mary Cover Jones (1924a, 1924b), Pavlov's classical conditioning was applied to humans, not only to condition certain responses, but to decondition unwanted responses. The therapeutic application of classical conditioning principles was realized.

## Operant Conditioning

B. F. Skinner's work has been immensely influential in the field of counseling and psychotherapy. He was a prolific writer and, in his works, he applied his experimental findings to personal, therapeutic, educational, social, and cultural situations. For example, in one of his last works, Skinner (1989), discussing the "operant side of behavior therapy," stated:

> The conditions of which behavior is a function are sometimes under control, in homes, for example, and in schools, workplaces, hospitals, and prisons. Therapists may change these conditions for their own purposes if they are part of a family or if they teach, employ workers, or administer hospitals or prisons. Professionally, they advise those who do so. They help parents with their children or spouses with their spouses; they advise teachers; they recommend new practices in hospitals and prisons. They can do so because some of the conditions under which people live can be controlled. (p. 79)

Skinner believed that his findings applied beyond the animal laboratory, where some of his groundbreaking technical work was done. In addition to describing his experimental operant conditioning approach (e.g., Ferster & Skinner, 1957; Skinner, 1938, 1953), Skinner wrote several books on the consequences of his work for culture and society (e.g., Skinner, 1948). His place in history as a major influence over psychotherapeutic practices is well deserved.

Skinner's operant conditioning approach very simply can be described as conditioning by reinforcements. In fact, one of Skinner's major contributions to learning theory was his emphasis on what happens after a behavior. It is the result of a behavior that is significant in affecting the behavior. Before his time, experimental psychologists, in the mold of Guthrie or Hull, attempted to find the way that a stimulus (S) and a response (R) were connected. They primarily focused on what went before a behavior in attempting to define its cause. Diagrammatically, the formula for human behavior before Skinner looked like this:

$$S \longrightarrow R$$
Stimulus          Response

But Skinner, following the lead of Thorndike (1905), began to look at what happens after a behavior to determine its contingencies. Skinner recognized it was the relationship of the response to a *stimulus following the response* that was primarily a predictor of the likelihood of a behavior occurring again. For Skinner, the formula of behavior looked like this:

$$S \longrightarrow R \longrightarrow S_r$$
Stimulus          Response          Reinforcing stimulus

The emphasis in this formula is on the reinforcing stimulus, that is, what happens after a response. If a man said "sit" to a dog, and the dog randomly or accidentally sat, the likelihood of the dog sitting on future commands is increased if the man gave the dog a reward (a dog treat) after his first command. In this example, the behavior or response is considered an "operant." **Operants are simply emitted behaviors—behaviors that happen**. The dog was rewarded for sitting on command with a dog treat; therefore, it is more likely that the dog will sit on command in the future. The operant behavior was reinforced. In effect, Skinner's major accomplishment was to take the emphasis off the behavior preceding a response. In fact, experimentalists before him seemed to be wearing blinders that prevented them from seeing anything related to a behavior except what came before it. Skinner's position required them to go beyond the S → R framework. Skinner focused on operants and the outcomes of the operant behavior.

It is no secret that animals and people are influenced by rewards. Individuals are frequently rewarded or punished for their behaviors. The rewards and punishments, obviously, come after the behaviors. Rewards and punishments have a major controlling effect on what is subsequently done. But it is not as simple as understanding that rewards and punishments influence behavior. Skinner went into great detail about how behavior is affected, primarily in his book *Schedules of Reinforcement* (Ferster & Skinner, 1957). Readers should also know that there are several excellent primers on Skinner's work, which are useful in providing quick summaries of Skinner's ideas (e.g., Reynolds,

1968). It is important to begin with an understanding that there are different possible outcomes to an action. Four basic outcomes were defined by Skinner:

1.  An operant can be positively reinforced. ***Positive reinforcement* is the process by which the likelihood of a response increases on the presentation of a stimulus.** A positive reinforcer is defined by its result. Giving a child candy when the child is behaving well, if good behavior follows, is an act of positive reinforcement. The candy, being a stimulus following well-behaved actions, is considered a positive reinforcer. Other examples of positive reinforcers are pay bonuses for exceptional employees, sales commissions for salespersons, medals for star athletes, and so on. Very simply, if something is rewarding, it is usually a positive reinforcer.

2.  An operant can be negatively reinforced. ***Negative reinforcement* is the process by which the likelihood of a response increases on the removal of a stimulus.** Assume for a moment that there is a rat in a cage with a painful electrical current running through the floor of the cage; the only way the rat can stop the painful electrical current is to press a lever. If the rat presses the lever, and the current ceases, then the rat's behavior has been negatively reinforced—meaning that it is more likely the rat will press the lever when again confronted by an electrical charge in the floor. Negative reinforcement occurs only when there is an aversive or painful situation. When an organism acts to stop the painful or aversive situation, and succeeds, then the behavior of stopping the painful situation is negatively reinforced. Using an umbrella in a cold rain is another example—when you use an umbrella, you avoid being soaked, and your umbrella-using behavior has been negatively reinforced—it's more likely to happen again when it's cold and rainy. But actually, there are three different types of negative reinforcement: (a) acts that stop an aversive stimulus; (b) acts of escape from an aversive stimulus; and (c) acts that prevent an aversive condition (see Kazdin, 1977). Any of these three behaviors can be considered negative reinforcement, because the behavior is more likely to occur in similar subsequent situations. Note that both positive and negative reinforcement *increase* the likelihood of behavior. Negative reinforcement should not be confused with punishment, which *decreases* the likelihood of a behavior.

3.  An operant can be punished. ***Punishment* is the process by which the likelihood of a response decreases on the presentation of a stimulus.** Punishment usually involves the presentation of an aversive stimulus. A son who had his wrist slapped by his mother on reaching for dessert before finishing dinner, who then avoids prematurely reaching for dessert in the future, has been punished. The likelihood of the child prematurely reaching for the dessert is decreased by the presentation of an aversive stimulus—the wrist slap. An athlete who is fined for misbehavior on a playing field, who then refrains from future misbehavior, has been punished. In both these examples, a stimulus was presented that was aversive to the individual, thereby decreasing the likelihood of future behavior.

4.  An operant can be extinguished. ***Extinction* is the process by which the likelihood of a response decreases on the removal of a stimulus.** Extinction usually involves removal of a rewarding stimulus. For example, a teenager who volunteers to cut a

neighbor's lawn, who has been paid in the past for doing the work, but who never receives subsequent payment, is less likely to volunteer in the future. A child reaching into what was previously an always full cookie jar, only to find on repeated attempts that there are no cookies in the jar, is less likely to continue looking in the jar for cookies. In both these examples, the likelihood of a behavior has decreased, because a stimulus (reward) has been removed.

Both punishment and extinction decrease the likelihood of a behavior.

Punishment is the most effective means for quickly preventing a behavior. But punishment has some very serious drawbacks. First, it must be consistently and continuously applied. If one instance in a sequence of behavior is overlooked (not punished) then there is a chance that it will be negatively reinforced (increased in likelihood because the punishment has been removed). Second, punishment does not instruct the subject (an individual or animal) about the appropriate behavior. The subject may appear confused. In this sense, it does not educate about the desired or expected behavior. Third, punishment is often followed by aggressive responses by the punished organism. Aggression is often an unwanted side effect of punishment. Skinner, accordingly, has convincingly argued against the use of punishment, and in favor of positive reinforcement and extinction as modifiers of behavior (Skinner, 1948).

To be a behavior therapist using operant conditioning, it is absolutely imperative to understand these four types of influence on behavior.

But beyond understanding the nature of what happens after a behavior and its subsequent influence on later events, Skinner also recognized that there are different schedules (ways) of maintaining a behavior, especially through positive reinforcement. There are five different *schedules of reinforcement* **(planned and systematic ways of introducing reinforcement)** that can be used to maintain a behavior. They are (numbered parenthetically):

A.   A continuous reinforcement schedule. (1)
B.   Intermittent reinforcement schedules.
   1.   Ratio schedules
      a.   Fixed ratio (2)
      b.   Variable ratio (3)
   2.   Interval schedules
      a.   Fixed interval (4)
      b.   Variable interval (5)

A *continuous reinforcement schedule* is the easiest to understand. Simply, each desired or wanted behavior is rewarded. No matter how fast or how slow, or in what time frame, **each emission of a desired wanted behavior is reinforced**. For example, every time a pet dog sits on command, it receives a treat.

*Intermittent reinforcement schedules***, on the other hand, require reinforcement of a partial number of responses**. There are four intermittent schedules (fixed ratio, variable ratio, fixed interval, and variable interval).

## RATIO SCHEDULES

A ratio schedule reinforces one of every so many responses. For example, if the ratio of rewards to behaviors is one reward for every five emissions of behaviors (a ratio equal to 1/5), then one fifth of the behaviors are reinforced. If it is the fifth response in the sequence that is always rewarded, then the reward is on a fixed-ratio schedule—every fifth response is reinforced in a fixed pattern. A fixed-ratio schedule of reinforcement is demonstrated by the following sequence of letters, where each X is an emitted response, and each R is an emitted response that is rewarded:

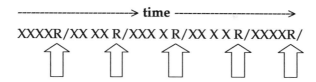

The fifth response in each sequence is indicated by an arrow underneath the letter and is also followed by a forward slash (/). Note that the time between the fifth responses may differ, but every fifth response received a reward. In this case each rewarded response was the fifth response. This is a fixed-ratio schedule.

A variable-ratio schedule still maintains a set ratio, say 1/5 (one reward in every five responses), but the response that receives the reward within the five emitted responses may vary. See the following sequence of letters, where, again, each X represents an emitted response, and each R is an emitted response that is rewarded. In this diagram each fifth response is followed by a forward slash (/). Each rewarded response is noted by an arrow.

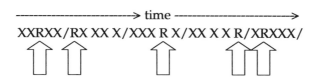

Note that one in every group of five responses received a reward. In the first group of five responses, the third response received a reward; in the second group of five responses, the first response received the reward; in the third group of five responses, the fourth behavior received the reward; in the fourth group of five responses, the fifth response received a reward; and in the fifth group of five responses, the second response received a reward. In each case, the ratio of one reward for every five responses was maintained, even though the event that was rewarded varied in each group of five responses. This is a variable-ratio schedule.

## INTERVAL SCHEDULES

Unlike ratio schedules, interval schedules do not involve counting responses. Rather, time is the issue. If an interval of time is set at 10 seconds, for example, then one reward occurs in every 10-second interval. The response that receives the reward within the time period is *fixed* at the response that is closest to the end of the time interval. This is a fixed-interval schedule of reinforcement. See the following sequence of letters, where, again, each X represents an emitted response, and each R is an emitted response that is rewarded:

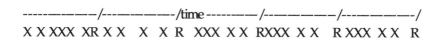

The 10-second intervals are noted on the timeline above the response letters X (response) and R (rewarded response), divided by the forward slash (/). Note that the behaviors that are rewarded are in all cases the behaviors occurring at exactly the end of the 10-second intervals, *or* the behaviors immediately or very closely following the end of the 10-second intervals. In this way, time is the factor setting the reinforcement pattern. About every 10 seconds, a response is rewarded, no matter how many or how few responses occur in the 10-second interval. This is a fixed-interval schedule.

A variable-interval schedule, like the fixed-interval schedule, does not involve counting responses. Time is the issue. Again, assuming that an interval of time for reinforcement is set at 10 seconds, then one reward occurs in every 10-second interval. The response that receives the reward, however, varies within the time period. It *is not* fixed at the response that is closest to the end of the time interval. It can occur any time within each 10-second interval. See the following sequence of letters, where each X represents an emitted response, and each R is an emitted response that is rewarded.

---------------- /---------------- /time---------- /---------------- /---------------- /
X X XXXR X R  X X  X  XXX X XXRXRXX  X X X XX  R X  X

The 10-second intervals are noted on the timeline above the response letters, divided by the forward slash (/). Note that the behaviors that are rewarded always occur sometime in the 10-second intervals, but the time of reinforcement in the intervals varies in each 10-second interval. In the first 10 seconds, the reward comes near the end of the period; in the second 10 seconds, the reward comes near the beginning of the period; in the third 10 seconds, the reward comes near the end; and in the fourth 10-second period, the reward comes at the beginning of the period. In the final 10-second period the reward comes about the middle. Time is the factor setting the reinforcement pattern. Within every 10 seconds, one response is rewarded, no matter how many or how few responses occur in the 10-second interval. But the time in each 10 seconds where the reward occurs varies for each 10-second interval. This is a variable-interval schedule.

Understanding these types of reinforcement schedules is very important, especially in clinical settings where continuous reinforcement of wanted behaviors becomes very expensive in time, effort, and resources. In fact, the **continuous reinforcement schedule (where every response is rewarded)** is very vulnerable to **extinction (a decrease in the likelihood of a behavior due to the removal of a reinforcing stimulus)**. The continuous reinforcement schedule is the easiest schedule of reward for the subject to *un*learn on removal of rewards. On the other hand, the variable ratio and variable interval schedules of reinforcement are the least vulnerable and most immune to extinction. In effect, the intermittent schedules have rewarded the subject for not being rewarded some of the time (interval schedules) or for not being rewarded for every response (ratio schedules). The variable ratio and variable interval schedule make the rewards less predictable. The subject then learns to be patient about rewards! Intermittent reinforcement schedules make the behaviors more enduring in the face of removal of positive reinforcement.

## SHAPING

So far, a great many details have been presented about how behaviors are affected by events that follow them, and how certain wanted behaviors can be maintained. Little has been said about how wanted behaviors first occur (are first emitted). In fact, the behaviors

**FIGURE 8.1** B. F. Skinner conducting a pigeon experiment with his operant conditioning chamber (Skinner box).
*Source:* Sam Falk/Science Source.

that are wanted by the behaviorist may not occur naturally. They may not exist in the subject's behavioral repertoire. In such cases, it is the responsibility of the behaviorist to encourage the wanted behavior. The behavioral method for encouraging new behaviors is called "shaping." ***Shaping*** **is the process by which a wanted behavior is successfully approximated—semblances of the wanted behavior are systematically rewarded, increasing the likelihood of the wanted behavior's occurrence.** In this way, the subject is rewarded for any behavior that comes close to the behavior that is desired or wanted, and, through a process of waiting for and rewarding appropriate operants (approximately like the wanted or desired behavior), the behaviorist slowly assists the subject in building the wanted behavior. Kazdin (1977) stated: "In shaping, the terminal behavior is achieved by reinforcing small steps or approximations toward the final response rather than reinforcing the final response itself" (p. 12). Skinner demonstrated this clearly with rats in what he devised as a ***reinforcement chamber*** **(what is now known as a "Skinner box"**; Figure 8.1). To get a hungry rat to push a lever to get food pellets, it is first necessary to reward any behavior of the rat that is close to the lever. As the rat gets closer to the lever, the rat is rewarded with a food pellet. Each subsequent approach to the lever is rewarded, until, finally, perhaps by accident, the lever is engaged by the rat, which produces an immediate reward. Shaping is a means of ensuring that wanted behaviors will be manifested.

## PRIMARY AND SECONDARY REINFORCERS

There are certain types of stimuli that act as reinforcers quite naturally. For example, a hungry rat will respond to food, a thirsty animal will respond to water, and so on. According to Reynolds (1968), when stimuli are **"able to reinforce behavior without**

**the organism's having any particular previous experience with them"** (p. 11), they can be considered *primary reinforcers.* In humans, deprivation-related primary reinforcers include food, water, sleep, and sex (broadly defined as skin-to-skin contact). Humans, for example, appear especially naturally attracted to foods with sugar, salt, and fat content. Moreover, other stimuli can become reinforcers. Reynolds (1968) stated that conditioned, or *secondary reinforcers,* **"acquire the power to reinforce operants through a procedure which is similar to that of respondent [classical] conditioning"** (p. 11). When an otherwise NS has been associated with a primary reinforcer consistent with the principles of classical conditioning, it can acquire reinforcing properties. The classic example of a secondary reinforcer is money. Money cannot be eaten or used as drink but it can be associated with (used to purchase) food or drink. Secondary reinforcers, as with money, are very powerful reinforcers.

Given these basic operant behavioral principles, behavior therapists can modify human behavior in mental health settings, as is described later in this chapter by means of Kazdin's (1977) Token Economy.

## The Target of Counseling

The object of counseling consistent with Behavior Therapy is a specified, identifiable, and measurable behavior. There is no assumption of psychological process beyond what can be observed. This basic principle was defined by Watson (1924/1930). Watson stated:

> We believed then, as we do now, that man is an animal different from other animals only in the types of behavior he displays. . . . The raw fact that you, as a psychologist, if you are to remain scientific, must describe the behavior of man in no other terms than those you would use in describing the behavior of the ox you slaughter, drove and still drives many timid souls away from behaviorism. (p. v)

Behaviorally oriented therapists, therefore, focus on observable behaviors, and they describe behaviors in operational terms. **An *operational term* is a definition according to actions—nothing is implied.** A behaviorist would say, "The man raised his finger to his eyebrow and scratched it three times in a downward fashion." A nonbehaviorist might say, "The man appeared to be thinking." Nonbehavioral hypothesizing is not consistent with the focus of Behavior Therapy.

## The Process of Counseling

The process of counseling is a process of defining maladaptive or distressful behaviors and then establishing procedures to stop or to lessen them. The counselor meets with the client to define behavioral objectives, and then the counselor acts in an ongoing process of behavioral assessment and environmental modification to change the external factors affecting an unwanted behavior. The behavior therapist is always viewed as responsible to develop reasonable, behaviorally sound, therapeutic means for influencing behavior. Therapeutic failure results from a poor assessment of the factors influencing behavior or a misapplication of behavioral techniques.

The process of counseling may differ according to the specialized technique used, and the reader is directed to the "Specialized Techniques" section of this chapter to gain a clearer understanding of the process of counseling according to specific techniques.

## Counselor Role

Behavioral tenets of practice are practical, concrete, and directive. Counselors are expected to attend to basic operant and classical conditioning principles in defining what is important in assessment and treatment. Targets for intervention are to be operational (measurable) and behaviors that are easily observable by trained professionals. Outcomes and goals are attainable, realistic, yet significant to client functioning in specified contexts.

The counselor role is that of technician and educator. The Behavior Therapist acts to coordinate a program designed to change behavior, primarily by implementing operant or classical conditioning principles. It is also important for the counselor to establish a **behavioral contract with the client, which essentially defines an agreement with the client and a consensus that the client's problem is anticipated to be modifiable by means of external influence on the client's behavior.** The counselor clearly defines the goals and objectives of counseling and the methods for achieving goals.

## Goals of Counseling and Ideal Outcomes

The goal of Behavior Therapy is a change in behavior. Because the behaviors undertaken for modification through behavioral techniques are measurable, the outcomes of therapy are measurable. Ideally, the client will leave therapy without symptomatic behavior, or at least with a lessening of unwanted behaviors. It is the behavior therapist's responsibility to assess whether the targeted behaviors have been diminished consistent with the patient's expressed interests at the beginning of therapy.

## Specialized Techniques

### JOSEPH WOLPE'S SYSTEMATIC DESENSITIZATION

**FIGURE 8.2**  Joseph Wolpe, speaking at the 1990 "Evolution of Psychotherapy" conference.

*Source*: Photo by R. Rocco Cottone

Joseph Wolpe's (1958, 1973, 1990) "Systematic Desensitization" technique is probably one of the best and most widely practiced examples of Behavior Therapy (see Figure 8.2). Wolpe, an MD psychiatrist, owing much to the works of Skinner (1953), Watson (1924/1930), Watson and Rayner (1920), and Eysenck (1960), took Behavior Therapy and adeptly applied it to mental health services. In fact, Systematic Desensitization builds on the works of Watson, and specifically one of Watson's students, Mary Cover Jones (Jones, 1924a, 1924b), who extended the classical conditioning model to the realm of deconditioning fear, as was discussed earlier in this chapter.

Wolpe, in his attempts to decondition anxiety in patients, tried several means to **ameliorate (improve or make better)** the anxiety response without using food as the deconditioning stimulus, as Jones (1924a) had done. Food, as it will be learned, is not the best stimulus to produce a response incompatible to anxiety. Wolpe was thwarted in his efforts until he learned of Jacobson's (1938) "Progressive Relaxation" technique. *Progressive Relaxation* **is a technique by which a deep-muscle relaxation is accomplished through a series of exercises.** Progressive Relaxation brings about a response in the client that is antithetical to the anxiety response. Also, progressive relaxation is a technique that is easy to do, can be taught to clients, and produces a response with practice that is strong enough to counteract an unwanted anxiety response. It also has the additional benefit of not requiring motor activity on the part of the patient in relation to the anxiety-producing stimulus. The patient, once relaxed, just has to relax and use his or her imagination. In effect, Wolpe combined the theoretical and practical work of Jones with Jacobson's "Progressive Relaxation" technique to produce "Systematic Desensitization." *Systematic Desensitization* **is a technique used primarily to decondition fear responses by pairing the stimulus that produces the unwanted anxiety response with a command to relax (which with practice can produce a deep-muscle relaxation).**

Theoretically, Systematic Desensitization is based on a principle of learning, "reciprocal inhibition," which Wolpe (1958) discussed in detail in his classic work, *Psychotherapy by Reciprocal Inhibition.* The principle of reciprocal inhibition is defined as follows:

> If a response antagonistic to anxiety can be made to occur in the presence of anxiety-evoking stimuli so that it is accompanied by a complete or partial suppression of the anxiety responses, the bond between these stimuli and the anxiety responses will be weakened. (p. 71)

Essentially, classical conditioning theory is extended through the principle of reciprocal inhibition to the realm of removing certain unwanted responses. Wolpe (1958) went on to describe several methods of applying the principle of reciprocal inhibition to human concerns, all without the use of food as a stimulus producing the response incompatible to the unwanted responses. The reason food is avoided is that the actual mechanism by which a response antagonistic to anxiety is produced by eating is unclear. Wolpe opted for more clear-cut anxiety-antagonistic responses, through direct relaxation, the sexual response, or even the assertive response.

Beyond introducing Systematic Desensitization and describing details of the approach in his 1958 work, Wolpe (1973) further refined and described the procedure in his book *The Practice of Behavior Therapy.* Four "separate sets of operations" are required in Systematic Desensitization:

1. Training in deep-muscle relaxation
2. The establishment of the use of a scale of subjective anxiety
3. The construction of anxiety hierarchies
4. Counterposing relaxation and anxiety-evoking stimuli from the hierarchies (p. 104).

These four operations are expanded on briefly in the following pages under three general headings, consistent with Wolpe's description in his text, for brevity's sake. What follows is modified and summarized from his 1973 text. The reader is referred to Wolpe (1958, 1973, 1990) as original sources for detailed descriptions of the technique.

1. *Training in deep-muscle relaxation.* Essentially, Wolpe (1973) recommended following Jacobson's (1938) approach with some modification. Wolpe shortened the

length of time required to learn the technique to about six sessions. He also instructs his patients to practice at home.

Progressive relaxation involves directives by the therapist for the patient to flex groups of muscles on command, followed by a command to relax the muscles. The procedure helps to produce a fatigued feeling in the muscles and demonstrates to the patient the difference between tension and relaxation in the muscle group. The procedure is summarized in the following paragraph, but as described, it is slightly modified according to the experience of the author.

The patient is asked to get into a comfortable position, preferably in a lounge-type chair or a therapy couch. The procedure is straightforwardly described to the patient, and the intent is simply described as educational, that is, to teach the patient how to relax and to experience a relaxation feeling through a mild exercise routine. The procedure is *progressive* because the therapist starts with one area of the body, usually the hands, and works systematically and logically through tangential muscle groups. For example, after the patient's hands have been tensed and relaxed on command of the therapist (sometimes with several repetitions of the same muscle group to ensure patient recognition of relaxation), then the therapist asks the patient to tense and relax the forearms, then the upper arm, then the shoulders, and subsequently, in sequence, the back of the neck, the face, the mouth and tongue, the front of the neck, the chest, the stomach, the groin, the front of the upper legs, and so on, around the body. In this way, all major muscle groups are systematically (sometimes repetitively) tensed and then relaxed. Finally, after all major muscle groups have been relaxed, the therapist instructs the patient to produce a total body tensing and relaxing with deeper and deeper feelings of relaxation (almost in a hypnotically suggestive way). With practice this technique can produce deep relaxation that is resistant to the effect of anxiety-producing stimuli.

Although Wolpe (1973) described a six-session process for teaching the patient Progressive Relaxation, whereby certain muscle groups are focused on each session, the preceding approach may facilitate an even quicker accomplishment of deep relaxation, and the approach can be easily learned by patients.

2.  *The establishment of the use of a scale of subjective anxiety and the construction of an anxiety hierarchy*. Operations 2 and 3 listed previously are combined in this section and modified, because they are related activities.

Because Systematic Desensitization is a procedure that is targeted to reduce anxiety consistent with classical conditioning principles, it is necessary to have clearly defined anxiety-producing stimuli delineated to associate with relaxation. The fact that Systematic Desensitization does not require the presentation of the actual anxiety-producing stimuli is in its favor from a practical standpoint. Actual *in vivo* (a real "live" situation) desensitization is often not possible within the confines of a mental health practitioner's office, and to go outside the office could involve a great expense both time wise and financially. Accordingly, Wolpe (1973) developed his technique so that the stimuli that trigger the unwanted response could be imagined—mentally conjured, so to speak—in order that the individual could be deconditioned to images of the stressful situations. Wolpe argued that deconditioning to imagery was effective at producing reduced anxiety in real-life situations. However, the images must be adequate, and it is noteworthy that some patients have difficulty conjuring adequate images, which would make them poor candidates for this technique. Regardless, the patient is asked to imagine the least anxiety-producing situation and the most anxiety-producing situation related to the experienced distress.

The therapist must act to clearly discern what it is that the patient fears. A fear of dogs, for example, may actually be a fear of the germs that dogs carry and spread through licking. A very different set of images would need to be developed (i.e., not of dogs, but of images of the spread of germs) if, in fact, germs were the stimuli producing the anxiety. Once the actual fear-producing situation is defined, the therapist asks the patient to assign a point value of 100 to the most fear-producing image, and 0 points to the least fear-producing image. This effectively constitutes a continuum of distress, from 0 to 100. A hierarchy of fear-producing stimuli is then developed with the patient defining images of situations somewhere between the two extremes on the continuum of distress. Most usually, patients are able to develop a hierarchy with about 10 or more images. The major task of the therapist is twofold: (a) to help the patient to develop a meaningful hierarchy of images from the least disturbing image to the most distressing image and (b) to ensure that the distress produced by going from one image to another along the continuum is approximately equivalent. In effect, hierarchy development allows for simultaneous development of what Wolpe calls *"subjective units of disturbance"* or *"suds"* **(p. 120). Patients must develop a subjective scale of distress and then communicate to the therapist approximate levels of distress using the subjective scale.** Wolpe (1973) stated:

> It is possible to use the scale to ask the patient to rate the items of the hierarchy according to the amount of anxiety he would have upon exposure to them. If the differences between items are similar, and, generally speaking, not more than 5 to 10 suds, the spacing can be regarded as satisfactory. On the other hand, if there were, for example, 40 suds for item number 8, and 10 suds for item number 9, there would be an obvious need for intervening items. (p. 120)

Once a hierarchy is developed and there is some consensus that the *suds* levels among items on the scale are nearly equivalent, then the therapist can move to the next step, which is the actual desensitization procedure.

3. *Counterposing relaxation and anxiety-evoking stimuli from the hierarchies.* Given a client who can relax on command after having followed the Progressive Relaxation procedures, and given an adequate hierarchy on a reasonable scale of subjective distress, then the therapist can initiate the Systematic Desensitization process. Wolpe (1973) described the instructions to the patient during the first desensitization session as follows: "I am now going to get you to relax; and when you are relaxed I will ask you to imagine certain scenes. Each time a scene is clear in your mind indicate this by raising your index finger about one inch" (p. 121). The therapist asks the client to stop imagining the scenes after about 7 seconds or so and continues to present relatively neutral images. This allows for practice with the client imagining scenes and communicating to the therapist the approximate level of *suds*. When the patient develops some proficiency during such exercises, then the therapist can move to the least anxiety-producing stimulus on the hierarchy. Usually, no more than one item from the hierarchy will be attempted in the first

desensitization session. Subsequent sessions slowly move up the hierarchy until the patient can experience near complete relaxation even with what was previously a highly anxiety-producing image.

Refining one's approach when applying Systematic Desensitization is important, and experience teaches that one must be patient and flexible through the process of desensitizing patients. Wolpe (1973) spelled out some very detailed concerns related to administration of this procedure. For example, the duration of an image should usually last only about 7 seconds, the spacing of sessions is usually once or twice a week, and the number of sessions needed varies depending on the patient and the patient's concern. To be effective as a behavioral therapist using Systematic Desensitization requires (a) much practice under supervision of experienced practitioners and (b) creativity in approaching the problems that arise in such a standardized procedure. Nonetheless, Systematic Desensitization is a very effective method for remedying phobic responses and is a useful armament for a counselor-generalist facing patients with such concerns.

## KAZDIN'S "TOKEN ECONOMY"

Alan E. Kazdin is a leader in the Behavior Therapy movement. He has written extensively on the application of behavioral theory in clinical contexts (e.g., Agras, Kazdin, & Wilson, 1979; Kazdin, 1982; Kazdin & Wilson, 1978). His book, *The Token Economy: A Review and Evaluation* (Kazdin, 1977), will be the focus of this section. In that book, Kazdin detailed the history, theory, and applications of token economies in applied settings. Kazdin (1977) described *token economies* as follows:

> The token economy is a type of behavior modification program which relies heavily upon the principles of operant conditioning. There are relatively few major principles of operant conditioning, although there is extensive research bearing on the effective implementation of the techniques derived from the principles. An understanding of the principles and diverse basic research findings is fundamental to the success of token programs. (p. 1)

Essentially, a token economy attempts to change the contingencies of behavior. Kazdin further stated that *a contingency*:

> Refers to the relationship between a behavior (the response to be changed) and the events which follow the behavior. The notion of a contingency is important because reinforcement techniques such as the token economy alter behavior by altering the contingencies which control (or fail to control) a particular behavior. (p. 1)

Overall, **a token economy is a system of supervision designed to reward certain client behaviors (as productive workers are rewarded on their jobs) so that a client is positively reinforced for behaviors that are wanted and desired by the supervising behavioral therapist.** The focus of token economies, therefore, is the same as the focus of operant conditioning—rewarding a desirable behavior after it occurs.

To reward behaviors, there are a number of options available to clinicians involved in behavior modification (Kazdin, 1977). Food and other primary reinforcers can be used.

Social reinforcers, such as praise, attention, and facial expressions, are useful conditioned reinforcers (if they have been associated with primary reinforcers, such as healthy physical contact, in the past). Specific activities can be used to reward other activities. For example, the *Premack principle* (Premack, 1959) can be applied; the **Premack principle is simply the giving of opportunities for the expression of a client's highly preferred activities, where such opportunities are made contingent on performance of target behaviors.** For example, if a child likes to play video games, making the child finish his vegetables at dinner in order to have time to play the games is application of the Premack principle (sometimes also called Grandma's law, since grandmothers have used that tactic for many years). But specific to token economies is the use of *tokens*—**"tangible conditioned reinforcers"** (Kazdin, 1977, p. 44), which are exchangeable for a variety of other reinforcers, including the ones previously described in this paragraph. Tokens are delivered immediately following the desired behavior, and they later can be traded for something the client desires. In this way, behavior patterns are not interrupted by eating, drinking, or activities that impede performance. Those activities are earned through the accumulation of tokens.

A token can be just about anything that is easily handled, such as a poker chip, tickets, stars, checkmarks, or toothpicks. But it is highly recommended that they should be something that clients cannot reproduce or purchase (or have purchased for them) on the outside. Some facilities choose to print their own currency as tokens, which can be easily controlled and handled. It is also wise to have the clinician place the client's initials on the currency when it is presented to prevent the transfer (voluntary or forced) of the tokens among clients. Regardless, Kazdin (1977) described several options in this regard, and his book should be consulted for the pros and cons of each option.

Once the tokens have been chosen, and once target behaviors have been identified, then it is necessary to associate the tokens with "back-up reinforcers" (Kazdin, 1977), which are items or events that are wanted by clients. These must be, to some degree, individualized for each client. They can be food, privileges, drinks, rest periods, or other rewards. But they should always be closely associated with the tokens. At first, only one or a few tokens may be required to obtain what is wanted. Later, more tokens may be necessary. The important initial issue is *repetition* and *contiguity* between the presentation of tokens and the presentation of what is wanted. The association of tokens with backup reinforcers, then, is accomplished through classical conditioning principles.

Once tokens have been clearly associated with the backup reinforcers specific to the client, then it is necessary to specify the contingencies for receipt of the token. Kazdin (1977) stated:

> The introduction of the program includes precise specifications of the responses that are to be reinforced and punished and the specific token values associated with each response. In addition, the specific back-up events, the prices in terms of tokens, and the periods in which back-up events are made available are specified. To introduce the program, client manuals are sometimes written to detail the contingencies. The contingencies may be described orally or displayed in a conspicuous place. The manner of introducing the program, verbal, written, or perhaps no formal introduction at all, in part depends upon the level of clients. (p. 51)

The contingencies essentially detail the consequences of certain behaviors, meaning that ultimately desirable and wanted behaviors are appropriately rewarded.

Consequences may be applied to individuals (most usually) or groups. And there can be rewards (presentation of tokens) or punishments (which take several forms). Kazdin said: "Token economies are based primarily upon positive reinforcement, i.e., the delivery of tokens for specified target behaviors" (p. 69). But he also described commonly used punishments, including "time out from reinforcement" (a pause in rewards), reprimands, overcorrection (requiring the client to exaggerate in a positive way the target behavior), and *response cost* **(the most common type of punishment, which usually involves the withdrawal of tokens or fines for unwanted behaviors).** Response cost is one of the most used and useful methods in token economy programs (Kazdin, 1977). However, Kazdin (1977) noted that it is probably unwise to use response cost as the main method in a token economy system. Kazdin seemed to favor more positive approaches. Remembering that punishments have adverse side effects—including possible client confusion, aggression, or the negative reinforcement of unwanted behaviors when punishment is not consistent—the use of punishments should be limited and wisely administered.

Related to client progress, Kazdin (1977) has recommended levels of programs where clients can progress up steps or stages. Level programs essentially require the planning of subprograms. Steps, stages, or subprograms are preferred to changing contingencies in the middle of one program. By including steps or stages, after a client has achieved a certain goal, a whole new subprogram is implemented, with different contingencies and different opportunities. It is the equivalent of allowing clients to graduate to new levels of accomplishment and reward. In this way, most clients do not stagnate, and they can continually progress to new levels of achievement. As long as the goals at each stage are realistic to the capability of clients in the program, success can be built into the program and expected of motivated and higher functioning clients. Levels are also useful in facilities where the ultimate goal is *discharge* **(graduation from the program)** of the client, such as psychiatric hospitals, vocational rehabilitation facilities (where job placement is the goal), or delinquency programs (where family reintegration may be the goal). All in all, step programs are useful in many settings.

The three widest applications of token economy programs have been with school children, the psychiatrically institutionalized, and the intellectually disabled. Regarding the effectiveness of token economy programs in these settings, Kazdin (1977) noted: "Research with each of these populations has firmly established the efficacy of token reinforcement in altering a wide range of responses" (p. 110). Other applications, with supportive but less conclusive outcome research, include work with delinquents, offenders, and the chemically dependent. Overall, token economies can be adapted to a number of settings.

The success of a token economy program to a large degree depends on the involved professional personnel. The individuals administering the program, those individuals doling out the rewards or punishments, must be well trained. Training should include didactic instruction on basic operant conditioning principles. Trainees should be given feedback by professional supervisors about their effectiveness. Moreover, the professional staff should be rewarded for appropriate professional actions in the workplace. Coordinators or program managers should ensure that the frontline token economy personnel are well prepared, monitored, and rewarded for attending to and reinforcing wanted client behaviors.

The ideal outcomes of most programs are: (a) **to have the client's behavior endure (*response maintenance*)**, especially when programs end; and (b) to have the wanted behaviors **generalize (spread)** to situations outside of the treatment setting. It is noteworthy that response maintenance cannot be assumed to be an ordinary outcome of the program. Research has shown that often, after the removal of token programs, client behaviors decline to a baseline (the level of behavior at the initiation of the program). In other words, although some research studies have demonstrated that wanted behaviors are maintained at a level above the baseline, this cannot be expected of all token economy programs with all client types. Therefore, when a program or client is expected to be terminated, it is wise to anticipate the end of the program, and to design the program so that rewards are *faded*. Essentially, *fading the contingencies* **is a process of programmed and systematic withdrawal of rewards,** usually moving from continuous to intermittent reinforcement schedules—to variable ratio or variable interval schedules where there are very few rewards. Also, contingencies can be transferred to the client himself or herself; in other words, the client can be reinforced for **self-reinforcement (the client learns to reward him- or herself for desirable behavior)**. Regardless, a well-planned approach can minimize the effect of program termination and ensure a lasting effect of the token economy.

Related to **generalization of wanted behaviors to other settings or situations (transfer or training)**, again, there are limitations. Kazdin stated: "In most token economies, altering behavior in one situation does not result in a transfer of those changes to other situations either while the program is in effect or after it has been withdrawn" (p. 177). One way to help ensure transfer of training is "to extend the program to settings in which transfer of training is desired" (p. 180). For example, where children have been involved in a token economy, parents or teachers can be trained to use token economy methods in the home or at school, respectively. Although it is difficult to design a smooth transition of a token economy program, it is incumbent on the program manager to anticipate the need for transfer of training and to implement appropriate interventions in the targeted settings.

Readers interested in using token economy programs are encouraged to read Kazdin's (1977) book. He explained many of the subtleties of using this technique, and his book is both scholarly and practical. Another useful and related resource that actually predated Kazdin's book is *The Token Economy: A Motivational System for Therapy and Rehabilitation,* by Ayllon and Azrin (1968). It, too, is both scholarly and applied, and should be required reading for individuals who plan to implement, to manage, or to work with token economy programs.

Overall, the use of token economies is probably the clearest behavioral approach consistent with operant conditioning. It is the most closely aligned therapeutic method with the work of Skinner, whose research findings led to the development of a theory of operant conditioning. As such, token economies represent a unique application of theory to professional practice.

## RECENT DEVELOPMENTS AND CRITICISMS

There are several criticisms of Behavior Therapy. One of the most serious criticisms of Behavior Therapy is that it can be inhumane. Behavior Therapy, consistent with behavioral theory, views the human being in a machinelike way, negating such internal concepts as free will and self-determination. The human is viewed as influenced primarily by external factors, and is almost exclusively modifiable by means of rewards, punishments, and associations. It is dehumanizing, especially from a humanistic psychology standpoint. Rogers, in a classic debate with Skinner in 1956, stated:

> To the extent that a behaviorist point of view in psychology is leading us toward a disregard of the person, toward treating persons primarily as manipulable objects, toward control of the person by shaping his behavior without his participant choice, or toward minimizing the significance of the subjective—to that extent I question it very deeply. My experience leads me to say that such a point of view is going against one of the strongest undercurrents of modern life, and is taking us down a pathway with destructive consequences. (Kirschenbaum & Henderson, 1989, p. 86)

Skinner responded by stating that the individual does not vanish according to behaviorism—that is, the individual is still viewed as a unique biological organism with a unique set of environmental influences—yet Skinner maintained that it is external objective experience that primarily directs behavior. In effect, free will and individual determinism vanish from the externalist framework. Where free will and self-determination are valued as human traits, behaviorism in fact does not value such traits.

A second related criticism of behaviorism is that it denies the internal, subjective psychological experiences of the individual. Subjectivity gives way to *objectivity* (focusing on observable behaviors). Subjective experiences are not valued according to behavioral doctrines. Some say this is denying the obvious *subjective, cognitive, and self-reflective* nature of human beings, that is, those human traits that differentiate humans from lower animals. However, the behaviorists maintain that human behavior is much like animal behavior—externally controlled—and even "thinking" and "self-reflection" are learned behaviors. The Cognitive Behavioral Therapists (see the summary in the next section) provide a response to the fully "external" approach of the purely behavioral therapists.

Finally, critics have attacked behaviorism by claiming that it is superficial. They claim that changing behavior is not enough, that, in fact, there are certain psychological processes that underlie behavior. It is these underlying processes that must be addressed in therapy, not just the behaviors themselves. Research evidence has supported the behaviorists, however, by demonstrating Behavior Therapy's effectiveness on objective measures of success in treatment.

Behaviorism has advanced to the degree that behavioral principles have been applied in many settings. Even marital relationships, the domain of systemic-relational theory, have been shown to be modifiable by behavioral techniques (Bornstein & Bornstein, 1986). And researchers continue to demonstrate the effectiveness of specialized behavioral techniques in specific settings (see Garfield & Bergin, 1986). Behavioral theory leads to objectively effective techniques for changing targeted behaviors.

It is noteworthy that recently there has been a movement in the field to acknowledge the close relationship between cognitive therapies and Behavior Therapy. All therapy is to some degree cognitive, as it involves language as a foundation for defining and targeting behaviors for intervention. *Cognition* **is the combination of language and perception,** and behavior therapies with humans involve a cognitive component that is undeniable. Wilson (2008) described a trend in Behavior Therapy, involving its cognitive aspects, as follows:

> The increasing tendency of behavior therapists to identify themselves as cognitive behavior therapists is reflected in the decision in 2005 to change the name of the Association for Advancement of Behavior Therapy (AABT) to the Association for Behavioral and Cognitive Therapies (ABCT). It is unclear if behavior therapy will continue to be practiced as a pure approach to therapy or if it will eventually become subsumed under the general rubric of cognitive behavior therapy. (p. 245)

So Behavior Therapy is evolving, and recognition of the cognitive aspects of treatment may be viewed by some as welcomed and by others as resulting in an illegitimate theoretical hybrid.

Overall, behavioral approaches are straightforward and practical. They are targeted and result oriented. They are unique in their emphasis on external factors affecting human behavior.

## COGNITIVE BEHAVIORAL THERAPY

As described in the previous section, Behavioral Therapy has been criticized as too purely behavioral. It is based on a theoretical position that downplays *human agency,* **the idea that humans can affect the courses of their lives and can make personal decisions based on thoughtful consideration**. Counseling is *not typically forced on clients by some authority* representing a governing agent that imposes treatment on clients (although in some legal contexts there is what is called **"compulsory therapy"**). *Compulsory therapy* **is a mandatory therapy required by a judge or legal entity for treatment of people who have endangered others or broken laws** (such as drunken drivers or sex offenders). In most cases, clients make a decision to attend counseling voluntarily or as influenced by significant other individuals in their lives. CBT recognizes human agency, yet it still holds to application of behavioral principles.

There is no clear-cut date that CBT was established. It has been an evolving movement in the counseling and psychotherapy field. One text that acts as a marker of the movement is the *Handbook of Cognitive-Behavioral Therapies*, edited by Dobson (2010, now in its third edition). The first edition of the book was published in 1988, and by then, a number of theorists had published works that inspired or instigated the movement (e.g., Beck, 1967; Ellis, 1962; Meichenbaum, 1977), while other theorists began to demonstrate that the agent called "self" could be viewed as a construct that had explanatory power in predicting behavior (e.g., Bandura's [1977, 1997] work on self-efficacy).

Dobson (2010, p. 4) summarized the three fundamental propositions of (CBT): (a) "Cognitive activity affects behavior"; (b) "Cognitive activity may be monitored and altered"; and (c) "Desired behavior change may be effected through cognitive change." Dobson stated:

The third CBT proposition is a direct result of the adoption of the mediational model. It states that desired behavior change may be effected through cognitive change. Thus, while cognitive-behavioral theorists accept that overt reinforcement contingencies can alter behavior, they are likely to emphasize that there are alternative methods for behavior change, one in particular being cognitive change. (p. 5)

Dobson went on to summarize efforts by CBT proponents to demonstrate that *cognitive mediation* (p. 5)—the idea that a change in thinking can create a change in behavior—did have an effect on behavior. Although Dobson argued that "the fact of mediation is no longer strongly contested" (p. 4), there are no clear-cut, methodologically sound, and unquestionable results that can be cited as definitive in this regard, which, according to Dobson, "renders these models subject to ongoing debate" (p. 6). Although the CBT therapists have come to agreement about the basic propositions of CBT, there are others who still feel the concept of cognitive mediation is open to review.

Practically speaking, CBT is best represented in the works and approaches of several well-known theorists. Ellis (1962) and his Rational Emotive Behavior Therapy (see Chapter 6) is probably the most well known. Ellis's approach is based on the foundation that thinking is crucial to how people feel. He believed that people have a propensity to think negatively, thereby trending emotionally to uncomfortable or dysfunctional emotions. He believed changing the way a person thinks—thinking more positively and more scientifically—could affect the person's tendency to experience negative emotions, which would be lessened. Beyond this, as with the behavioral therapists, there is no theory of personality. His approach is about behavior change as mediated by cognition. Beck (1967) is also credited with identifying cognitions as crucial to emotions and behavior (see Figure 8.3). However, Beck did not identify global irrational thoughts, as did Ellis. Rather, Beck was able to discern that different mental disorders were associated with specific thematic cognitive patterns. So the way depressed people thought was different than the way anxious people thought. Beck's 1976 book identified specific "cognitive distortions" associated with differing mental conditions (Beck, 1976). The works of Ellis and Beck were groundbreaking and are identified as early models of the CBT movement (Dobson, 2010).

Therefore, what differentiates a CBT counselor from a more purely behavioral therapist? The answer is the focus on cognition. CBT counselors use different names for the cognitive process, sometimes calling it thoughts, frameworks, schemata, rules, expectations, beliefs, attitudes, and so on. But the primary focus is on cognition,

**FIGURE 8.3** Aaron Beck.
*Source*: Judith A. Beck

which means there has been a definition applied to what a client perceives and experiences that becomes a focus of counseling. The "primacy of cognition" is the distinguishing feature of CBT—meaning that cognition is held in a high place in defining behavior and changing behavior. A more purely behavioral therapist would focus more on the actual behavior in question. He or she would clearly define the behavior and then identify the environmental contingencies (stimuli or external factors) associated with the behavior. A CBT counselor also would identify the problematic behavior, but would then define the cognitions or thoughts that precede or are simultaneously present with the problem behavior. The target for intervention is the cognition. The cognitive behavioral therapist will first and foremost address the cognition and will try to change the thoughts that are associated with problem behaviors. Importantly, the CBT counselor does not stop with changing the thought. Typically, a CBT counselor will direct actions by the client that require not only a change in thinking, but will facilitate a change in action. As with Rational Emotive Behavior Therapy (REBT) and as described in Chapter 6, the counselor will use any of a number of techniques to encourage new thinking and different actions than those defined as problem actions.

Although there are certainly counselors who identify with a more purely behavioral approach, there are also therapists that have aligned with CBT and hold to a mixing of philosophies—to a "both/and" approach to the debate of internal versus external factors affecting behavior. The more purely behavioral therapists will seek credentials, such as certifications in applied behavioral analysis, whereas CBT counselors will seek credentials in any number of approaches designated within the CBT umbrella.

## STUDENT–MENTOR DIALOGUE

**Student:**  It seems like Behavior Therapy is really different from the other approaches in the psychological paradigm. It's focused on what happens outside a person, not what goes on inside emotionally or cognitively. Does this mean that approaches that look inside the person for explanations of behavior are not valid?

**Mentor:**  No, it doesn't mean the other theories are not valid. It's just another way of looking at behavior. Human behavior is complex, and the behaviorists simply say that we need to look at what happens outside a person to understand behavior. They view human behavior as they view animal behavior—fully predictable based on external variables that affect the living thing. Behaviorists argue that human behavior can be completely understood by analyzing that which can be observed. They don't surmise about internal psychological processes. They are concerned with factors that affect the behavior from the outside. This is in contrast to those approaches that focus on what happens inside the person. It's a different philosophy, and no one is viewed by all mental health professionals as the "right" philosophy. Different mental health professionals make choices about theory that direct their practices.

**Student:**  What is the historical significance of Behavior Therapy?

**Mentor:**  It has major significance, especially against the backdrop of the internal model therapies—those focusing on the internal experience of thinking and feeling. The behaviorists basically challenged the prevailing mindset, arguing that behavior is predictable based on external variables. Behaviorism challenged well-regarded concepts like free will and self-determination. It presented a philosophy that to some theorists was tantamount to saying humans are nothing but machines. It relegated humans to a base level that has been criticized as animalistic. There is no agentic self—a self that directs behavior. Rather, the human is viewed as a malleable and programmable organism that behaves according to *environmental contingencies* **(rewarding or punishing stimuli connected with behavior)**. It does not present a lofty view of human nature, meaning humans are not viewed as intrinsically motivated by higher ideals. Therapy then becomes a method of modifying contingencies. Behavior Therapy is focused purely on observable behavior and surmises nothing about internal psychological processes. Historically, it represents a serious shift in philosophy.

**Student:**  What are the positive aspects of the movement?

**Mentor:**  Behaviorism clearly tied counseling and psychotherapy to science and the ideals of science. A scientific ideal is that of *measurability,* **meaning that scientists deal with observable phenomena that can be observed by all people and can be quantified.** It's a mechanistic model of behavior based on scientific ideals. Scientific ideals address predictability—they address phenomena that can be measured and re-measured to ensure that outcomes can be clearly associated with the variables under study. And importantly, there is a principle in science called *logical positivism* **that means theories must not only be provable, but they must also be able to be disproved** (Popper, 1959). It's about the ability to verify or to dispute a theory with data. For example, subjective theories of counseling and psychotherapy cannot be disproved—because they address the internal psychological workings of the individual. So to say that one's ego has been strengthened, or one's self-concept has improved, is not deniable if the client reports such. No one can challenge another person's internal psychological experiences. But in science, conclusions must be verifiable, meaning others can validate the experience of another person with one's own observation of something measurable. If it can't be challenged, it does not hold weight from a scientific standpoint. Science values verifiability, and behaviorism clearly aligns with classic scientific ideals. In a sense, behaviorism keeps counseling and psychotherapy "honest" with Western scientific ideals. It argues that counseling and psychotherapy must be something different than philosophy or religion.

**Student:**  So you view behaviorism in a positive light.

**Mentor:**  Yes, I believe it has offered the field something meaningful, and, to a degree, it does challenge the field to value a scientific base.

**Student:**  So, are you opposed to the ideas presented by the cognitive behavioral therapists?

**Mentor:**  No. I do not view my acknowledgment of Behavior Therapy's special place in the history of psychotherapy as any bias for or against the model or its competitors. The CBT movement is competitive to Behavior Therapy. It comes from a different philosophical place. It does offer a different perspective than pure behavioral theory. In a sense, the CBT movement recognizes the full effect of the influence of factors external to the individual as important and powerful. But it still holds that thoughts can mediate emotions and behavior. CBT is saying, "We shouldn't just focus on behavior." At one level that makes a lot of sense, because language and perception (cognition) are aspects of the therapeutic process. Counselors talk to clients. They define problems interpersonally and through language. They listen to clients' descriptions of problems and put them into context. This all happens through language. So in a way, the CBT counselor is both accepting of the external influence of the environment (stimuli from outside the individual) and is accepting of the need to put experiences into words, which may be reflective of the client's mental framework and may be part of the problem.

**Student:**  So you think that CBT is more aligned with the counseling process?

**Mentor:**  Well, it prevents the role of the counselor from being perceived as mechanical or nonresponsive to client thoughts or feelings. Whereas the behavioral therapist must downplay the role of thinking and feeling in problem definition and behavioral analysis, the CBT counselor can fully embrace such ideas. The choice between a more pure Behavior Therapy and CBT is a choice that reflects the counselor's alignment with a more pure external (environmental stimuli) philosophy of human influence, or a more internal (thoughts or feelings) philosophy of human influence. Regardless, the behavioral and cognitive behavioral approaches are some of the most highly researched and supported approaches in the field. As they derive from a scientific basis of theory development, they also perform well when evaluated on scientific criteria. From an ethical standpoint, a counselor is wise to choose an **empirically supported approach to treatment (an approach that performs well in research where objective measures of success are used as outcome criteria)**, and the behavioral and CBT approaches tend to be well supported by research.

## CONCLUSION

This chapter has presented, in some detail, two behavioral theories of learning—classical and operant conditioning—and two related specialized behavioral therapeutic techniques—Systematic Desensitization and Token Economy. The chapter diverged a bit from the organization of other chapters due to the unique nature of Behavior Therapy. Behavior Therapy is not a monolithic, consensually agreed-on approach. Rather, it is a conglomeration of many applications from basic learning theories and their practical applications. There are many proponents and specialized techniques that can be considered behavioral therapies. Consequently, this chapter should not be viewed as an overview of the field of Behavior Therapy. Rather, it focused on two approaches deriving from two basic learning theories. Many influential behaviorists have not been identified in this chapter.

Additionally, this chapter addressed the CBT movement in the field of counseling and psychotherapy. It was briefly defined and described, and classic theorists who have aligned with CBT were identified. The chapter attempted to define and to distinguish behavioral from CBT approaches on philosophical and practical grounds. Both are viewed as emerging from a Western scientific foundation, and both perform well when measured against objective criteria of success in counseling and psychotherapy, meaning they are generally empirically supported approaches.

## REFERENCES

Agras, W. S., Kazdin, A. E., & Wilson, G. T. (1979). *Behavior therapy: Toward an applied clinical science.* San Francisco, CA: W. H. Freeman.

Ayllon, T., & Azrin, N. (1968). *The token economy: A motivational system for therapy and rehabilitation.* New York, NY: Appleton-Century-Crofts.

Bandura, A. (1977). Self-efficacy: Toward a unifying theory of behavioral change. *Psychological Review, 84*, 191–215.

Bandura, A. (1997). *Self-efficacy: The exercise of control.* New York, NY: Feeman.

Beck, A. T. (1967). *Depression: Causes and treatment.* Philadelphia: University of Pennsylvania Press.

Beck, A. T. (1976). *Cognitive therapy and the emotional disorders.* New York NY: International Universities Press.

Bornstein, P. H., & Bornstein, M. T. (1986). *Marital therapy: A behavioral-communications approach.* Elmford, NY: Pergamon.

Dobson, K. S. (2010). *Handbook of cognitive-behavioral therapies.* New York, NY: Guilford.

Ellis, A. (1962). *Reason and emotion in psychotherapy*. New York, NY: Stuart.

Eysenck, H. J. (1960). *Behavior therapy and the neuroses*. Oxford, England: Pergamon Press.

Ferster, C. B., & Skinner, B. F. (1957). *Schedules of reinforcement*. New York, NY: Appleton-Century-Crofts.

Garfield, S., & Bergin, A. (Eds.). (1986). *Handbook of psychotherapy and behavior change*. New York, NY: Wiley.

Jacobson, E. (1938). *Progressive relaxation*. Chicago, IL: University of Chicago Press.

Jones, M. C. (1924a). Elimination of childrens' fears. *Journal of Experimental Psychology, 7*, 382–390.

Jones, M. C. (1924b). A laboratory study of fear. The case of Peter. *Journal of Genetic Psychology, 31*, 308–315.

Kazdin, A. E. (1977). *The token economy: A review and evaluation*. New York, NY: Plenum. Excerpts used with permission of Springer Nature.

Kazdin, A. E. (1982). History of behavior modification. In A. S. Bellack, M. Hersen, & A. E. Kazdin (Eds.), *International handbook of behavior modification and therapy* (pp. 3–32). New York, NY: Plenum.

Kazdin, A. E., & Wilson, G. T. (1978). *Evaluation of behavior therapy: Issues, evidence, and research strategies*. Cambridge, MA: Ballinger Publishing.

Kirschenbaum, H., & Henderson, V. (1989). *Carl Rogers: Dialogues*. Boston, MA: Houghton Mifflin.

Marx, M. H., & Hillix, W. A. (1973). *Systems and theories in psychology*. New York, NY: McGraw-Hill.

Meichenbaum, D. H. (1977). *Cognitive behavior modification*. New York, NY: Plenum Press.

Pavlov, I. P. (1957). *Experimental psychology and other essays*. New York, NY: Philosophical Library. (Original work published in 1916). Excerpt reproduced by permission of Philosophical Library, New York, and Peter Owen Publishers, London.

Popper, K. (1959). *The logic of scientific discovery*, translation of *Logik der Forschung*, London, UK: Hutchinson.

Premack, D. (1959). Toward empirical behavior laws: I. Positive reinforcement. *Psychological Review, 66*, 219–233.

Reynolds, G. S. (1968). *A primer of operant conditioning*. Glenview, IL: Scott, Foresman & Company.

Skinner, B. F. (1938). *The behavior of organisms*. New York, NY: Appleton-Century-Crofts.

Skinner, B. F. (1948). *Walden two*. New York, NY: Macmillan.

Skinner, B. F. (1953). *Science and human behavior*. New York, NY: Macmillan.

Skinner, B. F. (1989). *Recent issues in the analysis of behavior*. Columbus, OH: Merrill.

Thorndike, E. L. (1905). *The elements of psychology*. New York, NY: A. G. Seiler.

Watson, J. B. (1930). *Behaviorism* (Rev. ed.). Chicago, IL: University of Chicago Press. (Originally published in 1924)

Watson, J. B., & Rayner, P. (1920). Conditioned emotional reactions. *Journal of Experimental Psychology, 3*, 1–16.

Wilson, G. T. (2008). Behavior therapy. In R. J. Corsini & D. Wedding (Eds.), *Current psychotherapies* (pp. 235–275). Belmont, CA: Brooks/Cole.

Wolpe, J. (1958). *Psychotherapy by reciprocal inhibition.* Stanford, CA: Stanford University Press.

Wolpe, J. (1973). *The practice of behavior therapy* (2nd ed.). New York, NY: Pergamon Press.

Wolpe, J. (1990). *The practice of behavior therapy* (4th ed.). New York, NY: Pergamon Press.

# PART III

# Systemic-Relational Paradigm Approaches

This part of the book provides chapters addressing theories that align with the systemic-relational paradigm. They are all relationship-focused approaches. Satir's Conjoint Family Therapy is presented in Chapter 9—it is a trans-paradigmatic approach, as Satir broke new ground, moving from psychological theory to a relationship way of addressing problems. Chapters 10 and 11 on the works of Haley and Minuchin demonstrate that they conceptualized problems more purely relationally. Readers should get a firm understanding of how relationship-oriented treatments focus on what goes on between people, rather than what goes on inside them.

# CHAPTER

## 9

# Conjoint Family Therapy:
# Breaking New Ground

- To introduce a theory that was transitional from a psychological to a relational approach of treatment

- To provide a biographical sketch of Virginia Satir, the founder of Conjoint Family Therapy

- To describe Satir's basic ideas about relationships and their importance to mental health

- To provide a basic description of techniques and methods of Conjoint Family Therapy

- To outline the basic premises of a theory that crossed over into a more purely relational way of viewing counseling and psychotherapy

- To provide insight on recent developments and criticisms of this approach

Virginia Satir's *Conjoint Family Therapy* (1967) holds an important place in the history of theories of counseling and psychotherapy. Along with therapies such as Bowen's Family Systems Therapy (Bowen, 1978), it broke with the traditions of the psychological paradigm while seeding the fertile ground of the systemic-relational paradigm. Satir's work is seminal to the systemic-relational paradigm, as she reconceptualized the concept of deficient self-esteem within a relational framework. *Self-esteem* **is viewed as the positive value one places on one's self; it is usually viewed as resulting from a positive self-concept. A** *self-concept* **is one's internal self-definition, whether one's self is defined**

**positively, neutrally, or negatively.** Satir reconceptualized self-esteem from a psychological construct to a more relational concept that acknowledged the full influence of others on one's self-value. The reconceptualization of self-esteem as being highly socially influenced made her work unique and important to transitions between paradigms.

Actually, as Satir's ideas progressed, she began to deemphasize the idea of low self-esteem as a problem focus (Woods & Martin, 1984). She became more fully systemic- and process-oriented in her thinking in her later years. Yet, as late as 1982, in a chapter titled "The Therapist and Family Therapy: Process Model," she still acknowledged the importance of self-esteem to her theory. She stated:

> The central core of my theory is self-esteem. I now clearly see that without a direct link to the experience of the senses, there would be little change in feeling. Consequently, there would be little change in self-esteem, and therefore little real, dependable change in behavior. (pp. 21–22)

Her early works can best be described as transitioning or straddling psychological and systemic-relational paradigm propositions, while focusing on feeling and sensing as a means of engaging clients. She is also best described as a **humanist (someone who views human nature in a positive light),** as she has espoused an unyielding faith in the human potential to grow and to develop in positive ways.

Her therapy demeanor appeared at times to be a cross between those of Carl Rogers and Fritz Perls. Woods and Martin (1984) stated that she had "the warmth and acceptance of Carl Rogers" and the "strong experiential, here-and-now techniques reminiscent of Fritz Perls" (p. 8). Unlike these psychological theorists, however, she worked almost exclusively within a family context.

## VIRGINIA SATIR: A BIOGRAPHICAL SKETCH

Virginia Satir

Source: Photo by William Meyer at the English Wikipedia project. Wikimedia Commons.

Virginia Satir was born in 1916 in Wisconsin, and was the eldest of five children. She was raised on a farm. Evidently, she was inquisitive from an early age, as she often spoke about her decision at age 5 years to become a children's detective on parents. Satir (1982) stated:

When I was 5, I decided to become a children's detective on parents. There was so much that went on between my parents that made little or no sense to me. Making sense of things around me, feeling loved, and being competent were my paramount concerns. I did feel loved, and felt I was competent, but making sense of all the contradictions, deletions, and distortions I observed both in my parents' relationship and among people outside in the world was heart-rending and confusion-making to me. Sometimes this situation raised questions about my being loved, but mostly it affected my ability to predict, to see clearly, and to develop my total being. (p. 13)

At an early age, Satir was faced with adult responsibilities; her mother was ill, and she assisted in raising her siblings. Also, Satir suffered from illnesses, including an ear problem that left her hearing impaired for several years.

Satir attended the University of Wisconsin, where she earned a teaching degree, and later she taught and was the principal at a small school. She later attended the University of Chicago and earned an MA degree in psychiatric social work. After a failed marriage and a move to Texas, she returned to Chicago (in 1951), where she established an independent therapy practice. In 1955, she was employed by the Illinois State Psychiatric Institute to teach family therapy, which was her first formal experience theoretically conceptualizing her clinical applications. Soon after her second marriage, she left Chicago for California (in 1958). In 1959, she, Don Jackson, and Jules Riskin became the founding staff of the Mental Research Institute (MRI) in Palo Alto, California. Her ideas were refined at the MRI, and she systematically communicated her ideas through the publication of her seminal *Conjoint Family Therapy* (Satir, 1967). The MRI took an early lead and still maintains a favorable reputation as a pacesetter in the development of family therapy theory and practice. Satir later affiliated with the Esalen Institute in 1963 and finally returned permanently to independent practice.

During her lifetime, Satir earned many honors, including an honorary doctorate from her alma mater, the University of Wisconsin. She also received the American Association for Marriage and Family Therapy's "Distinguished Service to Families Award." She is frequently identified as a major leader in the marital and family therapy literature.

Satir has authored or coauthored many books, including *Conjoint Family Therapy* (1967), *Peoplemaking* (1972), *Helping Families to Change* (Satir, Stachowiak, & Taschman, 1977), *Self Esteem* (1975), *Making Contact* (1976), *Your Many Faces* (1978), and *Changing With Families* (Bandier, Grinder, & Satir, 1976). Satir is remembered by those who knew her best as a caring and feeling person. She was often referred to as "the Columbus of Family Therapy" (Banmen, 1988), as she traveled so many miles spreading the message of social systems theory and family therapy. She presented hundreds of workshops and over her lifetime saw thousands of families in therapy. She was energetic and productive till the end of her career.

Satir died on September 10, 1988, 4 months after being diagnosed with metastatic cancer.

## THE FOUNDATIONAL THEORY

### The Target of Counseling

In her book, *Conjoint Family Therapy*, Satir (1967) declared that family functioning was crucial to mental health and communication. Her ideas were greatly influenced by her work at the MRI in Palo Alto, California, where she worked closely with Don Jackson, MD, who, at that time, was the director of the institute. Satir, consequently, was very much influenced by the works of Bateson, Jackson, and Haley, who were at one time or another affiliated with the MRI group. These theorists have come to be associated with the *communications* school of family therapy.

Largely, then, Satir's (1967) focused on the family, a point she made clear in *Conjoint Family Therapy,* in which she described the **homeostatic (a dynamic equilibrium)** nature of family systems, the idea of "family pain," the identified patient as a symptom of a dysfunctional family, and the need to be family-holistic in conceptualizing the problems of "identified patients" (pp. 1–2).

Moreover, Satir (1967) was very clear about her view of parental responsibility in the development of a child's self-esteem. Broadly speaking, her view of self-esteem aligned her with psychological thinking, as she implicitly spoke of low self-esteem as a baggage that adults carry around from childhood. On the other hand, she defined self-esteem in relational terms. She stated:

> A person with low self-esteem has a great sense of anxiety and uncertainty about himself.
>
> a.   His self-esteem is based to an extreme extent on what he thinks others think of him.
> b.   His dependence on others for his self-esteem cripples his autonomy and individuality.
> c.   He disguises his low self-esteem from others, especially when he wants to impress others.
> d.   His low self-esteem comes from his growing-up experiences which never led him to feel that it is good to be a person of one sex in relation to a person of the other.
> e.   He has never really separated from his parents, that is, arrived at a relationship of equality with them. (p. 8)

Obviously, her conception of self-esteem is highly relational. The level of self-esteem is conceptualized as being critical to one's selection of a mate (low self-esteem begets mates with low self-esteem). Consequently, one's low self-esteem affects marital choice and is implicated in the transmission of low self-esteem across generations to one's children. Satir stated: "If the mates have low self-esteem and little trust in each other, they will expect their child to enhance their self-esteem, to be an extension of themselves, and to serve crucial pain-relieving functions in the marital relationship" (p. 45). She described those factors that are important to the development of self-esteem in children, almost all of which involve parental direction. She, ultimately, links a child's self-esteem to parental self-esteem as follows:

> The close relationship between parental validation, self-esteem, independence, and uniqueness shows up when one observes how a dysfunctional person (an unvalidated child who is now an adult) still clings to his parents, or to substitute parent figures, or relates to his sexual partner as if that partner were, in fact, a parent. (p. 54)

As **relationships are all about communication,** a person's poor self-esteem manifests itself in poor communication. It is through communication that the therapist attempts to undo the poor learning that has come primarily from dysfunctional parents—parents with poor self-esteem.

Poor self-esteem and poor interpersonal communication are correlative. In fact, Satir (1967) went so far as to conclude that low self-esteem *leads* to dysfunctional communication. Furthermore, she stated: "Dysfunction in communication will also follow when the individual is unable to handle different-ness" (p. 95). In effect, she believed that individuals should be accepting of others, no matter what the differences.

## The Process of Counseling

*Conjoint Family Therapy* **is a process of facilitating effective communication in a relational context.** The therapist acts as an *official observer* of family interaction and, more importantly, as a teacher of clear communication. It is assumed that client families are not able to see and to hear all that is communicated by the family members, and the therapist can assist in making messages complete and clear at all levels of communication. All communication has levels—and the research conducted at the MRI was instrumental in defining at least four levels—the formal, informal, nonverbal, and contextual levels of communication. **Formal communication is that which is communicated symbolically, through language or other symbol systems**—like a lecture. **Informal communication occurs outside structured or formal contexts,** such as going with a friend to a movie or spending time with friends in some spur-of-the-moment activity. **Nonverbal communication is that which is communicated through body language, one's appearance, and one's presence.** Finally, **contextual communication is about where it happens—in a classroom, at home, or at work.** Specifically, the therapist may intervene into interpersonal exchanges between the members of a family, helping clients to clarify messages, especially those that are inconsistent across levels of communication. For example, a husband may say to his wife that he loves her, but his lack of nonverbal expression of affection is communicating another message. When there is inconsistent communication at any level, the therapist might, for example, facilitate understanding among family members by having members enact roles to demonstrate the problem communication.

Actually, as Satir's ideas evolved, she moved away from a problem focus—that is, away from trying to correct deficient self-esteem—toward therapeutic process as a process unto itself (Woods & Martin, 1984). Where her ideas about process in her early works look remediative, in her later years, according to Woods and Martin (1984), she appeared to "invent process around an issue of relevance to the client; the process is the intervention" (p. 6). Regardless, even in her early works there is a process-oriented tone. She appeared to be primarily concerned with entering the family interaction to produce changes in interaction. Fundamentally, then, the difference between her early and later ideas about family therapy process is that *her early work was deficiency corrective, whereas her later work appeared to be primarily growth enhancing.* In both cases, the therapeutic interactive process seemed to predominate over the content of therapy. In other words, she did not try to do therapy with words alone; instead, she actively entered into interaction sequences (verbally and nonverbally) between and among family members as a primary intervention.

## Counselor Role

In *Conjoint Family Therapy,* Satir (1967) made 15 points about the role of the family therapist. Some of the most significant of those points are summarized in the following paragraphs.

First, Satir believed that a comfortable setting should be created in therapy. She felt that clients should, "perhaps for the first time, take the risk of looking clearly and objectively at themselves and their actions" (p. 160). One of the major tasks of the therapist is to facilitate a comfortable, threat-free, and sharing attitude.

Second, Satir stated that "the therapist decreases threat by setting the rules of interaction" (p. 165) and by the way the therapist "structures the interviews" (p. 167). Setting the rules of interaction is a critical issue to systemic-relational therapy. As experienced family therapists know, it is often difficult to control family interactions, especially in highly dysfunctional families. Consequently, a family's interactions may escalate during treatment to the degree it is deleterious to the family or to a member or members of the family. The therapist must structure the sessions and must make it clear that certain rules apply in the therapeutic setting.

Third, the therapist attempts to allay family and individual defenses. Satir (1967) said:

> In my opinion, the dysfunctional family operates within a reign of terror, with all members fearing they will be hurt and all members fearing they will hurt others. All comments are taken as attacks on self-esteem. Therefore, the therapist must reduce terror. So the therapist . . . exerts all his efforts to reducing terror, reducing the necessity for defenses. (p. 168)

The two ways in which the therapist can deal with defenses are: (a) by interpreting anger as hurt and (b) by explaining that pain is an acceptable and an expressible feeling in therapy. The therapist must, therefore, be an expert at "handling loaded material with care" (p. 169).

Fourth, the therapist "re-educates patients for adulthood, for accountability" (p. 171). The counselor assists the client in regaining a sense of self-accountability and self-control. By educating, the therapist is a teacher of what is expected of the patient. Accordingly, "the therapist delineates roles and functions" (p. 174) within the interpersonal context. Clients should be educated as to what their roles are within their family contexts.

Fifth, "the therapist completes gaps in communication and interprets messages" (p. 175). This is probably the most important counselor task, according to Satir. Any discrepancies in communication are interpreted: (a) about oneself—for example, saying one feels fine when one is acting distressed; and (b) between people—for example, focusing on nonverbal communication between the members of a family. According to Satir, the therapist should separate the content of a message (formal communication) from its relationship message (informal, nonverbal, and contextual). Satir made the point that every communication has a content message *and* a relationship message. For example, when a teacher says to a student, "You are a good student," two messages are communicated. First, there is the content of the message related to the student's performance; and second, there is the relationship message—that the teacher is in a position to judge the student. In just about every communication between people, there is both a content and a relationship message. Satir believed that the therapist should separate and openly make these communications clear to the communicator and to the receiver. Furthermore, Satir believed that the therapist "must also see himself as a *model of communication*" (p. 97).

Sixth, the therapist should avoid making judgments, and should be *congruent* in his or her responses. Although she uses the term *congruence* in a way that is similar to the definition of Rogers (1951), Satir never cited Rogers in her book. Instead, she referred to the classic "double bind" work of Bateson, Jackson, Haley, and Weakland (1956) in defining *incongruence*. **A double bind is a no-win situation in the context of relationships. A double bind is essentially an interpersonal trap.** Therefore, if a mother says to her child to "come sit on my lap" at the same time as she nonverbally freezes or signals discomfort, that is an incongruent and double-binding communication. Double-binding communication typically confuses or perturbs the message recipient. Essentially, Satir believed that a therapist should be in touch with his or her feelings and should behave consistently with feelings. Also, she believed that the content and relationship messages in communications should be consistent between counselor and clients, and between clients in family systems.

In sum, the role of the therapist is that of an effective communicator, a model of interpersonal interaction, and a teacher of what is expected of the clients in and outside of therapy.

## Goals of Counseling and Ideal Outcomes

Satir (1967) was very clear about what she felt was necessary as an outcome of treatment. She stated:

Treatment is completed:

- When family members can complete transactions, check, ask.
- When they can interpret hostility.
- When they can see how others see them.
- When one member can tell another how he manifests himself.
- When one member can tell another what he hopes, fears, and expects from him.
- When they can disagree.
- When they can make choices.
- When they can learn through practice.
- When they can free themselves from harmful effects of past models.
- When they can give a clear message, that is, be congruent in their behavior, with a minimum of difference between feelings and communication, and with a minimum of hidden messages. (p. 176)

Although the list is long and appears overly ambitious by many standards, one can summarize Satir's goals of therapy by stating that she attempts to help family members to manifest individual self-esteem and effective interpersonal communication.

## GENERAL PROCEDURES

### Assessment

Assessment and therapy occur at the same time, according to Satir. Her approach to assessment was much like Carl Rogers's (see Chapter 5). Essentially, Satir believed that *everyone* has the potential for growth and development. However, Satir (1982) believed that "any symptom signals a blockage in growth and has a survival connection to a system which requires blockage and distortion of growth in some form in all of its members to keep its balance" (p. 12). Accordingly, Satir paid special attention to symptoms, while defining them within family contexts. Doing assessment consistent with a conjoint approach requires entering the process of the family, defining significant triadic relationships, assessing rules and roles (both overt and covert), and defining relationship messages observed in communications between and among family members.

The assessment of triadic relational concerns was important to Satir (1967). In fact, in *Conjoint Family Therapy*, she devoted a whole chapter to "The Family Triangle" (p. 55). She specifically addressed the idea of marital discord and its influence on children. She was very alert to the issue of the child "identified patient" (IP), and she concluded that symptomatic behavior of a child was representative of parental/marital dysfunction (deriving from low parental self-esteem). Defining the identified patient as the "IP" she stated:

> I have been repeatedly struck by how readily the I.P. drops his role as intervener once family therapy is under way. Once he is assured that arguments do not bring destruction and that marital amicability lightens parental demands on him, the I.P. actively helps the therapist help his parents as mates, while at the same time he tries to get his parents to recognize him as a separate individual with needs of his own. As a matter of fact, the I.P. is often very helpful as "assistant marital counselor." (p. 56)

In a sense, Satir communicated that the **triangle (a three-person triad with three relationships)** is the building block of larger systems and is a unit requiring special assessment during the evaluation of symptomatic behavior. She believed that in a triangle, all three members could have "fears of being left out," and she felt that it was crucial, especially when dealing with children, to allay their fears.

Beyond assessing triadic structural concerns, Satir's (1967) ideas focused on assessing messages during communication, whether occurring within a triadic or **dyadic (a two-person relationship)** framework. As mentioned earlier, both content and relationship messages must be assessed, as it is the relationship message that is critical to the ongoing interactions within a family context. Satir (1967) stated:

> Communication is a complex business. The receiver must assess all the different ways in which the sender is sending messages, as well as being aware of his own receiving system, that is his own interpretation system.
>
> a.   When A talks, B assesses the verbal meaning of A's message.
> b.   He also listens to the tone of voice in which A speaks.
> c.   He also watches what A does; he notes the "body language" and facial expressions which accompany A's message.
> d.   He also assesses what A is saying within a social context. The context may be how B has seen A respond to him and to others in the past. It may also be B's expectations about what the requirements of the situation are. In other words, the receiver (B) is busy assessing both the verbal and the nonverbal content of A's message so that he can come to some judgment about what A meant by his communication. (p. 75)

Through communication analysis, Satir was an expert at defining rules (laws of interaction) of family communication (often unspoken rules). It was her contention that such rules should be brought into the open in the family.

Although there is no clear-cut diagnostic phase to the conjoint approach, it is evident that Satir originally believed that assessment should be highly relational and focused on both the triadic structure of systems and on communication (messages and rules).

## Treatment/Remediation

Satir's (1967) treatment program is one of adhering to several basic principles. First, it is assumed that positive changes result through the interpersonal process of therapy, which is a conclusion, primarily based on her humanistic attitude that people have honorable motives and that everyone is healable (Woods & Martin, 1984).

Second, interventions are aimed at relationships and communication. Individuals and their social contexts are inseparable. However, she did not go so far in her early works as theoretically denying the existence of individuals. *Consequently, her efforts toward remediation were dualistic: They were aimed at the individual, but simultaneously they were also aimed at relationships* of *significance.* Although this appeared to make practical sense to Satir, it also demonstrated her ***trans-paradigm theoretical thinking, meaning she was crossing paradigms and transitioning her theory from one worldview to another.*** Her transition was from the psychology of the individual (e.g., self-esteem) to the systemic (focusing on relationships). In her conceptualization of problems and in her approach to treatment, she was both individual *and* systems acknowledging, but she lacked a well-developed or well-articulated theory that allowed for acknowledgment of both in any systematic and comprehensive way. In other words, her theory did not weigh one influence (psychological or relational) against the other, so that predictions could be made as to the outcomes of targeted treatments. This issue is addressed more in the criticism section of this chapter.

Third, as will be more clear to the readers when specialized techniques are outlined in a following section of this chapter, Satir was very active in therapy, physically and linguistically. She entered the family with a sincere, active, and commanding presence, while she exuded love and kindness. She was a person to be reckoned with in therapy. She made no apologies for her "get in there and get your hands dirty" attitude about therapy. She encouraged emotional expression, touching, and feeling. She wanted her clients to experience their relations fully in the present. In videotapes of her sessions, she at times appears very directive about how families ideally could be.

Her therapeutic interventions can best be described as bringing forth and reorganizing emotions in a social and a linguistic context.

## Case Management

Satir (1967) was adamant about the need to have all family members, and especially the marital partners, in therapy. Even during pre-counseling phone contacts, she strongly encouraged all family members to attend.

During the first interview, Satir started by asking questions. She often asked questions to all family members in order to get all perspectives on an issue. Often, her questions addressed symptomatic behaviors, in order to place them in a relational context.

Satir also recommended strongly the use of "family life chronology" in the early sessions of therapy. Essentially, *a family life chronology is a family's social/relational history*. It begins with marital partners. The therapist must go back into the marital relationship history and explore issues from the very beginning of the relationship that might be significant to current concerns. Notes may be taken (or sessions recorded), but the important task of the therapist is to outline a kind of historical calendar on the marital relationship, with critical relational incidents recorded, including the first meeting, wedding plans, the marital ceremony, and so on. The therapist is alert to other past relational influences on the marriage as he or she explores the marital relationship. For example, if a parent-in-law was problematic early in the relationship, then it might be hypothesized that there might be continued strain in the parent-in-law relationship that might be influencing the marriage presently. Relationships with parents, siblings, in-laws, aunts, uncles, and any other individuals of significance are explored. Satir felt that *"different-ness"* **between marital partners (which can be interpreted as differences between the respective social systems of significance)** is a source of role strain. Conjoint therapy attempts to reconcile such *different-ness*.

The therapist continues therapy by asking children questions about their relational history, paying special attention to the events of social significance in their lives.

Children are very important, and Satir (1967) believed that children should be active participants in therapy. Regarding the management of children in therapy, Satir stated: "I found that a therapist has very few problems of control if he actively takes charge of the therapy process. If he knows how to do this, children respond as readily as their parents" (p. 139). However, she did acknowledge that certain unique problems arise when children are present in therapy, and she did address some of the most common difficulties in her book, including the commonly encountered disruptive behavior of children. In effect, Satir placed the parents in charge of disciplining their children, even though she maintained control over the rules of therapy.

Conjoint Family Therapy sessions are process-oriented, and assessment and treatment appear to go hand in hand. Importantly, interventions are aimed at affecting **family homeostasis (the dynamic equilibrium or balance of the family system).** Case notes should reflect the therapist's ongoing assessment (of family relationships, communications, and structure) and ongoing interventions.

Overall, the conjoint family therapist builds a relational history of client-systems, and then intervenes into the present dynamics of the system.

## Specialized Techniques

Probably the most concise summary of techniques used by Satir was presented by Woods and Martin (1984). Readers are referred to their excellent article on Satir's works for a straightforward presentation of her ideas. Five techniques are presented

1. *Verbalizing presuppositions (positive assumptions that the counselor makes about and communicates to the family).* The very presence of a family in therapy, unless the family is forced to attend by an outside party, can be interpreted as reflecting the hopes of family members that good outcomes result from treatment. Satir was a master at expressing what she assumed was being communicated by the family by its attending the first sessions of therapy. She would express her feeling that the presence of family members meant they were hopeful, desiring change, and willing to take steps necessary to solve problems. In other words, the family's actions demonstrated a presupposition (an antecedent assumption) about what could occur in therapy, and Satir made it a practice of verbalizing such presuppositions.

2. *Denominalization (making abstract terms concrete and descriptive of interactive behaviors).* Woods and Martin (1984) described denominalization as follows:

This involves obtaining specific behavioral descriptions for words such as love and respect. For instance, Satir wants to know exactly what must be done in order for the person to perceive that he or she is receiving respect. The clarified answer is often related to the individual's primary sensory-based representational system (i.e., visual, auditory, or kinesthetic). (p. 9)

Denominalization, then, is a means of taking global terms and making them behavior specific.

3. *Family sculpture (family sculpting is an artistic and therapeutic means of concretizing relational issues in a family).* L'Abate, Ganahl, and Hansen (1986) described sculpting as follows:

Family sculpting is a method in which family members are asked to arrange one another as a living statue or tableau. Drawing upon their creative instincts and using such nonverbal dimensions as distance, posture, visage, and gesture, the family members give concrete representation to their impressions of the family. Such a process is not new to the family. It occurs every day in such activities as seating arrangement, but is infrequently recognized or consciously controlled for an expressive effect. Due to its form this method achieves several purposes in therapy. In brief, it may actively involve inactive or non-vocal members; increase the clarity of communication within the family; enhance the expression of emotions; promote awareness of the internal and interactional experiences of the participants; allow new insights into family functioning/or both the therapist and family; intensify the family's experience in therapy; objectify and defuse some aspects of their experience; help family members differentiate; and bring them to a fuller awareness of their own interconnectedness in a way which linear verbal representations are incapable of achieving. (p. 166)

Satir frequently used sculpting by having one family member take a physical stance in therapy, and then she assisted the other family members to build a sculpture around the person's stance. She defined four basic stances that she felt could assist the sculptor in defining the operation of the system: blamer (an accuser), placater (an appeaser), superreasonable (a nonfeeler), and irrelevant (a seemingly uninvolved party). By sculpting, Satir hoped to integrate language with experience (Woods & Martin, 1984).

4. *Anchoring.* Dilts and Green (1982) defined *anchoring* as follows: *"Anchoring is the learned association between a stimulus and a response or between one response and another. When the stimulus or initiating response is triggered, the associated response will be elicited"* (p. 233). Essentially, a therapist's actions are used to connect client activities. Dilts and Green stated:

The anchor the therapist uses can be any external stimulus, a touch, a particular voice tone or gesture, or a snap of the fingers. We have learned that kinesthetic anchors (such as a specific touch on the client's knee, arm, shoulder) are the least difficult for the novice to learn. (p. 233)

Woods and Martin (1984) described how Satir might have used anchoring with a marital couple: Satir might ask her to look at her husband and "feel what she feels." When a positive response becomes evident in the individual (i.e., altered breathing, tears), Satir would touch her shoulder gently at the peak of positive emotion. Apparently, this helps connect the particular emotion with the touch, which makes the feeling more concrete for the individual (p. 10). Anchoring is a good example of how Satir brought feelings to the level of interpersonal physical experience.

5. *Reframing (reframing is a process of redefinition).* Satir used reframing mostly to redefine behaviors from negative interpretations to positive interpretations. If a client is feeling sad when discussing a concern with another family member, a positive reframe of the sadness is, "Your sadness is a way of expressing the depth of your concern." Satir used reframing to bring forth positive interpretations to individual actions. She felt that honorable motives were at the base of individual behaviors, and therefore, she always looked to express the positive viewpoint in therapy. In fact, Satir was a master of the positive reframe. It seemed to come quite naturally to her.

These five techniques are representative of Satir's way of doing therapy. However, specialized techniques were not the mainstay of her approach. Rather, as her approach matured, she began to focus more on the process of counseling as therapeutic in-and-of-itself.

## Recent Developments or Criticisms

One of Satir's last works was titled "The Therapist and Family Therapy: Process Model" (Satir, 1982). In this work, Satir moved away from the deficiency model of self-esteem that appeared to be a driving force in the book *Conjoint Family Therapy*. Although she continued to acknowledge the importance of self-esteem in her theory, she focused more on facilitating the growth-enhancing aspects of the individuals (and the system) rather than attempting to correct low self-esteem. It is as if she began to view clients less as a half-empty vessel and more as a half-full vessel. Her efforts then became more focused on means of facilitating growth within a family context. Satir (1982) stated:

> (a) Therapy is a process which takes place between persons and is aimed at accomplishing positive change, and (b) the therapist can be expected to be the leader in initiating and teaching a health-promoting process in the family. The therapist is not, however, in charge of the persons involved. . . . The process I initiate is heavily weighted toward each member of the family becoming as whole as possible. (p. 13)

Satir later stated: "I have been trained as a human pathologist. I am now working as a 'health developer', using the information of pathology to help me recognize trouble spots more or less . . . it tells me that something needs attention" (1982, p. 22). Symptoms, rather than being indicators of maladaptive systems needing correction, became more fully signals of blocked process and signs of the need for growth enhancement. It is as if Satir's frame of reference had been reframed to the positive—therapy is not therapy at all; it is education and opportunity. She stated: "I now see therapy as an educational process for becoming more fully human. I put my energies and attention on what can be added to what is present" (1982, p. 22).

Regardless of this switch in emphasis, Satir's approach can still be criticized as theoretically deficient. She still appeared, even in her latest works, to be straddling the psychological and systemic-relational philosophical fence. She was dualistic theoretically, as mentioned earlier. She attempted to make individuals more fully human, yet at the same time she defined personhood within a relational framework. She never fully identified whether individual psychological processes overshadowed relational dynamics, or vice versa. Instead, she tended to play a balancing act, using terms such as *self-esteem, self-worth,* and *congruence* almost flirtingly in a psychologically oriented way. At the same time, she always attempted to demonstrate the importance of relationships on the individual's concept of self. She was never able to fully cross over to more complete systemic-relational thinking, where there is no such thing as self-esteem—there are only relationships that affect human behavior. From a more fully systemic-relational framework, the term *self-esteem* is excess baggage. As communication and relationship are critical factors systemically, they are the focus of study. No psychological construct is necessary to account for human behavior, as relationship and communication are quite adequate. Self-esteem, for example, is interpreted systemically as one's social fit within a healthy interpersonal system. As can be seen, Satir never fully made the break with the theories that preceded her.

The focus of Conjoint Family Therapy is dualistic. Satir's (1967, 1982) work always focused on the individual and the social system of significance. She was interested in an individual's functioning within a social context. She studied both the individual's developmental movement toward wholeness and the system's homeostatic functioning, especially as related to the symptomatic behavior of an IP. She was both system- and individual-enhancing in her approach to therapy.

Reality appears to be simultaneously composed of individuals (as things) and relationships (which are processes that affect individuals). Satir, although learning a great deal from her contemporaries (like Gregory Bateson) about **systemic epistemology (the study of relationships),** tended to place great value on the individual. In a sense, she was as much a humanistic psychologist as she was a systems theorist and therapist. She was conceptually never able to reconcile systemic epistemology with her observations of self-determination and self-worth of individuals. Although she attempted to define self within a relational framework, a purist systems theorist might ask why such concepts needed defining at all. Psychological conceptualizations are not useful or relevant from a systemic-relational framework.

Historically, Satir's work bridges paradigms. In fact, Satir's (1967) *Conjoint Family Therapy* must be viewed as a seminal work in the development of the systemic-relational paradigm. Although it appears easy by today's standards to criticize her work on systemic-relational grounds, at the time, her ideas were groundbreaking and **trans-paradigm (transitioning to a new paradigm).** She was one of the few mental health professionals who were able to recognize the validity of intuitions about the inadequacy of purely individual interventions, although at the same time she developed techniques and methods for intervening into relational dynamics assumed to be at the root of symptomatic behaviors. She bridged paradigms in a very positive way.

Overall, analyzing Satir's work from a counseling paradigm perspective reveals theoretical crossover, which is laudatory historically but vulnerable theoretically.

## STUDENT–MENTOR DIALOGUE

**Student:**   What was it like to observe Satir as a counselor?

**Mentor:**   Satir was incredibly talented and interpersonally brave. Nothing seemed to scare her in the interpersonal realm. She viewed people in a positive light, so she always believed that people, no matter what their defined problem, had honorable motives. So she was both artful and gutsy in therapy. She presented as a very loving and caring person, and she never used techniques that were paradoxical or in any way meant blatantly to manipulate. She believed that the process of interpersonal therapy would take hold and move people closer together and in a healthy way. Her basic assumptions in this regard directed her.

**Student:**   So for her, it was all about interaction and getting people interacting in the therapy room. Is that correct?

**Mentor:**   To a large degree, yes. But she also believed that each had a "self," and that a self could suffer pain and discomfort. She also tried to acknowledge the pain individuals experienced and she would ask what pain they were experiencing. She wanted her clients to know that she was there to acknowledge their discomfort and she did it in a very open and loving way. She was inviting, and once a person expressed emotion, she would often contextualize it by having others make contact with the party in discomfort—by touching, supporting, or acknowledging the person in pain. She was very good at making contact with people, and she was very good at helping others make contact with other members of the family.

**Student:**   Yet it is true that she continued to straddle the philosophical fence by not being fully psychological or relational in her treatment.

**Mentor:**   Yes, that is true. But observing her work was revealing. In the end, she worked fully relationally, and even symptoms, pain, and expressed problems were interpreted within the context of the relationship system. At the end of her career, she seemed more fully relational in her thinking and approach to clients, and the concept of self-esteem seemed at most to be background rather than foreground. Yet self-esteem was the key to her recognition of the influence of relationships, as when she was a principal at a school and realized that many students with poor self-esteem had parents who communicated such. She hypothesized that self-esteem was passed through relationships, which was a breakthrough for her in approaching people. In a sense, she appeared grateful for the concept of self-esteem as a key to unlocking a method of treatment.

**Student:**  What is her significance today?

**Mentor:**  She has provided a model therapy that is both individual and system acknowledging. She was a model therapist, and demonstrated through her work how to positively approach clients. She was a transitional theorist, and her place as a groundbreaking theoretician and therapist is solid. She is a great example of a talented clinician who also was at the forefront of a theoretical revolution.

## CONCLUSION

The works of Virginia Satir are best viewed as a transition between two paradigms of counseling and psychotherapy—the psychological and systemic-relational paradigms. Satir was very alert to the influence of relationships on personal psychological functioning, although she also recognized the impact of faulty self-esteem on relationships. She became more fully process-oriented in her later years, as she relegated the idea of deficient self-esteem to a less than primary role in her theoretical statements. She began to view herself as a health facilitator and a growth enhancer in therapy. Satir's place in the history of paradigms of counseling and psychotherapy is secure, as she broke with the traditions of psychological thinking while entering the realm of systemic-relational philosophy.

## REFERENCES

Bandier, R., Grinder, J., & Satir, V. (1976). *Changing with families.* Palo Alto, CA: Science and Behavior Books.

Banmen, J. (1988, September/October). Virginia Satir: The Columbus of family therapy. *Family Therapy News, 19*(5), 23.

Bateson, G., Jackson, D. D., Haley, J., & Weakland, J. (1956). Toward a theory of schizophrenia. *Behavioral Science, 1,* 251–264. doi:10.1002/bs.3830010402

Bowen, M. (1978). *Family therapy in clinical practice.* New York, NY: Jason Aronson.

Dilts, R., & Green, J. D. (1982). Application of neuro-linguistic programming in family therapy. In A. M. Horne & M. M. Ohlsen (Eds.), *Family counseling and therapy* (pp. 214–244). Itasca, IL: F.E. Peacock. Excerpts © 2000 South-Western, a part of Cengage Learning, reproduced by permission of Cengage Learning.

L'Abate, L., Ganahl, G., & Hansen, J. C. (1986). *Methods of family therapy.* Englewood Cliffs, NJ: Prentice Hall.

Rogers, C. R. (1951). *Client-centered therapy.* Boston, MA: Houghton Mifflin.

Satir, V. (1967). *Conjoint family therapy.* Palo Alto, CA: Science and Behavior Books. Excerpts used with permission from Science and Behavior Books.

Satir, V. (1972). *Peoplemaking.* Palo Alto, CA: Science and Behavior Books.

Satir, V. (1975). *Self-esteem.* Millbrae, CA: Celestial Arts.

Satir, V. (1976). *Making contact.* Millbrae, CA: Celestial Arts.

Satir, V. (1978). *Your many faces.* Millbrae, CA: Celestial Arts.

Satir, V. (1982). The therapist and family therapy: Process model. In A. M. Horne & M. M. Ohlsen (Eds.), *Family counseling and therapy* (pp. 12–42). Itasca, IL: F.E. Peacock. Excerpts © 2000 South-Western, a part of Cengage Learning, reproduced by permission of Cengage Learning.

Satir, V., Stachowiak, J., & Taschman, H. (1977). *Helping families to change.* New York, NY: Aronson.

Woods, M. D., & Martin, D. (1984). The work of Virginia Satir: Understanding her theory and technique. *The American Journal of Family Therapy, 12,* 3–11.

# CHAPTER 10

# Strategic Problem Solving Therapy

**OBJECTIVES**

- To introduce a purely systemic-relational approach to counseling, meaning it exclusively focuses on problems as relational

- To provide readers with a basic overview of Jay Haley's approach, which has been called 'strategic therapy' and also 'problem-solving therapy'

- To introduce Jay Haley biographically as a historic figure in the fields of counseling and psychotherapy

- To present an approach that fully addresses issues within the context of relationship systems

- To outline the use of this approach in a way that is clear and focused on counselor assumptions and actions

Jay Haley is the founder of Strategic Problem Solving Therapy and a leader of the systemic-relational movement. Haley has been involved with the therapeutic application of social systems theory from his early days of research with Gregory Bateson (e.g., Bateson, Jackson, Haley, & Weakland, 1956). In 1956, Bateson et al. published a work that is now considered a classic in the mental health and psychotherapy fields—"Toward a Theory of Schizophrenia." In that work, which studied the relationship between children diagnosed as schizophrenic and their mothers, the authors defined the *double bind*, **which is a no-win situation within the context of relationships**. Haley was a crucial partner in the study, and the findings significantly affected his perspective of mental health and mental illness.

Haley has been a creative theoretician and an effective communicator of the systemic-relational viewpoint. His work is well respected and has thrived through the systemic "heyday," which lasted well into the early 2000s. Haley has been prolific, and his several books and many articles help to chronicle his development as a systemic therapist over the years (Haley, 1963, 1973, 1984, 1987; Haley & Hoffman, 1967). His 1987 book, *Problem Solving Therapy* (published in its first edition in 1976), is probably his most concise and definitive work. In fact, it is considered by many to be a milestone publication of the "strategic approach" to family therapy. As an introduction to strategic therapy, it also serves as an easy reading guide on the "how to's" of family therapy.

*Problem Solving Therapy* focuses on counseling families of triads or larger system structures. The issue of dyadic relational structures was dealt with in his earlier work, entitled *Strategies of Psychotherapy* (Haley, 1963). The summary of the work presented in this chapter is heavily based on *Problem Solving Therapy*.

## JAY HALEY: A BIOGRAPHICAL SKETCH

Jay Haley.
*Source*: Photo by R. Rocco Cottone.

Jay Haley was born in 1923. He received his BA from the University of California at Los Angeles in 1948 and pursued subsequent undergraduate training at the University of California at Berkeley, receiving a Bachelor of Library Science degree in 1951. He later worked as a librarian at Stanford University (1952–1953). In 1953, he earned an MA at Stanford University, where he studied communication, and, after graduation, worked on a "Project for the Study of Communication," which was directed by Gregory Bateson. During that project, Haley and others who were involved in the project studied hypnosis, animal behavior, films, schizophrenia, psychotherapy, families, and family therapy. About the same time, Haley entered into a private practice in hypnotherapy and marriage and family therapy.

His practice of psychotherapy was not only influenced by Bateson's relationship-focused philosophy, but he was also highly influenced by the master hypnotherapist, Milton Erickson, whom Haley studied as part of his work with Bateson's project. Erickson was known for a very directive style of therapy, and Haley, too, adopted a style of therapy that was directive and tactical in creating circumstances supportive of healthy relationships and mental health.

Over his professional career, Haley has held several academic appointments, including professorships at the University of Pennsylvania, Howard University, and the University of Maryland. He has served as the founder and codirector (with his then wife Cloe Madanes) of the Family Therapy Institute of Washington, DC.

Haley has published numerous books as an author, coauthor, or an editor. He has published numerous articles in professional journals on such diverse topics as film, hypnosis, schizophrenia, family therapy, religious power tactics, and communication. He founded the journal *Family Process*. He was actively involved in presenting family and individual therapy workshops.

He ended his career by moving to San Diego, California, in the 1990s where he worked with his third wife, Madeleine Richeport-Haley, and they produced a number of films relating to psychotherapy. Madeleine collaborated in the writing of Haley's final book, *Directive Family Therapy*. He died on February 13, 2007.

# THE FOUNDATIONAL THEORY

## The Target of Counseling

Haley (1987) clearly focused on designing interventions that involve the relational context of a problem. His viewpoint is highly behavioral within the context of a systemic-relational therapy. In other words, he focused on behavior *always* within its relational context, and focused on developing therapeutic "directives" to solve problems. Haley (1987) stated:

> If therapy is to end properly, it must begin properly—by negotiating a solvable problem and discovering the social situation that makes the problem necessary. The act of therapy begins with the way the problem is examined. The act of intervening brings out problems and the relationship patterns that are to be changed. (p. 8)

Thus, a relationally defined problem is the target of counseling. And interventions are aimed at solving the problem by affecting relationships within which the problem is manifest.

Haley (1987) went on to describe the importance of what is defined as *analogic communication*. Analogic communication is opposed to *digital communication*. According to Haley, analogic communication is communication that "has multiple referents" (p. 92). There is no one response to an analogic communication. In human behavior, **analogic communication is highly nonverbal, informal, and contextual**. It takes into account many variables. On the other hand, digital communication

> consists of that class of messages where each statement has a specific referent and only that referent. Something happens or it does not happen; there is *one* stimulus and *one* response. . . . If A, and only if A, then Z, and only Z. (p. 91)

**Digital communication is technical and formal**. So, when a girl says to her boyfriend, "I love you," while she looks seductively at another boy walking by, the digital message is contained in the words "I love you," whereas the analogic message is in her nonverbal behavior in the context of her interaction with a passerby. Haley and other theorists (e.g., Bateson, 1972; Watzlawick, Beavin, & Jackson, 1967; Watzlawick, Weakland, & Fisch, 1974) believed that analogic communication was very important to human interpersonal communication. Analogic communication is critical to the definition of a relationship. Consequently, the study of analogic communication is of major importance in understanding the relational context in which problems arise and maintain themselves.

Haley (1987) also viewed the family as a governed **homeostatic system (meaning the system maintains a steady operating state, like the human body maintains a temperature around 98.6°F)**. The idea of systems maintaining homeostasis is in keeping with systemic-relational propositions (Cottone, 2012). Accordingly, one of the tasks of the therapist is targeting the repeated sequences of behavior within which the symptomatic behavior is embedded, which may be maintaining an unhealthy homeostasis. Haley stated:

> When dealing with a governed, homeostatic system that is maintained by repeating sequences of behavior, the therapist changes those sequences by shifting the ways people respond to each other because of the ways they must respond to the therapist. (p. 126)

Consequently, the therapist attempts to affect the relationship dynamics that may be supporting the unwanted or symptomatic behavior, although the involved parties may be unaware of the relational context of the problem. The term *symptomatic*, in this sense, is family-dynamic symptomatic, not symptomatic in a classic organic-medical diagnostic sense. Haley believes that problems are relation-specific, and moreover, to change a symptom, one must change the involved relationships.

Problem Solving Therapy's alignment with systemic-relational philosophy is clear. Relationships are the focus of study. Systems of relationships that are significant to a problem (behavior) can be defined and isolated for study and intervention. Cause is nonlinear within defined relationships (e.g., mom or dad is not the cause of a son's problems; rather, their triadic relationship dynamics are out of sync). Change occurs through communication. **Communication is relationship, and relationship is communication**. Moreover, the focus is on analogic as opposed to digital communication. Individual disorders do not exist outside of relationships, as all psychological concepts are redefined within a relational explanatory framework. Finally, strategic problem solving therapists attempt primarily to influence relationships.

## The Process of Counseling

Haley (1987) believed that it was "sensible to interview the natural group where the problem is expressed and so to proceed immediately toward the solution" (p. 9). Usually, the natural group where a problem is expressed is the family (or in some cases, the household). In fact, the initial interview in Strategic Problem Solving Therapy is a structured family interview that has distinct stages. The five stages are: (a) *a social stage*, which involves greeting the family and making the family members feel comfortable; (b) *the problem stage*, where each member is asked to define the problem; (c) *an interaction stage*, which places the family members in dyadic or other interactions for observatory purposes; (d) *a goal-setting stage*, where the family members must operationalize their concerns and define what is to be changed through therapeutic interventions; and (e) the *ending the interview or "task-setting" stage*, which involves setting the next session and settling issues related to the logistics of the second session.

Through the stages of the first interview, the therapist gains needed information about the function of a symptom within a relational context, and the therapist then uses the symptom as leverage in changing the relational dynamics of the family. Importantly, *directives* are used throughout the course of therapy to influence relational change. **A directive is a recommended task, presented to the family as a means of studying or**

**affecting a problem.** However, directives are usually *not given* at the end of the first session, unless, of course, a highly experienced and skilled therapist is involved. In fact the first directive may not occur until the end of the second session. One of the therapist's major tasks in the first session is to get the family back for the second session in order that a planned therapeutic directive may be given by the therapist.

It is through directives that the therapist maintains control of what occurs in therapy, as he or she can always anticipate what results from the therapeutic directive. The therapist must always be one-step-ahead of his client-family. Although this sounds impossible, from a strategic standpoint it is quite plausible. Client-families only have several options when faced with a therapeutic directive: (a) to carry out the directive, (b) to fail totally to carry out the directive, and (c) to fail partially to carry out the directive.

As initial therapeutic directives are usually aimed at solving a problem, if the directive is carried out, the family is moving in the "right" direction after the second session, and the therapist's subsequent activities are aimed at maintaining and building on the good changes that have occurred. The therapist is solving the problem through the "front door." For example, if a couple has not been out alone together on a date (with no children, friends, or other family members), a counselor directive to go on a date together, with no one else accompanying them, would act to facilitate re-connection of the partners. Systemic directives always involve relationship interaction—they are never directed to one person alone, acting alone. Therefore, asking a couple to go on a date is systemic, whereas asking one person to self-monitor his or her mood is an example of a non-systemic directive. If a couple follows the systemic directive and reports success, then the therapist continues to provide directed activities useful in strengthening the couple's relationship (the front-door approach). On the other hand, if a client-system fails to carry out a directive, or fails even to give the directive a working chance, then the responsibility of failure is placed squarely on the shoulders of the family members. They are informed that they have missed an opportunity to begin to correct the problems that led to therapy. Follow-up directives may be formulated with the idea that resistance is a factor in the failure of the family to carry out the directive. **Resistance, in this case, is the action by one or more of the family members to act in a way that is not consistent with the therapist's directives—it is social, not psychological resistance.** Follow-up directives in subsequent sessions may be based on the assumption that resistance to therapeutic directives will persist. Resistance may be used strategically. In other words, the therapist may ask the family to do something that the therapist does not want the family to do—to approach the family through the "back door," so to speak. Back–door directives are designed to use the client-system's resistance to change behavior in a desirable way. Effectively, this makes full therapeutic use of the family's resistance. A classic example of a back-door directive is "prescription of the symptom." The client–family may be asked, in all seriousness, to demonstrate that it can produce the "symptom." The rationale for such a directive given by the therapist might be that, by producing the symptom, the family gives the therapist an opportunity to study the symptom within its context. Paradoxically, *resistant client-families may refuse to follow the directive, thereby changing in the wanted direction (removal of the symptom).* Therefore, back-door directives (such as the paradoxical task just described) allow the therapist to strategically make use of client resistance. Haley (1987) has described methods to ensure the success of such directives.

The third possible outcome to a therapeutic directive is that the client-family makes only a half-hearted attempt to follow the directive, which results in a failure. Such attempts are viewed as fully failed attempts (reflecting resistance) and are treated as in the previous example of the failed attempt.

Of course there is one other option: a failed faithfully carried out directive. In such a case, the therapist is accountable for a misapplied or mis-targeted directive. The therapist has the responsibility to develop a more effective means of dealing with the presented problems. This is enough of a reason for a novice therapist to delay giving a therapeutic directive until at least the second session. By the second session, the therapist has had the opportunity: (a) to study the audio/visual recordings of the first interview, (b) to formulate effective directives, and (c) to develop strategies for addressing the outcome of the directive (as previously described). Second, the therapist can use the beginning of the second session to test some rough hypotheses about the usefulness of the directives before one is presented to the family at the end of the session.

Obviously, Strategic Problem Solving Therapy attempts to "cover all bases" in approaching problems in their relational contexts. It is designed to put the therapist in full control. The appropriateness of directives are based on the symptomatic behavior. Haley (1987) is very alert to how symptoms are operationalized, and therapeutic progress is viewed according to the effect of therapy on symptomatic behaviors. He stated, "Therapists who have the goal of removing symptoms or solving problems, and who do so, have done their job and earned their pay" (p. 219). However, it is noteworthy that from the very beginning of his book, Haley made it clear that it is the relational context and sequences of interactions that are the focus of Strategic Problem Solving Therapy. This point cannot be overemphasized. He stated:

> Even though this approach assumes that the therapist has failed if he or she does not solve the presenting problem, and even though the symptom is defined in operational terms that are as precise as possible, the therapy focus is on the social situation rather than on the person. It is possible to define a "problem" in different social units. In this book a problem is defined as a type of behavior that is part of a sequence of acts among several persons. The repeating sequence of behavior is the focus of therapy. A symptom is a label for, a crystallization of, a sequence in a social organization. (p. 2)

Haley's approach, although behaviorally focused, is clearly systemic-relational in that all behavior is viewed in its interactional (communicational) context.

## Counselor Role

The counselor's role is that of a strategist. Haley believed that therapy is necessarily directive. His views on the directive and the strategic nature of therapy derived from his study of the skillful Milton Erickson, a master hypnotherapist (Erickson, Rossi, & Rossi, 1976; Haley, 1973). Erickson actively and spontaneously choreographed his therapy sessions, and he was strategic in targeting unwanted behaviors and ameliorating them through directive technique. His techniques were often straightforward in their intent, but he was especially skilled at what can be described as the **"back-door" technique, that is, directive techniques that place clients in therapeutic binds** (see Erickson et al., 1976). For example, Erickson might ask, "Do you want to go into a trance quickly or slowly?" Such a question appears to give a choice, but actually it gives no choice as to whether trance is achieved. This essentially constitutes *a therapeutic* double bind, a **trap the therapist uses to cause appropriate or wanted behavior.** According to Haley

(1987), the therapist, by the nature of the therapeutic context, cannot escape being directive, and this position is a direct offshoot of the position of Milton Erickson.

Haley also believed that the therapist should take a somewhat neutral role when
dealing with relationships in therapy. Haley (1987) stated:

> At the most general level, therapists should not side consistently with any-
> one in the family against anyone else. But that does not mean they should
> not temporarily side with one against another, because that is in fact the
> only way therapists can induce change. If they only place their "weight"
> in coalitions equally, they will continue the sequence as it was. In the same
> way, if they only join one person against another, they may maintain the
> system as it was by simply becoming part of the deadlocked struggle. That
> task is more complex: the therapist must temporarily join in different coali-
> tions while ultimately not siding with anyone against anyone. (p. 126)

The therapist, then, must play a relationship balancing act in sessions, leaning one
way when necessary, and another way at another time, but always maintaining the in-
between position when the act is over.

The strategic therapist is also a negotiator in a sense. He or she must be able to negotiate a therapeutic contract with a problematic family, when in fact, the family members
may see little connection between a symptomatic individual and their need to attend
sessions. Haley, however, does not negotiate about the presenting problem or the need
to redefine problems in relational terms. He appeared to believe that patients have difficulty thinking relationally, and he did the relational thinking for them. Consequently, he
often took the presenting problem at face value, even if it was focused on an individual
(related to a sole identified patient, IP). He then used the presenting problem as leverage to get the individuals in the problematic system to return so that he could target the
system for treatment. He attempted to influence change in the relational structure of the
problematic relationships.

In summary, the strategic therapist must be directive, tactical, relationally neutral,
and be able to negotiate the terms of therapy so that problems become the evident focus
of treatment.

## Goals of Counseling and Ideal Outcomes

The ideal outcome of Strategic Problem Solving Therapy is problem resolution. Haley
(1987) stated:

> The first obligation of a therapist is to change the presenting problem
> offered. If that is not accomplished, the therapy is a failure. Therapists
> should not let themselves be distracted into other matters so that they for-
> get this primary goal. Moreover, by focusing on the symptoms the ther-
> apist gains the most leverage and has the most opportunity for bringing
> about change. It is the presenting problem that most interests the client; by
> working with that the therapist can gain great cooperation. If a person with
> symptoms is offered as a problem, the therapist may believe that changes
> must take place in that family system before that person can change. Yet
> he should not try to convince the family that the real problem lies in the
> family and not in the person. Such a distinction is artificial. The therapist
> who engages in pointless debate with the family about the cause of the

> problem, attempts to educate them about family communication, or tries to persuade them to accept "family therapy" may fail to achieve his or her ends. The goal is not to teach the family about their malfunctioning system but to change the family sequences so that the presenting problems are resolved. (p. 135)

The actual mechanisms of change do not have to be understood. Only effective procedures and techniques for instigating and maintaining change need to be mastered by the therapist. The therapist, then, must be the consummate interpersonal technician.

# GENERAL PROCEDURES

## Assessment

Assessment occurs throughout strategic therapy, as the therapist continually reassesses whether clients are responding to directives or not. However, in the first session, the therapist makes a concerted effort to define significant relationship dynamics, primarily through the five-stage process. For example, in the first session, the therapist observes children closely, as they are reflective of the family's status. For example, a symptomatic child is viewed as reflecting a symptomatic parental relationship. Haley (1987) stated: "If there is a child problem in a family, the adults are usually in disagreement about how to deal with the child. Sometimes they show this disagreement immediately and sometimes they present a united front in the beginning" (p. 16). Haley is very alert to triadic interactions, and recognizes their significance to social systems theory. Triangles allow for coalitions. They also involve **hierarchy, the power structure of a family**. Parents, for example, are hierarchically one level up from children in terms of the potential to wield power. Power is an issue that Haley addresses directly in his work. He believed at the practical level that power cannot be denied in therapy. He disagreed with Bateson (see Bateson, 1979) on the issue of power. Bateson felt that power led to a false epistemology (focus of study), that it was seductive and was ultimately destructive when applied in interpersonal relations. He viewed interpersonal relations within a fully circular epistemological framework, which is inconsistent with the linear influence implied by *power*. Haley, on the other hand, made full use of power in his therapy, and he attempted to assess power hierarchy (primarily through triads) in the early stages of therapy. However, Haley's emphasis is more on communication than hierarchy. And if one were to define hierarchy according to his perspective, one would ultimately be describing the digital and especially the analogic communication patterns involved in cross-generational interactions.

As the therapist begins to get a sense of the relational dynamics of the family as organized around a symptom, he or she must maintain only tentative conclusions. Haley (1987) stated: "The therapist may be misled and therefore ideas should not be too firm. Observation gives information that can be tested as the session continues" (p. 17). And it is critical, from a strategic position, that the therapist should not share his or her observations with the family members. Haley stated:

> It is also important that the therapist should not share his observations with the family. If the problem child is sitting between mother and father, the therapist may make a tentative hypothesis that the child's problem serves

a function in their marriage. But that hypothesis should not be taken too seriously without further data, and the therapist should never comment to the family about the child's position. (p. 17)

Being able to observe changes in the family patterns at the analogic level means assigning digital explanations of problems to a secondary role. It is anticipated that family members demonstrate their changes through observable relational dynamics. The therapist puts his or her effort into observing and affecting analogic (informal, nonverbal, contextual) family communication, rather than simply presenting information digitally to clients in therapy.

## Treatment/Remediation

Strategic Problem Solving Therapy involves giving directives. Treatment is a process of giving directives and assessing client responses. Haley (1987) stated: "It is, of course, essential that a therapist know how to give directives so that they are carried out. It is a misfortune that most clinical training has not included this skill" (p. 56). The purposes of directives include: (a) to get people to behave differently; (b) to make the therapist important in the lives of clients—because the therapist has taken action that the family must react to; and (c) to gather more information—the response of clients to directives is educational of family interaction and dynamics.

**Directives are prescribed tasks.** Haley (1987) believed that they must be precisely and confidently given (not just suggested), targeted to involve everyone in the family, and reviewed before the family leaves the therapy session to ensure that everyone understands what is to happen. Directives may be straightforward (e.g., "I want you and your spouse to go on a date alone"); or paradoxical (e.g., prescribing the symptom and expecting resistance). The intent, however, is always the same, to change the relational dynamics around the symptom.

Some examples of directives used by Haley (1987) as described in *Problem Solving Therapy* include:

> A father who is siding with his small daughter against the wife may be required to wash the sheets when the daughter wets the bed. This task will tend to disengage daughter and father or cure the bedwetting.
>
> . . .
>
> A mother and father who need an excuse to be affectionate with each other may be asked to show affection to each other in an obvious way at set times to "teach their child" how to show affection.
>
> . . .
>
> A husband and wife with sexual problems may be required to have sex relations only on the living room floor for a period of time. This task changes the context and so the struggle.
>
> . . .
>
> A man who is afraid to apply for a job may be asked to go for a job interview at a place where he would not take the job if he got it, thereby practicing in a safe way. (pp. 68-69)

Assessment of family responses to directives always involves the three possible outcomes described by Haley: a faithfully carried out directive; failure to carry out a directive fully; or failure to carry out a directive partially. In every case, the therapist must be prepared to have an alternative action—another directive. In this sense, Strategic Problem Solving Therapy is a very structured treatment process.

## Case Management

Sessions are generally scheduled for about once a week, although if the family is demonstrating a great deal of emotion (a crisis), sessions may be scheduled more frequently. As problems begin to resolve, intervals between sessions may be lengthened, until there is termination. Usually, one goal of therapy is to have the client feel that he or she does not need the therapist anymore; it is wise to manage a case so that the client does not act dependently on the therapist throughout the process of therapy.

Sessions may last an hour, or they may be shortened or lengthened strategically. If a family has failed to carry out a directive, the following therapy session may be made longer (and more expensive). If a family has carried out a directive, the session may be shorter (and less expensive). In this way, clients are rewarded for doing what needs to be done.

Case recording is recommended. Case notes should record the presenting problems, the relational problem formulation, the directives given, and the actions taken by the family.

## Specialized Techniques

1. *Straightforward, front-door directives.* **Front-door directives simply direct the clients to do what is asymptomatic.** Some clients merely follow the directive of the therapist. However, a strategic therapist does not just give good advice. Rather, directives are always targeted at the sequences of interpersonal interactions that are at the foundation of problematic behaviors. Front-door directives, therefore, are directed tasks that attempt to straightforwardly affect relations of significance. To direct a husband to take his wife on a picnic at a time when otherwise she would be involved in problematic family interactions is a front-door directive. It affects relationships among family members, and it does so by asking the family members to do what the therapist really wants them to do.

2. *Back-door directives.* **Back-door directives ask the family members to do something when the therapist does not expect them to do it. A back-door directive anticipates resistance among family members**, or as Haley (1987) stated, the therapist "wants the [family] members to resist him so they will change" (p. 76). Paradoxical directives are classically back-door. To tell an insomniac to set his alarm every hour on the hour all night long to monitor and to record his wakefulness is actually an opportunity for a resistant client to rebel by not setting the alarm and by sleeping. To instruct a mother who is over-babying her child to continue to do this because she is doing it incorrectly, and then to direct her to baby the child in a way that is inconvenient, is a means of arousing resistance in the mother. In both of these cases, the therapist has anticipated that the client will rebel against the directive, thereby demonstrating appropriate resolution of the problem behavior.

3. *Front-door directives by metaphoric implication.* A front-door directive by analogy builds on the metaphoric nature of human interaction. Milton Erickson was a master of metaphoric directives (**a metaphor is something that is not literally true**). Sometimes, clients are unable to openly deal with their problems, and Erickson would use an analogous situation to direct clients as to what to do. Haley (1973) described one of Erickson's directives as follows:

> As a typical example, if Erickson is dealing with a married couple who have a conflict over sexual relations and would rather not discuss it directly, he will approach the problem metaphorically. He will choose some aspect of their lives that is analogous to sexual relations and change that as a way of changing the sexual behavior. He might, for example, talk to them about having dinner together and draw them out on their preferences. He will discuss with them how the wife likes appetizers before dinner, while the husband prefers to dive right into the meat and potatoes. Or the wife might prefer a quiet and leisurely dinner, while the husband, who is quick and direct, just wants the meal over with. If the couple begin to connect what they are saying with sexual relations, Erickson will "drift rapidly" away to other topics, and then he will return to the analogy. He might end such a conversation with a directive that the couple arrange a pleasant dinner on a particular evening that is satisfactory to both of them. When successful, this approach shifts the couple from a more pleasant dinner to more pleasant sexual relations without their being aware that he has deliberately set this goal. (pp. 27–28)

It is important to direct *actions and behaviors* (not just thoughts or feelings) through such metaphoric directives; in this way, actions are affected by the accomplishment of analogous actions.

4. *Encouraging controlled relapses.* Encouraging controlled relapses is a special kind of paradoxical strategy. The question arises: What does the therapist do when a client's unwanted behavior appears to spontaneously remit after a paradoxical maneuver with resistant clients? Haley (1987) stated:

> The therapist must accept the change when it happens and let the family put her down by proving her wrong. If she wants to ensure that the change will continue, she might say to the members that probably the change is only temporary and they will relapse. Then the family will continue the change to prove to her that it is not temporary. Talking about the change being temporary serves to block off a relapse. (p. 78)

The therapist might go so far as to plan a relapse, paradoxically asking the family members if they can find something valuable in their old "miserable" ways (Haley, 1973, 1987). A directed relapse also acts to plan a behavior that previously occurred spontaneously (symptoms), and paradoxically, a directed relapse acts to put symptoms under control. In effect, the therapist cannot lose. If the symptom returns, it has reappeared under the therapist's direction and, therefore, it is under control; if the symptom does not return, then the problems have been solved.

These four techniques represent some basic approaches to the directive counseling of the strategic problem solving therapist.

## Recent Developments or Criticisms

One of Haley's more recent works is a book by the title of *Ordeal Therapy: Unusual Ways to Change Behavior* (Haley, 1984). Again, as with Haley's book *Uncommon Therapy* (Haley, 1973), he referred heavily to the work of Milton Erickson. Erickson used "ordeals" to produce change in clients. He would direct clients to do something so burdensome as part of the symptomatic behavior that being symptom free was a relief. Haley described one of Erickson's cases—an insomniac, whom Erickson directed to polish the floors into the late hours of the night. Therefore, Erickson designed an ordeal that the patient would rather avoid by sleeping. Haley (1984) stated the "rather simple premise" of ordeal therapy as follows: "If one makes it more difficult for a person to have a symptom than to give it up, the person will give up the symptom" (p. 5).

Haley (1984) stated that ordeals should be "appropriate to the problem of the person who wants to change" (p. 6). It should be "more severe than the problem" (p. 6). Haley believed that it is best for an ordeal to be something that is good for the person. Just as polishing the floors is good for the insomniac (polished floors are always attractive), so too should other ordeals do something that is valuable in some way to the client. Ordeals should be something to which the person cannot easily object. Additionally, it should not violate a person's moral standards, and it should not harm the patient or other individuals. Haley stated: "Sometimes the person must go through it repeatedly to recover from the symptom. At other times the mere threat of an ordeal brings recovery" (p. 7). Regardless, Haley presents ordeals as effective strategies for facilitating behavior change.

At first glance, the idea of treating individuals through ordeals appears to indicate that Haley abandoned the systemic-relational framework so characteristic of his earlier works. Although he was amenable to working with individuals when creating therapeutic ordeals, he still framed concerns within a relational context. Haley (1984) stated:

> The ordeal is a procedure that forces a change, and there are consequences to that. The therapist needs to be aware that symptoms are a reflection of a confusion in a social organization, usually a family. The existence of a symptom indicates that the hierarchy of an organization is incorrect. Therefore, when a therapist resolves a symptom in this way, he or she is forcing a change in a complex organization that was previously stabilized by the symptom. If, for example, a wife has a symptom that helps maintain her husband in a superior position as the one taking care of her, that changes rapidly when an ordeal requires the wife to abandon the symptom. She and her husband must negotiate a new relationship contract that does not include symptomatic behavior. . . . It is best for a therapist to understand the function of a symptom in the social organization of the client. If not able to understand it, the therapist must resolve the symptom warily while watching for repercussions and changes. (p. 16)

In fact, Haley continued to take up the systemic-relational banner, arguing in support of the systemic-relational interpretations even when dealing with otherwise assumed organic-medical concerns (see the discussion in Cottone [2012] and the debate between Haley [1989] and Stein [1989]). Although Ordeal Therapy often targets the individual in therapy, it is still conceptualized within a systemic-relational problematic context.

There have been many criticisms of Haley's approach. His work has been portrayed as being highly manipulative and even deceitful, especially as related to back-door or paradoxical techniques. Haley (1987) devoted a full chapter of *Problem Solving Therapy* to the topic of ethical issues, in which he argued for the validity and usefulness of his approach. He argued that concealment of certain information in certain relationships is basic to human relations, and that to think otherwise is to deny the nature of human interaction. He also argued that all therapy is directive, no matter how nondirective it may appear at face value. He argued that the therapist must assess not only the short-term effects of interventions, but also their long-term effects on the therapeutic relationship. He stated:

> The question in this situation is not so much a question of whether the therapist is telling a lie but whether she is behaving unethically. Even if he is deceiving the patient for his own good, is it ethical to deceive a patient? If it is essential for the cure that deceit be used, it might be justified on that basis. However, one must also be concerned about the long-term effect of a person experiencing an expert as an untrustworthy person, which may be more harmful than the continuation of the symptom. (p. 226)

Haley essentially argued that a therapist must be ethically grounded in his approach, and client welfare (short and long term) must be a major determining factor of the appropriateness of therapeutic techniques. Effectively, then, it is considered ethical to "trick" a person out of a problem, "a method traditionally used by shamans" (Haley, 1987, p. 226), so long as it is in the short- and long-term interests of the client.

It can also be argued that Haley's approach, being highly interactionally behavioral, does not address underlying problems. For Haley, however, just solving the problem is not enough. He is alert to the underlying social-relational factors that might begin or maintain a symptom. He, on the other hand, does not believe in individual psychological problems or traits per se. He frames underlying processes in systemic-relational terms (e.g., family organization, interactive patterns), just as he frames presenting problems in systemic-relational terms. He would argue that the social context cannot be ignored when solving problems.

Although there has been some empirical support of the strategic approach with certain disorders (see Gurman, Kniskern, & Pinsof, 1986), and there is support for using paradoxical maneuvers with resistant clients (Beutler, 2000), the empirical jury is still out on Strategic Problem Solving Therapy.

Haley's approach has become very popular and is regarded as one of the leading therapies among systemic-relational paradigm adherents. However, his view and others with the same view have been criticized as being too warlike in their language and technique. It is as if the therapist is at odds with the client-system, attempting to out-maneuver and outwit the family. Haley's perspective places the therapist at odds with what might be considered the family's underlying relational dynamic, of which the family members might not even be aware. The therapist is continually attempting to stay one-step-ahead of the nonconscious relational process of the family, as if to prevent a defeat by the family. Some theorists view this as a dichotomized and contrived view of therapeutic interaction; and this view is especially criticized by those theorists who have attempted to incorporate problem formulation within the therapeutic system (see Hoffman, 1988).

Criticisms aside, the strategic approach has become a popular and highly used family therapy approach.

---

**STUDENT–MENTOR DIALOGUE**

**Student:**  This is really a different approach than we studied in earlier chapters of this book. It seems alien to the way people conceive of counseling. In many ways it makes counseling look cold, controlled, and contrived.

**Mentor:**  Haley believed all counseling and psychotherapy was directive. He would argue that even those approaches that claim to be non-directive cannot escape the therapeutic context, which is that of an expert earning a fee or salary in order to change behavior. It is naïve to believe that counselors and psychotherapists are licensed and employed to affect behavior and then are not in any directive sense responsible to do so. He made it clear that a therapist who changes behavior earns his pay. So his argument is compelling and aligns counseling goals fully with the counseling context—a highly trained specialist is engaged in using knowledge to change behavior using techniques that are designed and implemented to do so.

**Student:**  But doesn't the whole idea of using techniques designed to affect behavior without a client's awareness seem dishonest?

**Mentor:**  Most counseling approaches don't explain to clients the mechanism of change. In psychoanalysis, the analyst doesn't tell the client to have insight—it is supposed to happen through the therapeutic process. Likewise, Person Centered Therapists do not reveal to clients the intent of having the clients respond primarily affectively; it is supposed to happen due to the core conditions of treatment. So Haley's approach is no less honest than others. Few counseling approaches make it clear that the counselor must or should tell clients at the outset what outcomes are expected. Haley is just making full use of the therapeutic relationship for the benefit of the client. The fact that his intent is never revealed is not important, as his intent is always to change the relational dynamics—a mechanism of change that often is misunderstood by clients who primarily focus on the problematic behaviors of individuals.

**Student:**  But using paradoxical technique is so blatantly manipulative.

**Mentor:**  Yes, but research shows it works in very specific situations—where clients are resistant. It is a useful technique, perhaps as a last resort, for clients who act in opposition to logical and straight-forward therapeutic directions. Haley learned to use such techniques from

Milton Erickson, who was a master hypnotherapist. In many ways, Haley's work is a combination of the systems theory that Gregory Bateson purported and the very directive style of therapy that Erickson represented. The combination of the influence of Bateson and Erickson resulted in a relationship-focused directive approach to counseling.

**Student:**  Yes, one thing that is clear is Haley's confidence in relationships.

**Mentor:**  No question. In fact, counseling is a relationship. You have to believe in the power of relationships as a means to affect behavior to be a counselor, because that's what counselors do. They sit across the room from an individual, couple, or family and, by communicating, they are expected to influence behavior. The systemic-relational theorists, in many ways, make the obvious more than obvious. Haley didn't hypothesize beyond recognizing that behavior occurs in interpersonal contexts, and the contexts are crucial to the behavior. And the counseling context is also recognized as a means to strategically produce the results wanted by the client.

**Student:**  So do you think good counselors are master manipulators?

**Mentor:**  I think good counselors are masterful at connecting with clients, establishing a strong working relationship while establishing mutual goals, and designing interventions that facilitate change in a desirable way. If that's manipulation, I'm all for it. The term "manipulation," however, has a negative connotation. Perhaps systemic-relational counselors should be viewed as social engineers, not manipulators.

**Student:**  So do you think Haley's approach will continue to be used in counseling and psychotherapy?

**Mentor:**  Yes, surely. It is taught in many marriage and family therapy programs, and as more textbooks recognize Haley's unique contribution to the field, I believe it will continue to be applied, primarily in couple and family counseling.

## CONCLUSION

Haley's Strategic Problem Solving Therapy is one of the most paradigm-aligned therapies presented in this book. It is an excellent example of how systemic-relational thinking translates to practice solving problems that can be viewed by others as individual-specific. Although problems are the focus of study, individual problems are distinctly and consistently redefined within a relational context. Haley's approach targets reciprocal interpersonal interactions, attempting to alter the ways people act around each other in specified settings. Relationships, then, become the target of intervention.

Relationship issues are viewed as underlying presenting problems. Haley is a master of techniques designed to produce changes. He is the consummate interpersonal technician. And he is strategic in his attempts to help people to help themselves to change distressful situations.

## REFERENCES

Bateson, G. (1972). *Steps to an ecology of mind.* New York, NY: Ballantine.

Bateson, G. (1979). *Mind and nature: A necessary unity.* New York, NY: Bantam.

Bateson, G., Jackson, D., Haley, J., & Weakland, J. (1956). Toward a theory of schizophrenia. *Behavioral Science, 1,* 251–264. doi:10.1002/bs.3830010402

Beutler, L. E. (2000). David and Goliath: When empirical and clinical standards of practice meet. *American Psychologist, 55,* 997–1007. doi:10.1037/0003-066X.55.9.997

Cottone, R. R. (2012). *Paradigms of counseling and psychotherapy.* Cottleville, MO: Smashwords. Retrieved from https://www.smashwords.com/books/view/165398

Erickson, M. H., Rossi, E. L., & Rossi, S. I. (1976). *Hypnotic realities.* New York, NY: Irvington Publishers.

Gurman, A. S., Kniskern, D. P., & Pinsof, W. M. (1986). Research on the process and outcome of marital and family therapy. In S. L. Garfield & A. E. Bergin (Eds.), *Handbook of psychotherapy and behavior change* (3rd ed., pp.565–624). New York, NY: Wiley.

Haley, J. (1963). *Strategies of psychotherapy.* New York, NY: Grune & Stratton.

Haley, J. (1973). *Uncommon therapy.* New York, NY: W. W. Norton. Excerpt used with permission from W. W. Norton & Company.

Haley, J. (1976). *Problem solving therapy.* New York, NY: Harper & Row.

Haley, J. (1984). *Ordeal therapy: Unusual ways to change behavior.* San Francisco, CA: Jossey-Bass. © Jay Haley, excerpts used with permission of Stanford University Libraries.

Haley, J. (1987). *Problem solving therapy* (2nd ed.). New York, NY: Jossey-Bass. Excerpts republished with permission of John Wiley and Sons Inc.

Haley, J. (1989). The effect of long-term outcome studies on the therapy of schizophrenia. *Journal of Marital and Family Therapy, 15,* 127–132.

Haley, J., & Hoffman, L. (1967). *Techniques of family therapy.* New York, NY: Basic Books.

Hoffman, L. (1988). A constructivist position for family therapy. *The Irish Journal of Psychology, 9,* 110–129.

Stein, L. (1989). The effect of long-term outcome studies on the therapy of schizophrenia: A critique. *Journal of Marital and Family Therapy, 15,* 133–138.

Watzlawick, P., Beavin, J. H., & Jackson, D. D. (1967). *Pragmatic's of human communication: A study of interactional patterns, pathologies, and paradoxes.* New York, NY: W. W. Norton.

Watzlawick, P., Weakland, J., & Fisch, R. (1974). *Change: Principles of problem formation and problem resolution.* New York, NY: W. W. Norton.

# CHAPTER

## 11

# Structural Family Therapy

## OBJECTIVES

- To introduce a systemic-relational therapy that focuses on family structure

- To provide a biographical summary of Salvador Minuchin, the founder and proponent of Structural Family Therapy

- To outline the basic theory of the structural approach and to provide guidance on application of the theory

- To define some recent developments and criticisms of the approach

Structural Family Therapy is a systemic-relational therapy developed by Salvador Minuchin, MD, and his associates at the Philadelphia Child Guidance Clinic. Structural Family Therapy was developed in the late 1960s and early 1970s while Minuchin was the director (until 1975) of the Philadelphia Child Guidance Clinic. Minuchin refined his ideas in the years that followed as a trainer at the Family Therapy Training Center. In both positions, Minuchin would lead the development of a family counseling theory with an "emphasis on structural change as the main goal of therapy" (Colapinto, 1982, p. 112).

Structural Family Therapy is unique among the systemic-relational therapies because of its emphasis on the structure of families as a focus of study and as a target of intervention. Other systemic-relational therapies tend to focus more on communication as a target of intervention. Minuchin, who worked with severely disturbed and structurally different families from his earliest family practice (e.g., families of delinquents or

anorexics), became acutely aware of the differences and significance of family organization and roles as they influence human behavior. In fact, **the words *organization* and
*roles* aptly and simply describe what is meant by Minuchin for the term *structure*.
Structure refers to the patterns of interactions (which often become too rigid or ste-
reotyped) that can be observed in families within a therapeutic context**. Therefore, the
focus of study of Structural Family Therapy is "structure," which is clearly defined by
Minuchin as repeated patterns of interaction. Interpersonal interaction, within a family
context, is the focus of study. Even though *structure* is a term that is associated with
"thingness" in common usage, his definition of structure is clearly relational.

Minuchin's book entitled *Families and Family Therapy* (Minuchin, 1974) and his coauthored text entitled *Family Therapy Techniques* (Minuchin & Fishman, 1981) are used as
primary resources in summarizing "Structural Family Therapy." Readers are directed to
those books for a detailed discussion of theoretical tenets and techniques. For detailed
case studies, Minuchin's (1984) *Family Kaleidoscope* is recommended.

## SALVADOR MINUCHIN: A BIOGRAPHICAL SKETCH

Salvador Minuchin was born in Argentina on October 13, 1921. Little is known of his
childhood, but in a book Minuchin wrote with Fishman (Minuchin & Fishman, 1981),
there is a section that presents Minuchin's own family as an example of family theory.
In that section, Minuchin described a difficult period of his life and the importance of a
support system:

> When I was eleven years old, I needed to go to school away from home,
> since my home town had only five grades, and I lived for a year with the

> family of my Aunt Sofia. (Although
> my aunt was married for over fifty
> years to my Uncle Bernard, until his
> death, in my nuclear family the head-
> of-the-house position was always
> given to the member of my parents'
> family and not to the in law.) The
> year I spent in her house was the
> worst of my entire life. Away from
> home, friends, and familiar context,
> I grew depressed, had nightmares,
> felt isolated, was bullied in school
> by a bunch of "city kids," did poorly
> in my studies, and failed two sub-
> jects. I probably needed psychologi-
> cal help, only nobody noticed how I
> felt. The next year was somewhat bet-
> ter. I moved to the house of a cousin
> who had young children, shared a
> room with another cousin my age,
> and developed a friendship with

Salvador Minuchin.
*Source*: Photo by R. Rocco Cottone.

> three other adolescents. We formed a four-musketeers club that lasted
> throughout high school, so that by the time my family moved to the city,
> I had already developed a support system. (pp. 75–76)

Given his support system, Minuchin must have done very well, because he went from failing subjects to earning an MD degree (in 1947 at the University of Cordoba, Argentina). In 1948 he served as a First Lieutenant in the Israeli Army after a residency in pediatrics and child psychiatry at the University of Argentina. He later moved to New York, where he obtained a fellowship in child psychiatry, and he followed the fellowship with an additional residency in psychiatry (in Valhalla, New York). He received training in psychoanalysis, which he completed in 1967.

From 1952 to 1981, he held several positions that directly related to his theoretical propositions. From 1952 to 1954 he was the "Psychiatric Director" of the Youth Aliyah Department of Disturbed Children in Israel. From 1960 to 1966 he was the "Director of Training in Family Therapy" at the Wiltwyck School for Boys in New York. At Wiltwyck, he also directed a research unit. He, his wife (Patricia), and their two children moved to Philadelphia in 1965. From 1965 to 1975 he was the director of the Philadelphia Child Guidance Clinic and a psychiatrist with the Children's Hospital of Philadelphia. From 1975 to 1981, remaining at the Philadelphia Child Guidance Clinic, he took a position there as the director of the Family Therapy Training Center. During his time at the Philadelphia Child Guidance Clinic he was very productive: his most foundational theoretical works were published during his tenure there. While in Philadelphia, he also served as a professor at the University of Pennsylvania School of Medicine.

In 1981, Minuchin moved to New York City and established the Family Studies Institute. He was also a Research Professor of Psychiatry at the New York University Medical Center. The Family Studies Institute was renamed the Minuchin Center for the Family in 1995 when he retired.

Minuchin has received many awards and honors in his lifetime, including the "Distinguished Achievement in Family Therapy Award" in 1982 from the American Family Therapy Association. He received the "Family Therapy Award" in 1984 from the American Association for Marriage and Family Therapy.

# THE FOUNDATIONAL THEORY
## The Target of Counseling
Minuchin (1974) described Structural Family Therapy as follows:

> A body of theory and techniques that approaches the individual in his social context. Therapy based on this framework is directed toward changing the organization of the family. When the structure of the family group is transformed, the positions of members in that group are altered accordingly. As a result, each individual's experiences change. (p. 2)

Minuchin worked from the assumption that individuals are not bound by mentality into set ways of reacting; rather, he views the individual as an "acting and reacting member of social groups" (p. 2). He believed that to deal with a person's expressed problem individually is to build an artificial boundary between the person and his or her social context. His therapy further rests on three axioms: (a) "that context affects inner processes"; (b) "that changes in context produce changes in the individual"; and (c) "that the therapist's behavior is significant in change" (p. 9). As is evident, Minuchin's ideas are clearly consistent with basic systemic-relational tenets. The target of counseling is the relational context of a problem, most usually the family's organization and structure.

What makes Minuchin's (1974) approach unique as a marital and family therapeutic approach is the focus on family structure, substructure, and boundary. **Minuchin defines *"family structure"* as "the invisible set of functional demands that organizes the ways in which family members interact. . . . Repeated transactions establish patterns of how, when, and to whom to relate, and these patterns underpin the system"** (p. 51). Essentially these transactional patterns are communication patterns that come to regulate the behaviors of family members. Because Minuchin believes a "power hierarchy" is a universal rule governing family functioning, transactional patterns take the form of *roles,* **which are best understood as** *task orientations within rule structures.* These roles also help to define subsystems–relational **substructures within the family that are always composed of fewer relationships than the number of relationships in the larger family system.** Minuchin believed that **subsystems are** *"formed by generation, by sex, by interest, or by function"* (p. 52). Subsystems are very important to families, because they are the means by which a family "differentiates and carries out its functions" (p. 52).

Any person can belong to a number of subsystems in a family. For example, in a family of four with one male child and one elder female child, the female child can be considered part of the "children/sibling" subsystem. She is also a part of the "female" subsystem. In the female subsystem, the female child might have less power compared to the mother (who is a member of the parental/executive subsystem). The female child, however, may have more power in the children/sibling subsystem than the younger brother. Certain roles are carried out within these subsystems, as within the larger family system.

Minuchin (1974) defined **boundaries as** *"the rules defining who participates, and how"* **in family subsystems.** Fundamentally, these boundaries define the "shoulds" and "should nots" of individual behavior within and between subsystems. For example, in a household with a grandmother, her overinvolvement in parent-like decision making might be greeted by verbal or nonverbal expressions by the parents of a rule that her responsibilities are limited in this regard. Again, it is important to note that communication plays an important part in the determination of a boundary. Minuchin believed that boundaries, and thus rule communication, must be clear. He also strongly inferred that they should be fair. In regard to the fairness of a boundary, judgment enters in from a therapeutic standpoint. A therapist must assess whether, in fact, individuals are fulfilling their roles appropriately. For example, parents are expected to have some authority (power) over their children. Minuchin stated:

> Parenting requires the capacity to nurture, guide, and control. The proportions of these elements depend on the children's developmental needs and the parents' capacity. But parenting always requires the use of authority. Parents cannot carry out their executive functions unless they have the power to do so. (p. 58)

Certainly, Minuchin's ideas about structure, hierarchy, and boundaries must be viewed within a larger Western cultural context, where child rearing is primarily the responsibility of the parents and where children must reconcile their needs with the expressed needs of individuals in power positions in the family. At the same time, Minuchin believed that children should have some level of autonomy. This autonomy is manifest in the children/sibling subsystem, which should have rights to privacy, personal interests, and exploration. The fairness of boundaries, therefore, appears to be relative to societal context and the prevailing social mores.

Obviously, in certain situations, certain patterns or boundaries will be preferred; for example, with parents of young children, it is preferred that the parents, in coalition, fulfill the executive role in the family. In a one-working-parent family, an elder child may assume some of the executive function. There is role flexibility depending on the larger context of a family's functioning.

Although terms like *structure*, *subsystems*, and *boundaries* are useful in understanding how families operate, these terms relate to stabilizing factors within the family. In-and-of-themselves, they are not useful in understanding how family systems change. In fact, Minuchin (1974) went into great detail about the need for families to be adaptable, and he described the process of change as an accommodation of inside and outside stresses on the family. He hypothesized that stress comes from four sources: (a) contact by one family member with extrafamilial forces (e.g., a stressful employer–employee relationship for a family breadwinner); (b) contact by the whole family with extrafamilial forces (e.g., an environmental catastrophe or economic depression); (c) transitions in the family evolution (e.g., when development of individuals affects role function—children becoming adults, as a case in point); and (d) idiosyncratic factors (related to individual biological differences in the family, such as physical or intellectual disability). Stressors, of course, can produce healthy changes, unhealthy changes, or no change at all in a family. Family therapy becomes an issue when the family, or at least one of its members, becomes maladaptive or symptomatic; then change becomes necessary.

## The Process of Counseling

Colapinto (1982) described the process of Structural Family Therapy as follows:

> Therapeutic change is then the process of helping the family to outgrow its stereotyped patterns, of which the presenting problem is a part. This process transpires within a special context, the therapeutic system, which offers a unique chance to challenge the rules of the family. The privileged position of the therapist allows him to request from the family members different behaviors and to invite different perceptions, thus altering their interaction and perspective. The family then has an opportunity to experience transactional patterns that have not been allowed under its prevailing homeostatic rules. The system's limits are probed and pushed, its narrow self-definitions are questioned; in the process, the family's capacity to tolerate and handle stress or conflict increases, and its perceived reality becomes richer, more complex. (p. 121)

Essentially, the therapist attempts to *join* the family, to enter into its interactive process, and to affect its ways of operating.

Minuchin and Fishman (1981) described the *joining* process as follows:

> Joining a family is more an attitude than a technique, and it is the umbrella under which all therapeutic transactions occur. Joining is letting the family know that the therapist understands them and is working with and for them. Only under his protection can the family have the security to explore alternatives, try the unusual, and change. Joining is the glue that holds the therapeutic system together. (pp. 31–32)

Joining is the equivalent of establishing a therapeutic relationship. But joining the family does not mean that the therapist must act congruently with the family process. In fact, the therapist, once accommodated by the family, is left free to "jar" the family members (Minuchin & Fishman, 1981, p. 32). Joining, therefore, means the therapist will be accepted to some degree even if he or she begins to challenge the structure and rules of the family. Joining, therefore, also means that the family has become somewhat invested in the actions of the therapist.

Beyond joining the family, the process of Minuchin's (1974) Structural Family Therapy can be broken down into four dimensions. Note the word *dimensions* is used, instead of the word *stages*, as the presented dimensions may actually overlap in time. These dimensions *should not* be considered as sequential phases of therapy. The four dimensions are: (a) structural diagnosis; (b) probing within the therapeutic system; (c) sparking transformation; and (d) restructuring through a therapeutic contract. Essentially, Minuchin joins the family and analyzes its structure through exploring coalitions, subsystems, and the power hierarchy. He broadens the focus of the problem to include family interaction and structure, which in most cases will become the target of intervention. Importantly, he comes to an agreement with the family on the nature of the problem and on the goals for change (a therapeutic contract). And finally, he intervenes to create imbalance and to move the family toward a new, more adaptive structure.

## Counselor Role

Minuchin believed that the therapist must take a leadership role as he or she joins the family in therapy. Beyond developing a therapeutic alliance, the family therapist must *unbalance* the system to create change. This may be accomplished by forming a coalition with one or more family members against other family members. Although this may appear unfair, Minuchin believed that "when the therapist unbalances a family system by joining with one member, the other members experience stress" (p. 113). Furthermore, "change, through therapy, like any other family change, is accompanied by stress, and the therapeutic system must be capable of dealing with it" (p. 114). Stress, then, can be viewed as the family therapist's ally. In Minuchin's (1974) book, *Families and Family Therapy,* he gave the following example:

> A family comes into therapy because the husband has migraines. He is ashamed of his humble origins, having been the first of his family to go to college. He married a woman whose family he admired for their intellectual accomplishments, and he has great respect for his wife's opinions. She is the rule setter, to whom he accommodates and defers. The therapeutic goal in this case is to change the relative power positions of the spouses, transforming the family structure so that the man will gain status, securing more respect from his wife and achieving self-respect. To that end, the therapist affiliates with the man in the initial sessions, supporting him, and sometimes joining him in a coalition that is critical of the wife. (p. 114)

As is demonstrated in the previous quotation, taking sides through coalitions is done with the therapeutic goal clearly in mind.

Minuchin (1974) presented a number of varied therapeutic techniques to accomplish the therapeutic contract. In order to restructure the family, he believed that the therapist must accept the role of director as well as actor. In describing the role of the therapist, Minuchin stated:

> He creates scenarios, choreographs, highlights themes, and leads family members to improvise within the constraints of the family drama. But he also uses himself, entering into alliances and coalitions, creating, strengthening, or weakening boundaries, and opposing or supporting transactional patterns. (pp. 138–139)

In his text, Minuchin (1974) listed seven categories of "restructuring operations." Many of those operations are further described in Minuchin and Fishman (1981). They are listed and briefly defined in the "Specialized Techniques" section of this chapter.

His therapeutic method makes full use of the therapeutic relationship within the family context. Unlike the views of other theorists, the therapist is not looked at as outside the family looking in and attempting to create change. Rather, Minuchin's view is much more like the therapist engulfing himself or herself in the family patterns to affect change simultaneously from the inside and outside; that is, the therapist is viewed as an outside expert, yet the intent of Structural Family Therapy is for the therapist to enter the structure of the family and "to join" the family members, while holding an important place *within* the family. (See the definition of "joining" in the section Assessment, which follows.)

## Goals of Counseling and Ideal Outcomes

Minuchin (1974) defined a dysfunctional family as a system that has responded to "internal or external demands for change by stereotyping its functioning" (p. 110). He believed that structure in maladaptive families becomes so rigid that it blocks any possible alternative (healthy) transactional pattern. Often, there is involvement of an identified patient (IP; an individual in the family), and, in fact, the IP may have been treated by a mental health professional individually for expressed concerns. Given an identified patient with the possibility or likelihood of family involvement, or given a dysfunctional family as a presented problem, the family therapist's function is to help the identified patient and/or the family by facilitating a transformation of the family.

Colapinto (1982) defined the goals of the Structural Family Therapy as follows:

> The basic goal of structural family therapy is the restructuralization of the family's system of transactional rules, such that the interactional reality of the family becomes more flexible, with an expanded availability of alternative ways of dealing with each other. By releasing family members from their stereotyped positions and functions, this restructuralization enables the system to mobilize its underutilized resources and to improve its ability to cope with stress and conflict. (p. 122)

One of the main tasks of the therapist is to affect the structural homeostasis of the family that has supported the unwanted or symptomatic behaviors. Once the family organization and structure does not support unwanted behaviors, and once the family demonstrates its ability to sustain its changes in the face of family stressors, then therapy is no longer needed.

# GENERAL PROCEDURES

## Assessment

Assessment and the "planning" processes described by Minuchin and Fishman (1981) appear to go hand in hand. Planning, according to Minuchin and Fishman, is not a static process. They believed that the governing structure of the family only becomes known to the therapist as he or she "joins" the family, which takes time. *"Joining" is a term used by Minuchin to reflect the therapeutic alliance, that set of interpersonal factors that allows collaboration in defining the goals of treatment and the methods to be used to achieve therapeutic goals.* In Minuchin's most recent book on this approach, *The Craft of Family Therapy* (Minuchin, Reiter, & Borda, 2014), joining holds a high place in the theoretically derived clinical repertoire of the structural family therapist. Therefore, the therapist develops some preliminary hypotheses about the family, which he or she must be willing to discard as he or she becomes accommodated by the family. Minuchin and Fishman stated:

> The therapist forms an idea of the family as a whole upon first examination of certain basic aspects of its structure. From the simplest information gathered on a phone call setting up the first appointment, or recorded on a clinic intake sheet, the therapist can develop some assumptions about the family. For instance, how many people are in the family and where do they live? What are the ages of the family members? Is one of the normal transitional points that stress every family a factor here? The presenting problem may be another clue that suggests areas of possible strength and weakness in each client family. From these simple elements, the therapist will develop some hunches about the family to guide her first probes into the family organization. (p. 51)

Minuchin and Fishman (1981) described several "family shapes" that they felt were "commonly encountered" in therapy and helpful for beginning therapists to know, including "the pas de deux, three generation, shoe, accordion, fluctuating, and foster" (p. 51). The "pas de deux" structure is simply a dyadic family—husband and wife, parent and child, and so on—where there is great reliance on each other. The "three generation" family involves grandparents. "Shoe" families, named by the parable of the "old woman who lived in a shoe," are large, many-children families, in which often elder children carry some parental responsibility. "Accordion" families are those where the absence of one parent is common, for instance, military families, or families of a traveling salesperson. Accordion families must be able to change rules and structures around the presence or absence of the often-absent parent. "Fluctuating" families are characterized by shifting contexts (frequent geographic moves) or shifting composition (the serial love affairs of a parent). Fluctuating families must be able to adjust to almost continuous change and stress. "Foster" families are by definition temporary living arrangements for children. Minuchin and Fishman defined several other family structures, including stepparent families; families with a ghost (a death or desertion); out-of-control families (where the control of at least one family member is an issue); and psychosomatic families (where one member demonstrates nonorganic physical symptoms). Minuchin et al. have explored and given detailed guidance on treating many of these family types. For instance, Minuchin, Rosman, and Baker (1978) presented the results of detailed studies of psychosomatic families and provided useful information about how such families should be approached in therapy.

# Treatment/Remediation

Treatment is a process of challenging "the dysfunctional aspects of family homeostasis" (Minuchin & Fishman, 1981, p. 64). There are three main treatment "strategies" according to Structural Family Therapy. They are: (a) challenging the symptom; (b) challenging the family structure; and (c) challenging the family reality (Minuchin & Fishman, 1981). Each is briefly described as follows.

1.  Challenging the symptom is a means of influencing the family interactional patterns that have emerged around symptomatic behaviors. In fact, Structural Family Therapy has been developed around identified patients, usually children, and it is best applied in circumstances where there is an identified child patient. Remembering that "the problem is not the identified patient, but certain family interactional patterns" (Minuchin & Fishman, 1981, p. 67), symptoms can be used as a means to affect family functioning. Symptoms are viewed as a *family's response* to stress, and it is necessary to assess the interactional patterns around the symptom, and then to challenge the meanings associated with those patterns and the patterns themselves. The focus around a symptom, then, is dualistic—the symptom is viewed as representative of family dysfunction under stress, while at the same time the family's roles and operational organization around the symptom must be viewed. The targets, however, are the organization and roles operating around the symptom, and the therapist must challenge those roles and the family organization. For example, with a misbehaving and symptomatic child, the father might have taken the authority role and the mother the protective role; the therapist might attempt to realign those roles so that the parents are in an egalitarian authoritative relationship over the child, where decisions are overtly expressed as shared parental decisions. In this way, the organization of the family is altered around the symptomatic behavior of the child.

2.  Challenging the family structure often involves the strengthening or weakening of subsystem boundaries. For example, an overinvolved father and teenage daughter might be distanced through therapy, as the mother–daughter subsystem is strengthened. Or a parent–eldest child coalition may be weakened as the sibling subsystem is strengthened. Weakening or strengthening such boundaries involves rule setting and communication. Minuchin and Fishman (1981) stated:

    > By challenging the rules that constrain people's experience, the therapist actualizes submerged aspects of their repertoire. As a result, the family members perceive themselves and one another as functioning in a different way. The modification of context produces a change in experience. (p. 71)

    By changing the contexts of interactions, it is assumed that individual behavior will change.

3.  Challenging the family reality is essentially a means to construct a new meaning system, primarily by reframing current behaviors, interactions, or family organizational patterns. Minuchin and Fishman (1981) stated:

    > The therapist takes the data that the family offers and reorganizes it. The conflictual and stereotyped reality of the family is given a new framing. As the family members experience themselves and one another differently, new possibilities appear. (p. 71)

For example, with an anorexic patient, refusal to eat when commanded by her parents may be redefined as a sign that she is "strong enough to defeat both parents" (Minuchin & Fishman, 1981, p. 72), which thereby demonstrates a structural reversal of parent–child authority. Reframes, such as these, can produce a "startled new look at reality," according to the authors.

## Case Management

During the initial sessions the therapist essentially does "interactional diagnosis" (Minuchin, 1974). On understanding the identified problem within its relational context, Minuchin believes a "therapeutic contract" must be entered. Minuchin believed that, like diagnosis, the therapeutic contract evolves over time in therapy; it need not be a formal written thing, although Minuchin felt that it was necessary for treatment. In that sense, the therapeutic contract is an expressed consensus among family members about the nature of the problems and the goals of treatment.

Sessions can be arranged weekly, or more or less frequently as needed. Minuchin believes that videotaping is useful to beginner students (Minuchin & Fishman, 1981). Case recording should reflect the therapist's early hypotheses about the family structure and ongoing reassessments of structural factors affecting behavior. Interventions should be recorded in case notes, and case notes should reflect the structural emphasis. Results of interventions should be assessed in terms of structural changes in the family and resolution of symptomatic/unwanted behaviors.

## Specialized Techniques

1. *Actualizing family transactional patterns.* There are basically two purposes to actualizing family transactional patterns. First, Minuchin and Fishman (1981) described "enactment" as a special means of actualizing a transactional pattern. **Enactment is simply a therapist's request for the family to demonstrate a problem** within the therapeutic context, for example, asking family members of an anorexic to demonstrate what happens at dinner. Minuchin and Fishman (1981) stated:

   The therapist constructs an interpersonal scenario in the session in which dysfunctional transactions among family members are played out. This transaction occurs in the context of the session, in the present, and in relation to the therapist. While facilitating this transaction, the therapist is in a position to observe the family members' verbal and nonverbal ways of signaling to each other and monitoring the range of tolerable transactions. (p. 79)

   By facilitating enactments, the therapist provides an opportunity for the family's modes of operation to reveal themselves. Second, enactments essentially ensure that the family members are capable of performing the activities prescribed in the therapeutic contract. The therapist finds "considerable value in making the family enact instead of describe" (Minuchin, 1974, p. 141) functional behavior in the family context. The therapist may ask them to demonstrate what they can do "right" or to open communication channels by directing family members to address each other. The therapist may also move family members around physically, as space is a metaphor for closeness or distance in relationships. The important point here is to ensure that the family can do what it is supposed to do.

2. ***Marking boundaries or boundary making.*** Minuchin strived for a healthy balance between *enmeshment* (lack of subsystem differentiation that discourages individual autonomy) and *disengagement* (inappropriately rigid boundaries that prevent inter-subsystem stress crossover) in families. From the standpoint of the individual in a family, enmeshment translates to interdependency, whereas disengagement translates to autonomy at the expense of family involvement. In enmeshed families, rules must be clearly defined so that inappropriate crossover of roles is avoided. In disengaged families, new rules must be defined that present opportunity for effective interaction across otherwise impervious bounds. Essentially, **marking boundaries involves both: (a) establishing an amount of "psychological distance" between people and (b) affecting the duration of interactions between people (Minuchin & Fishman, 1981).**

3. ***Escalating stress.*** As was mentioned earlier, Minuchin (1974) believed that stress was a necessary concomitant to change. To create stress within the therapeutic context he uses techniques, such as blocking transactional patterns (to "dam the flow" in certain communication channels), emphasizing differences or highlighting disagreements, bringing forth hidden conflicts, or forming therapeutic coalitions. "Unbalancing," a specialized way of forming a therapeutic coalition, is a classic stress-producing technique. Minuchin and Fishman (1981) described unbalancing (as compared to boundary making) as follows:

> In boundary making techniques the therapist aims at changing family subsystem membership, or at changing the distance between subsystems. In unbalancing, by contrast, the therapist's goal is to change the hierarchical relationship of the members of a subsystem. (p. 161)

    **By aligning with one member of the family, for example, the therapist may affect the power hierarchy, thereby unbalancing the family homeostasis, and consequently the structure of the family.** Unbalancing has a stress-producing effect, but with a positive structural outcome.

4. ***Assigning tasks.*** Tasks may be assigned as part of the session or as homework in order "to create a framework within which the family members must function" (p. 150). However, Minuchin prefers to have families perform tasks as part of therapy. He prefers not to assign homework tasks to be accomplished outside of the therapeutic session. From Minuchin's perspective, restructuring occurs best when it occurs within the context of the therapeutic system.

5. ***Using symptoms.*** When it is evident that the family members are unable to make a therapeutic contract that focuses on anything other than the symptoms (of the identified patient or family as a whole), using symptoms becomes a reasonable therapeutic approach. **Symptoms can be made to be burdens, exacerbated within the therapeutic context, deemphasized, relabeled within a relational context, used to help parents become educators, or downplayed while other more manageable symptoms become the focus; in each case, the symptoms have been the focus of treatment and are used to change the family structure.**

6. ***Manipulating mood.*** The therapist may choose to raise or lower the level and/or type of mood in the family in order to trigger deviation counteractive forces or to model appropriate mood. Highly skilled and masterful therapists have been ob-

served to "manipulate mood" during sessions, whereas beginning therapists may be unable to operate on the unique plain that is required to apply this technique. In effect, a counselor by intent lifts or lightens his or her own mood to affect the interaction with a client (e.g., with a sad or a depressed client). Or a counselor may intentionally flatten his or her affect to mute the behavior of a highly active or emotionally agitated client. And the mood manipulation occurs while the therapist is simultaneously implementing other techniques.

7. *Support, education, and guidance.* The therapist takes on an executive function as a model or educator. This may work when parents are in need of direct guidance about what is behaviorally expected of them. Across all therapies, the importance of educating about appropriate or wanted behavior cannot be understated, as some clients may not know how to act in a healthy way and may need direct instruction on such.

In *Family Therapy Techniques,* Minuchin and Fishman (1981) defined several other techniques that are useful in family therapy, including: focus (zeroing in on therapeutically relevant data); intensity (techniques for increasing the affective component of interpersonal interactions); complementarity (demonstrating the interdependency of family members); constructions (changing the mental schema from which the family operates); paradoxes (directives that place clients in therapeutic double binds); and reframing (redefining behavior according to the therapeutic as opposed to the problematic reality). All of these techniques derive from a philosophy where relational context is the primary focus of study and treatment.

## Recent Developments or Criticisms

Minuchin's Structural Family Therapy has emerged as a major player among the predominant family counseling theories. Minuchin, in addition to delineating his model in detail related to both therapy and technique, followed a research agenda. His research results strongly support the effectiveness of Structural Family Therapy. His most comprehensive research project was reported in the book entitled *Psychosomatic Families: Anorexia Nervosa in Context* (Minuchin, Rosman, & Baker, 1978). In that book, Minuchin and his associates reported success rates with anorexics of 85.6%, which compares quite favorably to other studies of treatment of anorexics. Minuchin et al. cited the results of other research studies using other combined or individual therapies—success rates were in the 70% range. However, the Minuchin et al. study did not have a control group design, so the internal validity of the results is questionable. Regardless, the findings strongly support the use of family therapy along with medical methods in the treatment of anorexia. Minuchin published other works involving psychosomatic disorders, also showing the effectiveness of family therapy; but, unfortunately as of the mid-1980s, there were no known independent studies replicating the results (Gurman, Kniskern, & Pinsof, 1986).

Related to concerns about Structural Family Therapy, one of the major criticisms of Minuchin's approach is that it is not significantly different from the approaches of the communication family theories, specifically Haley's (1963, 1973, 1976) Strategic Problem Solving Therapy. It can be argued that Minuchin's "structure" ultimately reduces to communication (e.g., rules), which is more directly what the communication family theorists target in therapy. Minuchin has countered that structure is the operating dynamic in symptom manifestation, and he has argued against any approach that simply targets the symptom as the problem.

On the issue of taking sides or forming coalitions to unbalance the family system, Minuchin's (1974) Structural Family Therapy is clearly different than other systemically oriented family therapies. Notably, Minuchin's position is different from Haley's (1976) position about maintaining balance by avoiding extended coalitions. Minuchin's position is also inconsistent with the ideas of Satir (1967), another seminal systemic therapist. Minuchin's therapeutic coalition may be viewed as a hidden agenda by some theorists. It assumes that the therapist knows what is best for the family. It does not appear to be a mutual counselor–client activity. Regardless, the use of therapeutic coalitions demonstrates Minuchin's emphasis on the structure as a primary focus in therapy.

Minuchin's Structural Family Therapy can also be viewed as sexist, if it supports patriarchal attitudes about the power hierarchy in families. In a sense, his approach assumes that the therapist knows best what should occur structurally within a cultural context. This position is antithetical to the more egalitarian feminist stand, where power is viewed as ideally shared between men and women, regardless of cultural context.

Therefore, although Structural Family Therapy is a well-recognized and respected family counseling theory, it is not unaffected by criticism by theorists in the mental health field.

At the end of his career, Minuchin began to do much more social advocacy than therapy, although his 2014 book with Reiter and Borda in many ways restates the basic propositions of his classic approach.

## STUDENT–MENTOR DIALOGUE

**Student:**  I get that Minuchin's approach is relational, but it seems ironic that the way he looks at families is so structural. It almost seems like he makes relationships solid. I thought relationships were more like a process than something set in stone.

**Mentor:**  You are correct in seeing the problem of using structural terms to describe a relational process. In the end, Minuchin's structure does boil down to rules and patterns of interaction. But the structural descriptions of family interactions do offer clinicians a concrete language to apply to their observations. Western cultural language favors "thing-like" descriptors, and in this sense, Minuchin's theory and approach applies a level of abstraction that engages our cultural preference for tangible objects. If terminology that invokes structure helps counselors to conceptualize a problem in a way that is manageable, it is useful. Some theoreticians would argue that you don't need to interpret systemic-relational process with structural descriptors. Critics would argue that one should just focus on the interaction—the language and pattern of flow between and among individuals. They would argue that defining flow rather than structure better aligns treatment with a paradigm of relationship influence, because relationships are viewed as communication between and among people, and communication is not a one-way street with a stop-sign. Communication is multidirectional and continuous. So to some degree, even though most people would align Minuchin clearly with systemic-relational thinking, there still is a "thing-ness" about his structural interpretations.

**Student:** Minuchin must have been gutsy, because you hear stories about how he challenged families in a way that might be considered confrontational or perturbing. How can that be justified?

**Mentor:** Minuchin was a master of facilitating family discomfort in a way that relational dynamics fully emerged within the therapeutic context. He would challenge families, and in the moment of stress would "reframe" the situation so that the interpretation of the problem could be viewed more fully as relationship based (compared to medical or psychologically based). For example, getting a father to force an anorexic daughter to eat, only to create a crisis where the daughter refused to do so, led to an opportunity for Minuchin to redefine a problem from anorexia (a medical/psychological problem) to disobedience (a relationship problem). In this way, Minuchin translated a problem into interpersonal interaction, and then he treated the interaction. The problem became disobedience, not anorexia. Disobedience can be treated within the context of the father–daughter relationship. This theme emerges from much of his work—stressing the family, and then when the family is at a breaking point, reframing and treating the concern as a relationship problem. Minuchin was a master at this. And he was charming in a way that allowed him to "join" the family, essentially gaining the trust of family members and working from a strong therapeutic alliance.

**Student:** So is there something useful in accepting Minuchin's structural approach compared to other systemic-relational approaches that use less "thing-like" language?

**Mentor:** Yes. Some of his concepts, for example, "enmeshment" and "disengagement," are well respected descriptors of patterns of interaction that have been widely adopted by couples and family therapists. The terms have a structural "flavor," but they also are widely accepted and consensually defined patterns that are associated with any number of emotional problems. So Minuchin offers the field much in the way of language that may have a concrete undertone, but also is elegant at describing recurrent patterns of interaction. He was clearly observant of human interaction.

**Student:** So you see what Minuchin has to offer as valuable to the mental health professions.

**Mentor:** Oh yes. He not only gave us a language that helped us focus on interaction patterns, he also was a teacher by example. He was a great clinician, and his approach to clients offers anyone lucky enough to have observed him (in person or by recording) a lesson in the power of relationship-focused therapy as a directive, collaborative, and coherent approach to treatment. He was a major contributor to couple and family therapy and to the psychotherapeutic enterprise in general.

## CONCLUSION

Overall, Minuchin's (1974) approach is an example of a systemic-relational therapy. Structural Family Therapy focuses on relationships and relational networks. Its emphasis on recurrent patterns of interaction (structure) makes it distinct even among other systemic-relational therapies. Change is primarily instigated from outside the family, but the therapist has the unique opportunity to enter the family and to interact in a way that can significantly influence the internal workings of the family. The therapist, an expert of relationships, imposes a systemic-relational agenda on the family, which has been shown to be effective in diminishing symptoms.

## REFERENCES

Colapinto, J. (1982). Structural family therapy. In A. Horne & M. M. Ohlsen (Eds.), *Family counseling and therapy* (pp. 112–140). Itasca, IL: F. E. Peacock. Excerpts © 2000 South-Western, a part of Cengage Learning, reproduced by permission of Cengage Learning.

Gurman, A. S., Kniskern, D. P., & Pinsof, W. M. (1986). Research on the process and outcome of marital and family therapy. In S. L. Garfield & A. E. Bergin (Eds.), *Handbook of psychotherapy and behavior change* (pp. 565–624). New York, NY: Wiley.

Haley, J. (1963). *Strategies of psychotherapy.* New York, NY: Grune & Stratton.

Haley, J. (1973). *Uncommon therapy.* New York, NY: W. W. Norton.

Haley, J. (1976). *Problem solving therapy.* New York, NY: Harper & Row.

Minuchin, S. (1974). *Families and family therapy.* Cambridge, MA: Harvard University Press.

Minuchin, S. (1984). *Family kaleidoscope.* Cambridge, MA: Harvard University Press.

Minuchin, S., & Fishman, H. C. (1981). *Family therapy techniques.* Cambridge, MA: Harvard University Press. Excerpts reproduced by permission of the President and Fellows of Harvard College.

Minuchin, S., Reiter, M. D., & Borda, C. (2014). *The craft of family therapy: Challenging certainties.* New York, NY: Routledge.

Minuchin, S., Rosman, B. L., & Baker, L. (1978). *Psychosomatic families: Anorexia nervosa in context.* Cambridge, MA: Harvard University Press. Excerpts reproduced by permission of the President and Fellows of Harvard College.

Satir, V. (1967). *Conjoint family therapy.* Palo Alto, CA: Science and Behavior Books.

# PART IV

# Social Constructivism Paradigm Approaches

This part of the book is devoted to three counseling theories that reflect the development of the social constructivism paradigm of counseling and psychotherapy. *Social constructivism* **is an intellectual movement in the humanities, arts, and science that purports that relationships are crucial to understanding and establishing truths.** Truths are socially constructed, meaning that people come together and share experiences to develop their understanding of those experiences. Both Solution-Focused Brief Therapy (Chapter 12) and Narrative Therapy (Chapter 13) are excellent examples of approaches that have broken new ground and are aligning with the unique philosophy that social constructivist thought represents. Chapter 14 provides a model theory built on the most radical form of social consructivism; that chapter presents Cognitive Consensual Therapy. All of these approaches propose that truths are socially constructed. Counseling is a negotiation of socially constructed truths--some may be health enhancing and others may be problematic for clients.

# CHAPTER

## 12

# Solution-Focused Brief Therapy: Breaking New Ground

## OBJECTIVES

- To introduce an approach that is unique to counseling theory, based on its focus on solutions rather than problems

- To give an example of a model that is based on social constructivism philosophy

- To provide a brief historical introduction to the theory and its founders

- To provide guidance on methods, techniques, and the process of counseling

- To summarize recent research and outcome study findings on this contemporary model

Solution-Focused Brief Therapy (SFBT) represents a significant break with the underlying philosophy at the core of traditional psychologically oriented psychotherapy approaches. It also represents a unique philosophy that extends beyond that of classic social systems theory, which is at the base of the classic family therapy approaches. SFBT has been identified as a "constructivist" therapy by its founders Insoo Kim Berg and Steve de Shazer (Berg, 1993; de Shazer, 1985; see also Guterman's [2006] analysis). **Social constructivism is an intellectual movement in the mental health field that directs attention to the shared experience as a foundation for understanding—truths are defined through "communities of understanding"** (Cottone, 2012). This contrasts to the idea that truths are objective (knowable the same way by all people) or subjective (knowable to each individual as his or her own truth). Socially constructed truths are consensualized truths. SFBT purports that problems and solutions are not necessarily connected. The counselor and the client, rather than focusing on problems, collaboratively and socially construct solutions—behaviors, thoughts, and feelings that are identified with the nonproblem.

SFBT is unique in its focus on solutions to problems, and not the problems themselves. The solution-focused brief therapist is more concerned with the client's behavior when the client is not having problems—exceptions to problem behaviors. The focus of SFBT is to expand on, or to focus on, the good things happening in a client's life, or more specifically, the absence of symptoms or problems. The SFBT approach requires counselors to retrain their focus to those situations that represent times and circumstances when the problem does not pose a serious concern for clients. All clients have moments when they are symptom or problem free, and it is the circumstance and context of those moments that becomes the target for treatment of SFBT. It is all about what works, not what is broken. For example, if the goal of treatment is for a client to stop drinking, the solution-focused brief therapist would be very interested (a) in those times when the client does not drink; (b) in times when the client has resisted drinking; and (c) in those moments when the client has been sober; the focus would be on the behaviors, circumstances, and strategies of the client that are successful in maintaining sobriety.

SFBT was founded by Steve de Shazer (1982, 1985, 1994) and Insoo Kim Berg (1993). They together founded the Brief Family Therapy Center (BFTC) in Milwaukee in 1978, and soon after, they began to publish their ideas about SFBT. de Shazer is credited with publishing the first book on SFBT (de Shazer, 1982). In his 1982 book, de Shazer described a very directive therapy that theoretically built on the works of the theorists at the Mental Research Institute (MRI) in Palo Alto, California. That style of therapy was influenced by the famous hypnotherapist, Milton Erickson; it was very directive and initially was problem focused. In the 1982 work, de Shazer, however, began to manifest a theoretical transition to a focus on nonproblem behavior. He wrote:

> Simply the fingerprint involves transforming through reframing at least some aspect of the complaint from an involuntary, painful part of life into a deliberate, more useful part of life. The reframing changes the entire meaning of the person's situation, and a behavior change will follow. (p. 96)

The quote demonstrates his evolution from a problem-focused therapist in the mold of the MRI, to a more solution-focused practitioner. By 1994, he was "constructing stories of success" (p. 156) and was addressing something other than problem behaviors.

The Solution-Focused Brief Therapy Association (SFBTA) was founded by de Shazer, Berg, and a number of their colleagues in 2002. After the passing of Berg in 2007, the materials from their renowned clinic in Milwaukee, Wisconsin, the BFTC (which closed its doors soon after Berg died in 2007), were gifted to the SFBTA.

# STEVE DE SHAZER AND INSOO KIM BERG: BIOGRAPHICAL SKETCHES

Steve de Shazer was born on June 25, 1940. He was trained as a classical musician and played the saxophone. He earned a bachelor of fine arts degree, and later a master's degree in social work (MSSW), both at the University of Wisconsin in Milwaukee. He was a friend of John Weakland, a renowned theoretician who worked at the MRI in California, an institute that carried on the work started by Gregory Bateson and the group of researchers involved in a famous study of schizophrenia—the "double bind" study (a ***double bind* is a no-win situation in the context of relationships**). The "double bind" study in the 1950s implicated relationships as primary factors in the manifestation of mental illness. Much of de Shazer's early work was focused on the techniques embraced by the MRI, including paradoxical directives and the unique approach of the masterful hypnotherapist, Milton Erickson. In his 1985 book *Keys to Solution in Brief Therapy*, which is a defining text on SFBT, he infused ideas and techniques from the practice of Ericksonian hypnosis (the crystal ball technique and the confusion technique) with what can now be defined as more classic solution-focused techniques (see the "Specialized Techniques" section of this chapter). de Shazer married Insoo Kim Berg, who was a student of Weakland, and together Berg and de Shazer founded the BFTC in Milwaukee in 1978. At the BFTC they developed their ideas about SFBT. de Shazer died on September 11, 2005, in Vienna, Austria.

Insoo Kim Berg was born on July 25, 1934. She was trained as a pharmacist in Korea, and furthered her pharmacy studies in the United States at the University of Wisconsin—Milwaukee. She also earned a master of science in social work from the university, which in effect changed her career path. As a social worker, she began to focus

Steve de Shazer and Insoo Kim Berg
*Source*: Solution-Focused Brief Therapy Association.

on psychotherapy, and she studied at a number of centers to develop her skills, including the Menninger Foundation and the MRI, renowned for its focus on brief therapy and family therapy. At the MRI, she was mentored by John Weakland, known as one of the authors of the famous "double bind" paper ("Toward a Theory of Schizophrenia") coauthored by Gregory Bateson, Don Jackson, and Jay Haley (Bateson, Jackson, Haley & Weakland, 1956). That paper is considered foundational to the systemic-relational paradigm of mental health services. Weakland, and the MRI, had a profound influence on her ideas about psychotherapy, and the systemic view and focus on interaction in treatment significantly affected her approach to treatment. Berg met her second husband, Steve de Shazer, while at the MRI; de Shazer was a friend of Weakland's. She had one child, Sarah Berg, with her first husband, Charles Berg. She died on January 10, 2007 in Milwaukee.

# THE FOUNDATIONAL THEORY

## The Target of Counseling

An underlying philosophical tenet of SFBT is that change is inevitable—a constant of sorts (Berg, 1993; de Shazer, 1985). This, in effect, provides a positive outlook for treatment, as clients come to counseling with problems, and if change is inevitable, then improvement is possible. In effect, the targets for intervention are client resources. This is a resource model. The key to treatment is to target successes, not failures. It is about uncovering hidden resources and finding coping mechanisms, exceptions to problems, and solutions (actions that have worked in the past). Ironically, the "problem" is not the target of treatment. Rather, the target becomes the identification of the nonproblem, and the "construction of solutions" (de Shazer, 1985, p. 33). Early in treatment, it is important to establish the desired outcome and to define its manifestations currently. If a person presents as depressed, then the discussion becomes what it is like when the client is not depressed. Who is around when the client is not depressed? In what context is the client not depressed? Who can bring the client out of depression? Through the collaborative therapeutic relationship, the counselor and client begin to construct a context for the nonproblem. If the client states that he or she is never happy and is chronically depressed, then the discussion turns to *coping*—identifying those moments when the client successfully manages the depression or chronic disability. The counselor might focus on degrees of depression, and identifying those moments when depression is less intense or manageable. The target for the counselor is the identification of behavior, thoughts, or feelings that are manifest when the problem is not present or when the problem is diminished to some degree. In constructing solutions, de Shazer (1985) made it clear that "exceptions to the rules of the pattern [of unwanted behavior] are exactly the kind of information the therapist needs to know" (p. 34).

## The Process of Counseling

SFBT is, as its name implies, a "brief" therapy. The brief therapy movement of the MRI in Palo Alto, California, was a source of theoretical support for the development of SFBT. Weakland's findings at the Brief Therapy Center of the MRI supported a conclusion that therapeutic success can be accomplished in a very short time—nothing like the once weekly sessions for several years of the traditional analytic approaches.

de Shazer cited Weakland, Fisch, Watzlawick, and Bodin's (1974) findings that "72% of their cases either met their goal for treatment or made significant improvement with an average of seven sessions" (de Shazer, 1985, p. 4). Follow-up studies at the BFTC confirmed these findings (de Shazer, 1985) and also confirmed the enduring change experienced by clients. de Shazer argued that the changes were enduring and not just "palliative." de Shazer stated, "The quicker the problem is solved, the better" (p. 5).

SFBT can be done with individuals, couples, or families. It begins with the client being greeted by the counselor. For individual counseling, the counselor first asks what brought the client to treatment. Once the client has described a reason or reasons for attending counseling, the counselor focuses on the goals of treatment. de Shazer stated:

> I have found the idea that only a small change is necessary, and therefore only a small and reasonable goal is necessary, makes it far easier to develop a cooperative relationship between the therapist and client. One major difference between brief therapy and other models lies in the brief therapist's idea that no matter how awful and how complex the situation, a small change in one person's behavior can make profound and far-reaching differences in the behavior of all persons involved. Both clinical experience and research seem to confirm the idea that a small change can lead to other changes and, therefore, further improvement. Furthermore, it seems that the bigger the goal or the desired change, the more likely therapist and client will fail. (pp. 16–17)

SFBT seeks to start with "baby steps." It seeks to get some positive change, no matter how small, and to build on the foundation of even the smallest change to enhance healthy behavior.

When treating couples or families, the counselor might focus on differences of opinion around a problem, defining one person's perspective as illuminating of the nonproblem, and building on that perspective. Berg (1993) described a case where a husband left his wife 33 times. Her interest was not in his leaving, but in his return. That meant that he was attracted to his wife 34 times. The focus then becomes what factors were involved in the attraction, engagement, or reengagement. What did the wife do differently during those times of reengagement? What did the husband do differently leading up to the return? No matter how small the change in behavior, it is acknowledged and addressed and it becomes a focus of treatment. If a child is misbehaving within the context of family interaction, the question becomes, in what circumstances does the child show nonproblematic behavior, or even "good" behavior? Even misbehaving children have moments of calm or cooperation.

So counseling begins by addressing problems momentarily, and only as a means to begin to focus on the absence of the problem. Brief therapy, as a general rule, is typically 10 or less sessions. de Shazer (1985) stated:

> It has always seemed to me that if the average length of treatment is six to ten sessions, then I (or any other therapist) am ethically compelled to make the most use possible of that limited contact. As six to ten sessions is all that can be expected, then the model needs to be built on that reality. (p. 5)

So SFBT gets right to the point of redirecting clients to successes rather than failures.

## Counselor Role

The counselor role is that of a collaborator, a facilitator, and a questioner. The counselor acknowledges that the client knows his or her situation better than anyone, and the counselor is mindful of what the client brings to treatment, almost at face value. In other words, there is no reframing of a presenting problem as an internal psychological problem. Depression is not viewed as a mental disorder, for example; rather, it is viewed as a set of behaviors within a social context. Context is crucial to defining the problem and the solution. The client's frame of reference is acknowledged and accepted as a means to begin the focusing or refocusing process to healthy alternative behavior. The context of therapy is about the solution side of the problem–solution formula. Clients present with problems, yet the solution-focused brief therapist is there to facilitate a discussion of the context when the problem is not present or is diminished. The skillful solution-focused brief therapist does this in a tactful and positive way—it should not be a tense or adversarial process. It is about engaging with the client in a positive way and keeping a positive focus. The underlying philosophy that change is inevitable is a pillar of support for the therapist; it requires the counselor to be positive in establishing both a collaborative relationship with clients and a consensus about what outcomes are desired by clients.

## Goals of Counseling and Ideal Outcomes

The goal of SFBT is the replacement of symptomatic or problem behaviors with functional and wanted healthy behaviors. It is about moving past problems to solutions. The client is encouraged to build on past successful behaviors. If the client is unable to describe or identify exceptions to problems, the focus becomes coping mechanisms. The intent of SFBT is to use the client's repertoire of existing healthy behaviors, or to help the client to develop some alternatives to dysfunctional behavior. Ideally, little changes in the healthy direction act like the *ripple effect* in expanding the client's inventory of healthy options. The ultimate goal of treatment is to increase the client's focus on healthy thinking, feeling, and behaving to the degree that the client becomes satisfactorily functional within some personal or professional context.

# GENERAL PROCEDURES

## Questions as a Means to Probe for Solutions

Berg (1993) presented five different solution-focused questions that can help provide the therapist with a means for initiating treatment and interacting with clients. Each of the five types of questions is resource focused rather than problem focused.

Type 1. Pre-session change question. The counselor asks about the activities between setting the appointment and attendance at the first session. The intent of the question is to address any improvements over that period of time. "Has anything improved since you made the appointment?" "Has there been any change since the appointment was set?" It assumes that there has been a flurry of activities before the initial session, and the counselor is essentially probing for any communication from the client that something positive has happened.

Type 2. The "Miracle Question." Berg is credited with formulating this question (DeJong & Berg, 2008). The question is: "Suppose a miracle happened and the problem is solved . . . what would be different?" The intention is to have the client interact with the counselor describing what the situation looks like in the absence of the problem—assuming the problem has magically disappeared. How would the client behave differently? How would the client know the problem was solved? What would the client do in the absence of the problem? What changes would be noticed? The focus, therefore, becomes the vision of life without the burden of the problem.

Type 3. The exception finding question. This type of question is perhaps the most representative of the solution-focused approach. The exception finding question may be posed in a number of ways. The goal is to identify situations, behaviors, thoughts, or emotions that are active when the problem is inactive. To an alcoholic wanting to be sober, the question may be: "Where is the place where you find you do not drink and do not feel the need to drink?" Or to an anxious person, "Who calms you?" or, "When during the day are you typically not anxious?" For a woman complaining about anger toward her husband, a question might be: "What do you think at those moments when you are not angry at your husband?" The exception finding question searches for times and contexts that represent the absence of the problem.

Type 4. The scaling question. The scaling question typically involves description of a scale, usually from 1 to 10, that addresses commitment to solutions or degrees of symptomatology or distress. For example, if someone is fearful of a situation, the counselor might ask the client to place the fear on a scale of 1 (no fear) to 10 (intense fear) in a situation defined as a problem for the client. Once a number is defined, the scaling question is then followed by a second question, such as, "What would it take for you to move from that level of fear to one level lower on the fear scale?" Another example is: "How committed are you on a scale of 1 to 10 to solving your problem?" and then "What would have to happen for you to move up one place on the commitment scale?" The question can be asked about other people in a client's life; for example, asking a client, "How committed do you feel your spouse is to addressing your problem?" followed by "How would you know your spouse was more committed to solving your problem?"

Type 5. Coping questions. Coping questions are designed to address people in difficult situations that appear to have no exceptions, such as chronic debilitating illness or disease. It also can be applied to clients who are unable to identify any exceptions to their problem. The coping question is straightforward. "How is it that you cope with your problem?" It can be modified slightly in the following form: "What are you doing [feeling/thinking] when you are most able to cope with or accept your situation?" The idea behind the coping question is to help the client recognize that in his or her situation, there are means of managing, surviving, or dealing with the problem. The client is assisted in understanding that there are degrees of pain, discomfort, or dysfunction. Focusing on the most functional moments at a time when all seems hopeless is the intent of this technique.

These five types of questions are core to SFBT. The counseling process may largely involve the counselor asking these types of questions. Problems may be approached with just one type of question, or they may be explored though a number of lines of questioning. Skilled solution-focused brief therapists appear to be unrelenting in their use of these questions. They approach problems from any number of contexts, defining specific circumstances and times that provide a vision or model of the nonproblem.

## Specialized Techniques

A few of the techniques outlined by de Shazer (1985) as his "skeleton keys" are presented as follows.

### "DO SOMETHING DIFFERENT"

de Shazer described this technique as follows:

> Between now and the next time we meet . . . do something different . . . no matter how strange or weird or off-the-wall what you do might seem. The only important thing is that whatever you decide to do, you need to, do something different. (p. 123)

de Shazer believed that small changes in response to the generalized directive of the "do something different" command can prompt solutions. Clients may already perform a number of behaviors that may constitute the basis for solution to their problems. But if they do not have a repertoire of positive behaviors, thoughts, or feelings, the "do something different" directive may facilitate a new behavior, or a set of behaviors, that may be more functional than the dysfunctional behaviors that brought the client to treatment.

### "PAY ATTENTION TO WHAT YOU DO WHEN YOU OVERCOME THE URGE TO"

de Shazer described this as a technique to help with clients who act depressed, overeat, yell at a spouse, get drunk, and so on. Although problem conditions may exist, the intent of this technique is to find a set of conditions when the behavior does not happen. Because the behavior is already part of the client's repertoire of behaviors, it will appear to fit the therapeutic circumstance and provides clear examples of exceptions to the problem. The idea behind this approach is to help the client become observant of circumstances that allow an unhealthy urge to pass. Some feeling, thought, or behavior might act as a resource when there are temptations to behave in unhealthy ways.

### "THE FIRST SESSION FORMULA TASK"

The first session formula task starts with a question by the therapist. The question is described by de Shazer, and takes a form similar to the following: "Between now and our next session, I would like you to observe so you can describe what happens that you want to continue to happen." The idea behind this intervention is to get the client and the counselor to the same positive place—to set expectations not just about problems, but about good things that happen in the client's life. It is an affirmative command—it does not imply an "if" about wanted happenings. Rather, it implicitly communicates that something is likely to happen that is valuable to the client. Things are happening all around a client, and the intent of this technique is to get the client to focus on the positive and valuable situations or interactions in the client's life or sphere of activity.

## Recent Developments or Criticisms

There have been a number of publications summarizing the research on SFBT. In 2000, Gingerich and Eisengart published a review of the outcome research on SFBT. They summarized their findings as follows:

> All five of the well-controlled studies reported significant benefit from SFBT— four . . . found SFBT to be significantly better than no treatment or standard

institutional services. Since these studies did not compare SFBT with another psychotherapeutic intervention, we are not able to conclude that the observed outcomes were due *specifically* to the SFBT intervention as opposed to general attention effects. The other well-controlled study . . . compared SFBT with a known treatment (IPT) and found SFBT produced equivalent outcomes (no significant differences were found). Since none of the five studies met all of the stringent criteria for efficacy studies, and all five studied different populations (that is, there were no replications by independent investigators), we cannot conclude that SFBT has been shown to be efficacious. We do, however, believe that these five studies provide initial support for the efficacy of SFBT. The remaining ten studies contain methodological limitations that preclude drawing firm conclusions, but we note that their findings are consistent with the general conclusion of SFBT effectiveness. One of those studies . . . suggests that SFBT may be an efficient intervention (that is, successful outcome can be achieved with minimal intervention). (p. 493)

In effect, the studies up until the review were supportive, but not in any way conclusive about the efficiency and validity of SFBT as an effective psychotherapy.

In 2008, Knekt et al. published a "Randomized Trial on the Effectiveness of Long- and Short-Term Psychodynamic Psychotherapy and Solution-Focused Therapy on Psychiatric Symptoms During a 3-year Follow-Up" (p. 689). They concluded:

Short-term therapies produce benefits more quickly than long-term psychodynamic psychotherapy but in the long run long-term psychodynamic psychotherapy is superior to short-term therapies. However, more research is needed to determine which patients should be given long-term psychotherapy for the treatment of mood or anxiety disorders. (p. 689)

This study, which addressed psychiatric symptoms measured by a number of standard brief assessment instruments, was not overwhelmingly supportive, although the usefulness of the brief approaches in producing quick results was validated.

Also in 2008, Kim published a meta-analysis to evaluate the effectiveness of SFBT. Kim found that SFBT "demonstrated small but positive treatment effects" on outcome measures, but "only the magnitude of the effect for internalizing behavior problems" (p. 107) was significant statistically. Kim believed his study provided some definitive evidence of the effectiveness of SFBT.

A "practitioner review" of the effectiveness of solution SFBT with children and families was published by Bond, Woods, Humphrey, Symes, and Green (2013), which summarized publications from 1990 to 2010. The study addressed not only *quantitative* (empirically based research) studies, but also *qualitative* (nonempirically based research) studies. Bond et al. (2013) found:

Although much of the literature has methodological weaknesses, existing research does provide tentative support for the use of SFBT, particularly in relation to internalizing and externalizing child behavior problems. SFBT appears particularly effective as an early intervention when presenting problems are not severe. Further well-controlled outcome studies are needed. (p. 707)

Again, there was a tentative positive conclusion about the use and effectiveness of SFBT.

In 2013, Gingerich and Peterson published "A Systematic Qualitative Review of Controlled Outcome Studies" of SFBT. They concluded: "The studies reviewed provide strong evidence that SFBT is an effective treatment for a wide variety of behavioral and psychological outcomes and, in addition, it may be briefer and therefore less costly than alternative approaches" (p. 266). Furthermore, they concluded: "The strongest evidence of effectiveness came in the treatment of depression in adults where four separate studies found SFBT to be comparable to well-established alternative treatments" (p. 266). The Gingerich and Peterson conclusions were affirmative of SBFT as a viable, useful, and effective counseling theory.

Since 2000, there has been an expansion of publication and leadership in the SFBT movement. As examples, books have been published applying SFBT to the work of school counselors (e.g., Davis & Osborn, 2000; Murphy, 2015), to the treatment of anxiety (e.g., Quick, 2013), to work in end-of-life care and grief counseling (Simon, 2010), and in the treatment of domestic violence offenders (Lee, Sebold, & Uken, 2003), as well as other areas. There appears to be a "solution-focused" bandwagon of sorts, as many authors are addressing the application of this model to a myriad of mental health problems.

## STUDENT–MENTOR DIALOGUE

**Student:**  This approach seems really different than the other models we have studied. How does this approach fit with the other theories?

**Mentor:**  Well, this approach is different. In fact, it is associated with a different paradigm of mental health services—the social constructivism paradigm. That means that it doesn't assume that problems exist outside of interactions, but that problems are housed in social contexts, and therefore they can be addressed in a context of solution building. The therapist is a full partner in the collaborative effort to establish a positive frame of reference. The problem literally disappears as the counselor and client build a set of behaviors that represent the nonproblem. Behaviors, thoughts, and feelings associated with the goals of treatment are constructed and reinforced as a means to help the client establish a functional way of life.

**Student:**  How can a student of psychotherapy and a new practitioner switch gears? It seems like all or most of the other approaches focus on the problem that the client brings to treatment—the mental disorder or dysfunctional behavior. This is not the case with SFBT.

**Mentor:**  This approach is like a polar opposite to most of the organic–medical, psychological, or even some of the systemic-relational approaches, which keep the focus on the client's problems. In many cases, where counselors have been trained to be problem focused, they must unlearn that focus. This is not easy, because training programs tend to teach the traditional approaches first, and then, if SFBT is addressed at all, it is usually addressed as a newer or contemporary approach, and it may be lumped into one text chapter or one classroom lesson on a number of emerging approaches. But SFBT is now well established and has garnered some supportive research findings. It appears that it is as effective as any other model, and yet it is a brief and very positive model of treatment. The focus is distinctive and unique among the psychotherapies. It was one of the first approaches to build on social constructivism philosophy, meaning that it is socially focused and assumes that meaning comes from the interaction of the client and the therapist (and whatever they construct as solutions) rather than some pre-set outcome delineated in a theory of personality or mental health (such as a congruent self-concept or a strong and functional ego). So it holds a special place in the history of psychotherapy.

**Student:**  What do you see as problems of this approach?

**Mentor:**  I think counseling and psychotherapy students will have to change their perspective. It is hard for problem-focused counselors to ignore or to minimize "the problem." It seems alien to counselors who are new to this approach. Psychotherapies as a whole tend to be problem focused, so this contradicts the premise of most of the other theories that counselors are taught in their professional training programs. SFBT also requires close supervision, so that classically trained clinicians do not fall into the "trap" of the problem focus, and are able to focus on nonproblem behaviors and to formulate responses that facilitate solutions. Sometimes new-comers to this approach seem stifled at first, as they may have to unlearn what has been taught in beginning classes in the mental health professions.

**Student:**  Do you think this approach will survive?

**Mentor:**  I think it will survive and thrive. It is a brief therapy, and brief therapies have been embraced by third-party insurance payers for treatment of a number of problems covered by medical insurance. It appears to be an effective approach. It is positive. And it moves the mental health professions away from the established notions of what is considered mentally healthy or mentally dysfunctional. It is more accepting of the client's perspective of what can be healthy, and it thereby acknowledges the client's experience in moving the client to a different place that is valuable to the client. It is being adopted as a preferred model in any number of contexts. Berg was known to work with addictions, and she has published work on how this model can be used to address any number of addictions. It has been used in mental health contexts, schools, and private practices. It is a simple model once learned, and it is easily applied in any number of situations with any number of client problems. It can be used in individual, couple, and family therapy. It is, therefore, a flexible approach with broad applicability.

## CONCLUSION

SFBT is an example of a theory of counseling that is based on social constructivist thought. It is about the client and counselor socially constructing solutions to problems, rather than focusing on some preset or preconceived notion of a client's problem or circumstance. The relationship of the client and the counselor is collaborative. The therapist, rather than being an expert on mental health or dysfunctional behavior, is a facilitator of conversation that helps the client focus on the nonproblem. Little changes are encouraged and assumed to lead to bigger changes in client functioning. It is a positive approach, assuming that change is inevitable and that clients have resources that can be built on and expanded to act as a new foundation for improved and functional behavior, thoughts, or feelings. SFBT can be accomplished as an individual psychotherapy, as couple counseling, or as family therapy. Research is beginning to show that SFBT has great potential and is a viable, efficient, and effective approach to treating mental health issues.

## REFERENCES

Bateson, G., Jackson, D., Haley, J., & Weakland, J. (1956). Toward a theory of schizophrenia. *Behavioral Science, 1,* 251–264. doi:10.1002/bs.3830010402

Bond, C., Woods, K., Humphrey, N., Symes, W., & Green, L. (2013). Practitioner review: The effectiveness of solution focused brief therapy with children and families: A systematic and critical evaluation of the literature from 1990–2010. *Journal of Child Psychology and Psychiatry, 54,* 707–723. doi:10.1111/jcpp.12058

Berg, I. K. (1993). *IAMFC distinguished presenter series: Solution-focused Brief Therapy* [Video]. Retrieved from http://www.cmtipress.com/videos.htm

Cottone, R. R. (2012). *Paradigms of counseling and psychotherapy.* Cottleville, MO: Smashwords. Retrieved from https://www.smashwords.com/books/view/165398

Davis, T. E., & Osborn, C. J. (2000). *Solution-focused school counsellor: Shaping professional practice.* New York, NY: Bruner-Routledge.

DeJong, P., & Berg, I. K. (2008). *Interviewing for solutions* (3rd ed.). Belmont, CA: Thomson, Brooks/Cole.

de Shazer, S. (1982). *Patterns of brief family therapy. An ecosystemic approach.* New York, NY: Guilford.

de Shazer, S. (1985). *Keys to solution in brief therapy* (1st ed.). New York, NY: W. W. Norton. Excerpts used with permission from W. W. Norton & Company.

de Shazer, S. (1994): *Words were originally magic.* New York, NY: W. W. Norton.

Gingerich, W. J., & Eisengart, S. (2000). Solution-focused brief therapy: A review of the outcome research. *Family Process, 39*(4), 477–498. Excerpt republished with permission of John Wiley and Sons Inc.

Gingerich, W. J., & Peterson, L. T. (2013). Effectiveness of solution-focused brief therapy: A systematic qualitative review of controlled outcome studies. *Research on Social Work Practice, 23,* 266–283. Excerpt reprinted by Permission of SAGE Publications, Inc.

Guterman, J. T. (2006). *Mastering the art of solution-focused counseling.* Alexandria, VA: American Counseling Association.

Kim, J. (2008). Examining the effectiveness of solution-focused brief therapy: A meta-analysis. *Research on Social Work Practice, 18*, 107–126.

Knekt, P., Lindfors, O., Härkänen, T., Välikoski, M., Virtala, E., Laaksonen, M. A., . . . Helsinki Psychotherapy Study Group. (2008). Randomized trial on the effectiveness of long-and short-term psychodynamic psychotherapy and solution-focused therapy on psychiatric symptoms during a 3-year follow-up. *Psychological Medicine, 38*(5), 689–703.

Lee, M. Y., Sebold, J., & Uken, A. (2003). *Solution-focused treatment of domestic violence offenders*. Oxford, UK: Oxford University Press.

Murphy, J. J. (2015). *Solution-focused counseling in schools*. Alexandria, VA: American Counseling Association.

Quick, E. K. (2013). *Solution focused anxiety management: A treatment and training manual*. San Diego, CA: Academic Press.

Simon, J. K. (2010). *Solution focused practice in end-of-life and grief counseling*. New York, NY: Springer Publishing.

Weakland, J., Fisch, R., Watzlawick, P., & Bodin, A. (1974). Brief therapy: Focused problem resolution. *Family Process, 13*, 141–168.

# CHAPTER

## 13

# Narrative Therapy

*Ryan Thomas Neace, Christina E. Thaier, and Zachary Polk*

## OBJECTIVES

- To introduce Narrative Therapy (NT) as a theory that aligns with the social constructivism paradigm of counseling and psychotherapy

- To provide some historical context for the development of the theory and biographical sketches of Michael White and David Epston

- To describe the basic theory and define the terminology associated with this approach

- To specifically describe techniques used in NT

- To address recent developments, including the works of theoreticians who are expanding the application of this approach

- To define criticisms or concerns theoretically or practically

Since the late 20th century, many disciplines within the arts and sciences, including the field of psychotherapy, have embraced a "paradigm shift" from a modern to a postmodern worldview. Modern worldviews privilege realities and ways of knowing that are objective, universal, and certain. In contrast, a postmodern worldview understands reality and knowledge to be subjective, multiple, individual, fragmented, and co-constructed (Freedman & Combs, 1996). In postmodern thinking, there is no one way for people to understand experience; truth is socially constructed (Cottone, 2012). As such, humans living in a complex postmodern world need a means to make sense and meaning of their lives, to navigate their many available truths and choices, and to organize the fragments of their lived experiences. According to Narrative Therapy (NT), humans accomplish this through stories.

NT was developed by Australian social worker and family therapist Michael White and Canadian anthropologist/family therapist David Epston (Freedman & Combs, 1996). White and Epston were adventurous and innovative in their formation of theory, and integrated many emerging schools of thought. In their identification of "story" as the central metaphor of the theory, they emphasized the complexity in which stories are born, and, more specifically, gave direct attention to the importance of context, culture, and relationships in the formation of people's stories. As such, this chapter explores the context in which NT was born, and especially the way it was influenced by relationships with other scholars and the central ideas at the time of its inception and since.

A primary influence to NT was the work of Gregory Bateson and his illustration of the unique way in which humans make sense of the world. This approach, known as the "interpretative method," suggests that one must rely on interpretation of experience as objective reality cannot be known (Bateson, 1972; M. White & Epston, 1990, p. 2). In other words, reality is unique to each individual based on one's external influences (i.e., family, society, and culture); therefore, one's interpretation of reality is also unique. Coinciding with this belief is the narrative metaphor, a derivative of Milton Erickson's (the famous hypnotherapist) "teaching tales," that Epston encouraged White to implement into his practice. These "teaching tales" were Erickson's method of encouraging clients to expand and to enrich the stories about themselves, and to acquire a positive view from what may have once been seen as a negative experience (Erickson & Rossi, 1981; Freedman & Combs, 1996, p. 10).

Another major influence to NT was the work of French philosopher Michel Foucault and the philosophical movement known as post-structuralism. The primary foci of post-structuralism are the relationship between human beings and the world, and the practice of making and reproducing meaning within those relationships (Foucault, 1972; Madigan, 2011). This movement arose from literary theory, which asserts that meaning is not in the text, but lies in the interpretation of the reader. For example, three separate people can read the same passage from a literary work and have three different interpretations. This process can be explained through the use of *deconstruction*, a central concept originated from post-structuralist thinking that asserts that there is no fixed meaning, and it is the work of the reader to take apart the language being used and construct his or her own unique meaning (Foucault, 1972).

NT also incorporated Foucault's ideas surrounding power and discourse. Power, according to Foucault and Gordon (1980), is used to limit, deny, contain, or even disqualify individuals within a society and is responsible for shaping the lives and relationships of those individuals. Foucault declared that knowledge and power are inseparable terms. In this view, knowledge is the language used by the dominant voice of a society to implement power, and those who have acquired the power within the society control the knowledge shared by its people (Foucault, 1972; Foucault & Gordon, 1980). For example, white Europeans, who "discovered" the Americas many centuries ago, established their rule over the Native Americans who had previously established their own society, culture, and rich traditions. However, until recently, the history of the United States illustrated the Native Americans as savage and bloodthirsty animals who needed to be civilized. History is always biographical in nature, and the victors are the ones who have the power to share those histories (Freedman & Combs, 1996).

The distribution of power/knowledge in society also creates a widely agreed on "truth" to which both individual and communities of people are subjected. This "truth," or discourse, is a collaboration of ideas and intrinsic facts about the nature of people. According to Foucault (1972), discourse is conversation, and the meaning attributed to these conversations is agreed on by groups of people who hold common ideas. One's **dominant discourse** provides **a map on how one should live, think, act, and approach life in the most socially acceptable way.** Although not all individuals follow the script provided by the society, there are often negative consequences when one steps outside of these boundaries—often resulting in separation, marginalization, and oppression based on these choices or differences.

In summary, reality, truth, power, and language are constructed as a result of one's relational, cultural, and societal influences (Berger & Luckmann, 1966; Gergen, 2001), and these axioms form the central theses of NT. Furthermore, the nature of reality within the realm of NT can be described by the worldview of David Pare (1995), which stated, "the realities we inhabit are those we negotiate with one another" (p. 6).

As such, NT is a co-collaborative field of practice, where therapist and clients are empowered to share experiences and to create their own community of knowing. They work together through language to deconstruct the client's limiting or nonpreferred stories, co-research the significance of human relationships and the cultural beliefs that shape the stories they tell themselves, discover new meaning to old stories, and develop new preferred stories that reflect who they hope to become.

## MICHAEL WHITE AND DAVID EPSTON: BIOGRAPHICAL SKETCHES

Michael White was born in Adelaide, Australia, in 1948. He completed an undergraduate degree in social work from the University of South Australia in 1979. He worked as a probation officer, a welfare worker, and a psychiatric social worker at a children's hospital before founding the Dulwich Centre and beginning to work as a family therapist in private practice in 1998. In 2008, White founded the Adelaide Narrative Therapy Centre

Michael White (left) and David Epston (right) in Aukland, New Zealand, in 1984.

*Source:* Photo by Ann Epston. Reprinted with permission. All rights reserved by David Epston.

to provide counseling services and training in narrative practice. White was known for his work with children, indigenous Aboriginal communities, and those who nego-tiated narratives around trauma, violence, and diagnostic symptoms of schizophrenia and eating disorders. He continued to lead the narrative work (training, publishing, and community work) of the Dulwich Centre until his death on March 31, 2008.

David Epston was born in Peterborough, Ontario, Canada, in 1944. He began his undergraduate studies at the University of British Columbia, but left Canada at the age of 19 years. He relocated to New Zealand in 1964, and completed a bachelor of arts degree in sociology and anthropology at Auckland University in 1936. He went on to earn a diploma in community development from Edinburgh University in 1971, a MA in applied social studies from Warwick University in 1976, and received a certificate of qualification in social work in 1977. Epston has worked as a social worker, a family therapist, and is currently the codirector of the Family Therapy Centre in Aukland, New Zealand. Epston teaches at the School of Community Development, Unitec Institute of Technology, in addition to continuing his work with the Dulwich Centre.

White and Epston came to know of each other's work in the late 1970s, and "began their enduring friendship and intellectual partnership that was characterised by unshak-able optimism, a passion over ideas, what seemed like boundless energy, and a real dedication to assist the families with whom they were meeting" (C. White, 2009, p. 59). Although they did not live close to one another, conversations never ceased and the co-creation of their narrative practice began to blossom. Together they published *Narrative Means to Therapeutic Ends*, generally regarded as a seminal work in the development of NT (M. White & Epston, 1990). Both continued to write and publish, received numerous awards, and taught internationally about NT. However, they are often known to dismiss credit, stating, "We have been steadfast in our refusal to name our work in any consistent manner. We do not identify with any particular 'school' of family therapy, and are strongly opposed to the idea of our own contribution being named as a school. We believe that such a naming would only subtract from our freedom to further explore various ideas and practices, and that it would make it difficult for others to recognize their own unique con-tributions to developments in this work, which we regard to be an "open book" (Epston & White, 1992). White and Epston did not want to be seen as experts, but rather, they wanted to allow others to make contributions to the field, which is another reason this modality became influential. For them, the field belongs to all who have contributed, especially the clients who have sought them for consultation (Abels & Abels, 2001).

# THE FOUNDATIONAL THEORY
## The Target of Counseling

NT focuses on the stories individuals tell about the events in their lives. **A story or narra-tive is a mental account or chronicle of a person's experiences or life events.** Through the sieve of these stories, individuals filter the bulk of their experiences, and allow them-selves to be guided as to how they interact thereafter. If individuals have developed particularly problem- or failure-oriented stories, future events are storied through a problem- or failure-oriented lens. Conversely, if individuals have developed solution- or success-oriented stories, future events will be storied accordingly. It is important to note that the foundational idea within NT is that stories are comprised primarily not of the events themselves, but of an individual's interpretations of them. In this sense, NT aims to bring awareness to the stories individuals tell about themselves and their values.

According to M. White (2007), NT rests on at least five core assumptions: (a) All people have meaning-making skills that have been developed and employed over the course of their lives; (b) People are always telling stories, and these stories make it possible to attribute meaning to their lives. This is an active process of assigning meaning to life experiences, rather than a passive process by which individuals try to discover an implicit meaning (i.e., there is no implicit meaning, only what is assigned). The self-narrative or storyline is the primary frame through which this assignment of meaning occurs across the *landscape of action*, **which is a plotted sequence of events through time.** (c) It is this self-narrative or story-making across the landscape of action that shapes and constitutes life, and this occurs primarily nonconsciously. Relatedly, life is rich in experiences, but actually precious few of these experiences are directly attended to. This does not mean that individuals do not necessarily incorporate all of their experiences, only that they are highly selective about which experiences to acknowledge consciously—the rest may be incorporated nonconsciously or nondeliberately through the filter of previous stories; (d) Because of the plethora of experiences to be observed and given meaning to, there is likewise a plethora of opportunities for contradictory storylines. These provide a foundation for developing subordinate storylines which form the basis for therapeutic work when the dominant storyline speaks negatively about an individual's identity or is contradictory to an individual's values. (e) Life is multi-storied, rather than a single story. This means that although people experience life as a single-storyline in which they are stuck and attempts to deviate from it are futile, there are always subordinate storylines that can be developed into opportunities for actionable change and the production of a more fulfilling life.

Therefore, the target of counseling is the storyline or narrative that individuals have developed within the context of their lived experiences, about which they have developed negative meanings about their identities, or meanings that are otherwise incongruent with their values, that ultimately lead them to a sense of being stuck.

## The Process of Counseling

In NT, therapeutic conversation is seen as an artful science where client stories are laid out, examined, challenged, and expanded on interactively and collaboratively. As stories unfold, change is discovered as an ongoing process where humans are constantly being influenced through their relationship with their environment. Learning happens by the interpretation of one's experiences in the world, which are based on the influence from social discourse (Madigan, 2011). As a result of these influences, problems have the potential to arise. For example, when people subscribe to an objective standard of society and then fail to meet the standard, or if societal standards do not coincide with a person's beliefs and attitudes, problems become internalized and people see the problem as something flawed within them (Foucault & Gordon, 1980).

With this as a frame, NT posits that change occurs when one can find something unique within a client's problem-saturated story and build on that unique "sparkling moment" to create an alternative story (M. White & Epston, 1990). The rich development of a **subordinate storyline (a tangential mental account)** in this way provides a foundation for individuals to address their problems and to engage in actions that are potentially healing, as these actions are likely to be more consistent with what they actually value (M. White, 2007). **Re-authoring (rewriting)** storylines is the basis for change within NT as a person's story is full of gaps that must be filled in order for the narrative to be performed (M. White & Epston, 1990, p. 13). In other words, a re-telling of the narrative is required to derive new meaning. For example, an individual who has been incarcerated because of driving under the influence of alcohol may initially tell a story of failure, but re-authoring that story to include, for example, the lessons that the individual has learned, the changes he or she has made, and the people's lives he or she has impacted for the better while incarcerated tells a storyline of success.

NT efforts also incorporate work in the aforementioned *landscape of action*, as well as the imaginary territory of the *landscape of consciousness*, **where people place meaning, desires, intentions, and beliefs about their experiences, and ultimately, where individuals are able to assimilate a new identity** (Bruner, 1991; M. White & Epston, 1990). Re-authoring of stories occurs primarily through a five-stage process where individuals separate themselves from their storylines, challenge their ways of living according to those stories, and examine plausible subordinate storylines that are more positive or more congruent with their stated values (Epston & White, 1992). These stages are delineated as follows:

Stage 1.  Defining the problem
Stage 2.  Mapping the influence of the problem
Stage 3.  Evaluating and justifying the effects of the problem
Stage 4.  Mining for unique outcomes
Stage 5.  Re-authoring

## Counselor Role

Narrative therapists view their role as collaborative rather than corrective. The position of a narrative therapist is not to administer interventions or to practice techniques geared toward shaping a client's perception into an objective reality, but rather to listen to the client's story and privilege his or her experience. The therapist's goal is to capture the client's story, not the therapist's story about the client's story. In other words, narrative therapists have "a conviction not to speak for or on behalf of others, but instead to create conditions whereby they could speak for themselves" (Denborough, 2014, p. 111).

Narrative therapists take a decentralized but influential position in therapy. It is decentralized as the client's (and not the therapist's per se) knowledge is viewed as central and expert. It is influential as the therapist has knowledge of the process of therapy and asks questions that create space for the client to co-research the stories and investigate potential ways of understanding experiences. The therapist's knowledge is needed, but it is knowledge of the process of therapy and the significance of language, discourse, power, and the creation of truths. The client's knowledge and expertise is on the content and meaning of his or her life (Anderson & Goolishian, 1992).

A narrative therapist concentrates on listening, and allows clinical thoughts and speech to be guided by listening, which permits the therapist to question assumptions that are personally being made as the client speaks. For example, as the client tells his or her story, a therapist might ask, "What more do I need to know that would help me better understand this person's experience?" or "Am I beginning to fill in the gaps of my own understanding?" These questions are not asked with a predetermined assumption, but with a curiosity to understand what it is like to walk in this client's shoes. Listening and asking questions from a position of curiosity are viewed as intrinsically therapeutic and create space for clients to examine previously fixed meanings and settled certainties that have created problems in their lives (Freedman & Combs, 1996).

Finally, narrative therapists experience "the enrichment of [their] own lives, through the privilege of conversations [they] have with clients" (Crockett, 2008, p. 521). Just as clients might become "other than who they were" through the experience of therapy, the same is true of therapists also. Although this is not the primary intention of therapy, it is a natural part of the process that is acknowledged, embraced, and, when appropriate, shared with clients as part of the therapeutic process (Crockett, 2008; Freedman & Combs, 1996).

## Goals of Counseling and Ideal Outcomes

The sole and primary goal of NT is to assist the client and/or family in re-authoring problem-saturated stories (M. White & Epston, 1990). Through co-research with therapists, individuals uncover meaning behind instances that may have been forgotten or left out of their story (Bruner, 1991, p. 2). In the most simple terms, **re-authoring is looking at one's story from a preferred and often more favorable perspective**. In preferred stories, the client has power, not only in an imagined future, but also in the meaning and integration of past experiences. Metaphorically, the client is the author. This authorship allows clients to expand what is seen as possible for themselves and their lives. The ideal outcome is the experience that M. White (2004) calls ***"transport."*** This is **the mental movement that is experienced by clients and counselors through the witnessing of new experiences together, and the mutual construction of healthier stories that direct clients in a new way.**

# GENERAL PROCEDURES

## Assessment

However, NT is not a formulaic or normative approach; formal assessment or diagnostic procedures are not used except those that are germane to the questions asked in therapy itself (Tarragona, 2008). Instead, NT is a co-collaborative approach to counseling where the therapist is seen as a partner (rather than an expert) in therapeutic discourse (Polkinghorne, 2004). As a result, each therapeutic relationship is unique and holds the client's viewpoint about what is transpiring to be of paramount importance to understand the problem. In fact, clients serve as primary evaluators. As the expert witnesses to their own stories, they evaluate and explore both the problem(s) they are bringing to therapy and the ways they might best respond to overcome them. This means that clients use unique language to describe the phenomena they are encountering, and that this language rests on the way they understand themselves and their situations relative to their social, cultural, and historical experiences (Anderson & Gehart, 2006). Therefore, it is crucial to conceptualize **assessment in** NT as consisting primarily of **gaining an increasing understanding of the client's story**, rather than for the purpose of assigning pathology or labels (Stokes & Poulsen, 2014). In fact, NT rejects the modernist approach to understanding people by taking lengthy inventories and formal assessments, believing that "in terms of understanding an individual person's specific plight or joining in her worldview, this approach risks missing the whole point" (Freedman & Combs, 1996, p. 31). Instead, NT primarily employs different types of questions as a form of assessment (Freedman & Combs, 1996). According to Stokes and Poulsen (2014),

> Asking questions is meant to create space for both deconstruction of existing narratives and opening space for the development of new stories and meaning. Some of the types of questions include relative influence questions, deconstruction questions, opening space questions, preference questions, story construction/re-storying questions, and meaning questions. (p. 336)

In asking these questions, narrative therapists do not attempt to diagnose, predict, interpret, or use any other intervention that may usurp the primacy of the client's experience.

## Treatment/Remediation

Treatment occurs as a process of re-authoring a client's original narrative through the use of skillful investigation and questioning by the therapist, occurring across five stages which are designed to facilitate the development of a rich subordinate storyline. The *subordinate storyline* provides **an alternate point of view to the dominant storyline that is self-defeating and leads the client to feel stuck.** This re-authored storyline adds context and complexity missing from the original storyline, creating enough maneuverability for a client to begin to understand his or her life through a new, more positive, and value-congruent filter.

In Stage 1, NT involves building rapport and maintaining a sense that the client is the "privileged author" (Freedman & Combs, 1996; M. White & Epston, 1990). In this role, the client is encouraged to define the problem, and clinicians suggest that a name be ascribed to it (M. White & Epston, 1990). For example, M. White and Epston (1990) considered the case of a child suffering from **encopresis (involuntary defecation).** As the family felt that these incidences often came unannounced, they cleverly named the accidents "sneaky poo." NT asserts that by naming a problem, clients develop a sense of authority over it. This is especially relevant given that the target of counseling is a storyline over which individuals typically feel little or no power. Thus begins the process of *externalization,* **where the problem itself is seen as the problem** (encopresis), rather than some defect of character or identity (the child himself) which leads to the problem.

Stage 2 involves examining the role of the problem in the client's life through the use of *relative influence questioning* (Freedman & Combs, 1996), which helps the client and therapist to collaboratively **map the influence of the problem historically and presently,** as well as predict the future. This occurs through more ongoing investigative questioning on the part of the clinician. In particular, clients are encouraged to delineate and understand the impact and effects of the problem, and this is generally seen as an adjunct to the externalization that begins in Stage 1.

Central to Stage 2 is the concept of *thinness* or *thickness of stories.* M. White (2004) remarked that original narratives told by clients are often *thin,* meaning that while the client has ascribed some meaning from them, that meaning was derived with **an impoverished view of the complex nature of the world and the individual** (Morgan, 2002). As a modern-day metaphor, consider trying to understand an individual's personality simply by reading his or her posts on social media outlets like Facebook or Twitter. Although one certainly could trace some sort of basic outline, a complete and nuanced understanding of an individual is simply not possible without more context. However, this surface-level lack of nuance, the thinness of original narratives tends to lead to negative identity outcomes (e.g., self-blaming, self-criticism), and this same tendency may be extended to others involved in the story. Thus, mapping is designed to increase the *thickness* of stories, **where individuals incorporate the richness and complexity of life, humanity, and themselves,** thereby creating room for additional plausible storylines that are less pathologizing and individual-as-problem-focused. Acknowledging the thickness of stories helps clients to deconstruct their negative self-identities by adding the context missing from their original thin narratives, and begins a corner-turn toward a more active process in re-authoring the stories of their lives. This is designed to be, and typically is experienced as, empowering.

Following this trend of empowerment, in Stage 3 clients are encouraged to *truly evaluate their own involvement in the presenting problem* by examining whether their own actions have been congruent with their stated desired outcome. Simply, clinicians ask clients whether the negative outcomes of the problem are consistent with their stated goals.

In Stage 4, clients are encouraged to look at positive or **unique outcomes** (these may have been identified in earlier stages, as early as Stage 1)—**incidences when there are exceptions to the storyline,** or when a telling of the dominant narrative would not have been suspected to have ended in that particular way (M. White & Epston, 1990). As unique outcomes begin to surface within the person's problem-saturated story, the therapist helps client(s) to *thicken the plot* **(see the earlier description of thick stories).** Essentially, **thickening the plot involves helping the client to examine the process by which he or she overcame the influence of the problem in the case of unique outcomes** (M. White, 1995; M. White & Epston, 1990). This process is conducted by looking at the *landscape of action* and the *landscape of identity/consciousness* (Geertz, 1973; M. White & Epston, 1990). **The landscape of action is the sequence of events, the "who, what, when, and where" that led to the creation of a unique outcome in one's story.** Questions are asked with the intention of enhancing the aspects of an emerging preferred story so as to enable self-reliance. For example, if a client had a history of child abuse and discovered that there had been a time in her life when she was able to combat fear, the therapist might ask, "Who were the characters involved, what did you notice about your surroundings, how were you able to find strength in the face of fear?" Next, **the landscape of identity/consciousness is explored that consists of meaning, beliefs, intentions, or desires derived from the events that took place within the landscape of action** (Freedman & Combs, 1997; Geertz, 1973). As the client explores the answers from the aforementioned questions, the therapist might ask, "Having had endured such a challenge and finding strength in the process, how do you see yourself as a person?" As the therapist coauthors a story, he is constantly weaving back and forth, throughout the two landscapes, so as to solidify the counter story.

Finally, Stage 5 involves actual re-authoring of the original storyline. Consistent with the overall collaborative approach of NT, clients are invited to make a decision about whether to continue with the original narrative or author a new one. New stories are constructed with particular attention to thickness, and clients are encouraged to fold-in their new understandings of themselves, others, and life. They must be rich in detail, and the entire new narrative must pay particular attention to client values. Unique outcomes identified in Stage 4 are central to this process, and it forms the basis for a re-authored storyline. This is achieved primarily, although not exclusively, through therapist questions aimed at the reorganization of experiences (M. White & Epston, 1990, pp. 17–18). These carefully constructed questions are the tools used to necessitate change as well as generate experience among the client. They are not intended to gather information, but to fill in gaps of understanding and highlight areas of a person's story that would alter his or her perspective and open space for the construction of new meanings. The questions also form a scaffolding conversation, which make it possible for people to address the alternative narratives (M. White, 1995).

In order to assist with this process, therapists ask *story development questions* that invite clients to explore the process and detail of their story in relation to a time frame, context, and others (Freedman & Combs, 1996, p. 131; M. White, 1995). For example, a therapist may ask, "How did you prepare yourself to take this leap of faith and stand up against the problem?" "What exactly did you do?" "Did you make this decision on your own or did you have others to help you?" and/or "Who was present that helped you with this endeavor?" These questions would allow clients to see the event afresh in an expanse of time and space, and reexperience it in a more detailed (i.e., thick) way, thus creating a new storyline. Clients can begin to view their stories in a new light after having acquired the ability to experience their lives and themselves in these new ways, and focus is transferred to previously neglected aspects of their story (M. White, 1995).

*Meaning questions* are also asked in order for people to reflect on their stories, themselves, and other relationships while taking into consideration the implications of newly storied experiences, therefore constructing new experiences, or "stories of stories" (Freedman & Combs, 1996, p. 134; M. White, 1995). For example, a therapist may ask, "Now that you have acquired this new knowledge, in what context would it have the greatest impact?" "What does this new perspective say about you as a person?" and "What is the significance for you and your family that you are able to discuss these newly discovered strengths?" These questions help to insurrect local knowledge that has been dominated by cultural knowledge and take part in creating problem-saturated stories (M. White & Epston, 1990).

Solidifying the alternative story is done by eliciting *unique possibilities* and considering the effects that *new discoveries* might have on a client's life. M. White and Epston (1990) referred to this stage as *developing a history of the present* and extending the story into the future. Questions such as, "Having discovered strength, how do you see yourself facing similar challenges in the future?" "What do you predict happening in the next year after shedding light on this new discovery?" followed by "Who would be least/most surprised by the strength you have discovered within yourself?" would create a foundation in which a preferred story can withstand adversity as well as the test of time.

The therapist may also invite a *reflecting team* to comment on the strengths that were noticed or other unique outcomes that occurred while the client was sharing his or her story (Andersen, 1991). **The reflecting team approach essentially involves therapy conducted by a group of therapists rather than an individual, where some members of the team observe (sometimes through one-way mirrors or audio/video feed) and another member serves as the primary therapist** (Polkinghorne, 2004). However, unlike more traditional forms of observation in therapy that occur from behind a one-way mirror, NT reflecting team observers engage clients in discussion regarding their therapeutic experience at various intervals during therapy, and facilitate dialogue about whether what's transpiring is helpful, and what can be done on both the part of the therapist and the client to help the process (Polkinghorne, 2004). In addition, outside witnesses can also be involved with treatment, such as a partner or a family member. The therapist might ask this person(s) to identify how he or she viewed the client after having found new discoveries, and also to reflect on meanings derived from the new storyline. These kinds of collaboration between therapists, client, and others reveal further that NT "is a specialized discursive interpersonal activity, rather than a subject knower seeking to comprehend a client as an at distance object" (Polkinghorne, 2004, p. 56).

Finally, therapy terminates when the client's alternative story becomes the new dominant story of his or her life. During this phase, clients may be encouraged to commence with therapeutic letter writing (see Specialized Techniques section) or be provided with a certificate to acknowledge the client's accomplishments. Regarding follow-up, clients are always encouraged to return for treatment if they notice their problem-saturated story gaining momentum, or if they feel a decline of personal agency when faced with their old dominant story.

## Case Management

The narrative therapist takes great care to create an environment of collaboration, respect, and acceptance. As a rule, sessions are set up at the discretion of the client, as are the participants in therapy, although the narrative therapist may suggest the inclusion of particular other therapists (for participation in reflecting teams) or other outsiders. The duration of therapy can be short or long term, dependent on a variety of factors including the problem addressed or client-desired frequency of sessions. There is no prototypical length.

Case notes should reflect important details of client stories, including the problem-saturated narrative, the relative influence of the problem, important events that do not fold into that narrative or are exceptions to it, and dominant discourses around cultural, ethnic, socioeconomic status, religious, gender, and sexual orientation themes, as well as contextual themes that may be related to family, community, school, or other social arenas.

Although narrative therapists unquestionably avoid pathologizing, labels, and diagnosis, this does not preclude them from referring clients to appropriate outside resources for psychopharmacological intervention as necessary, particularly around the use antipsychotic medications (Dulwich Centre Publications, n.d.).

## Specialized Techniques

**NT is a modality centered on questions**. Most techniques in NT involve carefully constructed questions that are not meant to elicit information, but to generate an experience (Freedman & Combs, 1997; M. White & Epston, 1990). Questions offer an opportunity for the client to look at details of his or her story from a different point of view so as to create preferred ways of understanding experience. Nevertheless, NT does incorporate interventions, such as *deconstruction, externalization, outside witnessing*, and *therapeutic letters/certificates*.

### DECONSTRUCTION

One of the most important skills associated with NT is *deconstruction*. As clients tell their stories, therapists are encouraged to listen "deconstructively" (Freedman & Combs, 1997, p. 47), guided by the belief that one's story is laden with many meanings. In other words, a therapist's meaning of the story being shared may be completely different than the client's meaning. A technique referred to as *deconstructive questioning* encourages a therapist **to work from a place of curiosity (rather than assumptions) and**

**to look for gaps in his or her understanding of the story**. This line of questioning helps the client see his or her story from a different perspective and makes explicit how certain beliefs, attitudes, feelings, and practices have influenced the client's stories (M. White, 1995). For example, asking "In what situations do these kinds of ideas usually surface?" or "Are there locations where these beliefs are more strongly held than others?" exposes the whereabouts from which the problem is most likely found. Revealing the effects of these ideas allows the client to see the destructive nature of the problem and how it has impacted his or her life and the lives of the client's family (Freedman & Combs, 1996; M. White & Epston, 1990).

## EXTERNALIZATION

If the philosophy of NT can be described as constructivist and postmodern, then its core tenet is that people are not the problem—problems are the problem (M. White & Epston, 1989). **Externalization includes thinking, writing, and speaking of the problem in relational terms that create distance between the client and the problem** (Madigan, 2011; M. White & Epston, 1990). In externalization, the problem is transformed from being something within the client (a pathology or deficit) and is reframed as something outside of the client that they can take a stand against. The idea of the client seeing his or her self as separate from the problem is paramount in NT, as it challenges the dominant discourse.

For example, imagine a family seeking help with a daughter's **bulimia nervosa (an eating disorder where clients binge on food, purge food, or do a combination of binging and purging)**. The dominant discourse suggests that the family's image of "beauty and health" must be upheld. Using externalizing conversation, a narrative therapist would work to separate the family from the problem and bring awareness to the power that was influencing the problem. The power of social media and the pressure that western civilization places on a woman's body type would likely be explored, as well as how and why these images are experienced as important by the family. The meaning of *bulimia nervosa* would be deconstructed, and, through externalization, the problem might be re-described as "image." The family members would explore the "image's" influence on their lives as well as the behaviors, attitudes, and beliefs that have kept this problem a powerful part of their relationships. Rather than the daughter having a problem with her eating, the family is responding to the problem of "image."

The discipline of externalizing conversations is a crucial aspect of NT practice as it creates a platform for constructing questions that gives rise to the creation of alternative stories (M. White & Epston, 1990).

## OUTSIDE WITNESSING

**Reflecting teams, or outside witnesses (observers, in either case, to the treatment),** can be recruited so that the client may obtain multiple perspectives during the session (Epston, 1994; M. White & Epston, 1990). The teams may consist of professionals, family, and/or friends who are chosen by the client to act as witnesses. Witnesses offer substance or thickness to a client's preferred storyline.

Although it was a common practice in family therapy training centers for a team of professionals to observe therapy and discuss what was observed, it was rare that clients were invited to be a part of the process. The emphasis traditionally was on the therapist's learning. In NT reflecting teams, while learning is a part of the process, the emphasis is on the benefit of the client. These experiences are usually implemented at the end of the session (Epston, 1994).

When using a one-way mirror, the client(s) and therapist signal to the reflecting team, who begin discussing among themselves what they had witnessed during the session. The client and therapist listen—immediately able to witness how they were experienced by others. Next, the client has an opportunity to comment on the feedback he or she heard from the witnesses with the therapist. Finally, the reflecting team is invited into the session for a face-to-face discussion of the strengths that were witnessed in the client/family.

Outsider witnesses typically involve a smaller group or even an individual witness. They tend to be present in the therapy room with the counselor and the client, and may be consulted throughout the session to weigh in on what they are experiencing or offer other perspectives. A more formal processing is usually completed near the end of the session. The purpose of both experiences is to solidify the preferred narrative and to share with clients how they also "transport" others through the sharing of their story.

## THERAPEUTIC DOCUMENTS

Letter writing, an idea brought to NT by Epston, is said to be "worth 4.5 sessions of good therapy" as letters to clients sent in-between sessions or during the termination phase are useful for continuing preferred stories beyond the time in session (Freedman & Combs, 1997, p. 208; M. White, 1995). Letters, pictures, certificates, or other documents created either in or between sessions give the client an opportunity to stay immersed in the preferred story. They also provide the therapist a chance to think about the language and the questions that were being used during the session and to take a more reflective position. Document creating serves to "summarize the session, extend ideas that were partially established in conversation, and include people who did not attend the meeting," all of which thicken the plot, open opportunities to invite witnesses to share in the preferred story, and create more resonant and clear preferred stories (Epston, 1994; Freedman & Combs, 1997, pp. 208–215).

# Recent Developments and Criticisms

NT has been a staple in the postmodern world of psychotherapy since the last 25 years. Scholars and clinicians have been expanding on this practice and blending other evidence-based modalities in order to thicken the search for alternative stories. Furthermore, the incorporation of meaning making in these newly developed practices puts a new variation on modern ways of thinking.

## ATTACHMENT NARRATIVE THERAPY

Dallos and Vetere (2014) discuss the integration of NT, attachment, and family systems theory by considering the development and maintenance of human distress in relationships, aiming to provide new direction to psychotherapeutic intervention. Attachment NT (ANT) has shown promise in working with families who are having difficulty with children. May (2005) stated that the key allowing these theories to work together is emotional attunement. Emotional attunement is a highly sensitive state of emotional connection that stems from one's attachment to his or her parents, and, if trauma, such as abuse or neglect, had been experienced early in life, one's "internal thoughts and perceptions of external events" can affect how that individual relates to the world. In other words, a child's development can be altered as a result of these experiences. ANT allows an individual to name particular emotions associated with past traumas, expand understanding, and help with emotional regulation. Also, one can explore the significance of comfort, safety, and protection within a relationship, and create new meanings surrounding these states of being (Dallos & Vetere, 2014).

## NARRATIVE EXPOSURE THERAPY

Another expansion of NT that incorporates trauma-focused cognitive-behavioral therapy (TF-CBT) and testimonial therapy (TT) is narrative exposure therapy (NET), which has been used to treat individuals suffering from severe posttraumatic stress disorder (PTSD) as a result of exposure to mass violence and torturous conditions (McPherson, 2012). Also, mental health professionals were calling for a practice that was both evidence-based and culturally competent so as to work with individuals in refugee camps or war-torn countries. This modality is often referred to as pragmatic as it is brief and places emphasis on oral communication of the client, which removes the barrier of illiteracy.

The healing begins through habituation, which is a concept derived from TF-CBT (McPherson, 2012). The client is encouraged to recall his or her entire autobiography including both positive and negative experiences. As in TF-CBT, NET intends to expose the client to his or her own traumatic narratives, but contextualize the traumas as part of the client's story as a whole. The client then repeats the narration of the story, which leads to his or her habituation of more favorable emotional and physiological responses. This is accomplished through the restructuring and re-telling of a coherent narrative, which is the primary aim of NT. Finally, in the traditions of NT and TT, the therapist or the client documents the client's story and has it signed by all witnesses present (McPherson, 2012). The survivor now has a physical account of his story that talks of his struggles and strengths throughout life, which he may draw on whenever negative symptoms of his experience begin to surface.

## MINDFULNESS AND NARRATIVE THERAPY

Mindfulness meditation and NT have many similarities, especially in their views of human nature and the self. Mindfulness, which stems from Buddhist practices, along with NT, views the self as relational, not individualistic (Percy, 2008). In other words, the self cannot exist on its own; it is constantly being influenced by external stimuli as well as internal stimuli, such as thoughts and emotions that surround experience. The ever-changing mental and physical events shape a person's reality, and it is the emphasis on interrelatedness that diminishes an individual's impulse to attach, internalize, and objectify these bodily states. For example, as an individual enters a state of meditation, he or she becomes aware of these thoughts and feelings, and begins to view them as separate entities (Percy, 2008). In the tradition of NT, this shift allows the problems (the now-externalized thoughts and feelings) to be seen as the problems.

Percy (2008) provided a case example that showed the benefit of incorporating mindfulness and NT in the re-authoring of one's problem-saturated story. The client suffered from emotional and chronic physical pain caused by an automobile accident. He also stated that because of the physical injuries, this traumatic event left him "in a world of isolation," as well as in a state of "tortuous reflection" of his life thus far. The clinician used a 15-minute guided meditation to initiate each session, which gave the client an opportunity to be in touch with his "relational self." After meditation, the client and the clinician explored the events that had transpired. They began to re-author the painful memories as the meditation helped the client see himself as separate from the problems without having the therapist use externalization skills. The collaborative process of NT and mindfulness allows an individual to re-language the meaning of physical "pain" or "mental anguish" in an emotional context and alter one's relationship with it (Percy, 2008). For example, as one sees himself or herself as separate from the "pain," he or she will begin to notice how it fluctuates, and eventually relate to it with warmth and acceptance, rather than fear and tightness.

As seen in the aforementioned research, NT has much potential for future development. The possibilities that are made available within this practice allow the therapist and the client to experiment in the retelling of stories while incorporating many skills and interventions from various schools of thought. It also allows the client to move forward at his or her own pace without the limitations of more structured practices.

## Weaknesses

The previous discussion shows implicit and explicit strengths of NT, despite it having its weaknesses. A primary one is the confusing way that language encompasses the theory. The majority of terminology used within narrative theory is unique to each therapeutic relationship as it privileges each client's understanding of the problem. For example, if a client states that he or she is depressed, this symbolizes a whole array of problems, and only through investigating the client's intended meaning of "depression" can the therapist understand where the problem gets its power. However, privileging the client's language is a difficult skill to acquire and using universal language, such as "depression," is easier to communicate because it is "common" knowledge.

Another criticism of NT is that the theory is not systemic. Modern psychotherapist Salvador Minuchin published a particularly provocative article, which stated that he "could not see where the family was in narrative therapy" (Minuchin, 1998). Viewed through a modernist lens, one can see the difficulty in understanding the absence of family, as family dynamics and interactions between its members are not necessarily recognized within narrative practice. However, narrative therapists look beyond the interactions of family members and look for patterns of meaning within the family and the larger systems, such as culture and society.

Minuchin (1998) also criticized that NT focuses too much on the individual rather than the family, because of the practice of interviewing one family member at a time. However, looking through a social constructivist lens, one can see that narrative theory's understanding of an individual is that of a relational "self" who "exists within an ongoing interchange with others and continually co-creates itself with others" (Freedman & Combs, 1996). This concept explains the benefit of having each client act as a witness, or audience, while the other shares his or her story, as meaning can be understood and attributed to each person's experience. In spite of this explanation, Minuchin posited that the systemic nature of therapy is not present and that the co-creation of meaning cannot be accomplished through family members acting as witness to each other. Also, the assumption that narrative therapists "jump over the family" by privileging an individual's discourse may mean that the opportunity to create "family stories" is lost (Minuchin, 1998, p. 388).

The idea that responsibility of the problem is taken away from the client is another criticism regarding NT. Through the practice of externalization, NT encourages clients to see themselves as separate from the problem, so that agency is taken back into one's life (M. White & Epston, 1990). Although this at first seems to be removing them from responsibility, as clients acquire this skill, they are able to see how the problem influences actions, feelings, and thoughts as well as discover new possibilities to combat the problem. In other words, helping clients see their relationships with the problem from an alternative perspective may enable them to eventually take ownership for their actions in a more productive and less-shaming manner.

Finally, NT is most likely an inappropriate modality to use in crisis situations, as it is a free-flowing practice that progresses at the client's pace. During crises, action is typically taken to address the client's immediate needs, so as to create a safe environment as quickly as possible. Taking the time to deconstruct a suicidal client's dominant discourse in search of the location of the problem requires more patience and abstract thought than is generally capable in crisis. Although it may be true, for example, that an explanation of how a client has become suicidal related to the overwhelming power of his or her dominant discourse and lack of agency in the face of the problem might be helpful conceptually, it is too lengthy a process to be used during a time when help is promptly needed.

## STUDENT–MENTOR DIALOGUE

**Student:**   This approach appears to clearly fit within the framework of the social constructivism paradigm. What are your thoughts on this?

**Mentor:**   Well, there is clear alignment with social constructivism tenets, but at times the authors of works on Narrative Therapy and its derivatives appear to maintain the idea of self as entity. This is consistent with early constructivism theory, but it is less consistent with the more recent iterations of social constructivist theory. The authors don't fully present their approach as having radical theoretical implications, because a radical social constructivist might argue that one does not have to have a "self" if a story is in language, which is in the social domain (not the cognitive domain). As social constructivist thought has developed, purer non-psychological perspectives have emerged, as with Cottone's radical social constructivism (Cottone, 2013, in press). The self in social constructivism's radical form disappears as a structural concept and becomes socially constructed itself. So some writers in the narrative mode appear to maintain the concept of an agentic self, which is not at all crucial to radical social constructivist theory.

**Student:**   So you don't see this theory as social constructivist?

**Mentor:** I believe Narrative Therapy clearly fits within the social constructivism paradigm framework, and the practice is clearly constructivist in its intent and outcome. Just because some Narrative Theory proponents value the concept of "self" does not dislodge the approach from its paradigm roots. Clearly this is a collaborative approach where alternatives to sick or unhealthy frameworks are replaced by consensualized healthier truth claims.

**Student:** What do you believe are the valuable features of Narrative Therapy?

**Mentor:** It certainly is a creative approach that builds on client strengths. Like Solution Focused Brief Therapy, it asks questions of clients to build a new and healthier story with the client. It does not impose a truth about the nature of mental health or dysfunction. It is acknowledging of client experiences and builds upon those experiences as valid and acceptable foundations for the new story that is collaboratively created. This is a very positive approach to people's problems.

**Student:** Do you think the approach is viable?

**Mentor:** Yes, certainly. The movement has taken roots, as inspired by White and Epston. More and more people are jumping on the postmodern bandwagon, and this approach, as an early passenger, is a model for future generations of social constructivism theoreticians. This approach stands as a compelling example of how theory can emerge from philosophy that represents a dissociation from an earlier overarching philosophy.

## CONCLUSION

This chapter provides an example of a counseling theory that clearly aligns with social constructivism principles. The idea of using a story, a mental account that chronicles a person's life, as a vehicle for reframing a client's problems into something much more functional is unique among current psychotherapies. The approach is philosophically grounded and technically and practically refined, and its premise is being acknowledged and developed by a new generation of narrative theorists.

## REFERENCES

Abels, P., & Abels, S. L. (2001). *Understanding narrative therapy: A guidebook for the social worker*. New York, NY: Springer Publishing.

Andersen, T. (Ed.). (1991). *The reflecting team: Dialogues and dialogues about the dialogues*. New York, NY: W. W. Norton.

Anderson, H., & Goolishian, H. (1992). The client is the expert: A not-knowing approach to therapy. In S. McNamee & K. J. Gergen (Eds.), *Therapy as social construction* (pp. 25–39). Newbury Park, CA: Sage.

Anderson, H. D., & Gehart, D. R. (2006). *Collaborative therapy: Relationships and conversations that make a difference*. New York, NY: Routledge.

Bateson, G. (1972). *Steps to an ecology of mind: Collected essays in anthropology, psychiatry, evolution, and epistemology*. San Francisco, CA: Chandler.

Berger, P. L., & Luckmann, T. (1966). *The social construction of reality: A treatise in the sociology of knowledge*. Garden City, NY: Doubleday.

Bruner, J. (1991). The narrative construction of reality. *Critical Inquiry, 18*(1), 1–21. doi:10.1086/448619

Cottone, R. R. (2012). *Paradigms of counseling and psychotherapy*. Cottleville, MO: Author. Retrieved from https://www.smashwords.com/books/view/165398

Cottone, R. R. (2013, September). A paradigm shift in counseling philosophy. *Counseling Today, 56*(3), 54–57.

Cottone, R. R. (in press). In defense of radical social constructivism. *Journal of Counseling and Development*.

Crockett, K. (2008). Narrative therapy. In J. Frew & M. D. Spiegler (Eds.), *Contemporary psychotherapies for a diverse world* (pp. 489–533). Boston, MA: Lahaska Press.

Dallos, R., & Vetere, A. (2014). Systemic therapy and attachment narratives: Attachment Narrative Therapy. *Clinical Child Psychology and Psychiatry, 19*(4), 494–502. doi:10.1177/1359104514550556

Denborough, D. (2014). Michael White and adventures downunder. *Australian and New Zealand Journal of Family Therapy, 2014*(35), 110–120.

Dulwich Centre Publications. (n.d.). Commonly-asked questions about narrative approaches to therapy, community work, and psychosocial support: Collective paper. Retrieved from http://dulwichcentre.com.au/articles-about-narrative-therapy/common-questions-narrative-therapy

Epston, D. (1994). "Extending the conversation." *Family Therapy Networker, 18*(6), 30–37.

Epston, D., & White, M. (1992). *Experience, contradiction, narrative and imagination: Selected papers of David Epston & Michael White, 1989–1991*. Adelaide, Australia: Dulwich Centre Publications.

Erickson, M. H., & Rossi, E. L. (1981). *Experiencing hypnosis: Therapeutic approaches to altered states*. New York, NY: Irvington Publishers.

Foucault, M. (1972). *The archaeology of knowledge, and the discourse on language*. New York, NY: Pantheon Books.

Foucault, M., & Gordon, C. (1980). *Power/knowledge: Selected interviews and other writings, 1972–1977*. New York, NY: Pantheon Books.

Freedman, J., & Combs, G. (1996). *Narrative therapy: The social construction of preferred realities*. New York, NY: W. W. Norton.

Freedman, J., & Combs, G. (1997). Lists. In C. Smith & D. Nylund (Eds.), *Narrative therapies with children and adolescents* (pp. 147–161). New York, NY: Guilford.

Geertz, C. (1973). *The interpretation of cultures: Selected essays*. New York, NY: Basic Books.

Gergen, K. J. (2001). *Social construction in context*. London, UK: Sage.

Madigan, S. (2011). *Narrative therapy*. Washington, DC: American Psychological Association.

May, J. C. (2005). Family attachment narrative therapy: Healing the experience of early childhood maltreatment. *Journal of Marital and Family Therapy, 31*(3), 221–237. doi:10.1111/j.1752-0606.2005.tb01565.x

McPherson, J. (2012). Does narrative exposure therapy reduce PTSD in survivors of mass violence? *Research on Social Work Practice, 22*(1), 29–42.

Minuchin, S. (1998). Where is the family in narrative therapy? *Journal of Marital and Family Therapy, 24*(4), 397–403.

Morgan, A. (2002). *What is narrative therapy?* Adelaide, Australia: Dulwich Centre.

Pare, D. A. (1995). Of families and other cultures: The shifting paradigm of family therapy. *Family Process, 34*, 1–19. doi:10.1111/j.1545-5300.1995.00001.x

Percy, I. (2008). Awareness and authoring: The idea of self in mindfulness and narrative therapy. *European Journal of Psychotherapy & Counselling, 10*(4), 355–367. doi:10.1080/13642530802577109

Polkinghorne, D. E. (2004). Narrative therapy and postmodernism. In L. E. Angus & J. McLeod (Eds.), *The handbook of narrative and psychotherapy: Practice, theory and research* (pp. 53–68). Thousand Oaks, CA: Sage.

Stokes, L. D., & Poulsen, S. S. (2014). Narrative Therapy for adoption issues in families, couples, and individuals: Rationale and approach. *Journal of Family Psychotherapy, 25*, 330–347. doi:10.1080/08975353.2014.977681

Tarragona, M. (2008). Postmodern/poststructuralist therapy. In J. L. Lebow (Ed.), *Twenty-first century psychotherapies: Contemporary approaches to theory and practice* (pp. 167–206). Hoboken, NJ: Wiley.

White, C. (2009, October). Where did it all begin? Reflecting on the collaborative work of Michael White and David Epston. *Context, 105*, 59–60.

White, M. (1995). *Re-authoring lives: Interviews & essays.* Adelaide, Australia: Dulwich Centre Publications.

White, M. (2004). *Narrative practice and exotic lives: Resurrecting diversity in everyday life.* Adelaide, Australia: Dulwich Centre.

White, M. (2007, April). *Trauma and narrative therapy* [Video]. Presentation at a workshop of the International Trauma Studies Program, New York, NY. Retrieved from https://vimeo.com/34671797

White, M., & Epston, D. (1990). *Narrative means to therapeutic ends.* New York, NY: W. W. Norton.

# CHAPTER

## 14

# Cognitive Consensual Therapy

## OBJECTIVES

- To introduce a new theory of counseling and a new means to build theories through the paradigm framework

- To provide a model approach based fully on social constructivism philosophy

- To outline the philosophical underpinnings of this approach

- To provide details about how Cognitive Consensual Therapy is practiced

- To discuss potential criticisms of this approach with counterarguments

This chapter describes a therapeutic approach that is consistent with the social constructivism paradigm of mental health treatment. The *social constructivism* philosophy **purports that people understand their experiences through the social consensual process—people together socially construct meaning of their shared experiences.** As such, the focus is on the processes of cognition and consensus as involved in defining what is meaningful to clients. The purpose of this chapter is to describe further a counseling theory that was first introduced with publication of *Theories and Paradigms*

Robert Rocco Cottone in 1992, when he first published a chapter on Cognitive Consensual Therapy.

*of Counseling and Psychotherapy* (Cottone, 1992). This chapter acts as a refinement of the 1992 work.

Cognitive Consensual Therapy (CCT) is grounded on a social constructivist philosophy. Social constructivism is an intellectual movement in the humanities, art, and the social science that is part of a larger shift in philosophy from **modernism (where "things" are observed, analyzed, and understood)** to **postmodernism (where "relationships" are observed and the focus of study)**. Social constructivism is a special case of postmodern philosophy embraced by some theoreticians in the mental health field (Mahoney & Lyddon, 1988; Neimeyer, 1995). CCT is built on a radical form of social constructivism philosophy (Cottone, 2012, 2013, in press). Radical social constructivism purports that all understanding derives from agreement in social groups. There is no **objectivity (where all humans are capable of experiencing the same thing)** or **subjectivity (where each human has his or her own truth)**. Rather, there is "objectivity in parentheses" (Maturana, 1978), where what is known is objectively known only *within* a community of observers. Maturana (1978), a cognitive biologist, demonstrated that humans are structurally organized to come to consensus in their understanding of shared experience (see Figure 14.1). That consensual process (he called it the "consensual domain") is crucial to understanding that people interpersonally form the truths that guide them. Truths are not objectively true, and they are not subjectively held by individuals; rather, truths are consensual.

Cottone, building on the works of Gergen (1985, 2009) and accepting Maturana's ideas about how humans are structured to consensualize (Maturana, 1978, 1970/1980; Maturana & Varela, 1973/1980, 1987) further developed the idea of "communities of understanding," which he also called "consensualities" and "bracketed absolute truths"—truths that are unquestionable within the interactive boundaries of a community of believers (Cottone, 2010, 2012, 2014). Bracketed Absolute Truths take understanding off the questionable versus the unquestionable continuum and place it in a triadic position (see Figure 14.2).

**FIGURE 14.1**   Humberto Maturana at the 1990 Systemic Constructions conference.
*Source*: Photo by R. Rocco Cottone.

In effect, all understanding of experience is established through the consensual process—people understanding through their definition of shared experience. If truths are socially constructed, that means that any group (it takes at least two people) can socially construct their understanding of their shared experiences. To people inside a group, the truths that are constructed are accepted as unquestionable; but to people outside a group observing the group members, the truths may look questionable or debatable. So, for example, some religious groups accept an abortion philosophy that is "pro-life," but to others, a pro-abortion or "pro-choice" position might be acceptable. Essentially, truths are group bound and group relevant. Different groups of people can disagree on matters that are crucial to their daily lives, and they can disagree vehemently. Therefore, there are people who are pro-life and pro-choice, communist and capitalists, Democrats and Republicans, Israelites and Palestinians, Catholics and Protestants, pro-gun control and anti-gun control, and each group unquestionably holds to a truth or a set of truths. The list is endless. Each position represents a *consensuality*—**a belief held firmly as unquestionable within a community**.

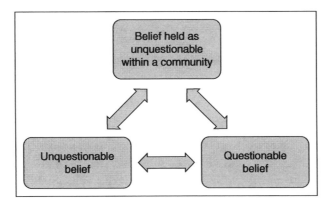

**FIGURE 14.2**   A "belief held as unquestionable within a community" is triadic to, and off the continuum of, "unquestionable belief" versus "questionable belief."

The relevance of consensualized truth to counseling is profound. When clients come to counseling, a cognitive consensual therapist assumes that the client is wedged between at least two competing and nonintersecting truths represented by two different communities. Counseling becomes a process of identifying the "truths" within which the client is enmeshed. Counseling becomes a process to help facilitate a client's connection to a group that best represents client healthy behavior within some socially acceptable context. Counseling becomes a form of social facilitation to: (a) engineer social "fit" for clients in healthy contexts; and (b) help to extricate clients from groups that are ill suited to the client's needs and goals.

Although some people might argue that a purely social philosophy conflicts with the commonly perceived concrete world, the fact remains that in the therapeutic realm, such a criticism is not so serious. The therapeutic enterprise is not a concrete enterprise. It is not the equivalent of constructing buildings. It is a social and linguistic enterprise (Szasz, 1974), where truths are housed in the understanding of shared experience. In this sense, the social constructivist philosophy at the foundation of CCT does not make claims of application beyond the social realm (where psychotherapy exists). Although CCT is based on an ontological position that relationships are real and are treatable processes, it is not meant to be applied to the debate over the nature of "reality"; rather, it is applied in a therapeutic context within which cognitive consensual therapists work.

Unlike other counseling theories, CCT requires a complete reordering of framework. It is a fully process-oriented therapeutic approach. Instead of focusing on organic–medical, psychological, or system structures, it focuses on the process of socially making sense of client experiences and defining healthy narratives for successful engagement in a socially safe and fitting place.

# THE FOUNDATIONAL THEORY

## The Target of Counseling

The target of counseling is the process of human interaction. Humans live in a continually evolving medium of *cognition* (**perceiving and languaging**) and social interaction. Counseling focuses on those truths socially constructed by individuals within specific social contexts. For example, a wife, after consulting with her friends, may argue that her husband is "uncaring," unavailable, and not empathic about the demands she faces. She and her friends have taken the position that being a homemaker, a mother, an employee, and a spouse is too demanding, and that her husband, who works one job, must share the household responsibilities. The husband, on the other hand, is in agreement with his boss and coworkers that his job is primary and that personal and family matters must be a lesser priority. Consistent with his work relationships, he argues that although he only works one job, he is the primary breadwinner, and all his efforts must be concentrated on the one job. In this scenario, there is a conflict of consensualities. Two different and competitive truths have been socially constructed.

In addressing a conflict of consensualities where different truths compete, the therapist must first identify social systems of significance, remembering that a person's understanding of experience results from both cognitive and social activity. The husband may be operating from a system of relationships that define the male breadwinner as dominant (a patriarchy), and he may be interacting in social contexts where perceptions and views on this topic are languaged or acted on from a patriarchal point of view. As described earlier, he works in a setting where there are few self-supporting or family-supporting female coworkers. The wife, on the other hand, may be operating from a context where there are professional and familial expectations placed on *both* husbands and wives. She may be socially interacting with others who demonstrate and communicate a point of view quite different from her husband's. Neither of these two perspectives is objectively right or wrong, but the fact that there has been lack of cooperation, at least from the perspective of one of the marital partners, means that there is a conflict of consensualities. The target of counseling becomes the interaction surrounding the conflict of consensualities.

It is noteworthy that the term *consensualities* is used in the plural sense. Practically speaking, it would be very unusual for a lack of co-operation to result from simply one conflict of one consensuality. There may be many consensualities operating at any one time, each evolving in its own way, and each within its own process of communication. Remembering that human interaction may be viewed as complex (involving verbal, nonverbal, informal, and contextual messages), several consensual positions may be communicated at one time. There may be an open verbal disagreement between spouses regarding the assignment of familial responsibilities. There may also be a nonverbal disagreement regarding the activities of one spouse's role in the home. And, there may be a larger social message that operates to prevent one or both spouses from operating in ways that would allow for a purely egalitarian marriage. All of these factors must be accounted for by the cognitive consensual therapist.

Where there is language, social interaction, and cooperation, there is an evolving consensuality. Where there is lack of cooperation, there is a differing or competing consensuality. The question arises as to whether people, as in the marital example, can come to consensus about differences in their understanding of shared experiences, and whether they can come to *agreement* as to how to reconcile them. The task of the cognitive consensual therapist is to facilitate such an agreement linguistically and interactively.

## The Process of Counseling

The counseling process is fully interactive. From the moment clients enter a counselor's office, interaction among involved parties is encouraged. For example, counseling invariably first involves the client's social system of significance (e.g., the family system). If a social system of significance has not been identified before therapy has been initiated, then the therapist attempts to define significant social systems and later to engage active social relationships in therapy. It is important to involve as many individuals implicated in "problems" as is practically possible from the very beginning of therapy, as the basic philosophy of CCT is that defined problems derive from *simultaneous cognitive* and *social* processes.

In therapy, the counselor interacts with the clients to probe their concerns and to define agreements and disagreements. The language used to express an agreement and/or disagreement is important; the use of specialized language by clients must be understood and analyzed, because it is likely reflective of a social system of significance. Social systems of significance often have unique social and linguistic traditions. Teenagers, for example, often speak differently from their parents (e.g., slang or jargon), reflecting different linguistic groundings. A specialized linguistic grounding is a clear message of involvement of other individuals. Determining which individuals external to those convened for therapy may be influencing the language and actions of individuals in therapy is critical. In this sense, linguistic dialects, jargon, and vernacular are very important to defining the interpersonal limits of a consensuality—the brackets of unquestionable truths held by clients in counseling.

Once consensualities or disagreements become openly expressed in therapy, the therapist begins to assess whether a new consensus can be facilitated. If a new consensus is not feasible, then the therapist must determine whether one of the positions taken by opponents in the group is more closely reflective of the larger sociolegal consensus by which the therapist is constrained. In fact, the therapist may be confronted with consensualities that are contradictory to the evolving sociolegal consensus. For example, in a patriarchal and incestuous family, forced to attend therapy by a legal authority, the father may take the position that incest is acceptable and that doing otherwise is against the family's wishes. In this case, the therapist is up against a consensus inconsistent with his or her role in a larger sociolegal setting. The therapist in such a situation must attempt to facilitate the societal consensus, clearly communicating the illegality of incest to the family members, and, where necessary, the therapist must act in accordance with the sociolegal consensus to help to ensure the incest does not recur and that family members are not harmed.

It is also possible that the therapist will be confronted with a family or group that defines the problem as due to one individual. Even the implicated (blamed) individual may agree that he or she is the problem; such an agreement may go so far as to define the implicated individual as "ill" or "sick." (Often this kind of agreement occurs after there has been some contact with an organic–medical therapist.) Although a cognitive consensual therapist prefers to define and to treat problems within social contexts, fully aware of the social and cognitive underpinnings of truth making, he or she does not necessarily argue against a consensus of individual blame, if such a consensus can lead to an ethical therapeutic resolution of a problem. In such a case, a psychiatric diagnosis is defined as a temporary means of identifying and solving problems, and it can be used to restructure social relations in a way that a new process of interaction is facilitated. In other words, any consensus that helps to resolve disagreements among involved individuals in therapy is useful, so long as it is considered ethical and not harmful by standards consensually agreed on by members of the professional and sociolegal communities, to which the therapist belongs.

This is not to say that CCT is an eclectic therapy that allows for an "anything goes" approach to treatment. Rather, it is instead a firmly philosophically grounded theory that allows for flexibility of response, with the understanding that the limits of professional activity are in some cases ethically and legally defined. Like eclecticism, any acceptable means of therapy can be used if a consensus is developed consistent with the approach, and so long as the approach is ethical, not harmful, and supported by the professional community. Unlike eclecticism, CCT is grounded philosophically in social constructivism and the consensual decision-making processes (cf. Cottone, 2001). CCT has specialized techniques all its own. As Keeney (1983) noted:

> One way of incorporating a diversity of views is to become an eclectic. For instance, a therapist may use "gestalt work" at one time and "strategic family therapy" at another. This therapist's theories and techniques are like an eclectic concert program—different music is played at different times.

> Another approach to incorporating diverse perspectives involves combination. Here the clinician takes bits and pieces from various approaches and "integrates" them into his own unified model. It is an illusion to view this as an eclectic approach. More accurately, any combination of views is itself a new theory. Combining Beethoven and Bach gives you neither, but something else. An "integrated theory" simply becomes another theory which an eclectic may add to his files. . . . However, as we mentioned, another jump in learning is possible. Third-order change . . . emerges when different epistemologies are discerned. Entering the labyrinth of epistemological comparison means going beyond theory and becoming aware of difference that may make the most profound difference in one's orientation to clinical understanding and action. (p. 160)

It is exactly this third-order type of change that the social constructivism philosophy represents, which is embodied practically in CCT.

Practically speaking, the process of CCT is a process of relationship analysis and negotiation. It attempts to resolve differences of opinion and action. It ideally provides for new definitions of concerns that will allow agreement about what activities should be undertaken by the therapist and clients to diminish or to resolve problems and to maintain client behavior within standards defined as acceptable within sociolegal standards. The cognitive consensual therapist proceeds from the assumption that change is inevitable, and that he or she is simply facilitating already progressing change. As long as the counselor represents a social and linguistic tradition different in some way from the problematic social and linguistic background of the client, and so long as the counselor maintains interpersonal contacts with the client, change is inevitable. Change of clients or change in their social systems of significance may be slower or quicker than what is occurring in a larger social context (out of sync with other changes), but it is change nonetheless, which is always the therapist's ally.

## Counselor Role

The counselor role as a cognitive consensual therapist is that of facilitating interactions (both behaviorally and linguistically) so that clients come to view and to understand different ways of acting and thinking. Basically, the counselor attempts to enter into coevolution with clients. The counselor recognizes that he or she will be educated in contact with the client's social system, and that the client, likewise, is influenced by the service delivery system of which the therapist is a part. Through behavioral and linguistic interaction, there can be an integration, and, hopefully, cooperation of the systems. Through therapeutic integration of ideas and actions, a newly evolving consensus may emerge, consistent with constraints imposed by relations with the larger service delivery system and the sociolegal context.

The counselor also plays the role of the professional authority. This role derives from his or her linkage to the larger professional community and the sociolegal system. The counseling relationship is viewed as a complementary relationship, where the therapist plays the one-up role. Regardless, this is not to say that the client does not influence what occurs in therapy. Whereas the counselor role is that of an educated authority, the therapeutic process is one of give and take. The therapist is alert to client needs and desires. The therapist is ethically obligated to serve the client primarily to solve expressed problems. However, problems are never defined in isolation by the therapist alone. They are defined through the process of therapy as a mutual activity. Once defined, problems are contextually interpreted as temporary means for moving the individual or the family along a developmental course.

*The counselor role, therefore, is largely* **trans-systemic, meaning that the counselor must be able to identify, analyze, and negotiate the influence of groups on the client's situation.** The counselor is continually cognizant of how things can be viewed from a *metaperspective* (**a higher order view** of the situation). This means that the therapist must be continually alert to social and biological influences on him- or herself, on the client, on the larger sociolegal system, and across professional mental health communities. It requires high-level intellectual work, because being trans-systemic requires educated abilities to understand, to analyze, and to negotiate the influence of relationships on behavior. It requires extensive knowledge of the cultural and subcultural factors operating in a community. The counselor is not simply an interpersonal technician. And the counselor role is not that of "the expert authority" imposing diagnoses and treatment approaches as if they were absolute truths. The role of the counselor is always relative to the professional community, the client system, and the larger social context. For example, broadly speaking, it is consistent with the professional role of the cognitive consensual therapist to define whether a client aspires to behaviors within the range of accepted social and legal standards. Such assessment is not absolutist, because it is recognized that social and legal standards change.

Take for instance a teenager (say age 15 years) who begins to abuse marijuana. The teenager is influenced by a group of teenagers who all smoke marijuana and who all agree that it is fun, not dangerous, and a way to have great social experiences. They have done research and ascribe to a position that marijuana is not as harmful as alcohol, a legal substance for adults. They experience the high of marijuana, and they find it to be stimulating and a social lubricant. But the 15-year-old lives with his parents who are drug prohibitionists. They hold a position that smoking marijuana is bad for a teenager, and they can quote research that shows that it affects the brain structures of young people. They believe smoking marijuana puts a child in contact with the drug culture, which can provide the teenager with more dangerous substances. They also fear that the social contacts made in a drug-abusing group may be less than desirable. This scenario represents a conflict of consensualities. The two groups (the teen group and the parental unit) hold to differing truths about the nature and the use of marijuana. The teenager is a part of both groups. The parents take the teenager to counseling. Marijuana use in the state of residence is illegal, so the counselor is confronted with a conflict of consensualities where one truth is counter to the sociolegal consensus (state and federal drug laws). In this case, the role of the counselor is trans-systemic, meaning that the counselor must understand the truths across the systems of significance—the teenager, family, and legal systems. The counselor then must address the teenager's behavior in a way that fully engages the teenager and yet fully and fairly represents the ideals held by the involved communities. A solution to this conflict is social, not psychological. It may involve connecting the child to a healthy nondrug abusing teen group. It may involve educating the teen about the legal system's treatment of teen marijuana abusers. It may mean the parents must come to understand how their family must be strengthened to provide an alternative attractive space for the child. Because of legal and ethical constraints, a solution cannot condone or support the continued use of an illegal substance. So this example demonstrates the social context of solution facilitation. Cognitive consensual therapists must be adept at assessing, negotiating, and navigating the social "truths" that apply to any conflict situation.

## Goals of Counseling and Ideal Outcomes

The ideal outcome of therapy is client cooperation in a desirable social context. This means there is client behavior consistent with social and legal standards in the contexts to which the client system has aspired, or to which the client is obligated (by law or otherwise).

Beyond client cooperation in desirable social contexts, it is also important that the client becomes integrated at a nonverbal and informal level in contexts consistent with his or her socially defined needs and desires. This means, at some basic level, there is communication from a group that the client is welcomed.

Ideally, clients demonstrate "acceptance of" and "acceptance in" a desirable social context. This is best assessed by means of observing whether the client is capable of appropriate two-way communication in the desirable social context. It is easily observed by assessing whether a client is viewed as attractive by other members of a new or acceptable social group.

# GENERAL PROCEDURES

## Assessment

Assessment occurs in *stages* in Cognitive Consensual Therapy. The *first stage* can be defined as the "trans-systemic stage." During the trans-systemic stage, the client is assessed in his or her present social, cultural, and subcultural contexts. Interpersonal relations of significance are defined. Language is assessed and matched with observed or described social group affiliations, past or present. In other words, the cognitive consensual therapist attempts to place the client in his or her social matrix, presently and historically. The therapist, accordingly, attempts to define which social groups the client or client group describes as meaningful, as groups to be addressed.

Once significant groups have been defined, they are analyzed at the level of linguistic traditions. The *second stage* of assessment, then, is linguistic. As cognition involves both perception and language, language specification is critical to understanding the consensualities that emerge, or potentially can emerge, within social groupings. If at some time it becomes obvious that there are linguistic limitations, perhaps through the intellectual or biological limits of clients or treatment groups, then a subphase of stage two is recommended. This subphase involves the taking of a client or treatment group history to assess whether there are potential genetic correlates to observed behaviors (e.g., a family history of schizophrenia, depression, or intellectual deficiency). CCT does not deny that professionals and clients may agree that a biological system is of critical importance to the definition of a problem or to treatment options.

The *third stage* of assessment involves defining agreement and disagreement among members of the therapeutic group. It is at this point that consensualities and conflicts of consensualities are defined. Any lack of cooperation is a hint of a failed attempt at consensus. Any challenge to the therapist is also a message of a different consensuality.

Additionally, when clients *blame* an individual or a group for a problem, in all likelihood a conflict of consensualities has been defined between the blaming individuals and the blamed party.

The *fourth stage* of assessment is not necessarily accomplished in all cases. The fourth stage is individual assessment of an identified patient or patients. It is used when a consensus about group involvement in the problem is not attained and when one person is clearly implicated as "the problem." It is a means of linking traditional diagnostic approaches, valued in Western culture, with the definition of the problem and the method of solution. It is viewed as a last-resort means of assessment. Accordingly, diagnoses are viewed as conventions, agreed-on criteria, deriving from the interactions of a group of experts acting to develop a professional consensus, which itself is changeable (e.g., the *Diagnostic and Statistical Manual of Mental Disorders*, Fifth Edition [*DSM-5*]; American Psychiatric Association, 2013).

## Treatment/Remediation

Treatment begins with the establishment of a professional relationship. The therapist should come across as a well-educated, experienced, confident, credentialed, and well-established professional. Beginning therapists should affiliate with therapists who can meet more mature qualifications.

The therapist's social skills are critical. The therapist must be able to interact with clients in a way that demonstrates that he or she understands (and if possible, speaks) the language of his or her clients at the cultural and subcultural levels. The therapist must also demonstrate that he or she understands *and* speaks the language of the larger service delivery and sociolegal systems.

Once clients or treatment groups have been assessed, it is necessary to determine the target of intervention. As stated earlier, the target will always be the process of human interaction. This means, at some level, the therapist will interject information into the therapeutic process that will affect the direction or speed of change occurring in the identified patient and/or the group of significance. Because all that is understood is cognitive and social, the therapist will attempt to engage the perceptual process, providing ample stimuli to clients as he or she defines the problems and solutions to be undertaken. For example, the therapist may make use of family assessment measures or individual diagnostic instruments and may make the assessment results generally known. Or the therapist may assist clients getting involved with outside groups or individuals that can be supportive through the process of change.

The therapist must always be cognizant of disagreements among members of a treatment group. It is not necessary to have an unquestioned consensus about the issues at hand in therapy among members of the treatment group, but it helps. It may be likely, however, that there will be an individual or individuals who are unable to perceive, to understand, or to behave consistently with the treatment goals as defined primarily by others. In such a case, the individual or individuals may be defined as socially out of sync with their group affiliation and unable to reconcile to group demands; such clients may be separated for individual, or, preferably, other group treatment. If that individual is defined as the "identified patient," then either psychological or organic–medical means of treatment may be undertaken.

Essentially, the cognitive consensual therapist defines a problem in a way that it is reasonable to clients, and then he or she treats the problem according to methods that would logically follow from the definition of the problem. For instance, if the problem of a child's misbehavior is defined by the therapist as resulting from parental conflicts, and the parents and the child openly or tacitly agree, then marital and family counseling would be a reasonable means of treatment. On the other hand, if the parents are resistant to a relational interpretation of the problem, and the child is diagnosed as hyperactive by school and other *authorities*, then either organic–medical treatments may be coordinated or a behavior modification program may be implemented. The therapist always yields to consensus, unless yielding means being unethical, illegal, harmful, or immoral according to professional, legal, and local standards. However, if it appears that no consensus is possible, then the therapist defines the inability of the treatment group members to come to consensus as the problem, which would seem indisputable. (Ironically, if one or more individuals disagree, then their actions verify the counselor's position.) In such cases, the goal of counseling would be the development of a means for assisting the family members to develop acceptable consensual positions (e.g., group communications training) so they can learn to agree.

## Case Management

Therapy is not necessarily a long-term process, although it can be long term if it is agreeable to both the client and the therapist and consistent with the goals of therapy. For instance, if both the client and the therapist agree that the goal of therapy is self-awareness, then more sessions may be necessary than with therapy aimed at solving a perceived situational problem. As a general rule, however, due primarily to socioeconomic constraints, shorter term problem-solving therapy is preferred.

Cases begin with the defined social group of affiliation. Essentially, every one of the group members is viewed as a client, just as the group itself can be viewed as a client. But the cognitive consensual therapist must focus on each individual in understanding the cognitive-consensual framework from which that individual is operating. Individuals do not exist in isolation. It is assumed that they are the sum of their ever-changing biological and social relations. Relatedly, co-therapy, or the use of treatment or observing teams, is highly recommended. In this way, treatment decisions occur in a consensual framework, which is fully consistent with the social constructivism philosophy.

Therapy may proceed as systemic, dealing primarily with a family system, for example. But individuals may be separated in counseling for several purposes, including the building of a consensus between the therapist and one client, or the building of consensus between several individuals. In fact, the therapeutic boundary of CCT is not the therapist's office. Instead, CCT may occur, through therapist coordination, in outside settings with outside individuals, or any place where an appropriate consensus among clients or participants may be facilitated.

Individual counseling, consequently, preferably involves another or other individuals in addition to *the client* and *the counselor*. Therapy is not simply dialogue between the therapist and the client. It is social, just as truths are viewed as highly social. Therapeutic understanding and therapeutic change are social activities, and, almost across the board, the cognitive consensual therapist engages other relationships in therapy.

The cognitive consensual therapist, then, may work with individuals or groups, switching between the two even while counseling one family or dealing with one problem. The cognitive consensual therapist defines the importance of his or her actions and conclusions consistent with the professional community of cognitive consensual therapists with which he or she associates (physically, geographically, socially, or theoretically).

Typically, individuals or families attend counseling approximately one session per week, as is mutually agreeable to the client and the therapist with the therapist's guidance. Sessions are designed to be pleasant and, to some degree, entertaining. Clients should feel good about coming to therapy. Counselors, therefore, are encouraged to use their social skills and a sense of humor when dealing with clients. This is not to say that the therapist should belittle the client or the client's problems, but it is to say that the client should feel positive about coming for therapy and confident about the counselor's ability to deal with concerns. Sessions may be scheduled at any frequency depending on the nature of the concern, the degree of consensus among treatment group members, or other factors that are discerned as important by the therapist (e.g., client financial concerns).

Case notes should describe individual cognitive and consensual frameworks, actions (including perceived nonverbal communications), and the interpersonal contacts that may constitute a social group of significance (in or outside of the therapy group). The therapist should also identify the conflicts in consensualities that he or she perceives and the actions he or she believes must be taken to facilitate changes. Recording of sessions (audio recording and especially video recording) is highly encouraged.

## Specialized Techniques

1. *Probing for consensualities*. This is a specialized assessment technique. The therapist essentially interviews the members of a system of significance, attempting to define agreements and disagreements among the clients (or outside individuals identified as significant) on issues of relevance. For example, the therapist might ask: "Who agrees with mother that father is not home enough?" Or, "Who takes up sides for Johnny when he argues with his sister?" Or, "What does Marie do when Jimmy and Tommy argue?" In these ways, agreements and disagreements on topics of concern can be identified, thereby revealing any conflicting consensualities potentially operating in the disagreements.

2. *Building consensus*. Building consensus is the process whereby the therapist attempts to design experiences supportive of a definition of the problem and, consequently, an appropriate way of behaving.

   The appropriateness of a behavior is defined within a social context by the therapist as a certified/licensed authority. A preferred behavior can never be illegal, should never be immoral according to reasonable societal and moral standards, and should never influence individuals by creating socially or physically painful experiences. As long as the wanted behaviors: (a) are not harmful to others; (b) are reasonable within an accepted social and professional (ethical) context; and (c) are consistent with the social context to which the client system aspires (by choice or legal mandate), then they are *appropriate*.

   Cognitive consensual therapists build consensus around their diagnosis of a problem and around their proposed solution to the problem. For example, assume that a teenage girl appears socially uncomfortable in the presence of boys her age. Assume further that her parents have brought her to therapy because they believe her "shyness" is to the extreme and is influencing her social relations in a negative fashion. The girl, however, seems a bit confused over her situation, and she is unsure what it all means. The cognitive consensual therapist, in this situation, might proceed by assessing the girl psychologically, or by observing her in social contexts, fully recognizing the power of the therapist's professional opinion (see Handelsman, Basgall & Cottone, 1986; Snyder, 1974; Snyder, Shenkel, & Lowery, 1977). Whenever possible, the therapist should incorporate professional information from outside sources to strengthen his or her position. While the therapist is assessing the girl, he or she is developing a relationship with her, and during this process, assuming that she is involved with therapy and communicates cooperatively, the therapist might communicate to her (verbally, nonverbally, and contextually) that she is interacting well, and that her condition is an adjustment concern that can be overcome by some behavioral exercises. The therapist then communicates the same message to the parents, who agree. The therapist then demonstrates a simple communication technique to assist the girl when meeting new people, and practices with her in the counseling setting. The therapist gives her a homework assignment and describes himself or herself as a teacher. The therapist then develops a therapeutic contract detailing approximately how long it will take to address the concern and outlining some of the other activities that will be involved. The parents are to be involved to some degree throughout the process. Through these actions, the cognitive consensual therapist has built a consensus around the definition of the problem as "shyness" and the solution as behavioral. According to CCT tenets, it would be predicted that the likelihood of success on this case would be enhanced through the development of a firm agreement among the parents, the child, and the counselor about the nature of the problem and the solutions to be undertaken.

On the other hand, if the parents were convinced that their daughter's behavior was because of an earlier diagnosed "schizophrenia," and the daughter disagrees and maintains a position that her problem is shyness, then the therapist's approach may have to be quite different. The therapist might have to support or challenge the previous definition of the problem, or he or she might have to attempt to develop a totally different consensus that is inconsistent either with a diagnosis of "schizophrenia" or "shyness." To do this, the therapist might have to develop a creative redefinition of her problem through a combination of techniques known as "challenging consensus" and "reframing" (defined as follows).

3.  *Challenging consensus.* The process of challenging a consensus is necessary when there are conflicts of consensualities. As stated earlier, lack of cooperation is a signal to a conflict of consensualities. In such a case, disputation of a consensually grounded position becomes necessary. Challenging a consensus *always* involves the presentation of an alternative position. Challenging a consensus may involve helping clients to come into contact with other individuals with different opinions and actions. It may involve activities that help the client to espouse a different position. But it *must* involve presentation of material that can be *perceived* as nonsupportive of the unwanted position. The client must come *to perceive* and *to understand* (linguistically) a different standpoint. As consensus involves both cognitive (perception and language) and social activities, it is important that stimuli are involved that can perturb a client's nervous system while there is simultaneous definition of what is perceived

within a social context (where at least one other person supports the wanted viewpoint).

4. *Reframing.* Reframing is probably the most universal therapeutic technique (L'Abate, Ganahl, & Hansen, 1986). Reframing is the process of redefining a concern. Reframing may involve redefining a perceived individual problem as a relational problem ("Your problem is your marriage"), or it may involve the opposite approach—redefining a relational concern as an individual one ("Your marital problem is really a problem of your spouse's alcoholism"). It may also involve a creative redefinition of concerns from one context to another ("Your problem is not in your marriage, it's in your relationship with your father"). Reframing can downplay problems ("Your depressions are your body's means of telling you something must change"), or reframing can emphasize a certain aspect of a problem ("It is not your feelings that are a concern, it's the way you think that needs to be changed"). L'Abate et al. (1986) provide a thorough discussion on the different types of reframing, and readers are referred to their book for additional information on the technique. In any case, reframing will always restate a concern in new ways so that a different consensus may be achieved.

5. *Spreading individual blame to relationships.* Spreading blame is the process of contextualizing a problem from an individual or an isolated group to a larger social context. It involves defining all of the individuals who may be perceived as implicated in a problem. It involves taking statements of an individual's fault (or blame), offered by one or several members of a group, and spreading the blame to several members of the group or to a larger social context. For example, a daughter who becomes involved in drug abuse, whose behavior begins to negatively affect family relations, may be defined by family members as the "cause" of the family problems. The cognitive consensual therapist, however, might choose to define her social group of affiliation (the peer group or drug culture) as the problem needing a remedy. If, in fact, a consensus around the new definition of causation is agreeable, then spreading of blame has occurred. Spreading the blame is actually a special kind of reframing where cause is redefined, usually from one individual to one or more relationships.

6. *Individual diagnostic techniques.* Individual diagnostic techniques include individual psychological assessment (of personality, interests, aptitudes, skills, values, psychopathology, intelligence, etc.). Individual diagnosis may involve the use of mental status examinations to assess the degree of "symptomotology." It may involve any interpersonal means of defining a problem within an acceptable counseling-theory framework. *In all cases, the use of individual diagnoses or assessment techniques is temporary, and the fleeting nature of the usefulness of evaluation is clearly communicated to the client by the cognitive consensual therapist.* The primary purpose of using such techniques is consensus building. The data provided by assessment devices may be very credible to clients during the therapeutic process.

7. *Relational assessment techniques.* Any technique used to define a relationship, such as structured interaction, may be used by the cognitive consensual therapist. For example, a therapist might ask a marital couple to engage in a discussion about perceived problems so that the therapist may observe the nature of

the relationships (e.g., whether it can be viewed as symmetrical or complementary). As with individual assessment methods, the purpose of such techniques is to assist in the building of consensus, remembering that cognition (perception and language) are involved. Assessment methods, therefore, are an easy way for counselors to facilitate relationship self-observation.

## Recent Developments or Criticisms

Obviously the major development related to CCT is its introduction as a counseling theory. This is a new theory of counseling and psychotherapy. Consequently, there have been no criticisms by other theoreticians or practitioners.

CCT has been presented for two purposes. First, it helps to operationalize the proposed social constructivism paradigm. Second, it demonstrates how closely theories of counseling and psychotherapy are linked to philosophy. CCT as a theory of counseling has been *purely deductively conceived.* Consequently, the development of CCT helps to validate the usefulness of paradigmatic thinking in the counseling field. This is not to say that paradigmatic thinking is the be-all and end-all of theory development in counseling and psychotherapy. Rather, it can be viewed as an opportunity.

Due to the newness of CCT, at this point it might be wise to address some potential criticisms of the theory. Some potential theoretical criticisms of CCT follow. First, it can be argued that CCT can never truly exist, because once a practitioner senses he or she grasps CCT, then it must have changed. This is true. CCT is not static. It is ever changing. It is changed in every communication about it, because individuals who learn of CCT and attempt to communicate its basic premises cannot help but modify it through their own experiences and sociolinguistic biases. It is fully anticipated that CCT will develop, if it survives, as a continually changing therapeutic approach, shaped within the context of a professional mental health community.

Second, some might argue that CCT is not unlike some psychological or systemic-relational therapies that are process oriented—for example, Rogers's Person Centered Therapy (cf. Rogers, 1951). However, there is much that is different between CCT and the therapies associated with the other paradigms presented in this book. CCT has no absolute conception of mental health. It also does not value the individual alone over the social system, or vice versa. There is no therapeutic ideal, such as Rogers's fully functioning person. Mental health, according to CCT, can never be a crystallized concept. Any conception of mental health is cognitively *and* socially founded. Mental health may vary according to local dictates and individual perceptions. CCT, therefore, provides a fully contextualized definition of mental health; however, there may be limits to this position. The CCT position that the definition of mental health is fully contextualized may lead to a conclusion that CCT is a relativistic theory, where right and wrong depend only on the demands of the moment. Consequently, it appears, according to CCT, that there is no single way to define what is valued in human interaction. However, any conclusion that CCT is relativistic is a naive conclusion. This is so because CCT does not negate the possibility of multiple consensualities or of a singular consensus, deriving primarily from bracketed absolute truths, which within a community are unquestionable or indisputable. CCT assumes that mental health may differ according to perceptions in different social contexts, but it does not deny the possibility of group centric truths about mental health (based on a pervasive underlying group consensuality).

A third criticism of CCT is that it is simply a highly refined eclectic philosophy. This argument was addressed briefly in a previous section of this chapter through a citation by Keeney (1983), which distinguished therapies based on epistemological positions as higher level approaches, going beyond either: (a) purely eclectic approaches that allow multiple therapeutic applications; or (b) approaches based on merged or combined theories. Patterson (1986), in discussing eclectic therapists, stated:

> Thus there seem to be as many eclectic approaches as there are eclectic therapists. Each operates out of his or her unique bag of techniques; on the basis of his or her particular background of training, experience, and biases; and case by case, with no general theory or set of principles for guidance. Essentially, it amounts to flying by the seat of one's pants. (p. 460)

Patterson's statement demonstrates a theoretically conservative stance about the nature of eclecticism. However, Patterson presented an optional, more liberal interpretation of eclecticism as well, saying that eclecticism could be a theoretical, comprehensive, and synthesizing approach. Nevertheless, whether one interprets eclecticism conservatively or liberally, eclecticism is quite different from CCT. CCT is formally and theoretically based. CCT is not loosely organized; rather, it is organized around specific, well-formulated theoretical and paradigmatic propositions and tenets. Although CCT and eclectic approaches are both integrative, CCT is integrative primarily at the levels of philosophy (social constructivism), whereas eclectic approaches appear to be integrative primarily at a practice-relevant level. Where some eclectic approaches are able to integrate theories within one or even two paradigms (e.g., Thorne's [1961, 1967] "Integrative Psychology"), they fail to incorporate (or to be able to integrate) all four paradigms, most usually excluding systemic relational or constructivism propositions. Because CCT is relational, at the practical level it is able to draw on any methods or techniques consistent with operating consensualities, while maintaining theoretical and philosophical underpinnings.

CCT can be criticized as too demanding for the therapist, requiring knowledge of many therapeutic methods and techniques. It is true that the cognitive consensual therapist must be a thoroughly educated and competent technician, but it is not necessary for the cognitive consensual therapist to be an expert in every therapeutic approach. Rather, it is recommended that the cognitive consensual therapist should have a firm understanding of paradigm propositions across the four paradigms (Cottone, 2012). Additionally, the therapist should be skilled in at least one, but preferably two approaches associated with each paradigm. This is, indeed, asking much of therapists, but it also reflects a faith in the capability and the level of professionalism of professional counselors. It requires in-depth training, social skill, intelligence, a professional attitude, and an intellectual spirit.

All-in-all, CCT is able to counter most attacks that would portray it as theoretically flawed, incomplete, or a hybrid. However, the test of time will be the critical test of CCT.

---

**STUDENT–MENTOR DIALOGUE**

**Student:**    This approach, as presented in this chapter, really seems like a proposition—is it really a practiced approach?

**Mentor:**    Yes, it has been used in practice by a few clinicians associated with the author. It has been refined since 1992, when it was first introduced, up until 2016, when this chapter was written. There have been no studies to assess the efficacy of this approach, so it must be considered an emergent and not fully developed or researched counseling theory.

**Student:**    I find it interesting, as it appears to be a fully theoretically directed approach. What I mean by that is that it was purely formed by following a philosophy. Is that true?

**Mentor:**    Yes. More than other theories, this approach was intentionally built on philosophy. Other theories tend to evolve as clinicians refine their ideas and then attempt to describe or fit their actions into a logical or theoretical framework. CCT is uniquely built on the social constructivism philosophy. Its development was meant to be a vehicle for transporting a method of theory building (the paradigm framework) as well as to provide another approach to treatment. So it does offer the field an example of a purely paradigm-consistent approach.

**Student:**    Don't you think that it is asking a lot of counselors, especially those in graduate training, to apply CCT. First, they have to learn a philosophy that might be alien to them—at least a philosophy that is different than the philosophies that undergird many other theories of counseling. Then, they have to have a large repertoire of technique so they can intervene as a relational therapist, a psychological therapist, or even someone applying psychiatric case management. That seems like a lot to expect.

**Mentor:**    Mental health practitioners are highly educated and licensed professionals. They all are educated in graduate programs. They are viewed as intellectuals, meaning they apply high-level abstract ideas to practice. The assumption is that they are highly capable professionals who will seek to learn and learn to apply theory-relevant technique. This is not unusual in any profession. The same is true for medicine or law. The good news is that once the social constructivism philosophy is embraced, its application becomes second nature to practitioners. Counselors must be adept at observing, defining, and conceptualizing the social factors clients bring to the therapy context. Once there is agreement about the nature of the problem and an approach to the solution, then the counselor can begin to implement a technique that stems from that consensus. The counselor does not have to be a master of every approach, but certainly the counselor must be trained, supervised, and skilled at approaching clients from a number of psychotherapeutic frames. In some sense, it makes counseling more complicated, but it also makes it interesting.

**Student:**    Beyond introducing a paradigm-consistent approach to theory building and offering a new treatment model, what does CCT hope to accomplish?

**Mentor:**    The hope is that others will embrace this new counseling model and learn to apply it. In time, if it gets some traction in the professional community, it can be assumed that others will assess it and determine whether it is a viable, effective, and useful approach. Researchers outside the CCT community will have to independently assess its efficacy, which will, if it is efficacious, help to establish the credibility of CCT.

## CONCLUSION

This chapter has presented a new theory of counseling and psychotherapy. CCT is a counseling theory designed around social constructivism tenets of practice. Some basic operational activities and techniques of CCT were presented, using the same organizational framework for chapters describing more established theories of counseling and psychotherapy. Potential criticisms of CCT were addressed. It is hoped that through this chapter, CCT has been operationalized to the degree that students and practitioners will have a sense of its implementation and that more experienced counselors may begin to experiment with its application as a therapy of choice.

## REFERENCES

American Psychiatric Association. (2013). *Diagnostic and statistical manual of mental disorders* (5th ed.). Arlington, VA: American Psychiatric Publishing.

Cottone, R. R. (1992). *Theories and paradigms of counseling and psychotherapy*. Needham Heights, MA: Allyn & Bacon.

Cottone, R. R. (2001). A social constructivism model of ethical decision-making in counseling. *Journal of Counseling and Development, 79,* 39–45.

Cottone, R. R. (2010). *Toward a positive psychology of religion: Belief science in the postmodern era*. Winchester, UK: John Hunt Publishing.

Cottone, R. R. (2012). *Paradigms of counseling and psychotherapy*. Cottleville, MO: Author. Retrieved from https://www.smashwords.com/books/view/165398

Cottone, R. R. (2013, September). A paradigm shift in counseling philosophy. *Counseling Today, 56*(3), 54–57.

Cottone, R. R. (2014). On replacing the ethical principle of autonomy with an ethical principle of accordance. *Counseling and Values, 59*, 238–248.

Cottone, R. R. (in press). In defense of radical social constructivism. *Journal of Counseling and Development*.

Gergen, K. J. (1985). The social constructionist movement in modern psychology. *American Psychologist, 40*, 266–275. doi: 10.1037/0003-066X.40.3.266

Gergen, K. J. (2009). *An invitation to social construction* (2nd ed.). Los Angeles, CA: Sage.

Handelsman, M. M., Basgall, J. A., & Cottone, R. R. (1986). The Barnum effect: Implications for testing in family therapy. *American Mental Health Counselors Association Journal, 8*, 80–86.

Keeney, B. P. (1983). *Aesthetics of change.* New York, NY: Guilford. Excerpt reprinted with permission of The Guilford Press.

L'Abate, L., Ganahl, G., & Hansen, J. C. (1986). *Methods of family therapy.* Engelwood Cliffs, NJ: Prentice-Hall.

Mahoney, M. J., & Lyddon, W. J. (1988). Recent developments in cognitive approaches to counseling and psychotherapy. *The Counseling Psychologist, 16*, 190–234.

Maturana, H. R. (1978). Biology of language: The epistemology of reality. In G. A. Miller & E. Lenneberg (Eds.), *Psychology and biology of language and thought* (pp. 27–63). New York, NY: Academic Press.

Maturana, H. R. (1980). Biology of cognition. In H. R. Maturana & F. J. Varela, *Autopoiesis and cognition: The realization of the living.* Boston, MA: D. Reidel. (Original work published in 1970)

Maturana, H. R., & Varela, F. J. (1980). Autopoiesis: The organization of the living. In H. R. Maturana & F. J. Varela (Eds.), *Autopoiesis and cognition: The realization of the living.* Boston, MA: D. Reidel. (Original work published in 1973)

Maturana, H. R., & Varela, F. J. (1987). *The tree of knowledge: The biological roots of human understanding.* Boston, MA: Shambhala.

Neimeyer, R. A. (1995). Constructivist psychotherapies: Features, foundations, and future directions. In R. A. Neimeyer & M. J. Mahoney (Eds.), *Constructivism in psychotherapy* (pp. 11–38). Washington, DC: American Psychological Association.

Patterson, C. H. (1986). *Theories of counseling and psychotherapy* (4th ed.). Cambridge, MA: Harper & Row.

Rogers, C. R. (1951). *Client-centered therapy.* Boston, MA: Houghton Mifflin.

Snyder, C. R. (1974). Acceptance of personality interpretations as a function of assessment procedures. *Journal of Consulting and Clinical Psychology, 42*, 150.

Snyder, C. R., Shenkel, R. J., & Lowery, C. R. (1977). Acceptance of personality interpretations: The "Barnum effect" and beyond. *Journal of Consulting and Clinical Psychology, 45*, 104–114.

Szasz, T. S. (1974). *The myth of mental illness.* New York, NY: Harper & Row.

Thorne, F. C. (1961). *Personality: A clinical eclectic viewpoint.* Brandon, VT: Clinical Psychology Publishing.

Thorne, F. C. (1967). *Integrative psychology.* Brandon, VT: Clinical Psychology Publishing.

# PART V

## Cross-Paradigm Approaches

This part of the book provides a summary of two theories of counseling and psychotherapy that cross paradigms. They were designed by theorists who specifically built in philosophy and methods showing that there was adherence to tenets that derived from different paradigms. The theorists were aware and apparently purposefully intended to mix paradigm propositions and tenets in a way that their theory could benefit practically.

# CHAPTER

## 15

# Dialectical Behavior Therapy

*Amanda K. Bohnenstiehl*

## OBJECTIVES

- To present the intricate work of Marsha Linehan that has shown much efficacy in treating a specific population of clients, as well as others

- To provide a historical perspective to give the reader a context for understanding and adopting the ideas that Linehan presented

- To give some biographical information on Linehan and give readers a sense of her personal history and how that influenced her ideas

- To list basic tenets of Dialectical Behavior Therapy (DBT) and the basic concepts used in conceptualizing and addressing a client's concerns

- To offer a dialogue on the theory, between a student and a mentor, on the significance of the theory for the mental health field

- To discern criticism and current or recent developments in the application of DBT.

*Dialectical Behavior Therapy* **(DBT)** was developed by Marsha Linehan, PhD, ABPP. It was first published as a manualized psychotherapeutic treatment in 1993. It is a skills-based approach first targeted toward and found through extensive research to be highly effective with those experiencing extreme emotional dysregulation patterns, suicidal ideation, and non-suicidal self-injury consistent with a diagnosis of

***Borderline Personality Disorder*** **(BPD).** The *Diagnostic and Statistical Manual of Mental Disorders,* 5th Edition (*DSM-5*; American Psychiatric Association, 2013) describes **BPD as, "A pervasive pattern of instability of interpersonal relationships, self-image, and affects, and marked impulsivity, beginning by early adulthood and present in a variety of contexts"** (p. 325). Since its inception, DBT has also been used and studied to be effective with additional populations, such as those with eating disorders, substance abuse issues, and in couples therapy (Dimeff & Koerner, 2007; Fruzetti, 2006; Safer, Telch, & Chen, 2009). In 2007, the adolescent version of the DBT manual was published by Linehan along with Alec Miller and Jill Rathus. Then, in 2014, Linehan published the second edition of the *DBT Skills Training Manual,* containing both new skills and new guidelines for skills training by therapists. A new edition of the adolescent manual was also published in 2015 (Rathus & Miller).

Linehan's approach displays the use of a combination of influences in mental health research and other disciplines found to bring relief to those suffering from an inability to manage painful emotions. She crosses paradigms by using a psychological lens as well as a family or environmental-systems approach to conceptualize the person and development of pathology (see ***Biosocial Theory*** that follows). Her theory is heavy on behavioral as well as Zen Buddhist principles, making it quite unique among other variations of Cognitive Behavioral Therapy.

## MARSHA LINEHAN: A BIOGRAPHICAL SKETCH

Marsha Linehan
*Source:* University of Washington.

A short biography of Marsha Linehan's professional life is provided on the website of her training company, Behavioral Tech, LLC (2017); her personal life was historically illustrated in a *New York Times* article (Carey, 2011). These two publications were used in the writing of this section as primary sources for describing Linehan's life.

Marsha Linehan was born on May 5, 1943, in Tulsa, Oklahoma. She was the third of six children. Her father was an oilman, and her mother did the child rearing along with participating in the Junior League and Tulsa social events. Linehan was a successful student from early on and a natural on the piano. She was described as "precocious" and often in trouble; she has described feeling deeply inadequate compared to her attractive and accomplished siblings. Her distress went unnoticed until she was struck with headaches in her senior year of high school.

Her younger sister, Aline Haynes, said, "This was Tulsa in the 1960s, and I don't think my parents had any idea what to do with Marsha. No one really knew what mental illness was" (Carey, 2011). At age 17 years, she was treated for "extreme social withdrawal" at the Institute of Living, in Hartford, Connecticut. She was often in seclusion due to repeated self-injury: burning her wrists with cigarettes and slashing her arms, legs, and midsection with anything she could find. Without such tools, her urge to die only deepened. Thus, she resorted to banging her head against the walls and floor. She described feeling completely out of control, empty, with no way to communicate her thoughts or feelings, and without her own understanding of what was happening. She received a variety of diagnoses and was treated with an array of powerful psychiatric medications, electroconvulsive therapy, and psychoanalysis. Nothing helped, and she remained in seclusion. After 26 months of hospitalization, her 1963 discharge summary described Linehan as one of the most disturbed patients in the hospital.

Linehan had several more suicide attempts and short-term hospitalizations before moving to Chicago to "start over." As a long-time Roman Catholic, she clung to her faith for guidance. She took odd jobs and began night classes at the Loyola University, Chicago. She has described having a visceral moment in prayer with God at a Chicago chapel that led her to love herself again. She later determined the only effective intervention for her would have been one based on facts, including which precise emotion led to which thought that led to what destructive act. She would have to learn to break the "chain" and use a brand new sequence of behavior.

She earned a BS (1968), MA (1970), and PhD (1971) in social and experimental personality psychology from Loyola. It took years of study to determine how she recovered: She had radically accepted herself as she was. "She had tried to kill herself so many times because the gulf between the person she wanted to be and the person she was left her desperate, hopeless, deeply homesick for a life she would never know" (Carey, 2011). She discovered that the only way to engage deeply suicidal people was to validate them. Their thoughts of death provided profound release given what they were suffering.

After leaving Chicago for New York, Linehan completed a postdoctoral internship at The Suicide Prevention and Crisis Service in Buffalo and a postdoctoral fellowship in behavior modification at Stony Brook University. Gerald C. Davison chose Linehan for her Stony Brook fellowship and highlighted her now well-known use of irreverence in therapy: "She could get people off center, challenge them with things they didn't want to hear without making them feel put down" (Carey, 2011). She served as an adjunct professor at both the University at Buffalo and then Loyola. She was then an assistant professor at The Catholic University of America in Washington, DC from 1973 to 1977, at which time Linehan took a position at the University of Washington as an adjunct professor in the psychiatry and behavior sciences department.

Linehan identified with the severely suicidal person's sense of being in hell; she developed her most central *dialectic*, **when two opposing opposites occur simultaneously**, of recovery coming only from "Acceptance and Change" and believed the only way to study this theory was to empirically test it with the most desperate population she knew. She determined that the diagnosis she most closely aligned with in earlier years was BPD; she chose this as her population of interest due to clinicians' generally low level of understanding and tolerance of these patients in therapy. Because of her recurring bouts of suicidality in her adult years, Linehan believed that the principles of acceptance and change in therapy would not be enough. Thus, she developed her approach of skills training for day-to-day use. Within DBT skills, all of the influences on Linehan's life and recovery can be found, from behavioral chaining to mindful meditation. Empirical studies at the University of Washington with suicidal clients in the 1980s and 1990s showed far fewer suicide attempts, hospitalizations, and higher commitment to outpatient therapy when compared with similar clients who received other experts' approaches.

Linehan's ability to connect to clinical as well as scientific audiences has been attributed to her interpersonal charisma. In 2011, she was able to transparently describe her own mental health struggle for the *New York Times*. Today, Linehan is a professor of psychology and a professor of psychiatry and behavioral sciences at the University of Washington; she is the director of the Behavioral Research and Therapy Clinics, a research consortium that develops and evaluates treatments for multidiagnostic, severely disordered, and suicidal populations. She is the founder of the Linehan Institute, a nonprofit organization that helps advance mental health through the support for education, research, and compassionate, scientifically based treatments; Behavioral Tech, LLC, a DBT training, consulting, and clinical practice; and Behavioral Tech Research, Inc., which develops online and mobile technologies to disseminate science-based behavioral treatments for mental disorders. She trains thousands of mental health professionals worldwide each year and leads many mindfulness workshops and retreats. She currently lives with her adopted daughter, Geraldine, and Geraldine's husband, Nate, in Seattle, Washington.

# THE FOUNDATIONAL THEORY
## The Target of Counseling

DBT is derived from cognitive behavioral therapy (CBT) with modifications specifically added for treating emotional dysregulation and related behaviors. These modifications are the inclusion of dialectics, validation, and mindfulness principles. For example, two skills taught to clients are to think dialectically (cognitive) and act dialectically (behavior). To *think dialectically* **means to get unstuck from black-and-white thinking (commonly known as cognitive distortions) and allow for the gray;** *acting dialectically* **occurs when one essentially compromises with herself or others in order to "walk the middle path" and find a solution to a problem.** Dialectics teaches that there is no absolute truth. The primary dialectic in DBT is "acceptance and change," which is woven throughout the therapy including but not limited to what is taught to clients as well as how therapists deliver the therapy. Linehan asserts that *validation,* **the sense that one's private experience exists and makes sense,** is the element missing from many people's lives. Lack of validation is the primary source of pain and distress. Another hallmark of DBT and the set of skills necessary for all other skills to be effective is Core Mindfulness. Mindfulness, the most obvious inclusion of Zen Buddhist teachings in DBT, also sets DBT apart from CBT. Linehan says, "the skills are psychological and behavioral versions of meditation practices from Eastern spiritual training" (1993b, p. 63).

Linehan's **Biosocial Theory** is the dialectical and transactional explanation for how emotional dysregulation and destructive problems come about, both in any given instance and over time. **Biological underpinnings called** *emotional vulnerability* **and social underpinnings called the** *invalidating environment,* **in combination, lead to problems.** Emotional vulnerability has three components, with which certain people are born (most often, people with BPD): emotional sensitivity, reactivity, and slow return to baseline. When a person who has these traits is sent the message in any manner that her emotional experience does not exist or is "bad," emotional dysregulation results; ". . . such an environment fails to teach the child when to trust her own emotional and cognitive responses as reflections of valid interpretations of individual and situational events" (p. 51).

As a result of Biosocial Theory playing out in clients' lives, they learn over time to maladaptively cope by engaging in three dialectical patterns, or dilemmas. *Dialectical dilemmas* **are the tendency for people to oscillate between extreme states of being, rather than existing in a regulated, middle ground, state.** The first is between emotional vulnerability (blaming the environment for unrealistic expectations) and self-invalidation (self-directed anger). Another dilemma is the tug of war between unrelenting crisis (frequent environmental triggers due to lack of structure) and inhibited grieving (overcontrol of sadness). Finally, active passivity (impulsivity or lack of problem solving) contrasts with apparent competence (minimization or stunted emotional expression). In DBT, therapists intervene both directly and indirectly on both clients and their environments to repair the effects of Biosocial Theory and reduce living in extreme states.

DBT holds a positive view of human nature that is considerably emotion-focused. Therapists using DBT conceptualize clients in terms of the eight primary emotions with which all human beings are born with capacities to experience. These are, according to Linehan: anger, sorrow, joy, surprise, fear, disgust, guilt or shame, and interest. Emotional experiences are made up of dialectical or nondialectical cognitive interpretations of prompting events leading to skillful or destructive actions and resulting consequences; it is a circular process. Further evidence of DBT's positive view of human nature is found in its *eight assumptions* **about emotionally and behaviorally dysregulated individuals** (Koerner, 2012, p. 22; Linehan, 1993a, pp. 106–108).

1.  Clients are doing the best they can.

2.  Clients want to improve.

3.  Clients need to do better, try harder, and be more motivated to change.

4.  Clients may not have caused all of their own problems, but they have to solve them anyway.

5.  The lives of suicidal, borderline individuals are unbearable as they are currently being lived.

6.  Clients must learn new behaviors in all relevant contexts.

7.  Clients cannot fail in therapy.

8.  Therapists treating borderline clients need support.

Holding these assumptions in mind assists immensely when both clients and therapists have low motivation for continuing the process of therapy together. DBT therapists remind each other of the assumptions continually, and they are also taught to the clients to help with self-judgment.

## The Process of Counseling

In DBT, the theory of change is one of a cognitive-behavioral nature. It comes about when clients learn new behaviors, and when those new behaviors are effectively reinforced over time, maintenance occurs. Reinforcement can occur internally and/or externally, and the therapist plays a major part in fostering and highlighting both. DBT provides this avenue for change through a transactional process of skill acquisition, skill strengthening, and skill generalization to be achieved over the course of about 1 year to 18 months of the first stage of treatment, the fundamental and most researched stage of DBT to date. DBT has four stages: Stage 1: moving from being out of control of one's behavior to being in control; Stage 2: moving from being emotionally shut down to experiencing emotions fully; Stage 3: building an ordinary life, solving ordinary life problems; Stage 4: moving from incompleteness to completeness/connection.

All beginning DBT clients start in *Stage 1*, **which consists of four components**: (a) weekly skills training group (skill acquisition); (b) weekly individual counseling (skill strengthening); (c) as needed phone coaching (skill generalization); and (d) weekly DBT consultation team meeting (during which individual therapist and skills group leaders must participate).

During weekly skills training, clients learn (or acquire), within a psychoeducational format, the DBT skills curriculum designed by Linehan. There are four modules of skills taught in order to increase skillful behavior and decrease corresponding sets of problem behaviors typical of those with BPD characteristics; the skills are helpful to all persons though, not those with BPD alone. As mentioned, the *Core Mindfulness* module is woven throughout the course of skills group; it is meant to create a stronger sense of self and control over thinking along with decreasing feelings of emptiness and confusion about self. The *Interpersonal Effectiveness* module aims at getting people what they want in relationships and addresses fear of abandonment. *Walking the Middle Path* is a fifth module that was formerly reserved for adolescent DBT clients; in 2014, Linehan integrated it into the Interpersonal Effectiveness module for adults to learn those skills in group as well. The focus is on finding common ground and learning to validate, which leads to a decrease in family conflict. The module of *Emotion Regulation* teaches labeling, acceptance, and changing feelings and discourages mood-driven choices and behavior. Lastly, in the *Distress Tolerance* module, crisis survival and reality acceptance skills are increased while decreasing desperate and impulsive actions. Linehan recommended that all clients receive two cycles of skills training, thus, learning each of the modules twice.

In weekly individual counseling, the primary therapist and client work to increase the likelihood of the client's skill usage in all contexts. The DBT therapist uses a variety of procedures, strategies, and techniques to be described later. During *case formulation*, **a client's problem behaviors are organized into the DBT "treatment hierarchy."** Life-threatening behaviors are the first tier, including self-injury, suicide, and aggression toward others; eliminating these behaviors (and urges as much as possible) is a *nonnegotiable goal* **(committing to DBT means these behaviors must be targeted)**. The second tier is therapy-interfering behaviors; these are also nonnegotiable with elimination as the goal. Examples include, and are not limited to, missing sessions, arriving late, being hospitalized, not doing homework, and rifts in the therapeutic relationship. Lastly, a negotiable third tier, is the quality of life-interfering behaviors. This includes everything else a client is struggling with and wants to change; clients decide what will be the quality-of-life targets of therapy. In any given session, the first tier is addressed first, as needed, then the other tiers subsequently. Individual therapy is where the therapist assists the client with how to apply what she is learning in skills group to her individual life; issues with client motivation to do so are also addressed by the individual therapist.

Skills coaching within phone calls between the client and her primary therapist (or a back-up, skills group leader) often also assist with issues of low client motivation. Clients are expected to call therapists for coaching *prior* to acting on destructive urges or when they are generally struggling to be skillful in their day-to-day lives. This component of the theory assists to achieve skill generalization in clients as the intervention is essentially leaving the typical setting and entering the typical environments of clients, where they need it in times of crisis. DBT therapists are expected to provide coaching after hours, keep calls short (about 5–10 minutes), and to keep the focus on finding skills to use.

Therapists delivering DBT engage in a weekly consultation team meeting, a group supervision component unique to DBT theory. Overall, a DBT program is considered a community of therapists treating a community of clients and doing the best they can with what they have been given. The meeting is where the team applies DBT to the therapists themselves in their work with clients; meetings mimic the structure of clients' individual sessions. The team meeting serves many purposes: to strengthen each other's work, cheerlead when dealing with difficult clients, provide client consultation when therapists are struggling to deliver high-quality DBT, enhance therapists' motivation, and more. The team addresses lapses in dialectical balance within a therapist, between therapists, and among the program as a whole. Linehan asserted that without a consultation team, therapists working with borderline and/or suicidal clients would likely stray from the model and burn out quickly, which would be highly ineffective for clients in desperate need of help.

## Counselor Role

The DBT therapist is highly flexible and uses a dialectical approach. "The therapist must balance the patient's capabilities and deficiencies, flexibly synthesizing acceptance and nurturing strategies with change-demanding strategies in a clear and centered manner" (Linehan, 1993a, p. 108). An individual session of DBT needs to display *warm engagement* (**validating and challenging**), a nonjudgmental stance, and a focus on emotions throughout. In addition, the therapist maintains the speed and flow through the treatment hierarchy. DBT therapists take several roles: They model dialectics, assess problem behaviors, teach the skills, and coach clients to use skills in an effort to reach their goals.

Linehan's **Therapist Consultation Agreements** (1993a, pp. 117–119; Koerner, 2012, pp. 186–187) further guide the DBT therapist's role with clients. Consultation team members commit to holding each other accountable to staying within a DBT framework by following these six agreements.

1. *Dialectical agreement.* We accept a dialectical philosophy; there is no absolute truth. When polarities arise, we search for the synthesis rather than for the truth.

2. *Consultation-to-the-patient agreement.* We agree to consult with clients on how to interact with other therapists and providers, not to serve as a go-between. We will not treat clients as fragile.

3. *Consistency agreement.* Our job is not to create a stress-free environment for clients; consistency among therapists is not necessarily expected. Mix-ups are inevitable; they are a chance for all to practice DBT skills.

4. *Observing-limits agreement.* We agree to observe our own limits and not judge others' limits. Clients can learn to figure out the limits.

5. *Phenomenological empathy agreement.* We agree to search for *nonpejorative* (**lacking contempt or disapproval**) and deeply empathic interpretations of clients', therapists', and our own behaviors. We will not judge therapists who are struggling to follow this agreement.

6. *Fallibility agreement.* We are all fallible and make mistakes as therapists. We can let go of defensiveness because we have probably done the problematic thing of which

we are being accused. We will inevitably violate all of the agreements here; we will then move toward synthesis with each others' help.

The overall message of the agreements is that any discourse occurring among a client and therapist, ancillary treatment providers, consultation team members, skills group members and leaders, and within a program as a whole are an opportunity for clients and therapists to practice their DBT skills. Linehan's theory comes full circle in this way. Ultimately, the DBT therapist serves to support people in experiencing their lives with emotional authenticity, accepting the wholesome and unwholesome, and everything in between.

## Goals of Counseling and Ideal Outcomes

As mentioned, Linehan's DBT has four stages. Stage 1 is the most intensive, as it occurs when a client is at the height of life-threatening behaviors (self-injury, chronic suicidality, aggression toward others, etc.); the goal is to decrease behavioral dyscontrol and increase behavioral control. It is intentionally highly structured given that clients' lives in this stage are typically very chaotic. Ideally, a client graduates after about 1 year to 18 months in Stage 1, once the client has significantly built her subjective **"Life Worth Living"** which Linehan characterizes as **a life the client does not want to lose and enjoys**. Clients work toward a Life Worth Living by abstaining from life-threatening behaviors, working toward skill generalization, and overall, increasing dialectical behavior patterns. Stage 1 is the fundamental blueprint for the theory. The goals of Stage 1 therapy remain throughout the other stages, because maintenance of new behavior is important.

Stage 2 is applied when a person is mostly free from safety concerns and ready to work on decreasing harmful effects of trauma and/or maintain new adaptive behaviors achieved during Stage 1; the goal is to decrease quiet desperation and increase *emotional experiencing* **(connection to the environment)**. Structured treatments for post-traumatic stress disorder (PTSD) are typically reserved for delivery during Stage 2 of DBT. Descriptions of Stage 3, which focuses on decreasing individual problems in living and increasing self-respect, and Stage 4, which focuses on decreasing sense of incompleteness and increasing capacity for joy, freedom, flow, and spiritual fulfillment, are much less represented in the existing literature.

## General Procedures

### Assessment and Problem Solving

Linehan's theory places a heavy emphasis on exhaustive initial and continual assessment of clients through the procedure of *behavioral chain analysis* **during which a problem behavior is intricately dissected and solution analysis is completed.** Therapists complete a behavior chain during each individual session, whether formally (written out, more detail) or informally (talking only, abbreviated), and clients learn over time how to behavior chain themselves. Behavior chaining stresses identifying factors occurring that are perpetuating clients' problem behaviors and preventing change from occurring. One perpetuating factor could be issues with motivation or commitment on the part of the client. For example, they could be lacking commitment to target suicide, to engage in requirements of treatment, or to practice or use certain skills necessary for change. Regardless of how lack of commitment is playing out, DBT therapists use Linehan's

**Commitment Strategies** (1993a, pp. 286–291; Koerner, 2012, pp. 81–84) to address the barrier to change.

1. *Pros and cons.* Helping the client consider reasons for and against change as well as the reasons for and against maintaining the status quo; exploring how change does or does not fit with goals and values.

2. *Devil's advocate.* Arguing for the status quo and stating doubts or drawbacks of changing. This enhances the client's position on why change is important; should be used to strengthen, not establish, commitment.

3. *Foot-in-the-door.* The therapist asks for small commitments first then increases requests in order to shape commitment toward the ultimate goal.

4. *Door-in-the-face.* The therapist asks for big commitments first then decreases a request in order to increase the likelihood of movement on at least something.

5. *Connecting present commitments to previous commitments.* Reminding the client of prior successes. Also, highlighting dissonance between current noncommitment and previously stated commitment.

6. *Highlighting freedom to choose and absence of alternatives.* The therapist emphasizes the client's right to choose along with undesirable consequences of not changing; natural consequences of choices will have to be accepted.

7. *Shaping.* The gradual strengthening of overall intrinsic commitment; client experiences more frequent, intense, or sustained behavior of wanting, acknowledging, and acting in line with the commitment to change.

8. *Cheerleading.* Especially during solution analysis, the therapist encourages the client, reinforces even minimal progress, and reminds her she has everything it will take to ultimately overcome her problems.

Commitment strategies are used heavily in the *pretreatment phase* of DBT treatment, *Orientation and Commitment,* in order to establish the minimum necessary commitment before beginning treatment.

Once in treatment, problem solving in DBT starts with assessment. The individual therapist completes a case formulation (described earlier) initially and at any given time to determine the client's current life-threatening, therapy-interfering, and quality-of-life-interfering behaviors. This case formulation informs what target behaviors will be transferred to the client's *diary card,* **a required self-monitoring tracking method with which the client keeps track of problem behaviors and skill usage on a daily basis.** Material on the diary card drives the content of individual sessions as therapists use it to determine which problem behavior(s), according to the treatment hierarchy, is going to be behavior chained that day. Effective solution analysis, toward the end of the behavior chain procedure, including use of commitment strategies, is imperative for change to occur. When the problem behavior is an urge to quit therapy, use of commitment strategies helps to prevent drop out.

## SUICIDE RISK ASSESSMENT

Linehan has specific procedures when it comes to suicide assessment of DBT clients, for the purpose of distinguishing between immediate risk and chronic urges as well as preventing death. The therapist obtains a very specific description of thoughts, urges, and plans, including frequency, intensity, and severity. A lethality assessment (Linehan, 1993a, pp. 519–523) is conducted, and the therapist works to gain commitment of the client to submit any items intended for self-injury or suicide purposes to the therapist. A behavior chain is completed in excruciating detail including heavy focus on solution analysis; therapists stress that there is *always* more than one solution to ending pain (while validating their pain) and are sure to reinforce nonsuicidal responses to distress. DBT therapists focus on the negatives of suicide, nonthreateningly, including the effect it would have on the therapeutic relationship. Lastly, they obtain commitment for a nonsuicidal plan and relate the client's current suicidality to overall patterns so as to link an episode to overall progress.

## CHANGE PROCEDURES

There are four procedures for eliciting change in DBT clients: contingency procedures, exposure-based procedures, cognitive modification, and the **didactic strategy of skills training** itself. Skills are taught and reinforced with clients constantly. Primary therapists conduct behavioral rehearsal of skills taught at group at any given time during corresponding individual sessions. Coaching calls are specifically for skills coaching, and anytime a client is actively dysregulated during group or individual sessions is considered an opportunity for skills practice through instruction and coaching from the therapist or skills group leader.

**Contingency procedures** in DBT are essentially the use of behaviorism principles (reinforcement, punishment, and extinction) to elicit change in clients. Some contingencies, while this is rare, are hard and fast rules that are not up for negotiation. For example, if clients miss either four individual or four group sessions consecutively, they are dropped from treatment. In addition, if clients self-injure or attempt suicide before seeking phone coaching, they cannot seek coaching from their primary therapists for 24 hours following the destructive act. Other contingencies and therapist observation of personal limits are used on a case-by-case basis. Contingencies are needed when ineffective behaviors are being reinforced in some way or when skillful behavior is being punished, such as a parent removing access to a phone, preventing a client from using phone coaching. They often take the form of an "If. . .then" statement, such as "If you kill yourself, then I won't be your therapist anymore." Orientating clients to contingencies and therapists' limits is essentially a training on behaviorism principles so that clients gain insight into how behavior changes.

**Exposure-based procedures** serve to reduce avoidance of negative emotions: fear, guilt, shame, and anger. Using exposure helps to increase the use of skills that have been avoided due to fear of pain and "emotion-phobia." Exposure in DBT can take many forms, such as mindfulness practice, and giving more focused attention to one's own internal experience (the opposite of dissociation). A therapist may **intentionally and gradually withdraw therapist support** (known as *fading*) to reduce fear of independence. All exposure techniques are intended to increase expression of painful emotions (e.g., crying) and enhance client control over aversive events rather than universal avoidance.

Lastly, in order to change nondialectical thinking, *cognitive modification procedures* are used. This practice is interwoven throughout the DBT process, it is informal (as opposed to traditional CBT), and it is always blended with validation of the existence of original thoughts. Cognitive restructuring intervenes through four steps: (a) teaching cognitive self-observation; (b) identifying and confronting maladaptive cognitive content and style; (c) generating alternative and adaptive cognitive content and style; and (d) teaching guidelines for when to trust and when to suspect cognitive interpretations.

The preceding general procedures along with the following specialized techniques are considered highly specialized and require years of training and practice in order to grow proficient at them.

## Specialized Techniques

There are several strategies used in DBT, which continue to distinguish it from traditional CBT. They are the bulk of what makes DBT what it is, along with the skills themselves. Here is an overview of the central concepts.

### DIALECTICAL STRATEGIES

The overall emphasis of dialectics in this theory has been established. There are also some specific dialectical strategies therapists utilize in DBT.

1.  *Entering the paradox.* The therapist does not "rescue" the client and avoids being drawn into extremes—embracing the notion that growing to accept and validate is actually a change on the client's part. The therapist balances being detached *and* intimate with the client—stressing that the client is not responsible for the way she is, *and* she is responsible for whom she becomes.

2.  *The use of metaphor.* An alternative means of teaching dialectical thinking and opening up possibilities of new behaviors. Redifining, reframing, and suggesting solutions to problems by taking something the client understands—such as two people climbing a mountain—and comparing it, through analogy, to something the client does not understand, such as the therapeutic process.

3.  *The devil's advocate technique.* Described earlier as a commitment strategy or general procedure. The therapist argues against change and commitment to therapy, paradoxically moving the client in favor of change and commitment.

4.  *Extending.* Taking the client more seriously than she takes herself; essentially, exaggerating a response when the client is exaggerating consequences of something.

5.  *Activating wise mind.* Guiding a client toward her *wise mind* **(when reason and emotion are in balance)** before responding to the therapist.

6.  *Making lemonade out of lemons.* Turning a problem into an asset or using the client's resistances. For example, suffering increases empathy; resistance reframed as persistence.

7.  *Allowing natural change.* Assuming the nature of reality is process, development, and change. Conditions of therapy may change: physical setting, appointment time, therapist inconsistencies, and so on. Exposure to safe change is therapeutic.

8.  *Dialectical assessment.* The therapist considers inside and outside influences on a person (Biosocial Theory), fitting the therapy to the client rather than fitting the client to the therapy. Embracing the idea that there is a culture into which a borderline individual can fit.

## VALIDATION STRATEGIES

Linehan asserts that acceptance of reality is a necessary condition for change to occur. Pain combined with nonacceptance results in suffering; pain combined with acceptance results in the pain itself (preferred over suffering). Validation strategies on the part of the therapist promote a value of acceptance and increase the likelihood of the client learning to self-validate. The measure of validation is whether the client *feels* validated; it is not based on the validator. Therapists oscillate smoothly from problem solving to validation as needed, depending on what is needed behaviorally in order to move the client along. There are six levels of validation (Koerner, 2012, pp. 122–124).

1. *Level 1: Listen with complete awareness, be awake.* Make eye contact, display a listening posture, turn phone off, and so on.

2. *Level 2: Accurately reflect the client's communication.* Paraphrase nonjudgmental-ly without interpretation.

3. *Level 3: Articulate nonverbalized emotions, thoughts, or behavior patterns.* State the unstated using the knowledge of the client to interpret her message and check accuracy.

4. *Level 4: Describe how the client's behavior makes sense in terms of past learning history of biology.* For example, "It makes perfect sense that you cut yourself, you couldn't think of anything else to do in that moment."

5. *Level 5: Actively search for the ways that the client's behavior makes sense in the current circumstances, and communicate this.* For example, "Of course you were terrified during that thunderstorm, anybody would be."

6. *Level 6: Be radically genuine.* Communicate respect for the client as a person and an equal, such as offering a tissue when crying or self-disclosing frustration with the client.

Linehan suggested validating at the highest level possible at any given time, as actions speak louder than words and higher levels tend to have more impact. *Functional vali-dation,* **responding to the client's experience as valid and compelling,** is imperative to the therapeutic relationship and, therefore, to reaching goals in DBT.

## STYLISTIC STRATEGIES

A final set of specialized techniques in DBT are Linehan's stylistic strategies. The thera-pist skillfully moves back and forth and synthesizes both reciprocal communication and irreverent communication. *Reciprocity* **is when the therapist is warm, vulnerable, gen-uine, highly responsive, and self-discloses.** *Irreverence* **serves to provoke the client to go "off balance" or to get her attention.** There are many examples of such, all of which a therapist has to commit to its delivery for it to be effective. A classic example is asking, "And how's that working for you?" when a client is arguing in favor of problematic behavior. The therapist must be in constant assessment of what style of communication is needed in any given moment in order to avoid damaging the therapeutic relationship and use communication style as a therapeutic strategy. Reciprocity can be safer in the short run and detrimental in the long run, whereas irreverence is risky in the short run and can produce a breakthrough in the long run.

Again, these specialized DBT strategies take much practice and guidance from a consultation team in order to use them effectively. Linehan has drawn on many philosophical and research-based influences to develop DBT's treatment targets, process, procedures, and techniques, which have proved to be highly effective through clinical trials since the early 1990s.

## Recent Developments or Criticisms

One concern with DBT is its unknown efficacy with a wide variety of mental health concerns. Linehan originally developed it for women struggling with chronic suicidal ideation and exhibiting BPD; this is also the population it has had the most empirical evidence of helping. Many components of DBT are directly related to BPD. Although in many ways it could be applied to any mental health concern, it may be considered too intensive for many clients of higher functioning. However, DBT does have the concerns of women at the forefront, making it compatible to a feminist audience. Linehan uses the pronoun "she" consistently in her writing to convey that DBT is most often conducted with females, as seen in this chapter as well. In addition, while the DBT therapist is in large part a teacher, there is no power differential between therapists and clients, like the equal relationship endorsed in feminist theory. For example, a therapist is just as susceptible to being chained on therapy-interfering behaviors as a client.

DBT has been expanded in use with additional populations: adolescents, substance abuse disorders, eating disorders, couples therapy, in inpatient settings, and more. Once modifications are made to the original model, however, it is uncertain how effective the therapy has the potential to be, as modifications have not necessarily been thoroughly tested. Chapman, Turner, and Dixon-Gordon (2011) agree that there is value in combining DBT with other approaches, but that therapists need to adhere to the theoretical foundations of DBT and deliver it as researched in order to be the most effective. An area of growing development is combining DBT with treatment for PTSD during Stage 1 treatment, rather than waiting for Stage 2. Melanie Harned, a colleague of Linehan, has published several articles explaining this modification with positive results in clinical trials (Harned & Linehan, 2008). The modification is preventing those with co-occurring BPD and PTSD from dropping out of DBT prematurely due to complications of PTSD; using the protocol, clients' self-injury and suicidal behavior are extinguishing at faster rates in order to be eligible for the prolonged exposure portion of the treatment.

From a multicultural lens, there are several components of DBT that are culturally sensitive. There is a spiritual focus throughout many of the skills, and no one form of prayer or meaning seeking is prioritized over another. Prayer is taught as a skill, toward higher beings when applicable and also to one's own "wise mind." Also, Level 4 Validation operates by linking current behavior to previous learning, which could be culturally driven. That said, while some literature is taking a specifically multicultural focus on DBT, such as expanding to the deaf population, further research is warranted in this area. DBT is being modified for various clinical presentations, but there is a lack of specific implications for various multicultural identities. Finally, despite ways that DBT intervenes on clients' environments and conceptualizes with a family system or environmental lens, the ultimate focus is on the individual learning to cope with her reality, regardless of who created that reality. Finally, clinical trials with samples of primarily male participants need to be conducted, in order to evaluate whether DBT has a high efficacy with men as it does with women.

Regardless of criticism or limitations of DBT, Linehan has revolutionized mental health services with a previously underserved, and even avoided, clinical population. DBT is a newer psychotherapy, compared to others, that is growing in popularity due to its evidence-based nature. Its cross-paradigmatic nature allowed Linehan the freedom to create a treatment without restriction of a narrower lens.

## STUDENT–MENTOR DIALOGUE

**Student:**   What are your thoughts on Marsha Linehan?

**Mentor:**   I think Linehan's place within psychotherapy theory research is well-established and continuing to grow, as she is actively researching, training, and practicing today. She is an expert in Borderline Personality Disorder, as she experienced its symptoms in her life as well. She has trained others in DBT all over the world, and it is gaining popularity. Among the cognitive-behavioral therapy community, she is a major contributor.

**Student:**   But what about her theory—what do you think about her ideas?

**Mentor:**   I find her ideas to be highly intricate and complex. There are many concepts, principles, procedures, and strategies for a DBT therapist to learn and to practice as compared to other theories. It takes a lot of willingness and commitment on the part of a DBT therapist to want to work with a personality-disordered population involving risky subject matter of suicide and self-injury. Due to a borderline person's tendency to attack the therapeutic relationship, it can be a frustrating position for the therapist at times. However, the consultation team component buffers that frustration a lot. In addition, DBT is known as the "gold standard" of treatment for those with BPD, a diagnosis to which Linehan has brought more attention. Therapists are more accurately diagnosing their clients with BPD, as opposed to, say, bipolar disorder. This intricate and detailed approach provides the necessary structure and guidelines for treating such a complex and chaotic population of clients.

**Student:**   How does it explain such life-threatening behaviors of suicide and self-injury?

**Mentor:**   Linehan's Biosocial Theory holds that chronic emotional dysregulation patterns result from a biological quality of emotional vulnerability, when combined with invalidation from the environment. People with BPD, and others with intense paralyzing emotional pain, often use destructive methods of cutting or entertaining thoughts of suicide as a means of escaping their pain. They get relief, and despite harmful consequences, they are negatively reinforced to continue these destructive acts in order to get relief from pain. Thus, DBT teaches clients means for getting relief in other, nondestructive ways so as to keep them alive as well as to build a higher quality life. This increases motivation for effective problem solving.

**Student:**  Why is there such an emphasis on dialectics in her model? What is a dialectic?

**Mentor:**  A dialectic is a synthesis of two opposing forces. Dialectics are found in DBT almost everywhere, from the way therapists deliver the therapy to how clients are taught to think and behave. Judgments and rigid black-and-white thinking lead to dysregulation and distress whereas dialectical behavior leads to willingness and acceptance of reality. Linehan pulled the concept of dialectics into her theory from cognitive behavioral research and the Buddhist emphasis on embracing contradictions, finding synthesis, and "walking the middle path."

**Student:**  So what do you see as good about this theory?

**Mentor:**  This theory is highly structured, and it is highly flexible. It has a protocol for essentially any scenario that can come up in therapy; it also allows for therapist and consultation team discretion to observe their limits, follow their own wise minds, and apply the model in the best manner they can with what they are given. It values adherence to the model and does not judge when that is not possible or when therapists make mistakes. It is good that DBT has shown high efficacy in clinical trials with suicidal and self-injuring clients, most often consistent with a diagnosis of BPD. This makes it highly attractive to consumers, insurance companies, and nonprofit funding sources that want to pay for services that have shown success. DBT is also being modified and studied with additional populations, which is quickly increasing its efficacy with a broader range of mental health concerns.

**Student:**  Thank you.

## CONCLUSION

This chapter has served as an overview of DBT by Marsha Linehan, a theory that crosses paradigms. According to Chapman et al. (2011), DBT has influences from not only CBT and Zen practices, but also humanistic, existential, and even psychodynamic principles. Linehan pulled from her personal experiences with mental illness and religion along with cognitive behavioral research and Buddhist principles to create DBT. It has a focus on the individual as well as systems, families, and larger environments. Linehan found a way to apply qualities of several philosophically grounded theories to produce consistently positive results. DBT is an evidence-based therapy that, since 1993, has significantly grown in popularity in the research community, among clinicians, and within various clinical populations.

The DBT-Linehan Board of Certification has created a national certification for individual therapists, skills group leaders, and DBT programs as a whole. Information on the process of meeting national standards for delivery of this treatment in high demand can be found at https://dbt-lbc.org.

# REFERENCES

American Psychiatric Association. (2013). *Diagnostic and statistical manual of mental disorders* (5th ed.). Arlington, VA: American Psychiatric Publishing.

Behavioral Tech, LLC. (2015). Marsha Linehan biosketch. Retrieved from http://behavioraltech.org/about/trainerdetails.cfm?tid=1

Carey, B. (2011, June 23). Expert on mental illness reveals her own fight. *The New York Times*. Retrieved from http://www.nytimes.com/2011/06/23/health/23lives.html?pagewanted=all&_r=0

Chapman, A. L., Turner, B. J., & Dixon-Gordon, K. L. (2011). To integrate or not to integrate dialectical behaviour therapy with other therapy approaches? *Clinical Social Work Journal, 39,* 170–179. doi:10.1007/s10615-010-0283-4

Dimeff, L. A., & Koerner, K. (2007). *Dialectical behavior therapy in clinical practice: Applications across disorders and settings.* New York: NY: Guilford.

Fruzzetti, A. E. (2006). *The high-conflict couple: A dialectical behavior therapy guide to finding peace, intimacy & validation.* Oakland, CA: New Harbinger Publications.

Harned, M. S., & Linehan, M. M. (2008). Integrating dialectical behavior therapy and prolonged exposure to treat co-occurring borderline personality disorder and PTSD: Two case studies. *Cognitive and Behavioral Practice, 15,* 263–276. doi:10.1016/j.cbpra.2007.08.006

Koerner, K. (2012). *Doing dialectical behavior therapy: A practical guide.* New York, NY: Guilford.

Linehan, M. M. (1993a). *Cognitive-behavioral treatment of borderline personality disorder.* New York, NY: Guilford.

Linehan, M. M. (1993b). *Skills training manual for treating borderline personality disorder.* New York, NY: Guilford.

Linehan, M. M. (2014). *DBT skills training manual* (2nd ed.). New York, NY: Guilford.

Miller, A. L., Rathus, J. H., & Linehan, M. M. (2007). *Dialectical behavior therapy with suicidal adolescents.* New York, NY: Guilford.

Rathus, J. H., & Miller, A. L. (2015). *DBT skills manual for adolescents.* New York, NY: Guilford.

Safer, D. L., Telch, C. F., & Chen, E. Y. (2009). *Dialectical behavior therapy for binge eating and bulimia.* New York, NY: Guilford.

# CHAPTER

## 16

# Emotion-Focused Therapy

*Andrea R. Cox*

## OBJECTIVES

- To present the emotion-focused work of Leslie Greenberg and Susan (Sue) Johnson, which has shown to be efficient in the treatment of couples' distress and depression, and for helping clients deal with the aftereffects of trauma and abuse

- To provide a historical perspective to give the reader a context for understanding the ideas presented by Greenberg and Johnson

- To give some biographical information on Greenberg and give readers a sense of his personal history and how that influenced his ideas

- To list basic tenets of Emotion-Focused Therapy (EFT) theory and the basic concepts used in conceptualizing and addressing a client's concerns

- To offer a dialogue on the theory, outlining the conversation between a student and a mentor on the significance of the theory for the mental health profession

- To discern criticism and current/recent developments in application of EFT

Leslie (Les) S. Greenberg, PhD, CPsych, and his then doctoral student Susan (Sue) M. Johnson began developing the EFT approach together (Greenberg, 2011; S. M. Johnson, 2004) at the University of British Columbia. *EFT is a practice of therapy that is informed by the understanding of emotions and their role in psychotherapeutic change* (Greenberg, 2011). Initially, EFT looked at the role of emotions on interpersonal conflicts within couples and marital relationships (Greenberg, 1979; Greenberg & Clarke, 1979; Greenberg & Webster, 1982; Johnson & Greenberg, 1985). In 1984, Sue Johnson, EdD, completed her doctorate in counseling psychology and she and Les Greenberg wrote the first *EFT Manual* (S. M. Johnson & Greenberg, 1985). In the manual, S. M. Johnson and Greenberg (1985) provided information on the first outcome study comparing EFT to untreated couples and couples who completed a skills training and behavioral communication intervention (S. M. Johnson, 2004). The compelling results of this study sparked decades of continued research.

In the field of counseling and psychotherapy, interest in the role of emotions on therapeutic change continued to develop. There was an expansion of research on the topic. During this time, emotion-focused, process-oriented treatments were used to study depression (Greenberg, Watson, & Goldman, 1998), interpersonal problems (Paivio & Greenberg, 1995), intimate partner happiness and distress and couples therapy (Gottman, 1994, 1999; M. D. Johnson & Bradbury, 1999; S. M. Johnson & Greenberg, 1985), the effect of trauma (Paivio & Nieuwenhuis, 2001), and the effect on human attachment (Bowlby, 1988). Beyond the original EFT theorists, many have worked to advance the study of emotions (Lewis & Haviland-Jones, 2000; Plutchik, 2000; Tomkins, 1991). Greenberg, Rice, and Elliot (1993) explored the experiential process of emotions in psychotherapy, which outlined **the original name for individual** EFT (*process experiential psychotherapy*), and Greenberg and Johnson (1988) used the term **emotionally focused therapy (the original name for the** EFT **couples therapy approach)** to explore vulnerable emotions and help reestablish the emotional bond between couples (Greenberg, 2011). These additions to the field of psychotherapy helped to highlight and to validate the value of emotions in treatment, and they enhanced the necessity for increased research and exploration of emotions as a significant part of the human experience and the process of change.

In conjunction with the prominent research of the time, focusing on the effectiveness of process experiential, emotion-focused approaches to therapeutic intervention (Greenberg, 2011), Greenberg (2002) coined the term *Emotion-Focused Therapy*. This term is now used to capture both individual and couples therapy approaches designed to evoke *emotion-focused coping* (**strategies used to alleviate distress by minimizing, decreasing, or preventing the emotional factors related to stressors**). As studies continued to explore EFT, Greenberg began to focus on treatment of individuals, while Johnson focused on treatment of couples. Despite this difference, since 2002 the terms *Emotion-Focused Therapy* or *EFT* have been adopted to encompass both individual and couples therapy. This chapter primarily focuses on treatment of individuals.

The foundation of EFT is in the exploration of emotions as well as the meaning and influence that feelings have on the human experience and in therapeutic change. EFT postulates that emotions are innately adaptive and, if activated, they are able to help clients to reclaim emotional control related to previously undesirable personal experiences, as well as to alter maladaptive emotional states and exchanges (Greenberg, 2011). EFT counselors work to help their clients become more tolerant of emotions that have been previously avoided and encourage clients to use their understanding of emotions to provide information about desired needs, concerns, and goals; this is a key principle of EFT. A central assumption of EFT is that avoidance of previously experienced emotions is linked to dysfunction. For this reason, EFT counselors believe it is imperative that clients fully experience rather than avoid their emotions.

## LESLIE (LES) S. GREENBERG: A BIOGRAPHICAL SKETCH

Leslie (Les) Greenberg
*Source:* Leslie Greenberg.

Leslie (Les) Greenberg (Greenberg, 2014), now a Canadian citizen, was born on September 30, 1945, in Johannesburg, South Africa. In 1967, he graduated with a bachelor's degree in engineering from the University of Witwatersrand in South Africa, and in 1970 he completed his master's in engineering from McMaster's University in Toronto, Ontario. In 1975 he earned a PhD in psychology from York University in Toronto, Ontario. Following graduation, Greenberg began teaching at the University of British Columbia.

Early influences on his career came from the work of Juan Pascual-Leone, who used a neo-Piagetian constructivist model of the mind to understand clients. Greenberg was also influenced by his mentor, Laura North Rice, who studied with Carl Rogers. Greenberg was initially trained in a Client-Centered Therapy approach, and then trained in Gestalt Therapy. He was also exposed to a plethora of other approaches including psychodynamic, systemic-interactional, and cognitive therapy.

Greenberg has received a host of awards, including the Distinguished Research Career Award (from the Society for Psychotherapy Research in 2004), the Professional Award in Distinguished Contributions to Psychology as a Profession (from the Canadian Psychological Association in 2007), the Award for Distinguished Professional Contributions to Applied Research (from the American Psychological Association, 2012), the Carl Rogers Award (from the American Psychological Association, 2010), and the award for Distinguished Contribution to Psychotherapy (from the American Psychological Association, 2013). He is also a founding member of the Society for the Exploration of Psychotherapy Integration (SEPI). Additionally, Greenberg has written a plethora of academic articles and authored multiple books on EFT.

Greenberg is a distinguished professor and is currently functioning as a professor emeritus in the Department of Psychology at York University in Toronto. He is also the director of York University's Emotion-Focused Therapy Clinic, which is a state-of-the-art community mental health and training center. At the center, therapists are supervised in their learning of the practical application of EFT, which is provided to both individuals and couples from the surrounding community.

# THE FOUNDATIONAL THEORY

## Target of Counseling

The scientific basis for the growth tendency in EFT is linked to a contemporary emotion theory (Frijda, 1986; Greenberg, 2002, 2011; Greenberg & Paivio, 1997; Greenberg & Safran, 1987), which suggests that emotion is fundamentally adaptive in nature. Greenberg essentially has based much of his theory on *affective neuroscience* (the scientific study of the structures and processes in the human nervous system that are involved in emotions). Emotion theory suggests that emotion helps organisms to rapidly and automatically process complex situational information so that the organism can produce actions necessary to meet basic needs. Furthermore, emotions allow for the rapid automatic evaluation of the significance of a given situation to a person's overall well-being, thus guiding adaptive action (Greenberg, 2011). Overall, then, EFT has a foundation in the biological sciences. It connects affective neuroscience to everyday experiences that may be problematic or even healing.

As people experience the world, they develop emotion schemes that help them to better understand varying situations. These schemes develop into internal emotion structures. They combine motivational, affective, behavioral, and cognitive elements into internal organizations with the purpose of identifying and understanding relevant cues within one's environment. The ability to learn from a previously defined emotional schema allows emotions to be flexible, which also leaves them open to possibly becoming maladaptive (Greenberg, 2011). EFT uses various interventions to help manage maladaptive emotional schemes. These interventions help clients learn to regulate their emotions. In EFT, the view of emotion regulation is that the cognitive system gets information from the emotion system. In this way, the emotion system guides both cognition and action (Greenberg, 2011).

EFT holds a positive orientation of human nature. Humans are seen as capable of being creative and having agency as well as being able to engage in awareness and choice. This is different from other theories that view humans as being ultimately determined by innate drives, biologically reinforced contingencies, or the past. EFT postulates that people are oriented toward growth and survival. It also suggests that people are best understood as (a) having the capacity for or tendency toward adaptation and (b) being capable of succeeding within the environment in which they live.

## The Process of Counseling

In EFT, the process of counseling consists of a process of successfully following and leading the client in an exploration of emotion that will deepen the client's understanding of the self. This process is aided by two core treatment principles, which are the provision of the therapeutic relationship and the facilitation of therapeutic work. During the process of counseling, the client feels comfortable with the establishment of the therapeutic alliance and believes the therapist is attuned to his or her needs and experiences. Additionally, the client's emotions are explored using differential interventions that align with the specific needs of the client.

According to Greenberg et al. (1993), EFT has two major principles that undergird EFT interventions: the development of the therapeutic relationship and the facilitation of therapeutic work. EFT's therapeutic style consists of a person-centered approach

(Rogers, 1957, 1959) in which the therapist works to enter and respond empathically to the client's internal frame of reference and is merged with a guided, process directive experiential and gestalt therapy approach (Gendlin, 1996; Perls, Hefferline, & Goodman, 1951). The combination of these two approaches allows for a deepened therapeutic experience. Additionally, this approach promotes a **"following" and "guiding" experience** in which **both the therapist and the client are influencing one another in a nonimposing manner**. The goal of following and guiding is to help deepen the client's experience as well as to explore and encourage the processing of emotions.

For the therapist, following always takes precedence over leading. The amount of guiding and structure provided varies by client and situation based on the degree of emotional dysregulation presented by the client (Greenberg, 2011). The level of emotional dysregulation is often represented by the client's in-session state. These in-session states are viewed as *markers* **(which are performance indicators of a task or concern presently being worked on or a current observable state)** of potentially unaddressed affective or cognitive processing concerns. Markers create an opportunity for the therapist to provide differential interventions that are designed to best meet the presenting need of the client (this is further discussed in the section Markers and Tasks).

Clients with increased distress and avoidance tend to benefit from more emotion coaching and process guidance. Clients who have a greater internal locus of control, are more fragile, or are more reactant will benefit from less guiding and more responsive following. Culture may also influence the degree of leading and following that is expected by the client during a therapy session (Greenberg, 2011). Overall, it is the therapist's responsibility to help facilitate a balance between guiding and following that will create a synergetic flow and will encourage therapeutic growth.

## Markers and Tasks

A defining feature of the interventions that are used in EFT is that each intervention is guided by an in-session marker (Greenberg, 2011). The strategy of using marker-guided intervention has been demonstrated in research. This research suggests that clients enter into specific identifiable in-session problematic emotional processing states, which include statements and behaviors that mark underlying concerns related to affect and that these markers provide opportunities for specific types of effective interventions (Greenberg et al., 1993; Rice & Greenberg, 1984). Markers can also provide information about a client's readiness to address a specific problem. EFT therapists are trained to identify different types of markers and to understand which intervention will best help the client process the underlying concern linked to the specific marker.

Greenberg (2011) identified the following main markers and their accompanying interventions:

1.  Problematic reactions are expressed through confusion about a given behavior or emotion related to a specific situation (e.g., "I saw a billboard the other day, the picture had a lot of dark colors. After looking at it I began to feel down, but I'm not really sure why."). This type of marker creates an opportunity for *evocation* **(the process of activating an experience)** in order to help promote reexperiencing the original situation. This allows the reaction to arrive at the implicit meaning, thus allowing the client to make sense of the situation. Resolution of this marker involves a new view of self-functioning.

2. An unclear but **"felt sense" (experienced sensation)** is related to the client's difficulty with getting a clear sense of his or her personal experience (e.g., "I'm feeling something, but I just can't put my finger on it."). In this case, the person is confused about or on the surface of the felt sense but is unable to clearly understand the experience. **Focusing (a process of paying attention to one's bodily felt sense;** Gendlin, 1996; Greenberg, 2011) is a strategy used to help clients generate a more clear understanding of their felt sense. Resolution of this marker involves a shift in the bodily felt sense and the formation of new meaning.

3. Conflict splits occur when one aspect of the self is in opposition with another aspect of the self (e.g., "I can never be as good as them and that makes me mad, because I know I do some stuff right."). This is often represented by having one part of the split self that is coercive and critical of the other part of the split self. When this marker occurs, a *two-chair dialogue* **(a process of having two opposing parts of the self encounter one another)** is used. This intervention allows the critical voice to become softened through the exploration and communication of the thoughts and feelings linked to each of the selves. Resolution of this marker involves integration between the two sides.

4. Self-interruptive splits occur when one part of the self constricts or interrupts an emotional experience or expression (e.g., "I was so mad I could have cried, but instead I just sat there. I was not going to let them see they got to me."). A two-chair dialogue is used to help clients begin to identify how parts interrupt. Clients are then guided to reenact this interruption via a physical act (shutting the voice down), verbally (saying things like "shut up, you can't handle this"), and/or metaphorically (confining or enclosing) in order to allow the client to experience the process of being an agent in the interrupting process. Then the client works to react to and challenge that portion of the self. Resolution of this marker involves the expression of previously blocked experiences.

5. An unfinished business marker involves one's unresolved feelings connected to a significant person in his or her life (e.g., "my grandmother died before I could tell her I was sorry for not visiting more frequently, and now I will never get to apologize."). This type of marker calls for an *empty chair dialogue* **(which is the process of having a person speak to an imagined other).** This intervention allows the client to activate an internal view of the significant other. It also allows the client to explore, experience, and make sense of his or her emotional reaction to the significant other. Understanding of the client's unmet need (in this case, possibly acceptance) and shifts in the views of the other and the self typically occur. Resolution of this marker involves holding the significant other accountable, or forgiving/understanding the significant other.

6. Vulnerability consists of a state in which the self is experienced as insecure, fragile, or deeply ashamed (e.g., "I just don't think I can do it. I can't go on like this."). When vulnerability is the marker, the therapist must work to provide affirming empathic *validation* **(a process of confirming another's experience).** The client needs to experience empathic attunement from the therapist. The therapist must be able to capture the content of the client's feelings, note the vitality or significance of the emotions, and mirror the tempo, rhythm, and tone of the experience. Additionally, the therapists need to normalize and validate the client's experience of vulnerabil-

ity. Resolution of this marker involves the strengthened sense of self, which results from the mirroring of the client's self-experience.

Additional markers and interventions including trauma and narrative retelling, self-contempt and compassion, alliance rupture and repair, confusion and clearing a space, and emotional suffering and self-soothing (Elliott, Watson, Goldman, & Greenberg, 2004; Greenberg, 2002; Greenberg & Watson, 2006). Greenberg (2011) identified these markers as "the same old stor(ies)" (p. 88) and describes them as self-explanatory. These markers may be of untold stories, empty stories, or even broken stories. Despite the type of story, the marker represents a repetitive story where the client is stuck. In order to help the client become unstuck, the therapist encourages the client to reexperience memories of specific events. Thus, the marker is dealt with through empathic exploration of the client's story in order to promote a coherent understanding of the client's previous experience.

## Counselor Role

In EFT, the role of the therapist is to help the client change his or her emotion by accessing new emotions. Greenberg (2002) has outlined a number of ways in which this process can occur including: exploration of emotions, enactment and imagery, and generating new emotional responses (Greenberg, 2011). Greenberg (2002) viewed therapists as "emotion coaches." He suggests that the EFT therapist is to accompany the client on a journey of identifying feelings, determining the validity and origin of the emotions he or she feels, accepting emotions, allowing feelings to provide information and facilitate thought, developing emotional knowledge, and reflecting on and expressing emotion. The therapist explores previously and presently (in-session) felt emotions and guides the client toward creating adaptive emotional schemas that free the client of burdensome maladaptive internal emotional structures.

One way to access new emotion is by helping the client to identify and to explore his or her emotions as they occur in the present moment (in-session markers). When this happens, the therapist works to draw the client's attention to the emotion that is being expressed. The therapist also encourages the client to label the emotion. For example, while experiencing abuse, the client may have felt helpless. This feeling of helplessness may be present during a therapy session. The therapist would help the client determine if helplessness is functioning as a primary or secondary emotion. Through exploration it is likely that the therapist and client would resolve that feelings of helplessness were functioning as secondary to fear. In this example, both helplessness and fear are maladaptive emotions. For this reason, the therapist would work to help the client establish a new adaptive emotion (e.g., possibly anger).

Developing new adaptive emotions helps to change the client's original maladaptive structure. In this case, the new feeling (e.g., anger) is likely an emotion that was felt but not expressed during the original situation (e.g., abuse), or is a feeling that is being felt in the present and is functioning as an adaptive response to the original situation. Creating the space for the client to develop adaptive emotions allows the client to assume a relational position that is different from the position held during the original situation. This allows the client to hold the abuser(s) accountable. It may also help clients to see themselves as worthy of protecting rather than guilty (Greenberg, 2011).

If no emotion appears to be present (which is an in-session marker), the therapist helps the client determine whether or not the client had needs that were not being fulfilled (e.g., needs for love, safety, and security; Greenberg, 2002). With the establishment of new adaptive emotions, the client may direct the new emotion (e.g., anger) toward the perpetrator (in the case of abuse) instead of inward. In this case, clients may blame the perpetrator for not keeping them safe. This realization will likely help the client feel stronger rather than weak and unsafe (Greenberg, 2011).

Another way the therapist helps the client access new emotions is through enactment and imagery. In EFT, enactment and imagery consist of helping clients remember previously experienced emotions (e.g., helplessness), helping clients create alterations in the way they view a given situation (e.g., believing they are worth protecting rather than believing the abuse was their fault), or providing an expression of emotion for clients (e.g., helping clients determine adaptive emotions; Greenberg, 2002). Once new emotions have been identified, clients are able to challenge the validity of the maladaptive emotion they previously held toward the self and/or others. Before checking the validity, these maladaptive emotions influence the client's perception of a situation (e.g., "the abuse was my fault"). Checking the validity of the maladaptive emotion helps to weaken the control the maladaptive emotion has on the client. This helps to disconfirm maladaptive beliefs and emotions (Greenberg, 2011) and allow the client to develop a more balanced view of the situation.

Additionally, the therapist may help the client access new emotions through the generation of new adaptive emotional responses. In this process, the therapist helps the client explore a previously emotion-latent situation and generate new emotional responses, as well as to help the client to incorporate the new responses into memory. The EFT therapist believes it is important to help the client arrive at an emotion before leaving it. This means the client is encouraged to fully experience the emotion before adapting a new emotion. Fully feeling the emotion while in the safety of a therapeutic, supportive, empathic relationship creates a powerful reconsolidation of the client's past memories. Nadel and Bohbot (2001) suggested that the reconsolidation happens because the client is having a new in-session experience with the therapist while activating memories from past experiences. In this situation, memory is transformed due to the assimilation of the new material (the presence of the therapist) on past memories. In addition to the restructuring of the old memory by the new experience, the client also experiences the co-activation of adaptive emotional responses (e.g., warmth and kindness from the therapist) and an increased ability to cope with the original situation.

## Goals of Counseling and Ideal Outcomes

The most fundamental overarching goal of EFT is to increase the client's awareness of emotions. According to Greenberg (2002), EFT focuses on helping clients strengthen their emotional intelligence and emotional literacy. Greenberg (2011) also outlined the concept of *emotional competence*, **which is seen as the ability to access emotional experiences, regulate and transform maladaptive emotions, and develop a positive self-narrative**. The management of maladaptive schemes is achieved by activating the schemes in order to verbally describe their influence. Then the client works to explore and reflect on his or her understanding of the influence the maladaptive schemes held with the key purpose of creating new meaning (Greenberg, 2002, 2011; Greenberg & Safran, 1987). Although exploring maladaptive schemes can be difficult and sometimes scary, mastery of reexperiencing emotions that were previously intolerable provides a deeper level of change. This process of focusing on and exploring emotional experiences helps the client to access primary adaptive emotional responses to various situations.

An ideal outcome for an EFT client would be one in which the client has successfully garnered the key components of EFT. This would be a client who has approached, attended to, regulated, used, and transformed his or her emotions. This client would also have learned when to engage the emotion change process. This client would feel comfortable navigating these experiences both in and out of the therapy setting while understanding that the therapist is a source of support and that the therapeutic relationship provides an avenue by which corrective emotional experiences can take place.

# GENERAL PROCEDURES

## General Strategies for Working With Emotions and Principles for Emotional Change

The two major tasks associated with the general strategies for working with emotions are helping people either access more emotion or contain their excessive emotions. In this case, people with too little emotion are taught how to access more emotions, and people who express too much emotion are taught how to contain their emotions (Greenberg, 2011). EFT identifies this as a focus, because EFT assumes that having too much or not enough emotion is a source of people's problems. As this is problematic, it is important for EFT therapists to help clients learn to regulate their emotions. Examples for how therapists help their client's access or contain their emotions are outlined later in the chapter.

## Assessment and Problem Solving: The Development of the Therapist's Perceptual Skills

The EFT model provides a system by which the therapist is able to make distinctions among differing types of emotional experiences and expression. Based on the presentation of the client and the situation that presents during the session, the therapist is trained to select the intervention that best fits the presenting need (Greenberg, 2011; Greenberg & Paivio, 1997).

In order for the therapist to successfully accomplish this task, the client must be able to identify the type of emotion being expressed. Emotions may be primary, secondary, maladaptive, or adaptive. First, the therapist must determine if the emotion is a *primary emotion* (an initial, automatic emotional reaction—the client may be aware or unaware of this initial emotional reaction) or a *secondary emotion* (a reaction to an earlier internal stimulus—often functioning as a reaction to an earlier emotion). Additionally, primary emotions are the fundamental reactions to a situation (e.g., sadness or loss) and secondary emotions are more a function of a reaction about the thoughts or feelings that are connected to the situation. Secondary emotions do not focus directly on the situation itself (e.g., feeling angry because of one's own sadness). Secondary emotions should be explored to better understand its predecessor (the primary emotion).

According to Greenberg (2011), the therapists use their experience and personal knowledge of general human emotional responses as well as their understanding of the sequences of emotion and their awareness of their own typical emotional reactions to specific situations to help determine which emotions are likely to be primary emotions.

Next, the therapist must determine if the emotion is an *adaptive emotion* (**an emotion that is functional and aiding in survival**) or a *maladaptive emotion* (**an emotion that is no longer functional**). Maladaptive emotions typically are repetitive and do not change despite changes in circumstances (e.g., feeling anger about losing a job even after finding a new job). Additionally, when maladaptive feelings are experienced they do not allow the client to generate solutions to problems that would be viewed as adaptive. Because maladaptive emotions do not provide adaptive direction it is important to assess primary adaptive emotions, which are often better for helping generate adaptive direction. This process of replacing maladaptive emotions with adaptive emotions is discussed later in the chapter.

In the spirit of guiding and following, the therapist works to understand the client's thoughts and feelings about the nature of the types of feeling being expressed. In EFT, this is a respectful collaborative process in which goals for treatment are defined and the development of tasks work to promote a therapeutic experience in which both the therapist and the client strive together to overcome the client's presenting problem.

## The Therapeutic Relationship

In EFT, the therapeutic relationship is seen as curative. The acceptance and empathy shown by the therapist toward the client promotes self-acceptance, strength, and validation, and decreases feelings of isolation. The therapist engages clients (Geller & Greenberg, 2002) in an **I–Thou dialogue (in which each person is viewed as important;** Buber, 1958, 1965) in which the therapist responds sensitively to the client's emotions and is actively engaged and highly attuned to the client's experiences. This approach allows the therapist to convey acceptance, respect, and congruence. During sessions, the therapist actively works to validate and to confirm the client's emotional experiences, thus helping the client to synthesize and solidify an identity (Greenberg, 2011). This process allows clients to develop a comfort level that enables them to feel safe enough to participate fully in self-exploration, exploration of emotion, and to engage in new learning. These are all vital tasks involved in achieving therapeutic movement and change. Additionally, a respectful collaborative process of goal and task development helps to promote an experience in which both the client and therapist are working collectively toward overcoming the problem. Therapists exude empathy as they work with clients to develop an *EFT goal agreement* (**an agreement designed to work on resolving the chronically enduring pain experienced by clients**). Coming to an agreement on the EFT goals and tasks requires that the therapist understand the client and the client's needs (Greenberg, 2011).

Engagement in this type of therapeutic relationship allows clients to begin to understand and to regulate their painful, overwhelming, and disorganized emotions (Greenberg, 2011). Participating in therapy with a therapist who is attuned and responsive provides the development of emotion regulations and interpersonal soothing. As the therapeutic relationship continues to develop, the interpersonal regulation of affect will become internalized to represent self-soothing as well as the ability for internal regulation of emotion (Greenberg, 2011; Stern, 1985).

## The Facilitation of Therapeutic Work

The facilitation of therapeutic work is linked to three *task principles* (**promoting differential processing, task completion, and agency and choice**). These principles are based on the assumption that humans are "agentic, purposeful organisms with an innate need for exploration and mastery of their internal and external environment" (Greenberg, 2011, p. 67). These task principles assist therapists in helping clients to pursue the work of resolving internal, emotional concerns while working on ***therapeutic tasks*** (**affective/ cognitive problems that clients work to resolve**) and personal goals. This consists of the therapist identifying markers related to the client's level of functioning and then deciding which intervention is best suited to facilitate effective resolution of the client's problematic state (Greenberg, 2011).

During therapeutic work, the therapist makes suggestions encouraging the client to experiment with specific behaviors, then solicits information about how the client was ***experiencing*** (**the result of attending to and awareness of the continual flow in the body)** the experiment. In EFT, experiments are designed to help clients articulate primary emotions and needs accessed during the process of experiencing, to promote acceptance and transformation of painful unresolved emotions, and to encourage the clarification of implicit feelings and meaning. The use of the therapeutic relationship and the facilitation of work highlight the therapist's use of the perceptual skills needed to successfully implement EFT.

## Specialized Techniques

In addition to the perceptual skills used by the EFT therapist, there are also several intervention skills that are used to help move clients toward living more emotionally healthy lives. According to Greenberg (2011), the interventions used in EFT are guided by the understanding of the emotion process, the principles of emotion intervention, and the descriptions of distinctive interventions for varying problem markers. The following techniques are used by EFT therapists.

Greenberg (2011) identified intervention skills used by EFT therapists as:

1.  ***Awareness. Awareness* is the process of exploring what an experience symbolizes**. In EFT therapy, helping clients to increase emotional awareness is the most fundamental goal of treatment. According to EFT, it is important to become aware of and understand the symbolic importance of one's emotions and to articulate this in session. This helps clients to access adaptive information as well as information about emotional **action tendencies (desires to behave in given ways based on a particular feeling).** As clients work to achieve awareness, they are encouraged not only to think about the emotion, but to feel the emotion in awareness. This is the purposeful act of being intentional about experience emotions. Once people are aware of what they are feeling, they are able to reconnect to their needs and thus are motivated to strive toward meeting their own needs. Therefore, the ultimate goal of awareness is the acceptance of emotions.

    There are three stages of change related to emotional awareness as it relates to problematic emotions. These are awareness, reduction, and recognition. The first stage consists of being aware of the emotion after the event. Learning to become aware of emotions in the present can help people navigate strategies for successfully responding to future emotion-latent situations. Often times this is where traditional insight-oriented therapy stops; however, EFT postulated that it is important to delve further into awareness. That being said, the second stage helps clients to reduce the amount of time it takes them to determine their feelings. The third stage is connected to recognizing the urgency of an emotion as it begins to arise. Once this is accomplished, the client is able to transform the emotion before it fully arises. When clients have become keenly aware of their emotions they are able to more successfully manage their emotions and emotional triggers.

2.  *Expression. Expression* **is the act of engaging one's body in the topic being discussed**. Humans have a natural tendency to avoid experiencing and expressing difficult emotions. The expression technique is used to encourage clients to overcome avoidance and approach painful emotions during a session. This is done by encouraging the client to incrementally attend to his or her bodily experience as emotions are explored during the session. As this is done, the client is encouraged to sit with or tolerate the impact of the emotion. This process of *approaching and tolerating* **uncomfortable emotion is consistent with the notion of exposure.** Research by Foa and Jaycox (1999) supported the effectiveness of exposure of work related to previously avoided emotions.

    Greenberg and Safran (1987) suggested that the function of this technique is to help clients overcome avoidance of previously experienced events. Additionally, this technique helps clients to effectively and appropriately express primary emotions that were previously constricted. Helping clients successfully experience the benefit of this technique typically includes helping clients change their explicit beliefs (e.g., crying equates weakness), which are often perpetuating their avoidance. Using expression as a form of coping (Folkman & Lazarus, 1988) may help clients identify and clarify core concerns as well as help direct clients toward pursuing their goals.

    The usefulness of arousal and expression in therapy (or life) often is dependent on the following things: which emotions are being expressed, the issue linked to the emotion, the actual expression or behavior linked to the emotion, who is expressing the emotion and to whom, when and under what conditions the emotion is expressed, and the affect and meaning that follow the expression of emotion. In life, outward expressions of problematic emotions are not often helpful, while in therapy it is often necessary but, according to this model, not sufficient for therapeutic change. The belief of EFT therapists is that in order for optimal emotional change to occur, the integration of both cognitive and affective processing are required (Greenberg, 2002; Greenberg & Pascual-Leone, 1995; Greenberg & Safran, 1987). Additionally, transformation of affect (explored later in this chapter), which is different from tolerance of affect, must also occur (Greenberg, 2002).

3.  *Regulation. Regulation* **of emotion can be defined as a process of helping clients identify which emotions need to be regulated and generating strategies for how to best regulate those emotions.** Given that emotion regulation and expression is not always appropriate or helpful in life or in therapy, it may be necessary for some clients to learn to downregulate their emotion so that they are able to function successfully. When one's distress level is elevated such that emotions are no longer informing adaptive action, it is necessary to help the client utilize emotion regulation skills. In such cases, the need for training in downregulation may precede or accompany exploration of emotions.

    Providing a safe, calming, validating, and empathic environment are key factors in helping clients learn to regulate their emotions. Facilitating this type of therapeutic environment helps to strengthen the self and soothes automatically produced underregulated distress (Bohart & Greenberg, 1997). Being able to self-soothe is initially developed within healthy interpersonal relationships in which one develops internal security by feeling one exists in the heart and mind of others (Schore, 2003; Sroufe, 1996; Stern, 1985). This can be learned as early as infancy (Perry & Szalavitz, 2006). The internalization that happens in the soothing of these interpersonal relationships over time can help individuals develop implicit *self-soothing*, **which is the ability to spontaneously regulate feelings without deliberate effort.**

Once able to self-soothe, the client is taught emotion regulation and distress tolerance skills (Linehan, 1993). This includes trigger identification, avoidance of triggers, identifying and describing emotions, allowing and tolerating emotions, developing a working distance (meditation and self-acceptance), increasing emotions that are viewed as positive, self-soothing, breathing, and using distractions. One's ability to regulate breathing and to observe feelings while letting emotions come and go is important in the process of regulating emotional distress.

4.  *Reflection. Reflection* **(creating meaning through a process of abstracting meaning)** allows the client to make narrative sense of his or her experiences. Once clients have made sense of their experiences, they are able to assimilate their understanding of the experience into their personal ongoing self-narrative. The process of reflection fosters an understanding about the psychological make-up of the self. That is to say, how one understands one's emotional experiences will influence how one views oneself. Reflection helps clients to create new meaning, thus allowing clients to generate new narratives for understanding their experience (Goldman, Greenberg, & Pos, 2005; Greenberg & Angus, 2004; Greenberg & Pascual-Leone, 1997; Pennebaker, 1995). The narrative organizes the client's experiences, allows the client's experiences and memories to form a meaningful coherent story, and provides a sense of identity.

5.  *Transformation. Transformation* **is a process of changing one's emotionally based self-organization.** This intervention focuses on helping the client to arrive at previously painful emotions with the intention of allowing the maladaptive emotion to be changed or transformed by a new, more adaptive emotion. Although humans have a tendency toward not embracing negative emotions, in EFT it is imperative and clients are encouraged to experience or reexperience negative feelings from their past.

In EFT, it is believed that changing one's emotional state is not possible unless the individual fully experiences the maladaptive emotion (which is linked to maladaptive schemes or internal organizations) and then is able to successfully use another emotion to undo or transform it. This differentiates EFT from other treatment models that focus solely on catharsis, exposure, purging, or attunement of emotions. Primary maladaptive emotions are best managed through the transformation process. This is a process in which new emotions are able to undo previous responses instead of attenuating them (Fredrickson, 2001). This process speaks to a basic principle of EFT, which suggests that one must first arrive at a place before leaving it.

Maladaptive emotional schematic memories from previous experiences are activated in the therapy session and are changed by memory restructuring. Nadel and

Bohbot (2001) found that new present experiences paired with activated memories of previous events may lead to memory transformation through a process of assimilating the new information into previous memories. Because the old memories are activated in the present, they are able to be restructured via assimilation by the addition of new experiences including the safety of the therapeutic relationship, the co-activation of adaptive emotional responses, and new resources (skill development) for how to cope with the previous situation. Memories are reconsolidated by the presence of these new components. This allows for a change in one's emotional *self-organization* **(the changing experience of self)** allowing the client to view the self and the situation from a different perspective.

There are many ways in which therapists help clients access new emotions to change previous emotions. One way in which this is done is shifting the client's attention toward emotions that may be "on the periphery" (Greenberg, 2011, p. 80) of his or her awareness; another option, in the absence of emotion, involves focusing on the needs held by the client at the time of the initial emotion (Greenberg, 2002; e.g., in cases of abandonment, the need for safety may be explored). Enactment and imagery is another way in which a therapist may help a client change a previously maladaptive emotion. This includes helping the client remember a time he or she felt a particular emotion, changing the client's view of things, and may also include expressing an emotion for the client (Greenberg, 2002).

6.  *Corrective emotional experience.* A *corrective experience* **is when an old experience is changed in a positive way by a new experience.** Therefore, a corrective emotional experience is one in which a person, who has previously experienced some type of negative emotional event or situation, has that emotion corrected through the engagement of a new positive emotional experience. For example, when clients are able to fully experience previous negative emotions (e.g., shame) in the presence of therapists, and the therapists respond in a warm, caring, compassionate manner rather than responding with distain or repulsion, this experience has the power to change the negative feelings (e.g., shame). Additionally, expressing anger and having it accepted rather than rejected by the therapist can be experienced as a corrective emotional interaction. This experience provides interpersonal soothing, offers new successful experiences, disconfirms pathogenic (unhealthy) beliefs (linked to maladaptive schemes), and shifts the client's personal experience from powerless to powerful. It also encourages the client to feel comfortable expressing emotions, without reservation, in the presence of the therapist. Each time the therapist is attuned to and validating of the client's internal world, the client is engaged in a corrective interpersonal emotional experience. The implication here is that having new experiences (in this case with a therapist) can be especially important in offering an opportunity for an interpersonal corrective emotional experience.

## Phases of Treatment

Greenberg (2011) outlines three major phases within the EFT treatment intervention. Each phase has a set of steps that describes its course across time (Greenberg & Watson, 2006). **In the first phase, the focus is on bonding and emotional awareness.** This phase involves four steps: "(a) attending to, empathizing with, and validating the client's feelings and current sense of self; (b) providing a rationale for working with emotions; (c) promoting awareness of internal experiences; and (d) establishing a collective focus" (Greenberg, 2011, p. 82). **The second phase involves evoking and exploring the client's core maladaptive emotional schemes.** This phase also has four steps: "(a) establishing support for emotional experiences, (b) evoking and arousing problematic feelings, (c) undoing interruptions of emotions, and (d) helping the client access primary emotions or core maladaptive schemes" (Greenberg, 2011, p. 82). **The final phase is the transformation phase. In this phase, the client is encouraged to both develop alternatives through the generation of new emotions and to reflect on the emotions that have been aroused during the session in order to create new narrative meaning.** This phase involves three steps: "(a) generating new emotional responses to transform core maladaptive schemes, (b) promoting reflection to make sense of the experiences, and (c) validating new feelings and support(ing) an emerging sense of self" (Greenberg, 2011, p. 82).

## Recent Developments or Criticisms

### LIMITATIONS

According to Greenberg (2011), EFT strives to meet clients where they are; however, due to the nature of this particular therapy, people who are very emotionally restricted or those who are self-conscious or highly controlled may find it difficult to participate in this therapeutic approach. It is likely that individuals with this type of presentation will have difficulty accessing their feelings and engaging in role-play and enactment activities. Additionally, clients who are looking for quick practical solutions or who need rapid symptom-focused relief may find the process of exploring their emotions unfavorable. Nevertheless, initially these clients would be worked with using a more behavioral approach and given coping strategies. Although clients with this type of presentation would initially develop coping strategies, it would be important to keep in mind that the goal of EFT is to come to a deeper level of change through the process of focusing on issues of unresolved emotional pain. Additionally, EFT may not be the best entry-level treatment model for individuals who are highly fragile, highly dysregulated, those who are engaging in self-harming behaviors, or those with complex trauma histories. In the case of these populations, stabilization would likely be necessary before the initiation of EFT as a treatment.

### CRITICISMS

According to Greenberg (2011), there are three major criticisms of EFT. The first highlights the fact that working with emotions can be dangerous. Because emotions can be disorganizing or overwhelming, it can be dangerous to activate them; however, EFT promotes adaptive emotions, which are far from destructive. Additionally, due to the nature of emotions, EFT therapists understand the need to develop a positive healthy therapeutic relationship before accessing painful emotions. The second criticism of EFT is related to the rational nature of people. This criticism suggests that because people tend to be rational beings they may not be responsive to an emotion-focused approach, may view being emotional as a sign of weakness, may see emotions as irrational, or may not form a strong therapeutic alliance. This may be especially relevant when considering culture and gender. When thinking about culture and gender, it is important to understand the ways in which social roles (e.g., East Asian cultures where rules govern social expression) influence one's willingness to experience and to express emotions. That is to say, the emotional schemes developed about emotions may need to be explored based on the client's cultural background and/or gender. Despite this criticism, it is important to note that all people, regardless of the need for rationalization, gender, or culture, have feelings, and people need to know how to deal with their feelings. The third criticism is that the empathic explorations and conjectures that are deeply rooted in the EFT interventions are seen as intrusive, too leading, and may possibly distort the client's experience. At the heart of this criticism is the concern that the client may engage in the act of complying with whatever emotion or emotional experience is led by the therapist. This criticism is countered by the therapist's focus on following rather than leading during therapy sessions. EFT therapists are aware of the criticisms of their preferred therapeutic approach and have worked toward, and will continue working toward, understanding, inspecting, and addressing these criticisms.

## STUDENT–MENTOR DIALOGUE

**Student:**  I'm not sure I understand why this approach is considered a "cross paradigm" approach. Why is it in this section of the book?

**Mentor:**  You have to know that this approach, more than most theories of counseling, has a definite focus on the biology of emotion. Greenberg clearly links his ideas to the study of affective neuroscience. He believes that there is a "primacy of emotion" that undergirds behavior and thinking. Emotion, rather than being just feeling, is deeply rooted in human biology. So his approach is a combination of an organic-medical proposition (emotion is grounded in biology) and some combination of psychological and social theory tenets. Greenberg holds to a "self," which is a psychological construct; yet he places strong emphasis on the therapeutic relationship, which is social. And, in 1995, in a chapter he wrote with Pascual-Leone, he took a position that can clearly be viewed as constructivist, as emotional experiences are re-narrated through the relationship with the counselor. When you look at Greenberg's history, you find a number of influential factors that appear aligned with different paradigms. His work is really a reflection of those competing and sometimes overlapping influences.

**Student:**  What are your thoughts on Leslie Greenberg's contribution to psychotherapy?

**Mentor:**  I think Greenberg's place within psychotherapy theory and research has been well-established. This statement is supported by the theory being identified as an evidence-based treatment for depression. It also has support in the treatment of couple/marital distress and trauma. Additionally, Greenberg is an expert in understanding emotions, emotional responses, and the schemes that influence both. He has trained others in EFT through the Emotion-Focused Therapy Clinic at York University, and EFT is continuing to gain popularity. Within the Emotion-Focused Therapy community, he is a major contributor.

**Student:**   But what about his theory—what do you think about his ideas?

**Mentor:**   I find Greenberg's ideas interesting. EFT feels like an intentionally integrated approach to helping clients live more effective lives. It is easy to see the influence of the Person Center and Gestalt approaches as well as the underlying foundation of Piagetian schematic development on the influence of emotion. He also certainly brings in the biological by addressing the brain structures involved in emotional experience. And there are also constructivist ideas in his work.

**Student:**   How does it explain emotion?

**Mentor:**   EFT explains emotions by recognizing that all humans experience emotions. Emotions are biologically grounded. Also, it suggests that emotions are developed within interpersonal experiences that begin early in life. These experiences create schema that get organized into internal organizations or schemes. Schemes can be adaptive or maladaptive. When schemes are maladaptive they must be explored in order to help understand function and generate new adaptive meaning.

**Student:**   Why is there such an emphasis on maladaptive schemes in his work?

**Mentor:**   In EFT, maladaptive schemes are at the root of dysfunction. Working to understand and to explore these schemes helps the client to become more aware of the influence of emotion schemes. As awareness is the fundamental goal of EFT, understanding these emotion schemes allows the client to begin to understand the "how" and "why" of emotional expression.. To some degree, one must assume that EFT reprograms the biological mechanisms of emotion.

**Student:**   So what do you see as good about this theory?

**Mentor:**   The theory's focus on emotions with the intention of undoing previously maladaptive schemes is a very important function of this theory. Earlier to the research supporting this theory, the engagement of emotions typically stopped at exploration. Additionally, this theory rightfully assumes, despite cultural social training and expectations, that all humans experience emotions and that it is helpful for humans to learn to deal with emotions.

**Student:**   Thank you.

## CONCLUSION

EFT is viewed through the lens of modern biological, cognitive, and emotion theory and grew out of person-centered, gestalt, experiential, and existential therapies (Greenberg, 2011). It was initially derived from a research-based approach designed with the focus of understanding the change process that occurs within psychotherapy (Greenberg, 1979, 1986, 2011; Rice & Greenberg, 1984) and has come to be identified as an evidence-based treatment for depression (Greenberg, 2011). It has been proven to be effective for clients dealing with trauma and for distressed couples (Baucom, Shoham, Mueser, Daiuto, & Stickle, 1998). A major goal of EFT is to create a therapeutic environment in which the client feels safe to fully experience emotions in order to engage in the process of transformation. During the transformation process, the client is able to successfully tolerate maladaptive emotions and generate new adaptive emotional responses to previously harmful maladaptive schemes. This is done through a series of interactions between the client and the therapist, which includes guiding and following and allows the therapist to help the client both cognitively and affectively process deeply felt emotional experiences.

## REFERENCES

Baucom, D. H., Shoham, V., Mueser, K. T., Daiuto, A. D., & Stickle, T. R. (1998). Empirically supported couple and family interventions for marital distress and adult mental health problems. *Journal of Consulting and Clinical Psychology*, 66, 53–88. doi:10.1037/0022-006X.66.1.53

Bohart, A. C., & Greenberg, L. S. (1997). *Empathy reconsidered: New directions in psychotherapy.* Washington, DC: American Psychological Association.

Bowlby, J. (1988). *A secure base.* New York, NY: Basic Books.

Buber, M. (1958). *I and thou* (2nd ed.). New York, NY: Scribner's.

Buber, M. (1965). *The knowledge of man.* New York, NY: Harper Torchbook.

Elliott, R., Watson, J. E., Goldman, R. N., & Greenberg, L. S. (2004). *Learning emotion-focused therapy: The process-experiential approach to change.* Washington, DC: American Psychological Association. doi:10.1037/10725-000

Foa, E. B., & Jaycox, L. H. (1999). Cognitive-behavioral theory and treatment of posttraumatic stress disorder. In D. Spiegel (Ed.), *Efficacy and cost-effectiveness of psychotherapy* (pp. 23–61). Washington, DC: American Psychiatric Publishing.

Folkman, S., & Lazarus, R. S. (1988). Coping as a mediator of emotion. *Journal of Personality and Social Psychology, 54*(3), 466–475. doi:10.1037/0022-3514.54.3.466

Fredrickson, B. L. (2001). The role of positive emotions in positive psychology: The broaden-and-build theory of positive emotions. *American Psychologist, 56*, 218–226. doi:10.1037/0003-066X.56.3.218

Frijda, N. H. (1986). *The emotions.* New York, NY: Cambridge University Press.

Geller, S., & Greenberg, L. (2002). Therapeutic presence: Therapists' experience of presence in the psychotherapy encounter in psychotherapy. *Person Centered and Experiential Psychotherapies, 1*, 71–86.

Gendlin, E. R. (1996). *Focusing-oriented psychotherapy: A manual of the experiential method.* New York, NY: Guilford.

Goldman, R. N., Greenberg, L. S., & Pos, A. E. (2005). Depth of emotional experience and outcome. *Psychotherapy Research, 15,* 248–260. doi:10.1080/10503300512331385188

Gottman, J. M. (1994). An agent for marital therapy. In S. M. Johnson & L. S. Greenberg (Eds.), *The heart of the matter: Perspectives on emotion in marital therapy* (pp. 256–296). New York, NY: Brunner-Mazel.

Gottman, J. M. (1999). *The seven principles of making marriage work.* New York, NY: Grown Publishers.

Greenberg, L. S. (1979). Resolving splits: Use of the two chair technique. *Psychotherapy, 16,* 316–324. doi:10.1037/h0085895

Greenberg, L. S. (1986). Change process research [Special issue]. *Journal of Consulting and Clinical Psychology, 54,* 4–9.

Greenberg, L. S. (2002). *Emotion-focused therapy. Coaching clients to work through their feelings.* Washington, DC: American Psychological Association. doi:10.1037/10447-000

Greenberg, L. S. (2011). *Emotion-focused therapy.* Washington, DC: American Psychological Association.

Greenberg, L. S. (2012). Leslie S. Greenberg: Award for distinguished professional contributions to applied research. *American Psychologist, 67,* 695–697. Retrieved from http://psycnet.apa.org/index.cfm?fa=buy.optionToBuy&id=2012-30216-032

Greenberg, L. S., & Angus, L. (2004). The contributions of emotion processes to narrative change in psychotherapy: A dialectical constructivist approach. In L. Angus & J. McLeod (Eds.), *Handbook of narrative psychotherapy: Practice, theory, and research* (pp. 331–349). Thousand Oaks, CA: Sage.

Greenberg, L. S., & Clarke, K. M. (1979). Differential effects of the two-chair experiment and empathic reflections at a conflict marker. *Journal of Counseling Psychology, 26,* 1–8. doi:10.1037/0022-0167.26.1.1

Greenberg, L. S., & Johnson, S. M. (1988). *Emotionally focused therapy for couples.* New York, NY: Guilford.

Greenberg, L. S., & Pascual-Leone, J. (1995). A dialectical constructivist approach to experiential change. In R. A. Neimeyer & M. J. Mahoney (Eds.), *Constructivism in psychotherapy* (pp. 169–191). Washington, DC: American Psychological Association. doi:10.1037/10170-008

Greenberg, L. S., & Paivio, S. C. (1997). *Working with the emotions in psychotherapy.* New York, NY: Guilford.

Greenberg, L. S., & Pascual-Leone, J. (1997). Emotion in the creation of personal meaning. In M. J. Power & C. R. Brewin (Eds.), *The transformation of meaning in psychological therapies: Integrating theory and practice* (pp. 157–173). Hoboken, NJ: Wiley.

Greenberg, L. S., Rice, L., & Elliott, P. (1993). *Facilitating emotional change: The moment by moment process.* New York, NY: Guilford.

Greenberg, L. S., & Safran, J. D. (1987). *Emotion in psychotherapy: Affect, cognition, and the process of change.* New York, NY: Guilford.

Greenberg, L. S., & Watson, J. (2006). *Emotion-focused therapy of depression*. Washington, DC: American Psychological Association.

Greenberg, L. S., Watson, J. C., & Goldman, R. (1998). Process-experiential therapy for depression. In L. S. Greenberg, J. C. Watson, & R. Goldman (Eds.), *Handbook of experiential psychotherapy* (pp. 227–248). New York, NY: Guilford.

Greenberg, L. S., & Webster, M. C. (1982). Resolving decisional conflict by gestalt two-chair dialogue: Relating process to outcome. *Journal of Counseling Psychology, 29*, 468–477. doi:10.1037/0022-0167.29.5.468

Johnson, M. D., & Bradbury, T. N. (1999). Marital satisfaction and topographical assessment of marital interaction: A longitudinal analysis of newly wed couples. *Personal Relationships, 6*, 19–40.

Johnson, S. M. (2004). Attachment theory: A guide for healing couple relationships. In W. S. Rholes & J. A. Simpson (Eds.), *Adult attachment: Theory, research and clinical implications* (pp. 367–387). New York, NY: Guilford.

Johnson, S. M., & Greenberg, L. S. (1985). Emotionally focused couples therapy: An outcome study. *Journal of Marital and Family Therapy, 11*, 313–317. doi:10.1111/j.1752-0606.1985.tb00624.x

Lewis, M., & Haviland-Jones, J. M. (2000). *Handbook of emotions* (2nd ed.). New York, NY: Brunner-Mazel.

Linehan, M. M. (1993). *Cognitive-behavioral treatment of borderline personality disorder*. New York, NY: Guilford.

Nadel, L., & Bohbot, V. (2001). Consolidation of memory. *Hippocampus, 11*, 56–60.

Paivio, S. C., & Greenberg, L. S. (1995). Resolving "unfinished business": Efficacy of experiential therapy using empty-chair dialogue. *Journal of Consulting and Clinical Psychology, 63*, 419–425. doi:10.1037/0022-006X.63.3.419

Paivio, S. C., & Nieuwenhuis, J. A. (2001). Efficacy of emotion focused therapy for adult survivors of child abuse. A preliminary study. *Journal of Traumatic Stress, 14*(1), 115–133. doi:10.1023/A:1007891716593

Pennebaker, J. W. (1995). *Emotion, disclosure and health*. Washington, DC: American Psychological Association. doi:10.1037/10182-000

Perls, F., Hefferline, R. F., & Goodman, P. (1951). *Gestalt therapy*. New York, NY: Dell.

Perry, B. D., & Szalavitz, M. (2006). *The boy who was raised as a dog: And other stories from a child psychiatrist's notebook*. New York, NY: Basic Books.

Plutchik, R. (2000). *Emotions in the practice of psychotherapy*. Washington, DC: American Psychological Association.

Rice, L., & Greenberg, L. (Eds.). (1984). *Patterns of change: An intensive analysis of psychotherapeutic process*. New York, NY: Guilford.

Rogers, C. R. (1957). The necessary and sufficient conditions of therapeutic personality change. *Journal of Consulting Psychology, 21*, 95–103.

Rogers, C. R. (1959). A theory of therapy, personality and interpersonal relationships, as developed in the client-centered framework. In S. Koch (Ed.), *Psychology: A study of a science* (Vol. 3, pp. 184–256). New York, NY: McGraw-Hill.

Schore, A. N. (2003). *Affect dysregulation & disorders of the self*. New York, NY: W. W. Norton.

Sroufe, S. A. (1996). *Emotional development: The organization of emotional life in the early years*. New York, NY: Cambridge University Press.

Stern, D. (1985). *The interpersonal world of the infant*. New York, NY: Basic Books.

Tomkins, S. (1991). *Affect, imagery and consciousness* (combined volumes). New York, NY: Springer Publishing.

# PART VI

# Conclusion

Chapter 17 provides an overview of matters of psychotherapy effectiveness. It addresses research. It addresses the limitations of outcome measures in counseling research. It describes both modernist and postmodern research models. It calls for a new era in research on counseling and psychotherapy.

# CHAPTER

## 17

# The Future of Counseling and Psychotherapy

## OBJECTIVES

- To surmise that traditional counseling approaches may not be easily translated to electronic service delivery models

- To describe the evolution of psychotherapy across paradigms

- To address the "common factors" movement in psychotherapy research

- To summarize the "good news" of psychotherapy effectiveness

- To challenge the Western scientific tradition and to introduce a postmodern view of research in counseling and psychotherapy

This textbook was written and designed to provide a contemporary accounting of the major theories of counseling and psychotherapy as organized by the paradigm framework. Organic–medical, psychological, systemic-relational, and social constructivist approaches have been identified and described. Approaches that cross paradigms were also described and outlined. The intent of each counseling theory chapter was to provide a clear philosophical foundation and enough information to allow clinicians to apply techniques and to implement the approach confidently.

# TECHNOLOGY AND TELEHEALTH

One wonders whether textbooks like this book will be viewed in a different light in a few years, as the technological revolution continues to influence the practice of counseling and psychotherapy (Cottone, 2015). It is very predictable that face-to-face, one-on-one counseling will be (to some degree) replaced by distance counseling or tele-counseling. The **telehealth movement (health treatment by a professional in a remote location through electronic communications with patients)** has taken hold, and it will likely affect the delivery of mental health services as it has affected medical service delivery. It may be that those psychotherapeutic approaches that translate easily to the electronic medium survive and thrive. For example, some approaches may be more easily packaged for programming of virtual treatment and electronic protocol methods. Research is showing that computer-assisted counseling is an effective alternative to **in vivo (live) in-person** counseling for a number of problems in a number of contexts (see the discussion on ethics regarding this matter in Cottone & Tarvydas, 2016). However, the verdict is still unclear on the overall efficacy and usefulness of computer-assisted counseling in general mental health clinical practice. Professionals who use electronic means of communication with clients need to continue to assess and to confirm the validity and safety of their approaches.

# EVOLUTION OF APPROACHES

In the meantime, psychotherapy has evolved over the course of about 116 years. Since Freud's first works (in 1900 and 1901), there have been several revolutionary changes in counseling philosophies. In psychology, the field began to consider humanistic and behavioral approaches as alternatives to the dominant insight-oriented therapies that emerged after Freud's initial works. Then the systems theorists began to challenge psychology itself; they argued that relationships are crucial to mental disturbance and mental health, and they began to offer relationship-oriented approaches to treatment. Couples and family therapy approaches emerged from systemic ideas. Most recently, the social constructivism philosophy is finding its way into clinical practice, as is evidenced by some novel approaches purporting that truths are known through a **consensualizing (social agreement)** process, such as establishing agreement on solutions rather than focusing on problems, or establishing healthy narratives of clients' lives. Therapies have changed and philosophy has been powerful in affecting change in counseling theory.

# COMMON FACTORS

It is also possible that theory will become less emphasized in treatment, as researchers continue to define the *common factors* associated with successful treatment, aside from the theory that is applied. As common factors are identified, they may be taught as predominant factors in treatment, which may challenge the historical, educational focus on theories. Mental health professional educators are faced with choosing to focus on theories, to focus on common factors primarily, or to do some combination of teaching theory and common factors as a means of preparing practitioners. Research is giving the field broad hints about how the common factors movement interfaces with theories of counseling and psychotherapy. It can be argued that common factors are present, regardless of theory, but it can also be argued that theory directs clinicians in a way that common factors are engaged. For example, therapeutic alliance to some degree involves the client's view of the counselor as an expert (demonstrating confidence in the practice of counseling). Clinicians may gain confidence if they have a clear theoretical roadmap that guides them in challenging moments, which they encounter in everyday practice. Therefore, theory—rather than being counter to, or opposed to, common factors—may be intimately intertwined with the common factors in producing positive results for clients. In other words, there may be interaction effects where theory, therapist traits, the context of treatment, and other variables all add into the equation. Researchers are attempting to answer questions related to the isolated versus interactive nature of variables that are associated with successful treatment.

## PSYCHOTHERAPY EFFECTIVENESS

Overall, the news about psychotherapy effectiveness is good. In a chapter entitled "The Efficacy and Effectiveness of Psychotherapy," Lambert (2013) summarized some very encouraging findings. Using formal, theory-driven psychotherapies, 40% to 60% of clients report benefits when there are carefully controlled research protocols (benefits in routine practice settings may be lower). He also documented that long-term therapy has longer lasting effects, but relatively short-term treatment (14 sessions or less) produces significant benefits. Therapy is also better than no therapy. Control group participants do not improve to the degree that participants in "bona fide" treatment conditions improve. This is all good news. Interestingly, differences across therapies are not pronounced, lending less credence to those who are encouraging the idea of using only "empirically supported treatments." In effect, all psychotherapy provided by a competent, ethical therapist has benefits. Lambert stated: "To advocate empirically supported therapies as preferable or superior to other treatments is probably premature" (p. 205). Lambert also concluded that "Positive affective relationships and positive interpersonal encounters, that characterize most psychotherapy and are common across therapies, still loom large as stimulators of patient improvement" (p. 206).

On the matter of adherence to a specific theory as a positive outcome variable, research has shown "mixed results," whereas alliance factors show a strong relationship to positive outcome (Baldwin & Imel, 2013). Although researchers can say with some confidence that working alliance (therapeutic alliance) is clearly associated with successful treatment, strict adherence to one form of therapy is not clearly and consistently associated with success. In fact, the evidence reviewed by Baldwin and Imel (2013) was not sufficient to draw conclusions that theory adherence was effective at all.

The big picture conclusion about the current state of psychotherapy outcome research is that the counselor–client relationship cannot be ignored. It makes sense that a **caring, ethical, guiding, and collaborative relationship** between a client and a counselor is valuable. Almost everyone can agree that over the course of a lifetime, each person has experienced a relationship with another person that has had a significant positive effect on one's life. Sometimes that person may be a parent. Sometimes the person may be a teacher or a preacher who takes interest in one's well-being. Perhaps it was someone who recognized the strength in the other person. Perhaps it was a school counselor. It is clear that disturbed relationships can affect mental health; it is also clear that a helping relationship can have just as powerful an effect. Aside from research, common sense communicates a message of the power of relationships in affecting human lives. This is encouraging for the field of counseling and psychotherapy, because therapy is a relationship.

Beutler (2000) also provided an interesting perspective on the effectiveness of treatment. In his paper published in 2000, he reported on a project that began with a thorough literature review on therapy factors associated with successful treatment. Then he did a cross-validation study with clients diagnosed with depression to test these factors. He was able to validate a number of "optimal and enhancing" guidelines—empirically informed and cross-theory principles for treating depressed patients. The first principle on his list is crucial. He stated:

> The first such principle reflects on the nature of the therapeutic relationship and on the importance of the therapeutic alliance. Although this is only one principle, it is . . . probably the foundation for much or even most treatment. Indeed, the other principles, at least those identified as optimal, may well be dependent on this first principle to become active. (p. 1005)

Beutler identified seven other "optimal" principles. According to Beutler, therapeutic change is greatest: (a) when there is exposure to the objects/targets of emotional avoidance; (b) when skill-building and symptom-removal methods are used with "externalizing" clients, and when insight and relationship-focused methods are used among "internalizing" patients; (c) when the initial focus of treatment is skill-building and symptom disruption; (d) when procedures do not produce resistance in the client; (e) when counselor directiveness is inverse to the level of resistance or when resistance is approached through prescription of symptom continuation (a paradoxical maneuver); (f) when the client's level of stress is between extremely high and extremely low levels; and (g) when the client is aroused in a safe environment until problem behaviors diminish or disappear. Beutler's work is a model of the way research methods can be used to rise above theory and simple empirical validation of technique.

## RESEARCH TRENDS

Research, however, is not without biases. In fact, the nature of research derives from the Western culture's intellectual tradition. It is modernist in its tradition, meaning it holds to standard tenets of objectivist science. The Western modernist ideal is as follows: There is a nature that is separate from humans, and can be measured objectively and in a way that humans can apply language as a means of exact understanding. Postmodernists (e.g., Cottone, 2012; Gergen, 2001) have begun to challenge the traditions of modernist science as applied to counseling and psychotherapy. Gergen's arguments were compelling, because they came at a time when his published paper, "The Social Constructionist Movement in Modern Psychology" (Gergen, 1985), was beginning to arouse emotion and reaction among researchers in psychology and social sciences (e.g., Smith, 1994). Constructivist-oriented research is not about finding objective evidence that applies in all contexts. Psychotherapy research is unlike research in the hard sciences. Measures of success in psychotherapy are often self-report measures (subjective measures of feelings, for example), and even when instruments are used, those instruments may actually reflect culturally imbedded values. For example, sadness and pessimism are viewed negatively in the American culture. Too much sadness is viewed as pathological, yet sadness may have a message value. Maybe sadness has value in helping to change a person's life. Maybe pessimism has value in making people cautious, which can have survival implications. Any measure that quantifies sadness or pessimism as pathological, then, may be more a reflection of the culture than of any objective measure of psychopathology (Cottone, 2012). Any researcher that purports such measures as carrying the weight of objective science is not recognizing the social context of research and of the human condition. The social constructivism movement would prioritize defining the "context" of research as important both in hypothesis generation and interpretation of results.

Research should not be held as the final arbiter of truth claims about counseling and psychotherapy. The most important criterion in the assessment of psychotherapy may be the benefit to clients and to a society that values human freedom and dignity. *The final arbiter might be the ability of counseling approaches to solve problems or to help clients solve problems.* This criterion is not significantly studied or mentioned in outcome research. Counseling is a socially imbedded practice. The self-report of clients stating that counseling helped them to solve problems that otherwise baffled them may be as valuable as any outcome measure that attempts to objectify subjective emotional experience. In other words, the story of psychotherapy research is only partially written, and new chapters need to address new ways of measuring the value of counseling to individuals and to society.

## CONCLUSION

This chapter provides an accounting of the current status of outcome studies on psychotherapy effectiveness. Although there have been numerous studies on psychotherapy outcome, few studies produce findings indicating the superiority of one approach against another. Yet psychotherapy is effective in-and-of-itself, and it is more effective than no treatment or control/wait group interventions. One of the most interesting findings of outcome research is the consistent and significant effect of therapeutic alliance in producing positive outcomes. Therapist interpersonal skills and working alliance factors appear to be the most influential factors in counseling. New philosophies, and new ways of conceptualizing outcome, are needed to address the professional need to establish the credibility and validity of current psychotherapeutic methods.

## REFERENCES

Baldwin, S. A., & Imel, Z. E. (2013). Therapist effects: Finding and methods. In M. J. Lambert (Ed.), *Bergin and Garfield's handbook of psychotherapy and behavior change* (6th ed., pp. 258–297). Hoboken, NJ: Wiley.

Beutler, L. E. (2000). David and Goliath: When empirical and clinical standards of practice meet. *American Psychologist, 55,* 997–1007. doi:10.1037/0003-066X.55.9.997

Cottone, R. R. (2012). *Paradigms of counseling and psychotherapy.* Cottleville, MO: Author. Retrieved from https://www.smashwords.com/books/view/165398

Cottone, R. R. (2015, April). The end of counseling as we know it. *Counseling Today, 57*(10), 48–53.

Cottone, R. R., & Tarvydas, V. M. (2016). *Ethics and decision making in counseling and psychotherapy* (4th ed.). New York, NY: Springer Publishing.

Gergen, K. J. (1985). The social constructionist movement in modern psychology. *American Psychologist, 40*, 266–275.

Gergen, K. J. (2001). Psychological science in a postmodern context. *American Psychologist, 56*, 803–813. doi:10.1037/0003-066X.56.10.803

Lambert, M. J. (2013). The efficacy and effectiveness of psychotherapy. In M. J. Lambert (Ed.), *Bergin and Garfield's handbook of psychotherapy and behavior change* (6th ed., pp. 169–218). Hoboken, NJ: Wiley.

Smith, M. B. (1994). Selfhood at risk: Postmodern perils and the perils of postmodernism. *American Psychologist, 49*, 403–411.

# Index